COOL DESIGN HOTELS

DISEGNO COOL: HOTELS
HOTELES DE DISEÑO
DESIGN DE HOTÉIS COOL

Edited by Macarena San Martín

Art director:
Mireia Casanovas Soley

Editorial coordination:
Catherine Collin

Project coordination:
Macarena San Martín

Texts:
Macarena San Martín

Layout:
Claudia Martínez Alonso

Translations:
Lydia de Jorge (English), Quirino Di Zitti (Italian), Mariana Sousa Moreira (Portuguese)

Editorial project:
2007 © LOFT Publications l Via Laietana, 32, 4.°, Of. 92 l 08003 Barcelona, Spain
Tel.: +34 932 688 088 Fax: +34 932 687 073 l loft@loftpublications.com l www.loftpublications.com

ISBN 978-84-95832-96-2   Printed in China

LOFT affirms that it possesses all the necessary rights for the publication of this material and has duly paid all royalties related to the authors' and photographers' rights. LOFT also affirms that it has violated no property rights and has respected common law, all authors' rights and other rights that could be relevant. Finally, LOFT affirms that this book contains no obscene nor slanderous material.

The total or partial reproduction of this book without the authorization of the publishers violates the two rights reserved; any use must be requested in advance.

If you would like to propose works to include in our upcoming books, please email us at loft@loftpublications.com.

In some cases it has been impossible to locate copyright owners of the images published in this book. Please contact the publisher if you are the copyright owner of any of the images published here.

COOL DESIGN HOTELS
DISEGNO COOL: HOTELS
HOTELES DE DISEÑO
DESIGN DE HOTÉIS COOL

Edited by Macarena San Martín

KOLON

"You can design and create, and build the most wonderful place in the world. But it takes people to make the dream a reality."

Walt Disney, American producer, director, screenwriter and pioneer animator

«Puoi progettare, creare e costruire il luogo più meraviglioso del mondo. Ma ci vuole gente per trasformare il sogno in realtà.»

Walt Disney, produttore, regista, sceneggiatore e animatore nordamericano

«Puedes diseñar y crear, y construir el lugar más maravilloso del mundo. Pero se necesita gente para convertir el sueño en realidad.»

Walt Disney, productor, director, guionista y animador norteamericano

«Pode conceber, criar e construir o lugar mais maravilhoso do mundo. Mas são necessárias as pessoas para transformar o sonho em realidade.»

Walt Disney, produtor, director, argumentista e animador norte-americano

12	EAST HOTEL Jordan Mozer & Associates	22	OSTRACO SUITES Nikos Pitsos & Dimitris Mantikas
30	AUGARTEN HOTEL Günther Domenig	36	NEBESA REAL Engineering
42	INTERCONTINENTAL DÜSSELDORF HPP – Hentrich-Petschnigg & Partner HBA – Hirsch Bedner Associates	48	THE MANDEVILLE HOTEL Stephen Ryan

52 LIFE GALLERY ATHENS Kline Haller & Vassillis Rodatos Architects	58 THE LALU Kerry Hill Architects
68 GRAND HOTEL CENTRAL TMA Arquitectura	74 HOTEL GANSEVOORT The Stephen B Jacobs Group
78 RADISSON SAS 1919 HOTEL Björn Guobrandsson	84 THE BLACKET Edmund Thomas Blacket

92	THE GRAND Gail Behr	98	THE CHEDI MUSCAT Jean-Michel Gathy/Denniston International Architects & Planners
106	BENESSE HOUSE Tadao Ando	112	THE LYALL Bruce Henderson Architects
118	OPUS HOTEL Paul Merrick Architects	124	CRAM L'HOTEL GCA Arquitectes Associats

134 FAENA HOTEL & UNIVERSE
Philippe Starck

142 FRESH HOTEL
Zeppos-Georgiadi+Associates

148 THE COMMUNE BY THE GREAT WALL
Designed by 12 renamed
Asian architects

156 THE PRINCE
Allan Powell Architects

162 THE SPIRE QUEENSTOWN
Martin Hughes Architecture Interiors

166 AMAN I KHAS
Jean-Michel Gathy/Denniston
International Architects & Planners

172	MOJIKO HOTEL Aldo Rossi	182	STRAF HOTEL Vincenzo de Cotiis
188	F1 KASSEL GRIMM RESORT MoHen Design International	192	W SEOUL WALKERHILL Studio Gaia
200	HOTEL BARCELONA PRINCESS Oscar Tusquets Blanca	210	DAR LES CIGOGNES Charles Boccara

214	THE PARKER PALM SPRINGS Jonathan Adler	220	PURO Álvaro Planchuelo
226	THE DORSET HOTEL Günther Domenig	236	CONRAD TOKYO Takenaka Corporation
244	VATULELE RESORT Doug Nelson & Martin Livingston	254	ARCHITECTS DIRECTORY

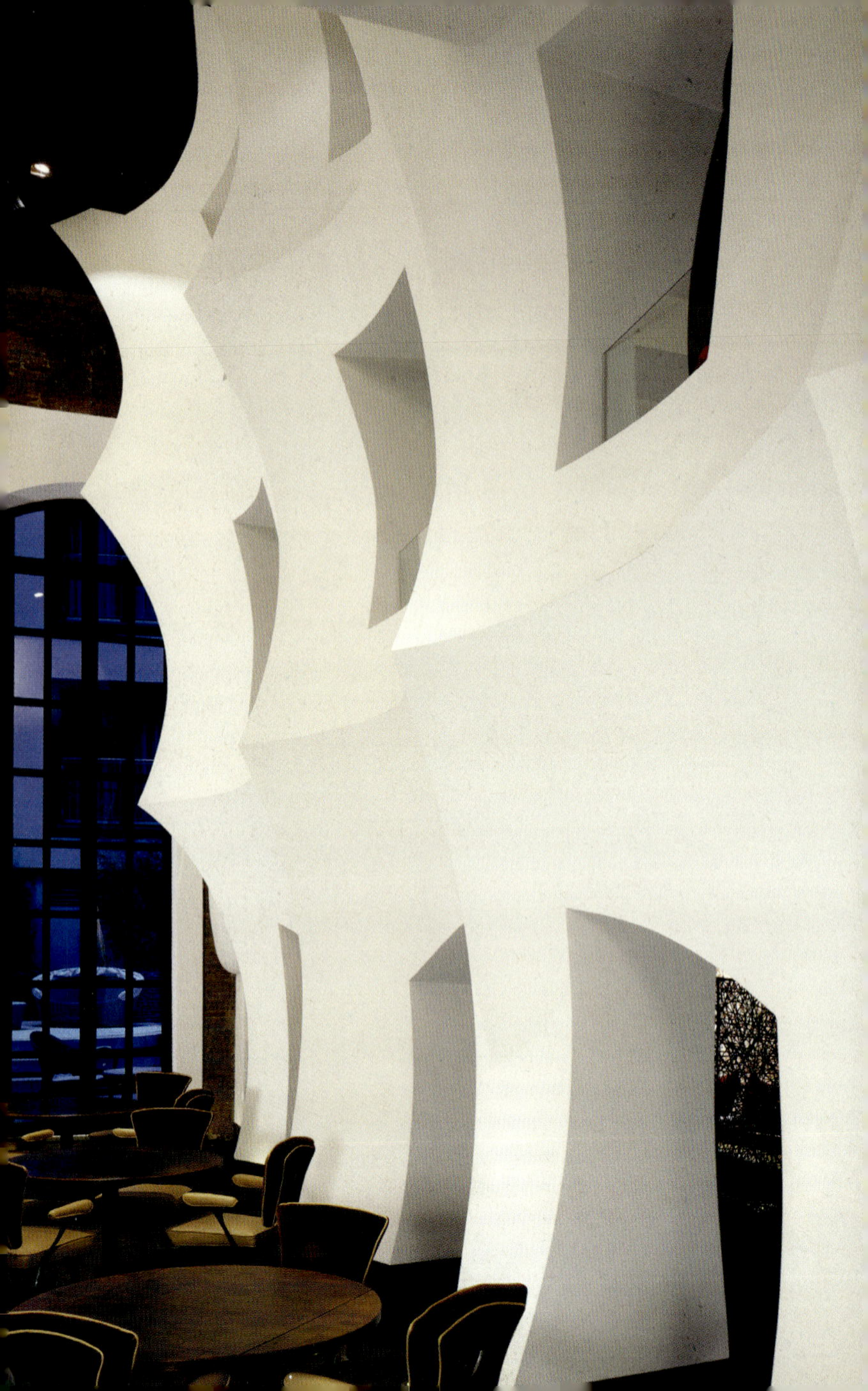

EAST HOTEL
The Sun Rises in the East

Architects: Jordan Mozer & Associates

Date: 2004
Address: 31 Simon von Utrecht Strasse, 20359 Hamburg, Germany
Tel.: +49 40 30 9930 Fax: +49 40 30 9932 00
www.east-hamburg.de
Photos: © Doug Snower

Location: Urban
Style: Contemporary design
Rooms: 125
Special features: Bars, restaurants, conference rooms, sauna, spa, gym, outdoor putting green, roof terrace

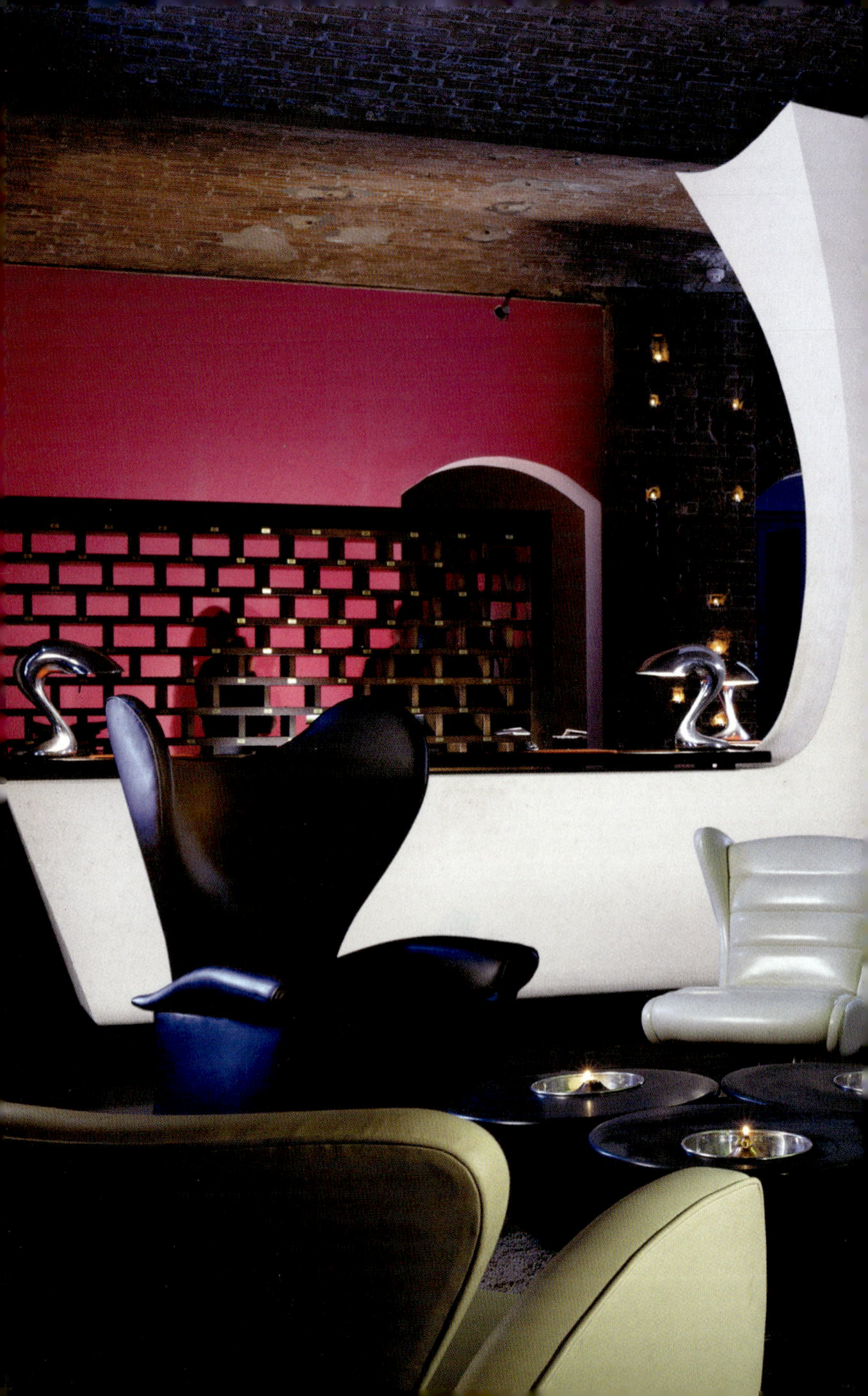

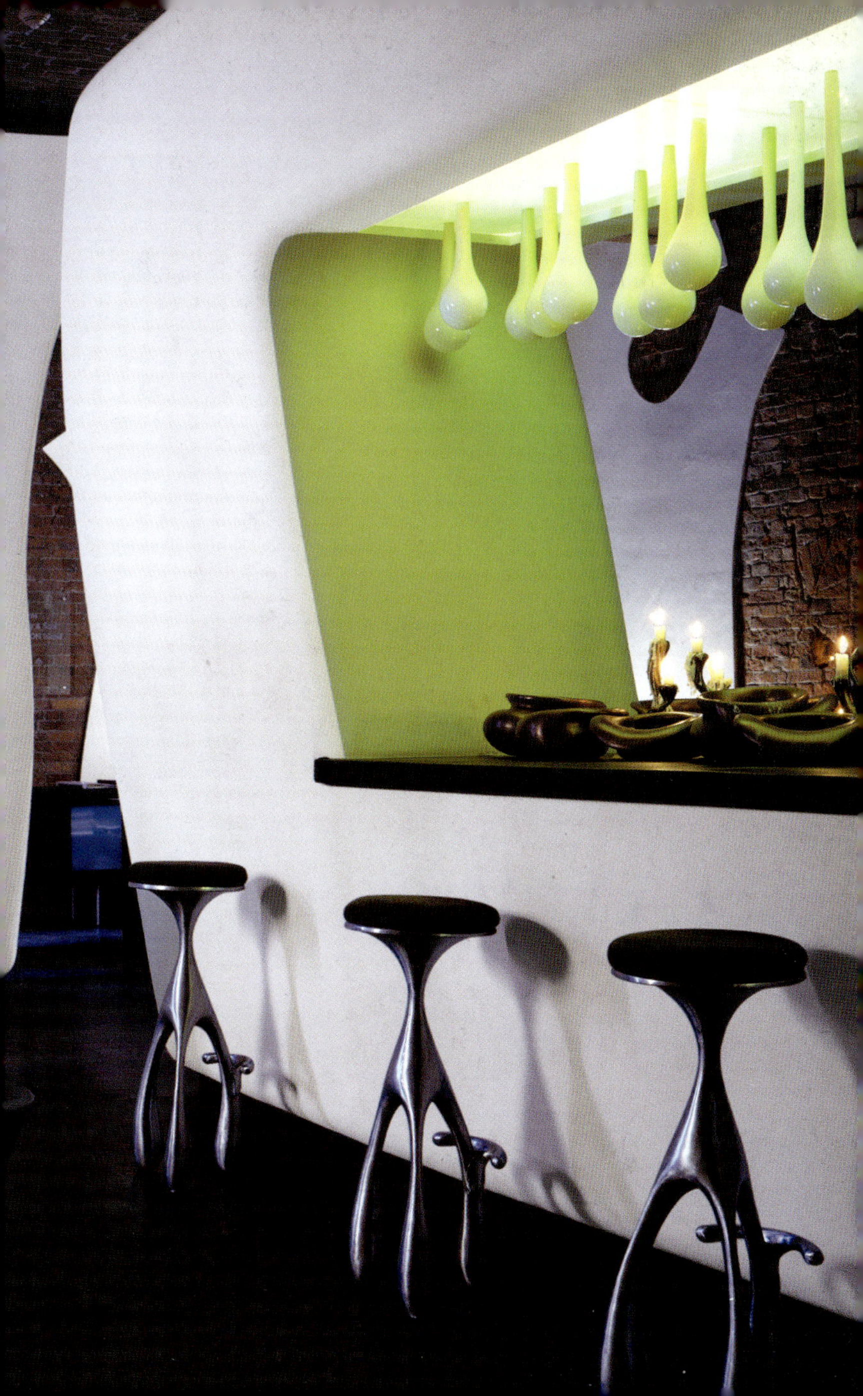

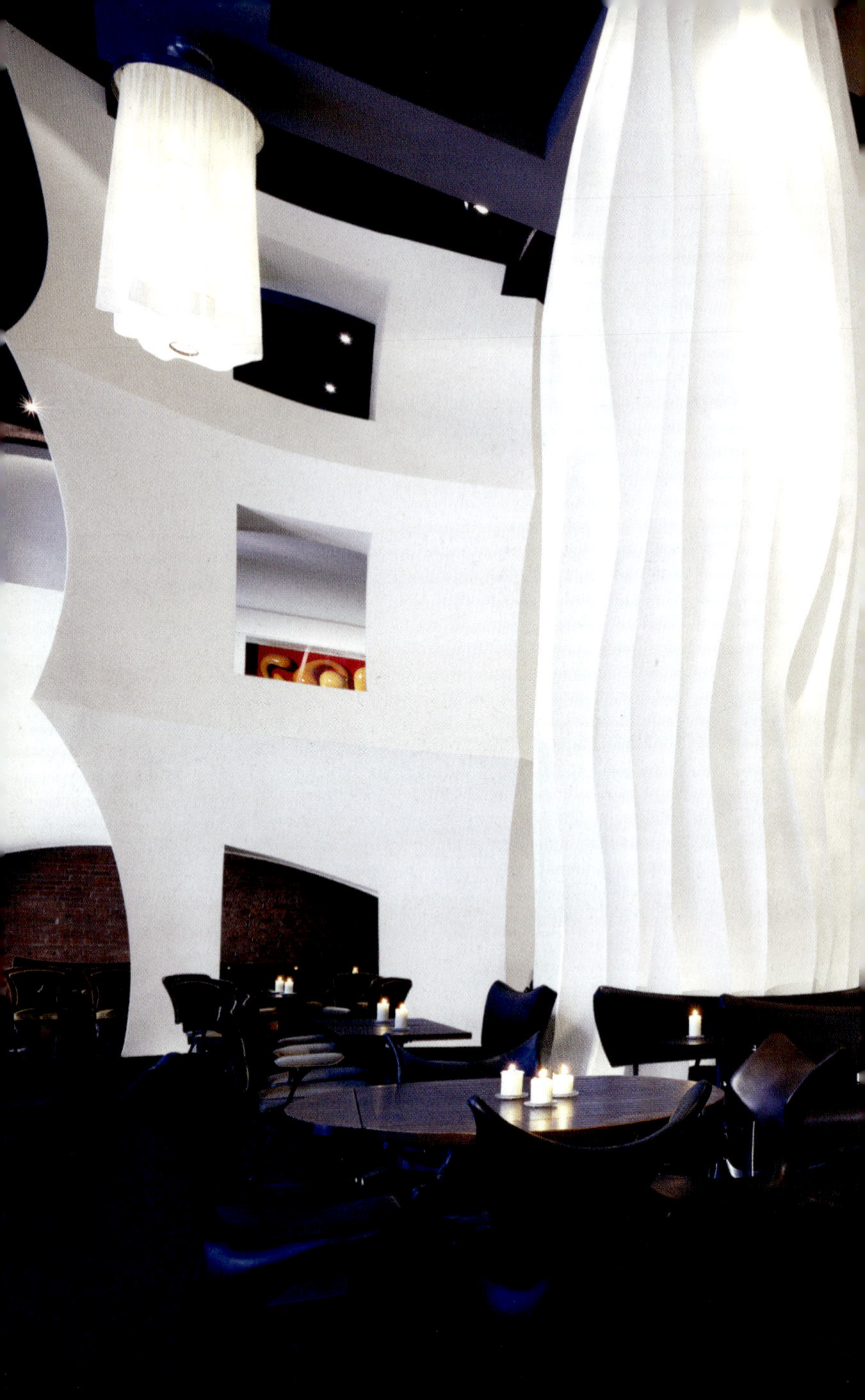

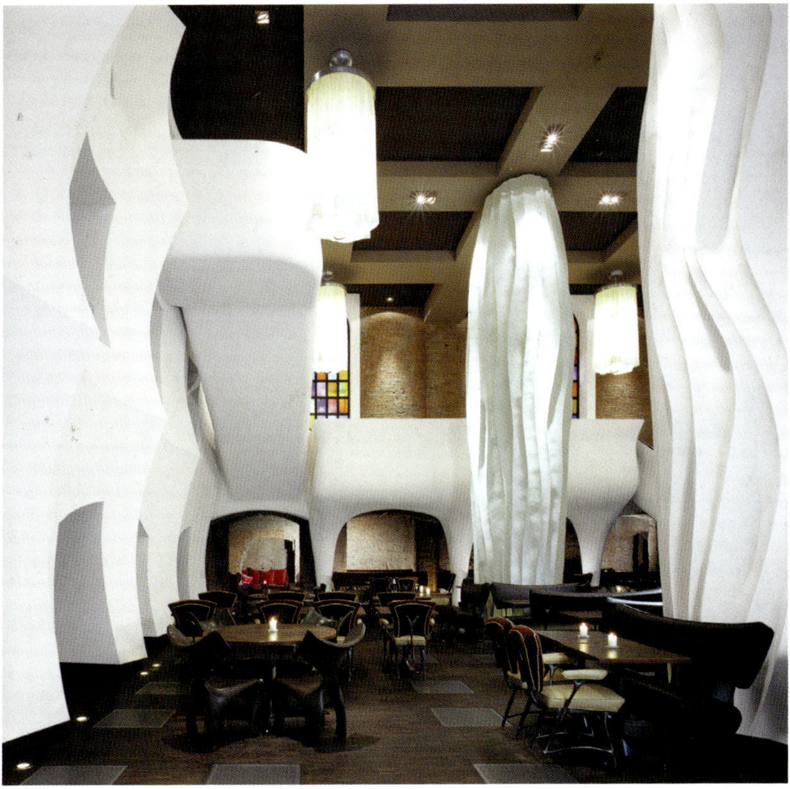

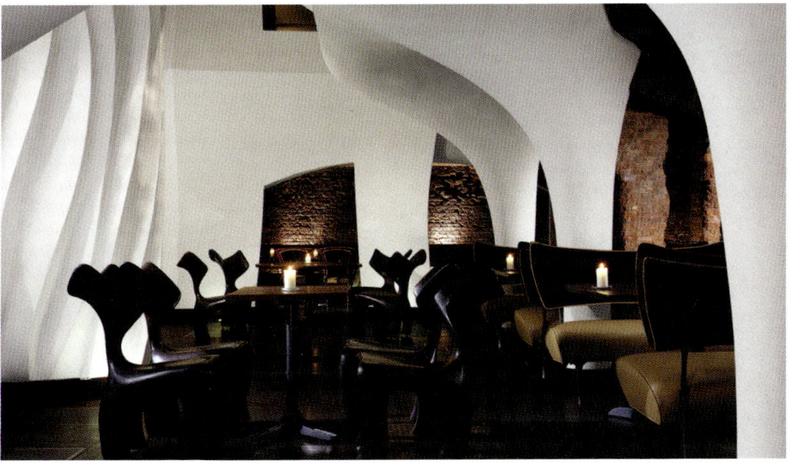

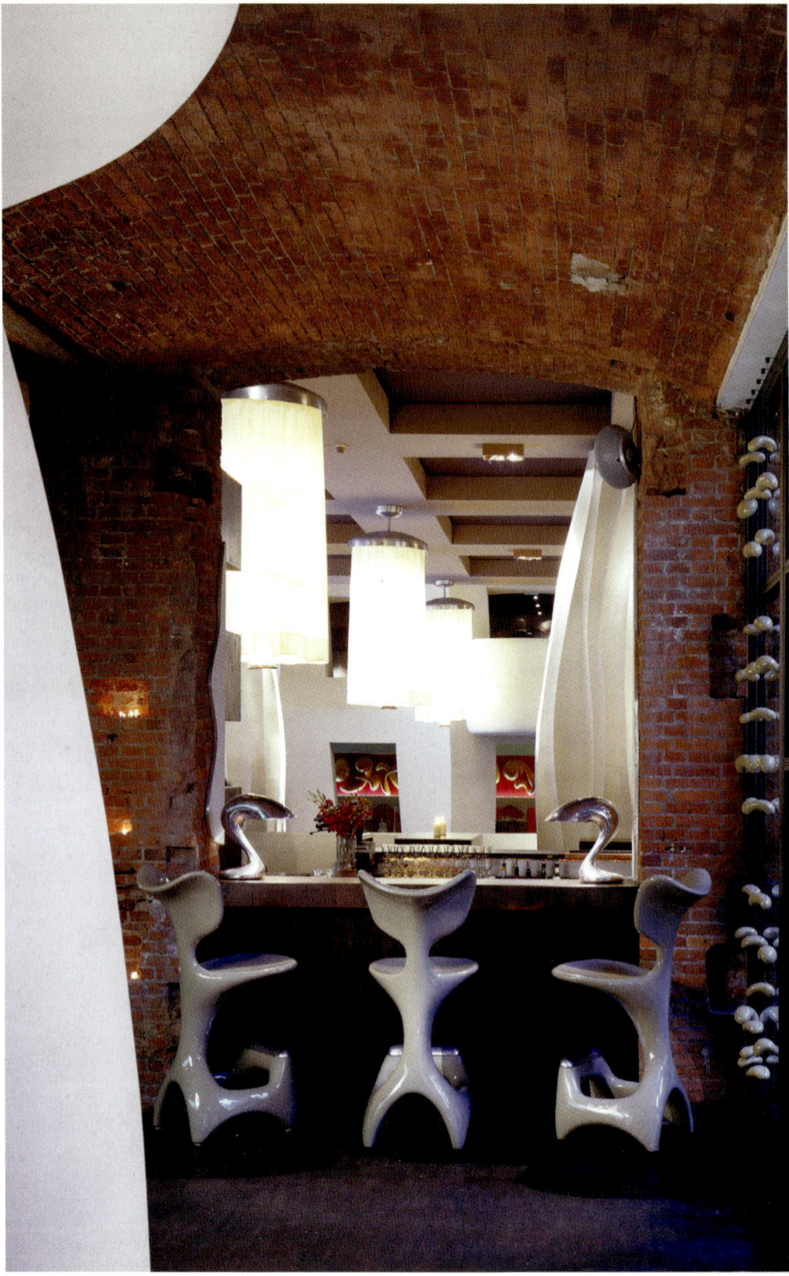

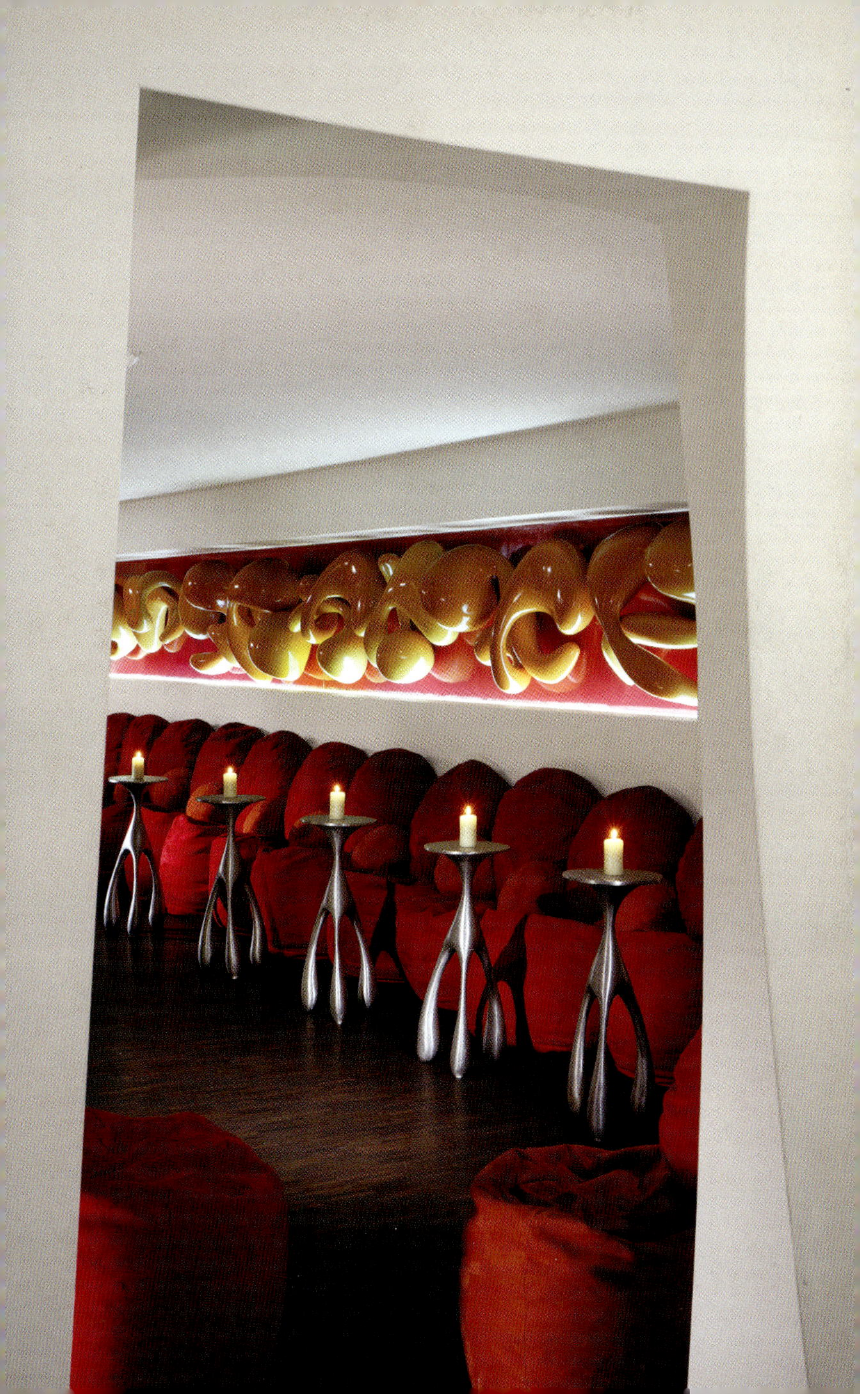

1. Entrance
2. Lobby
3. Registration
4. Bedrooms area
5. Elevator to lobby
6. Garden
7. Restaurant
8. Colours lounge

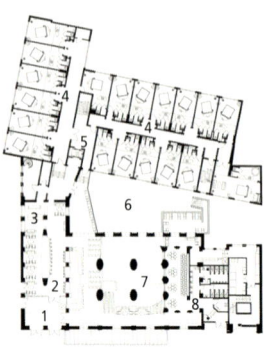

Ground floor

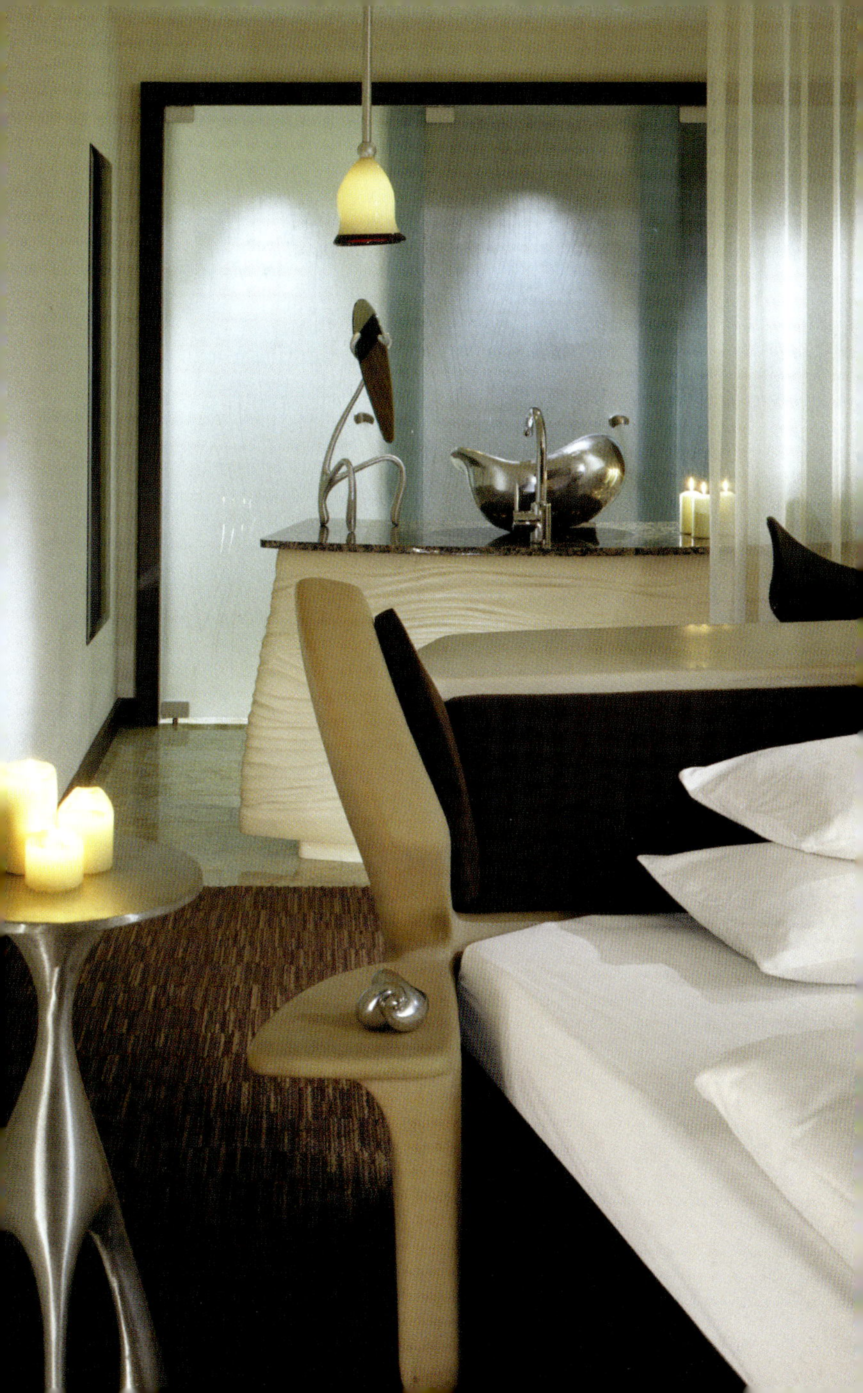

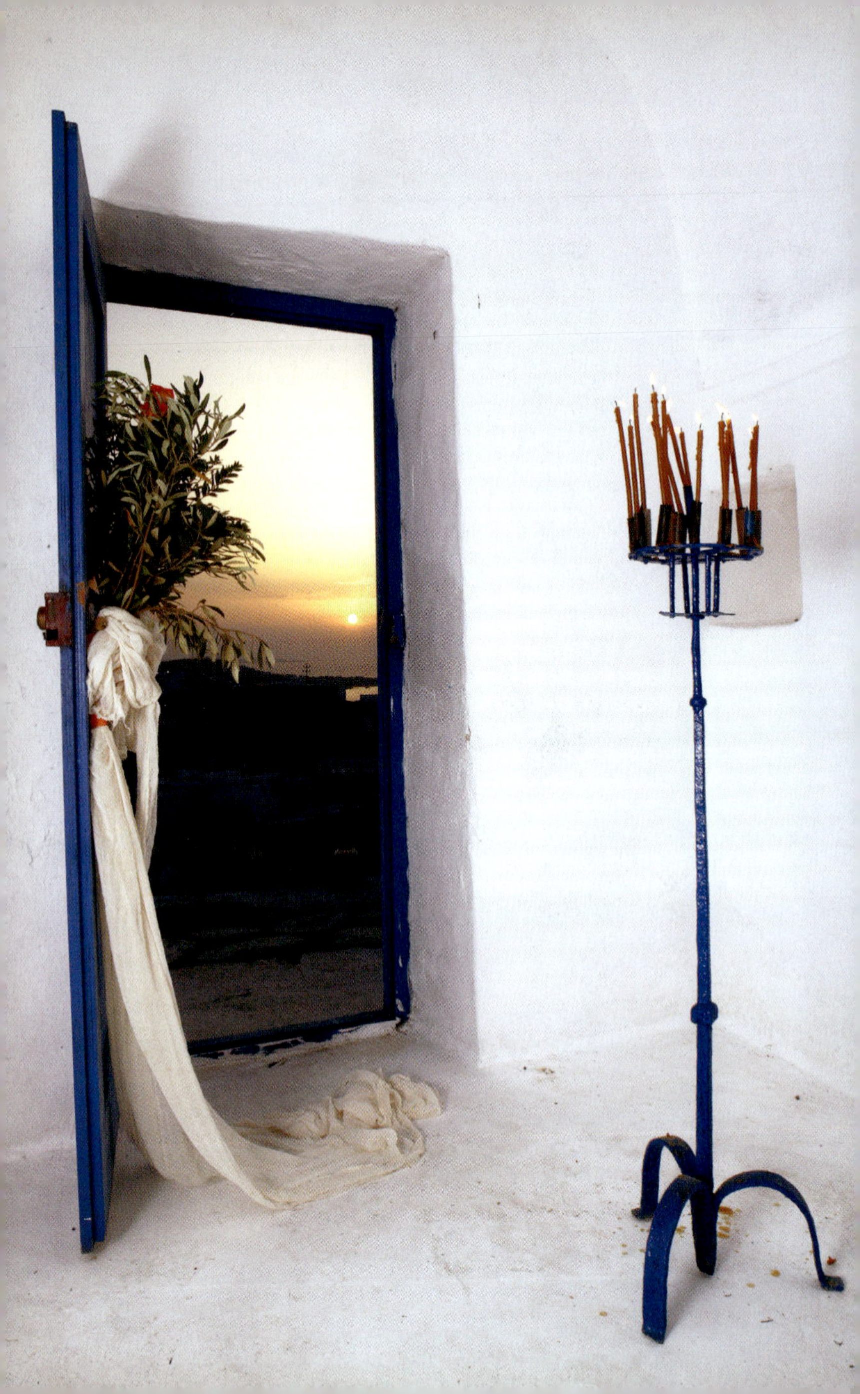

OSTRACO SUITES
Relaxing and Dreaming

Architects: **Nikos Pitsos & Dimitris Mantikas**
Designer: **Angelos Angelopoulos**

Date: 2004
Address: Drafaki, 846 00 Mykonos, Greece
Tel.: +30 228 902 3396 Fax: +30 228 902 7123
www.ostraco.gr
Photos: © Ostraco Suites

Location: Beach
Style: Contemporary Mediterranean
Rooms: 24
Special features: Individually styled rooms, pool bar, BBQ, boat and plane excursions, two traditional for wedding ceremonies chapels

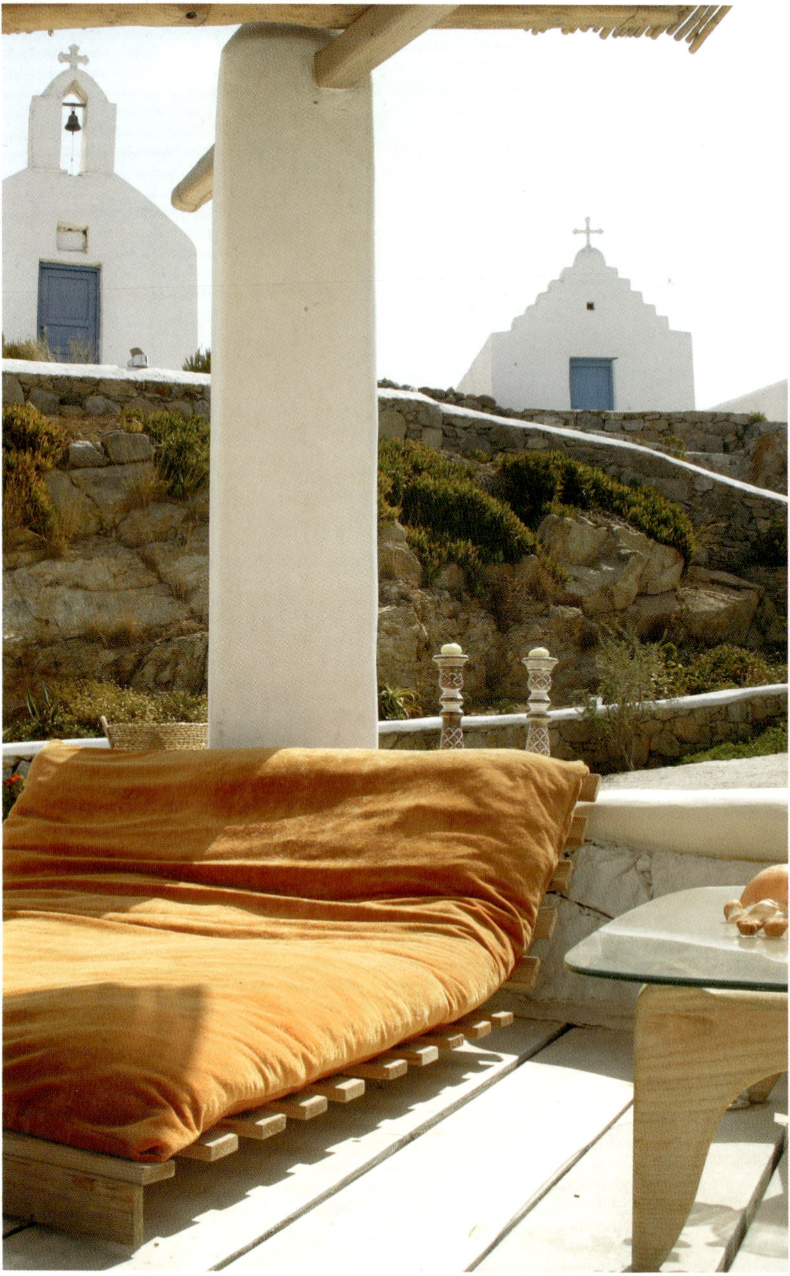

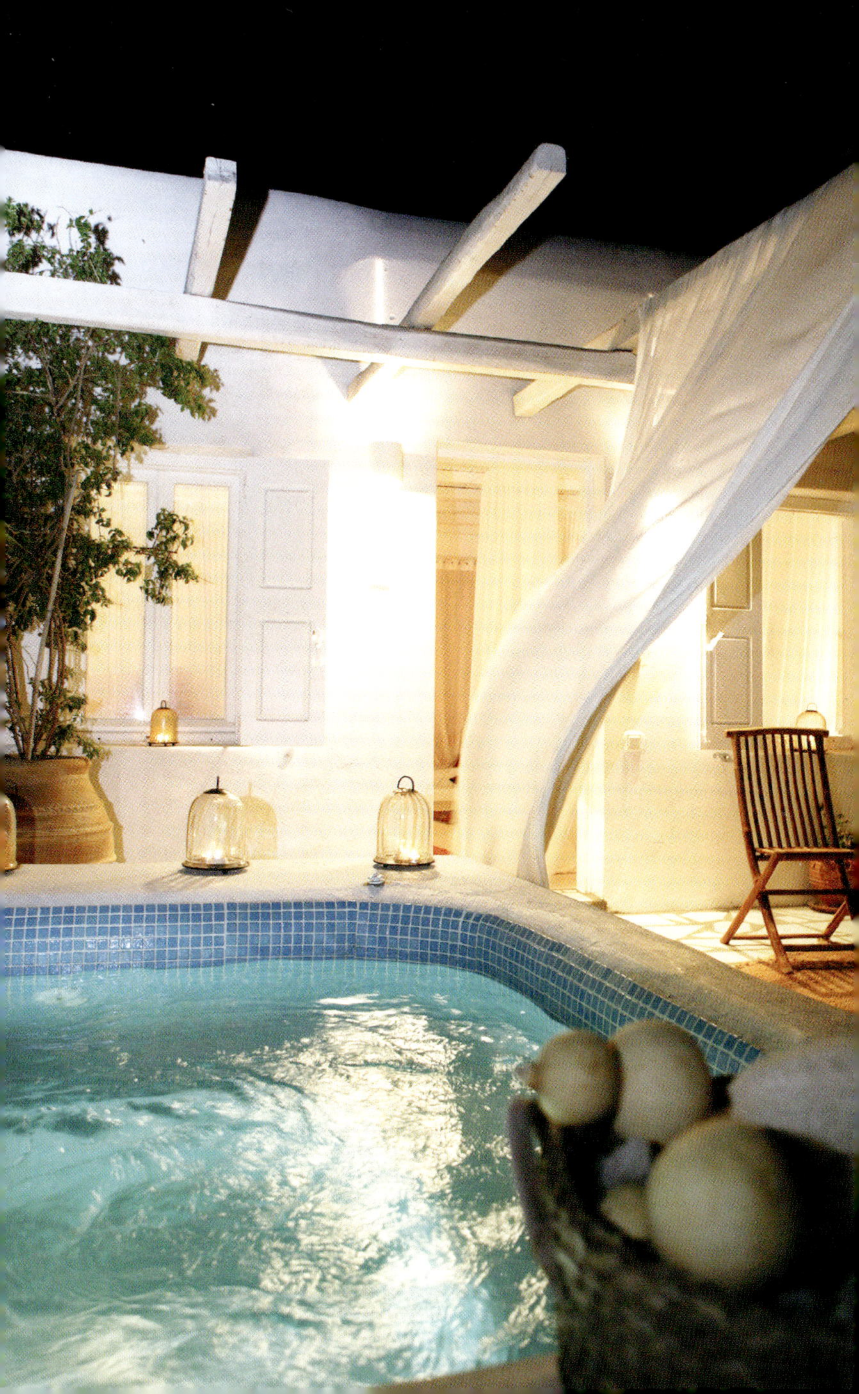

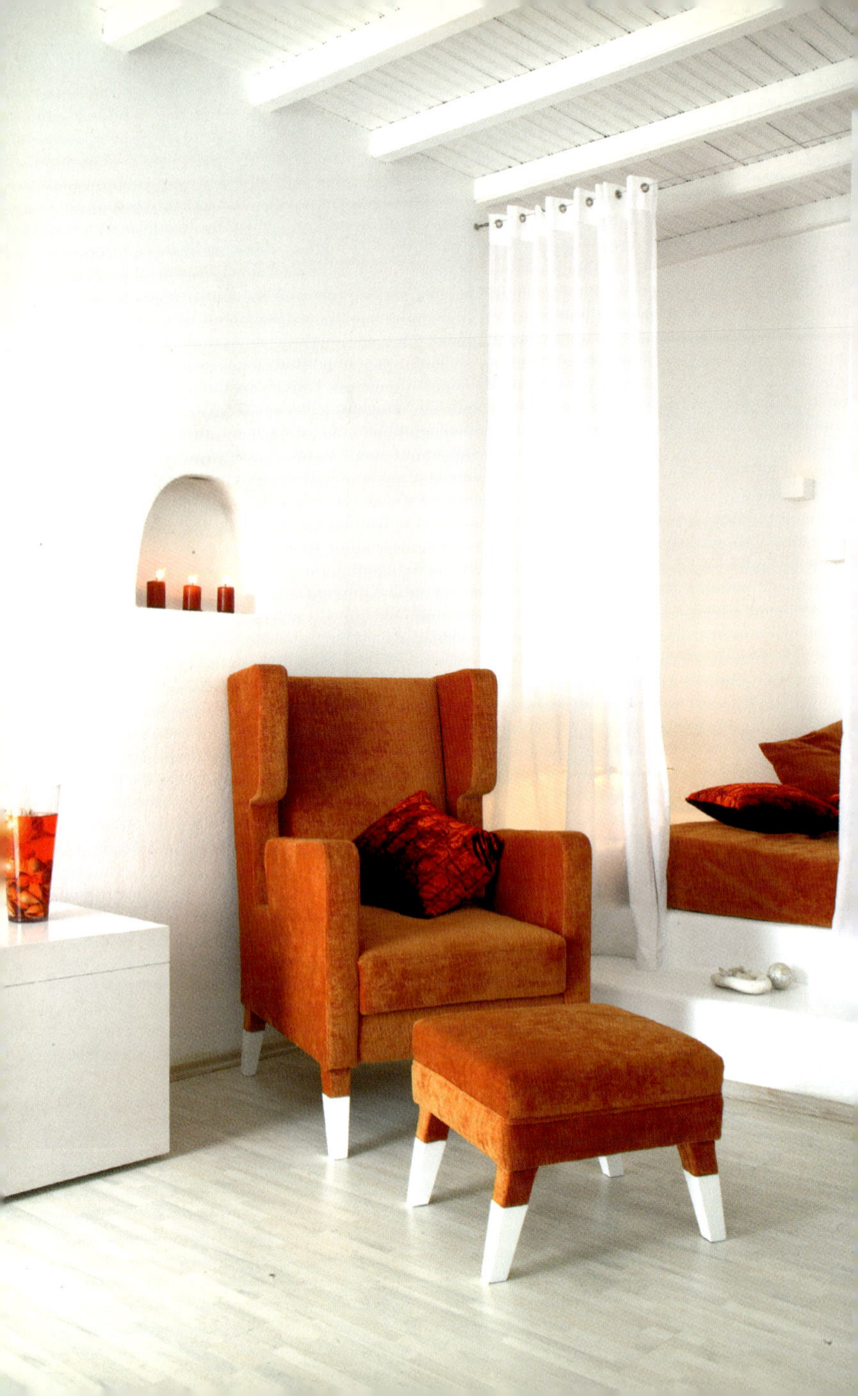

27

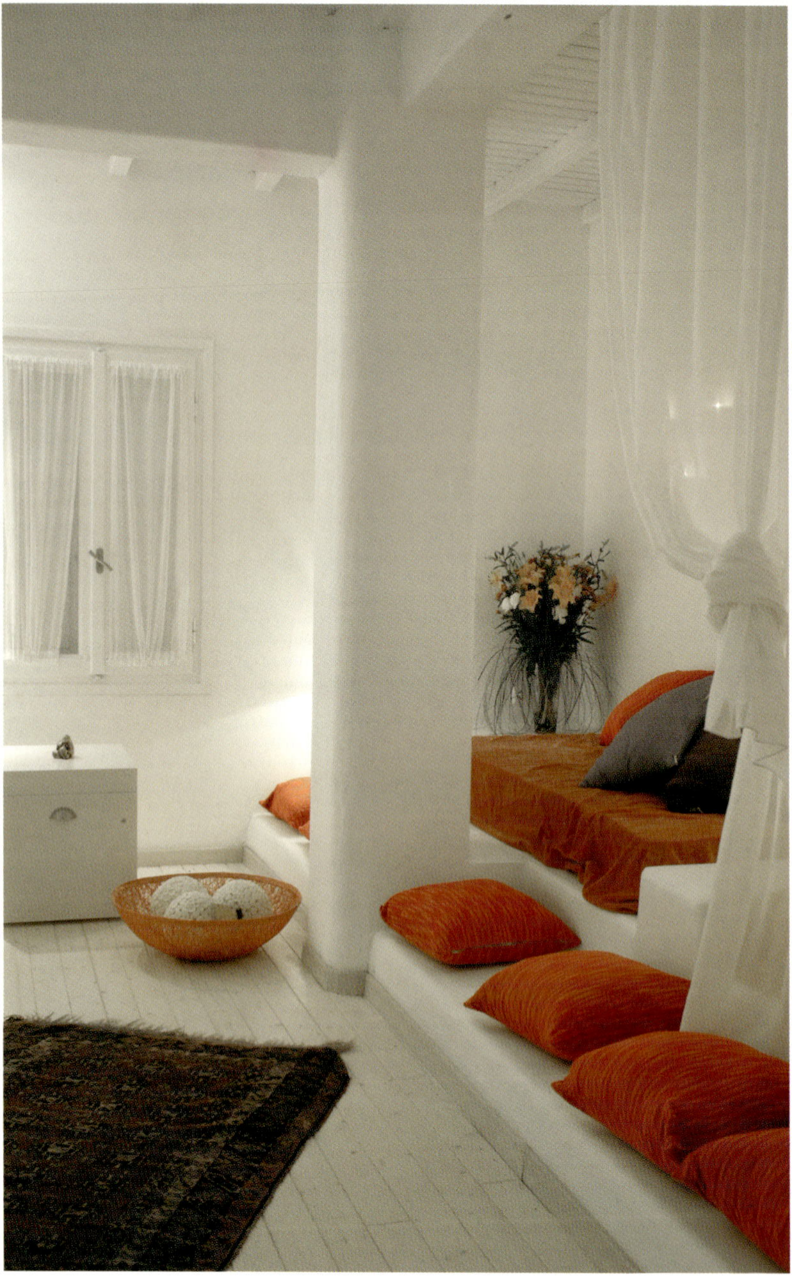

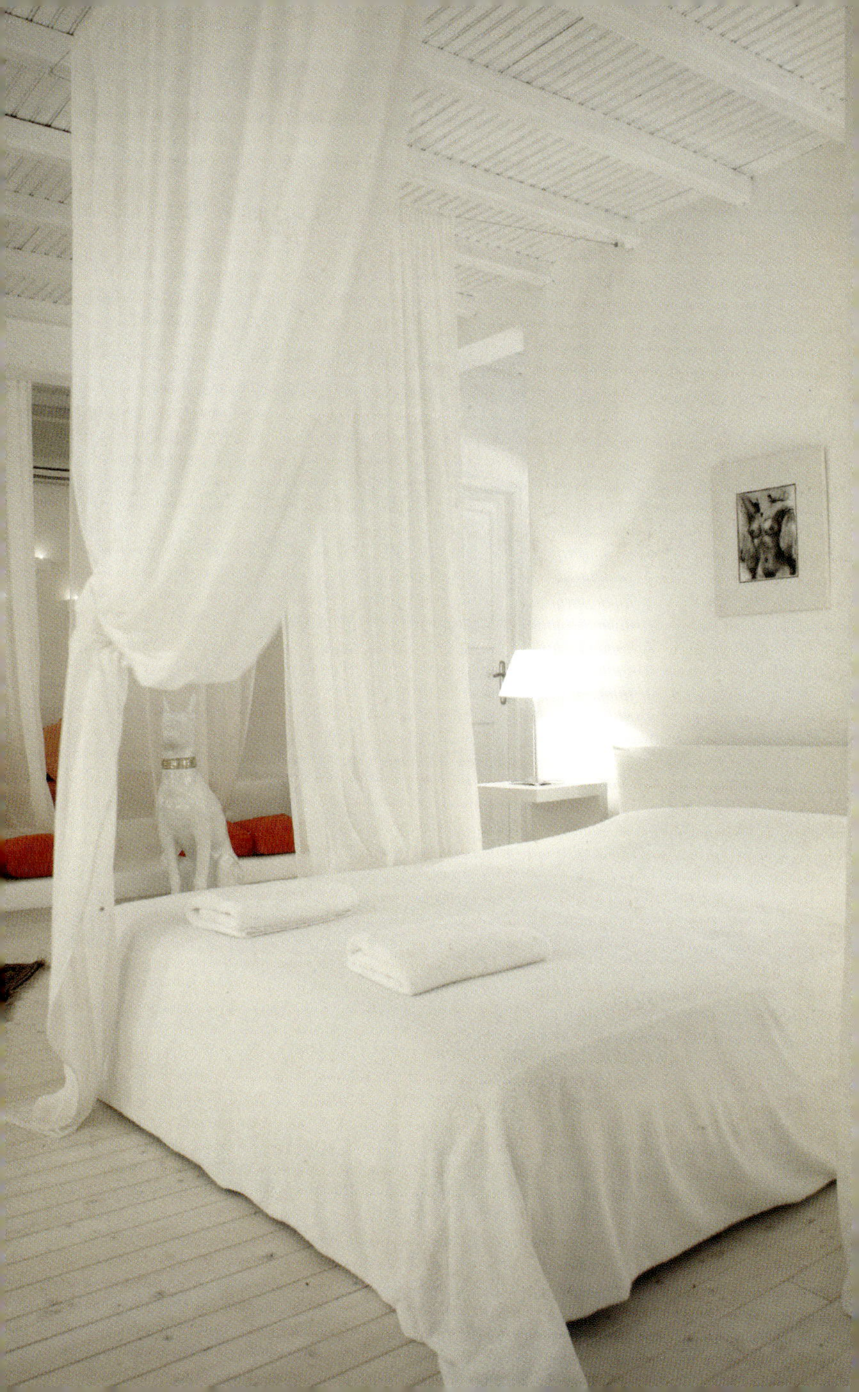

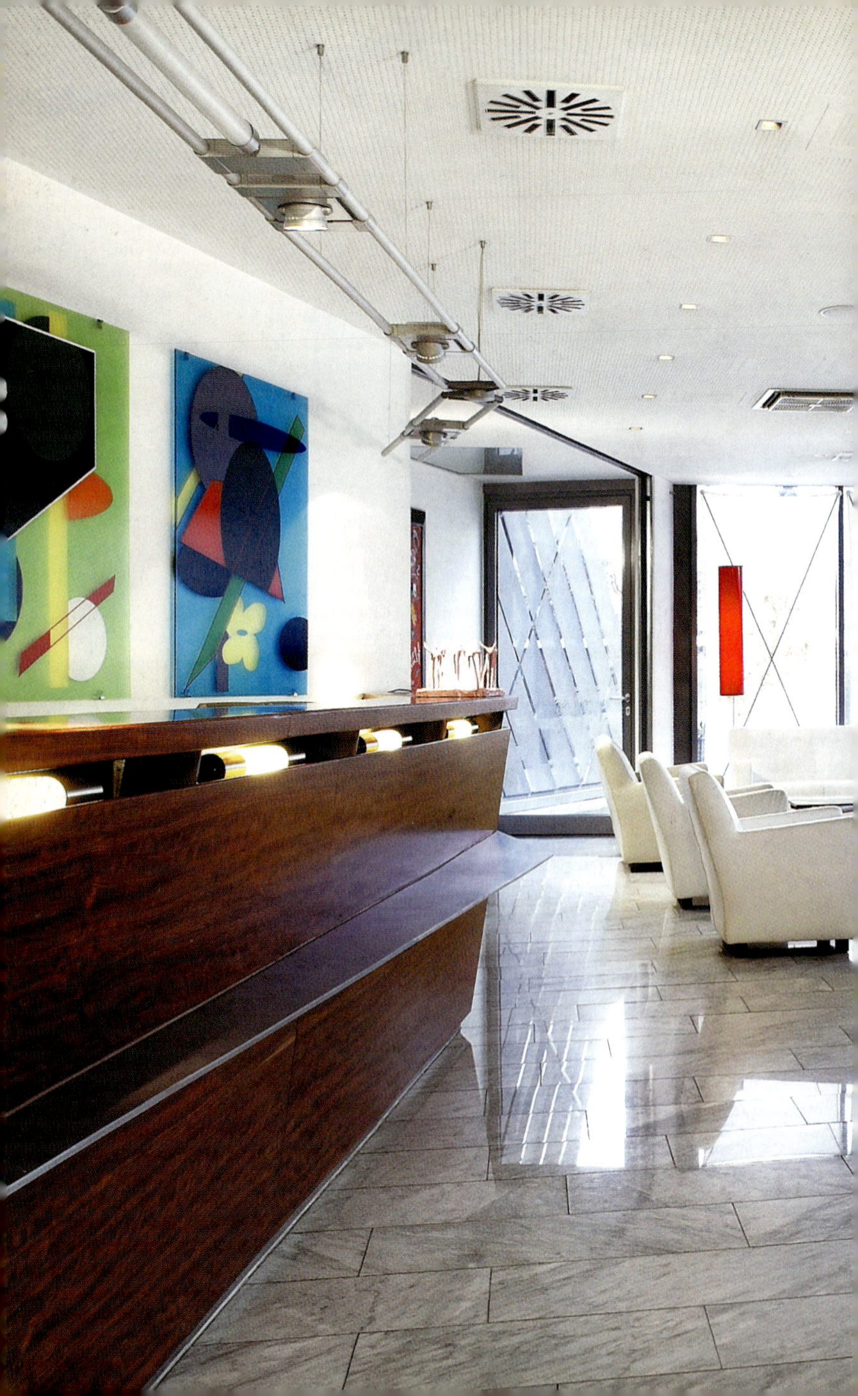

AUGARTEN HOTEL
Art and Design

Architect: **Günther Domenig**

Date: 2000
Address: Schönaugasse 53, A-8010 Graz, Austria
Tel.: +43 316 20 800 Fax: +43 316 20 800 80
www.augartenhotel.at
Photos: © Augarten Hotel

Location: Urban
Style: Modern
Rooms: 56
Special features: Indoor pool, sun terrace, sauna, solarium, rooftop terrace

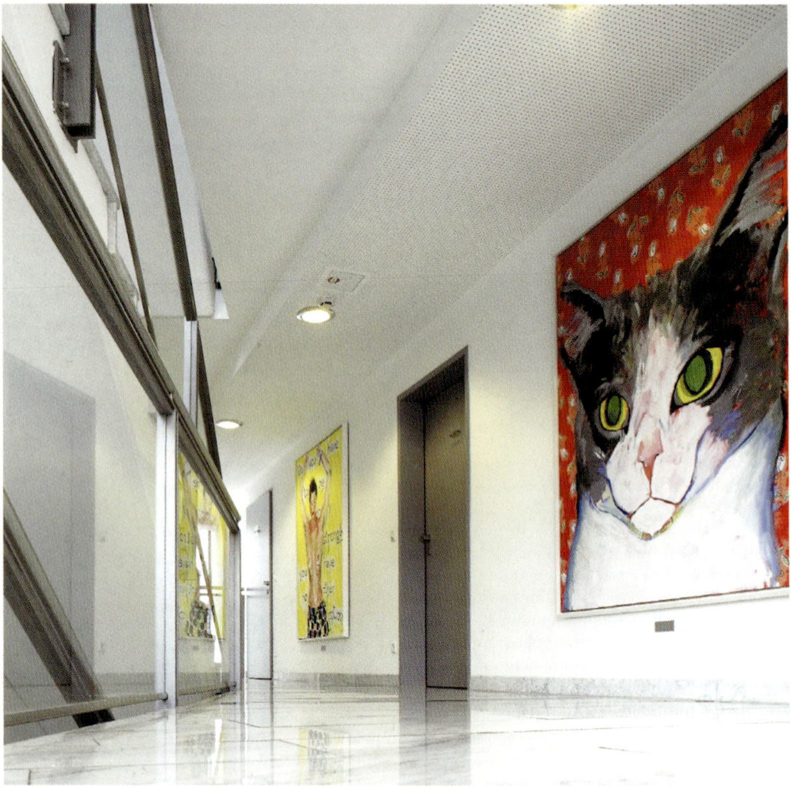

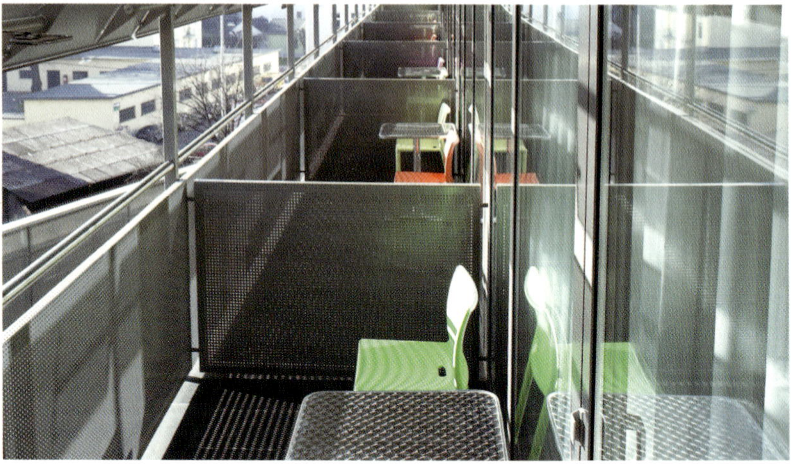

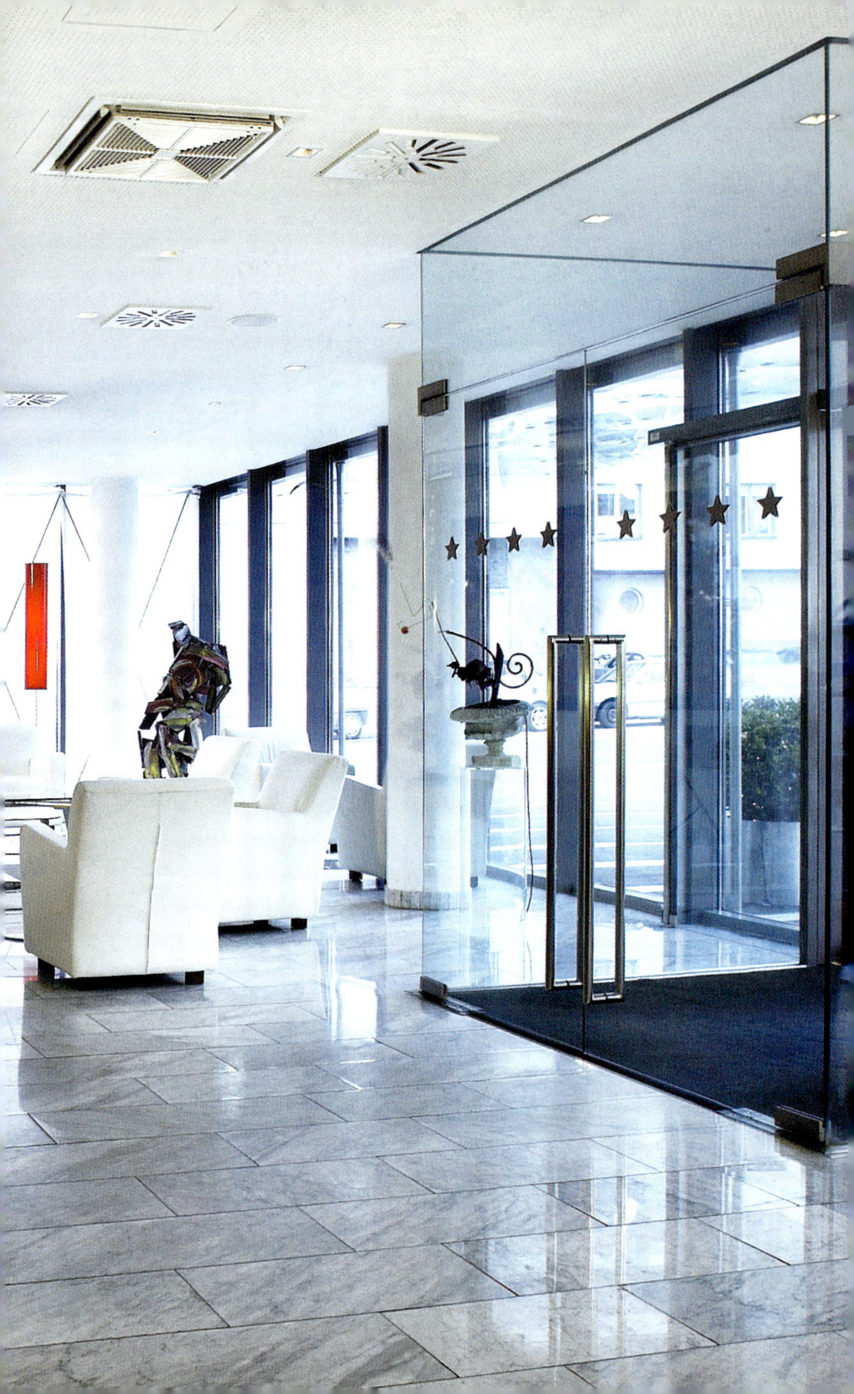

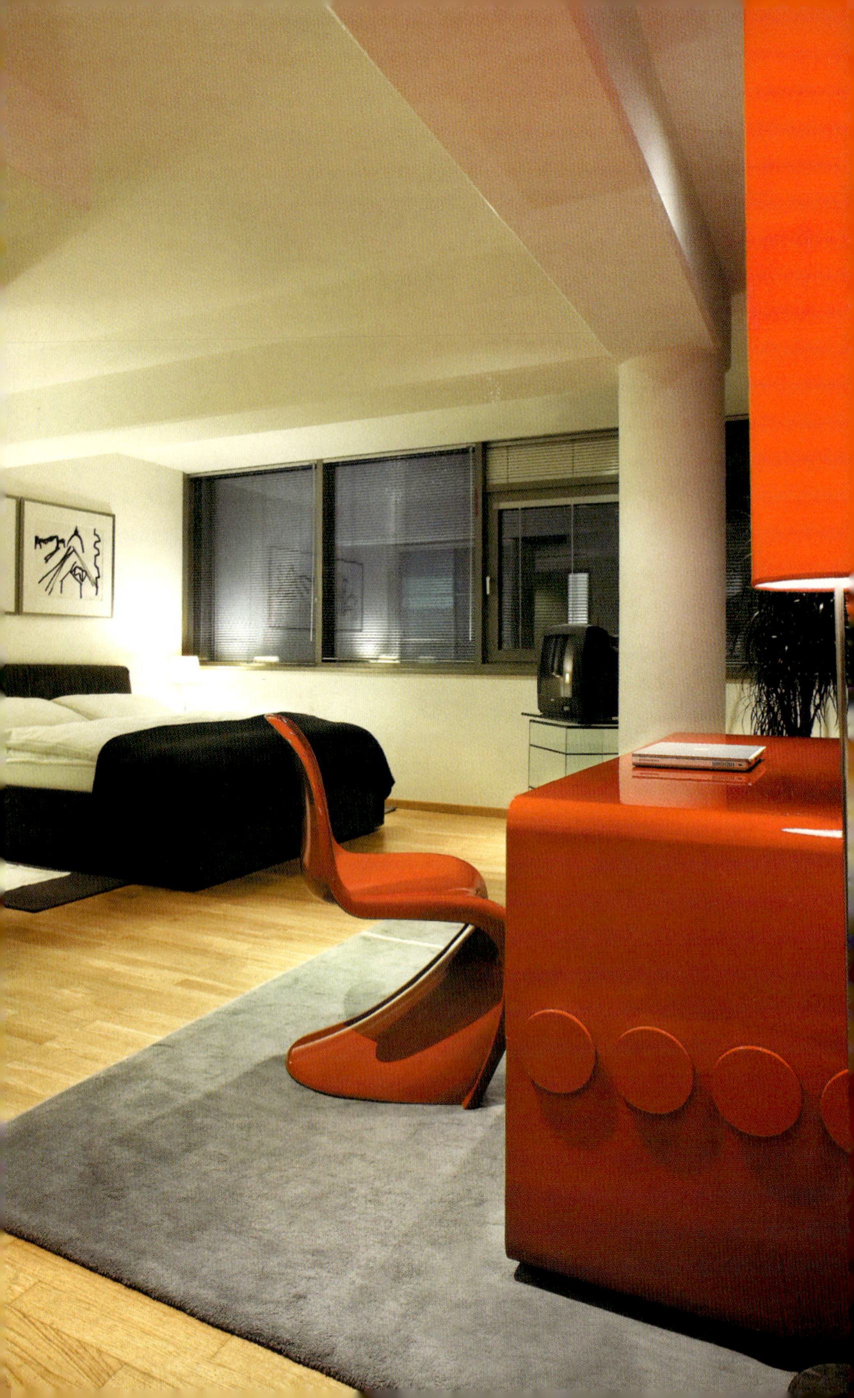

35

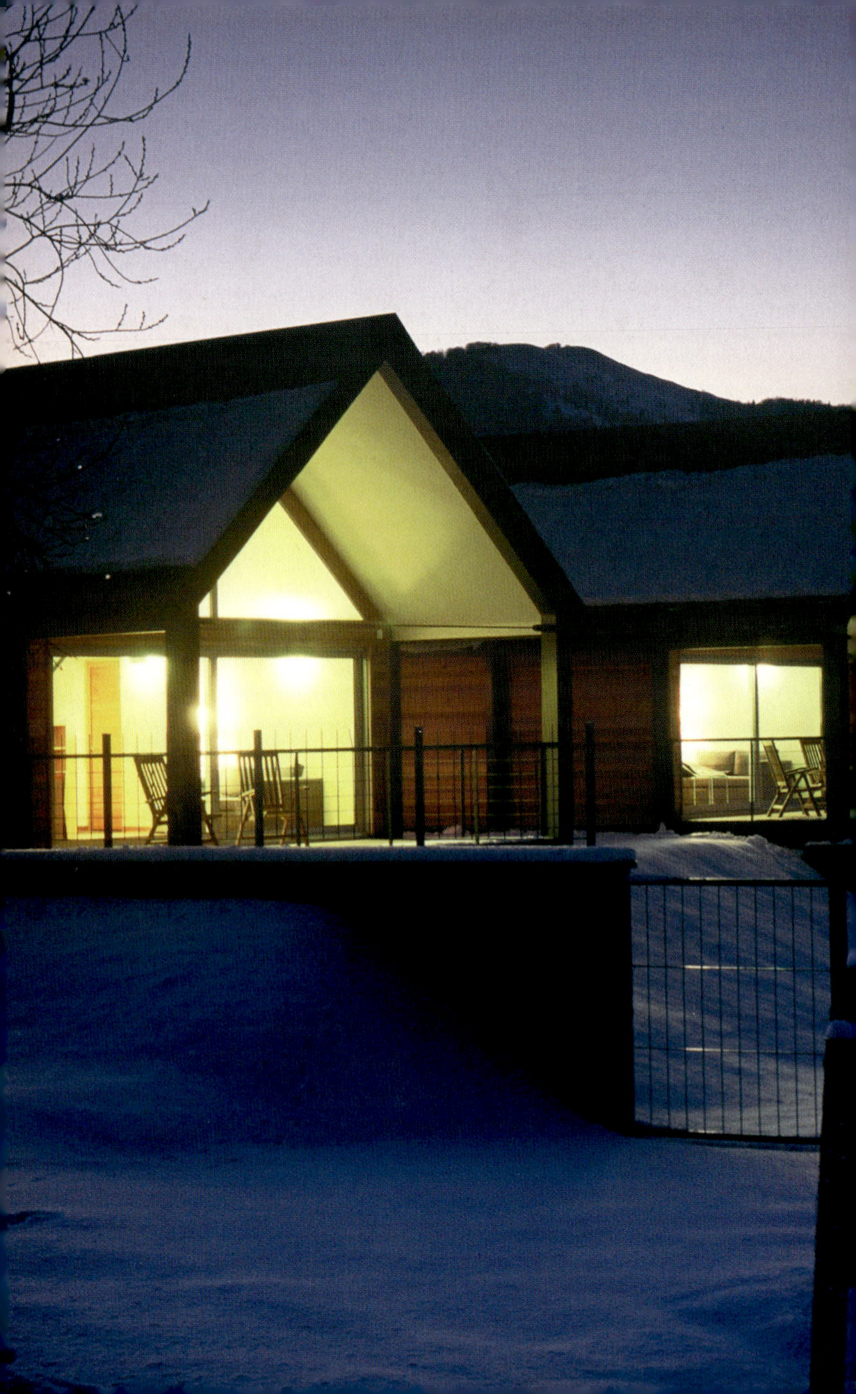

NEBESA
Comfort with Panorama

Architect: **REAL Engineering**

Date: 2004
Address: Livek 39, 5222 Kobarid, Slovenia
Tel.: +386 53 844 620
www.nebesa.si
Photos: © Nebesa

Location: Countryside
Style: Contemporary mountain retreat
Rooms: Four two-person houses (51 m^2)
Special features: Individual houses with living room and terrace, social area with fireplace, wellness centre

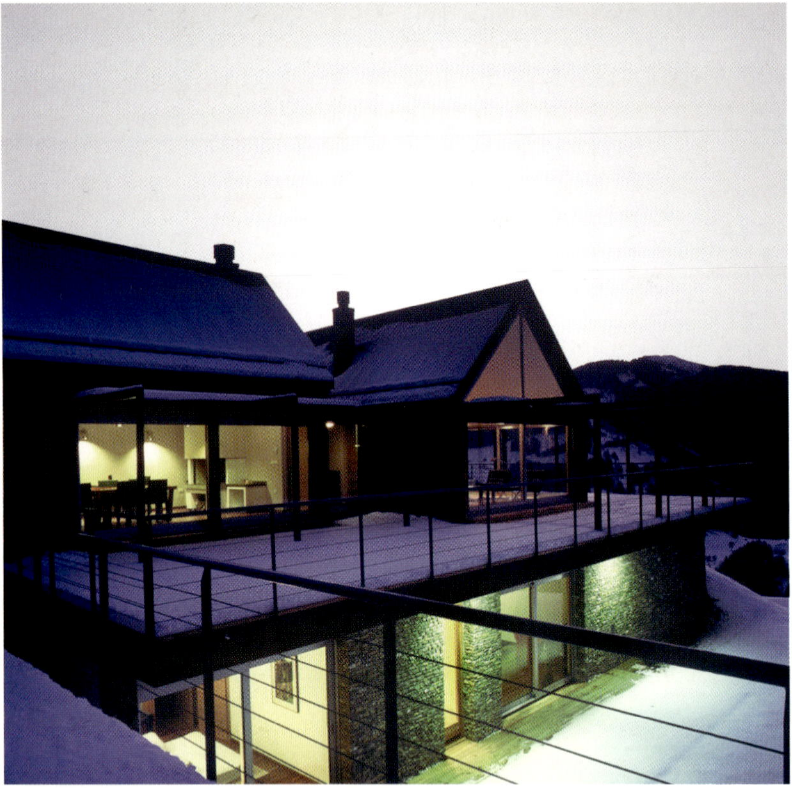

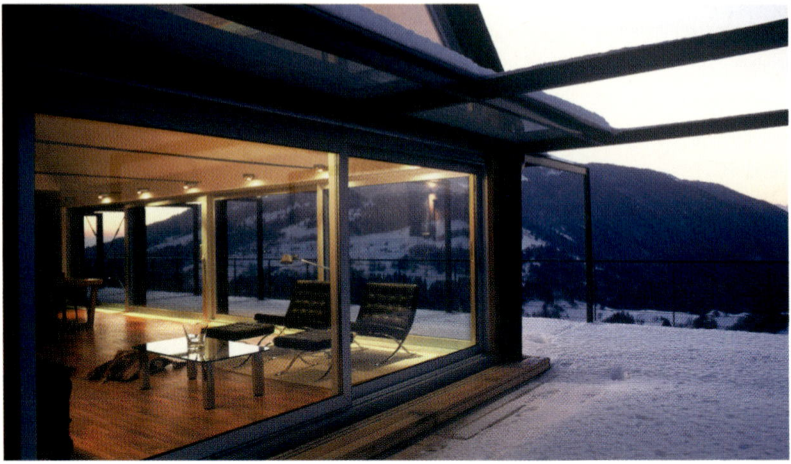

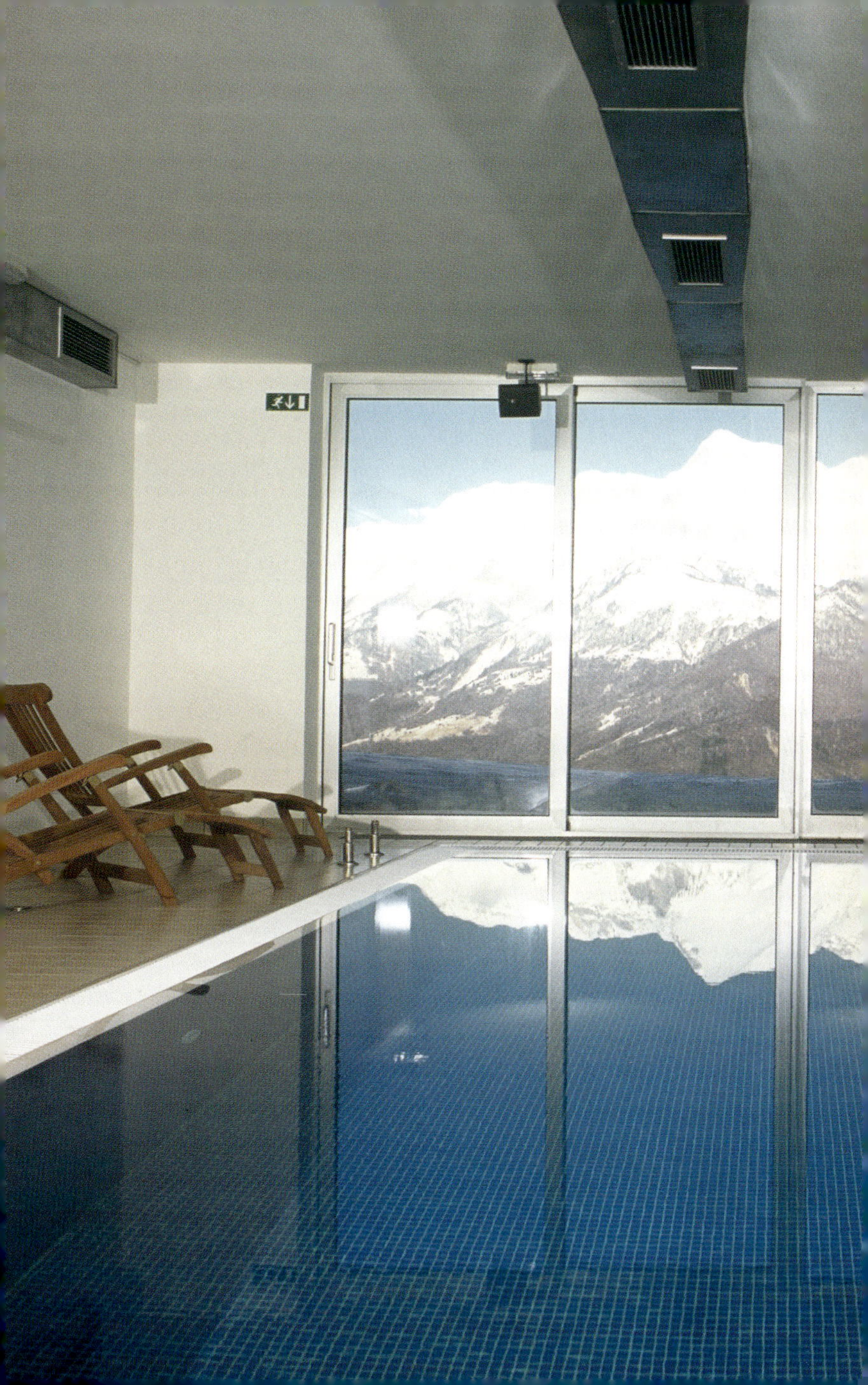

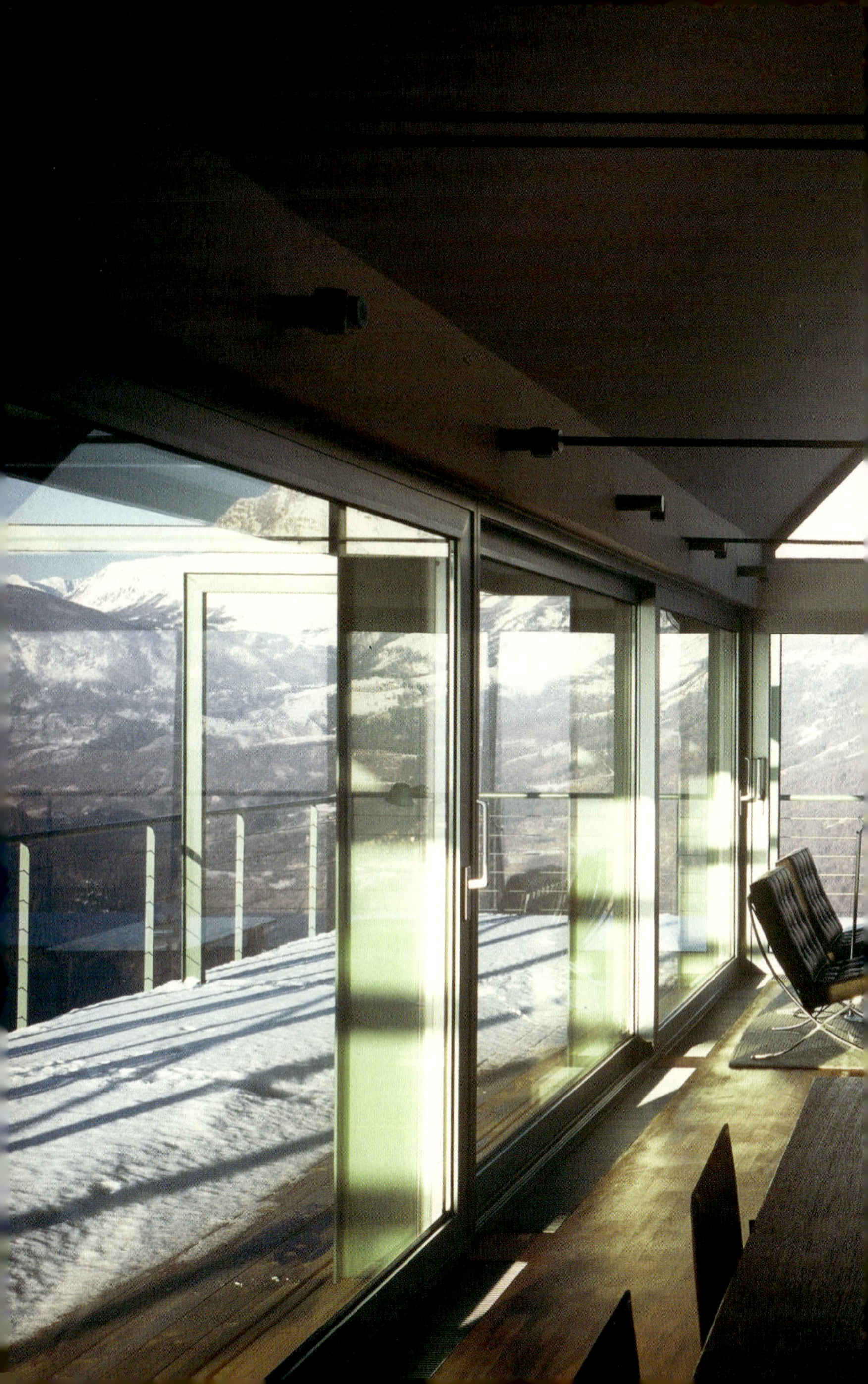

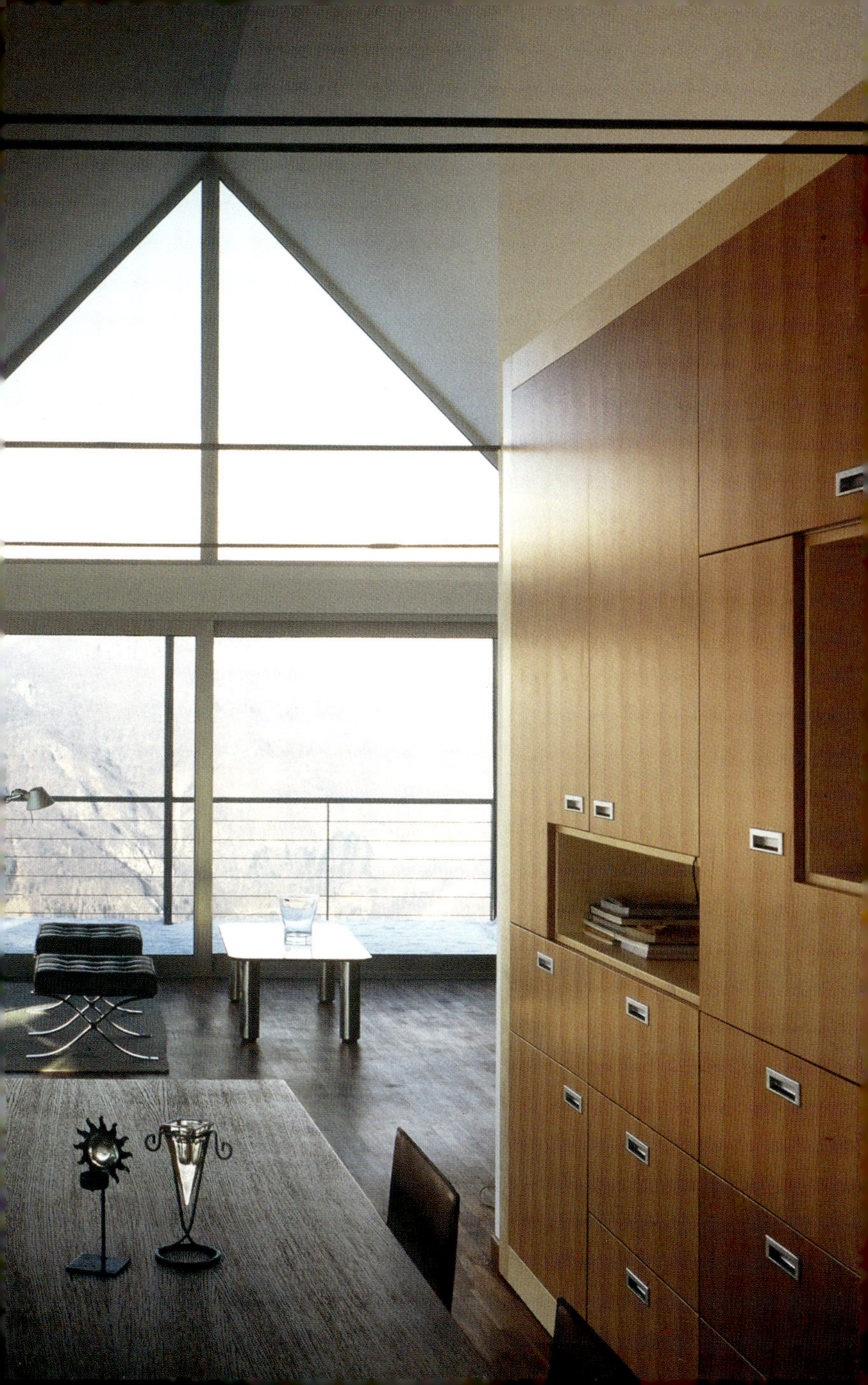

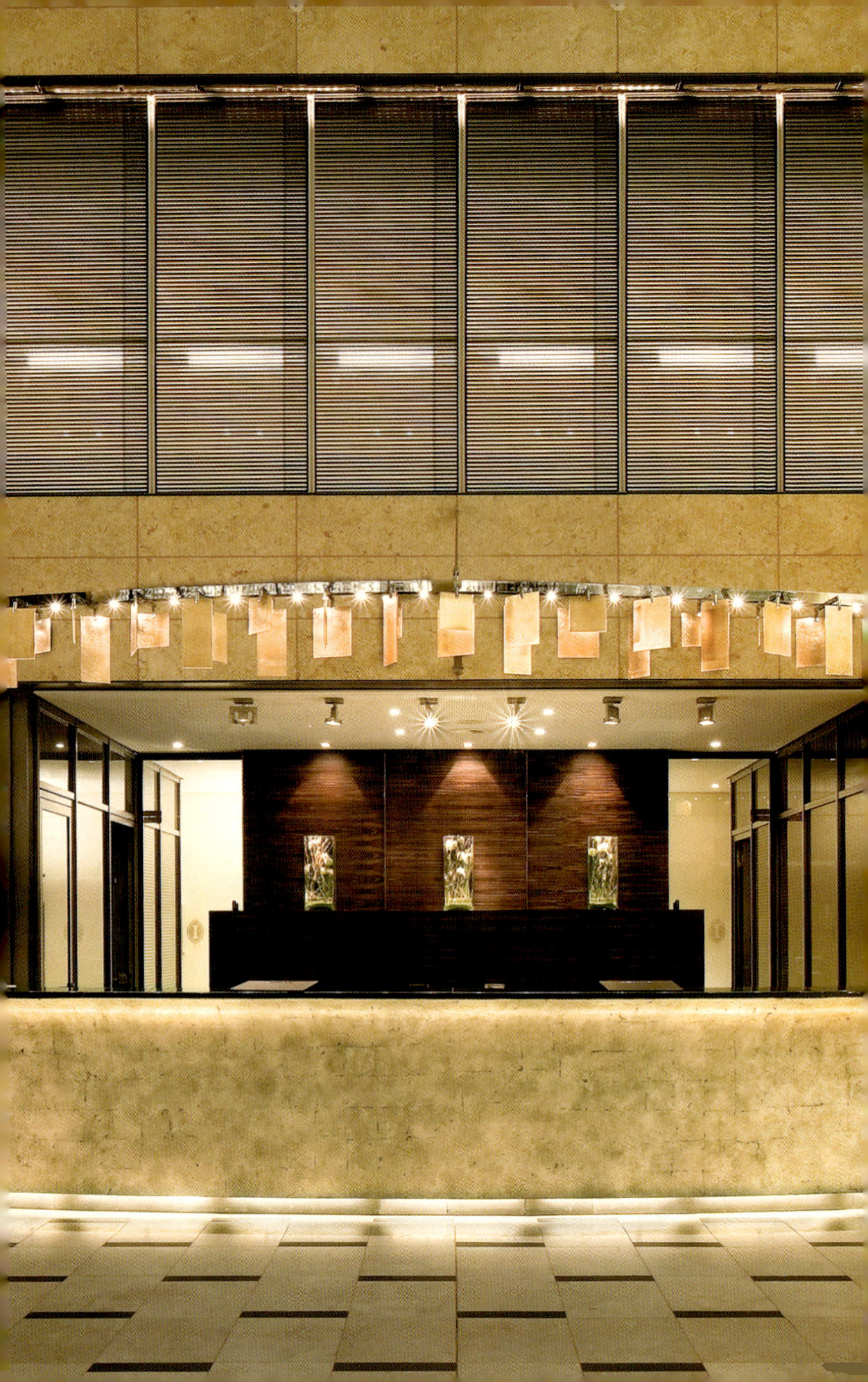

INTERCONTINENTAL DÜSSELDORF
Comfort and Exceptional Service

Architects: **HPP – Hentrich-Petschnigg & Partner**
HBA – Hirsch Bedner Associates
Collaborators: **Tombusch & Brumann (interior)**

Date: 2005
Address: Königsallee 59, 40215 Düsseldorf, Germany
Tel.: +49 211 8285 0 Fax: +49 211 8285 1111
www.ichotelsgroup.com
Photos: © Olaf Schiemann

Location: Urban
Style: Modern luxury
Rooms: 286 guest rooms and 32 suites
Special features: Ideal location on the main shopping boulevard of Düsseldorf, surprising art concept, largest ballroom in the city

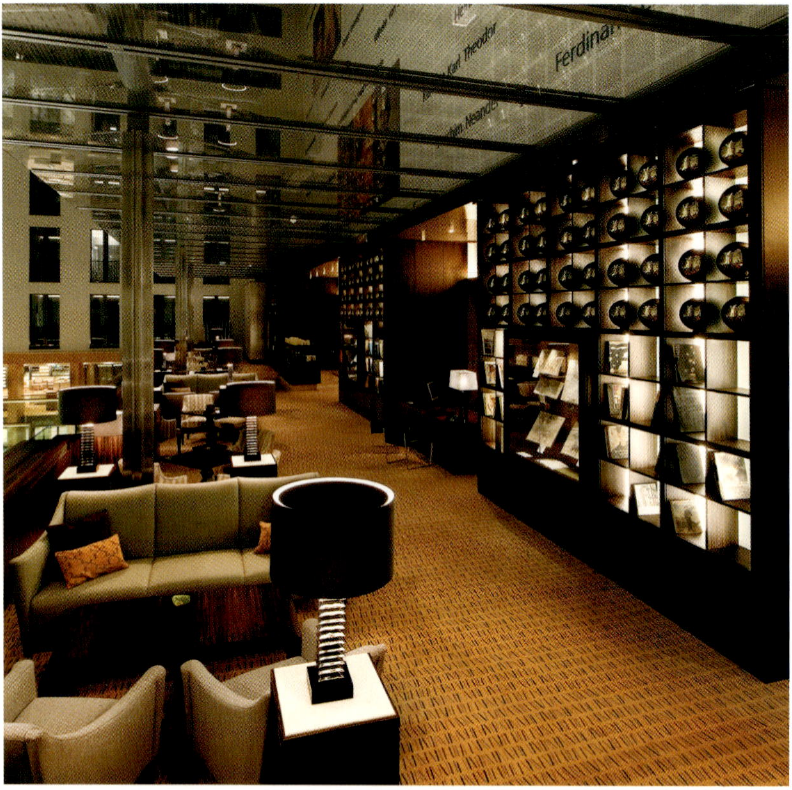
Karl Theodor
Neander

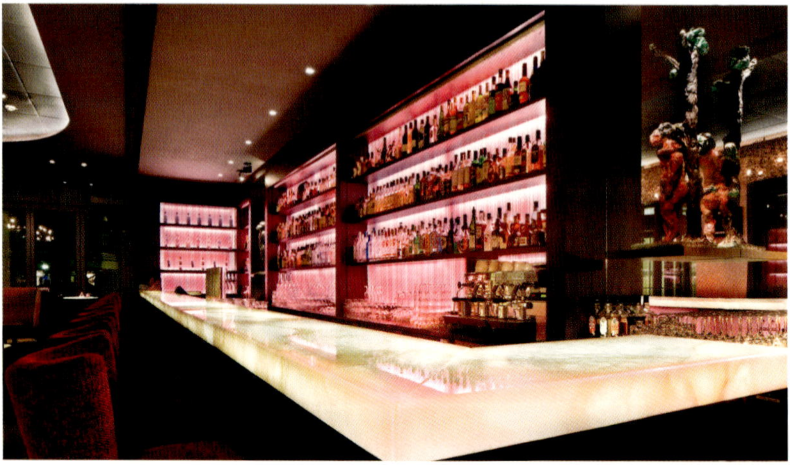

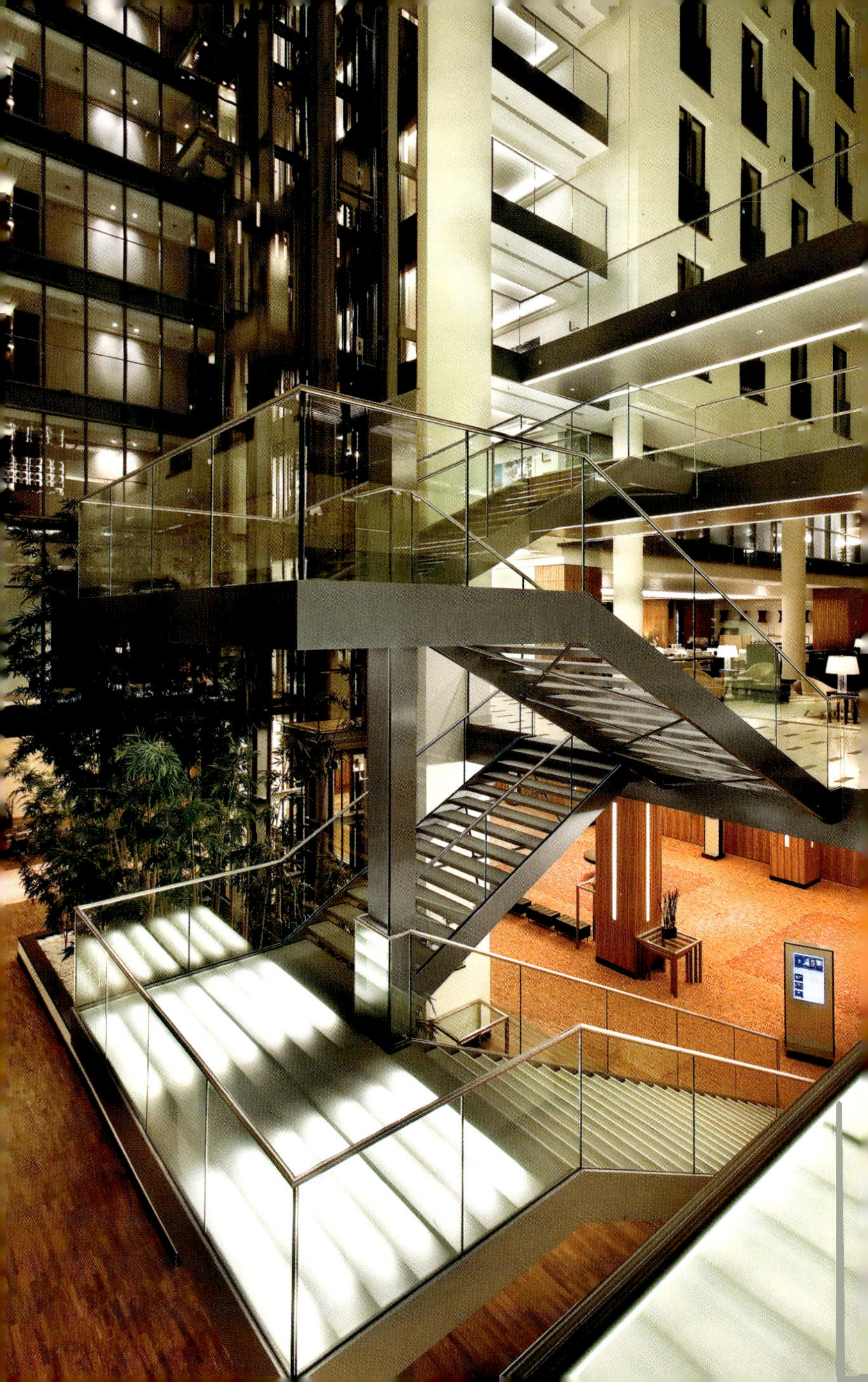

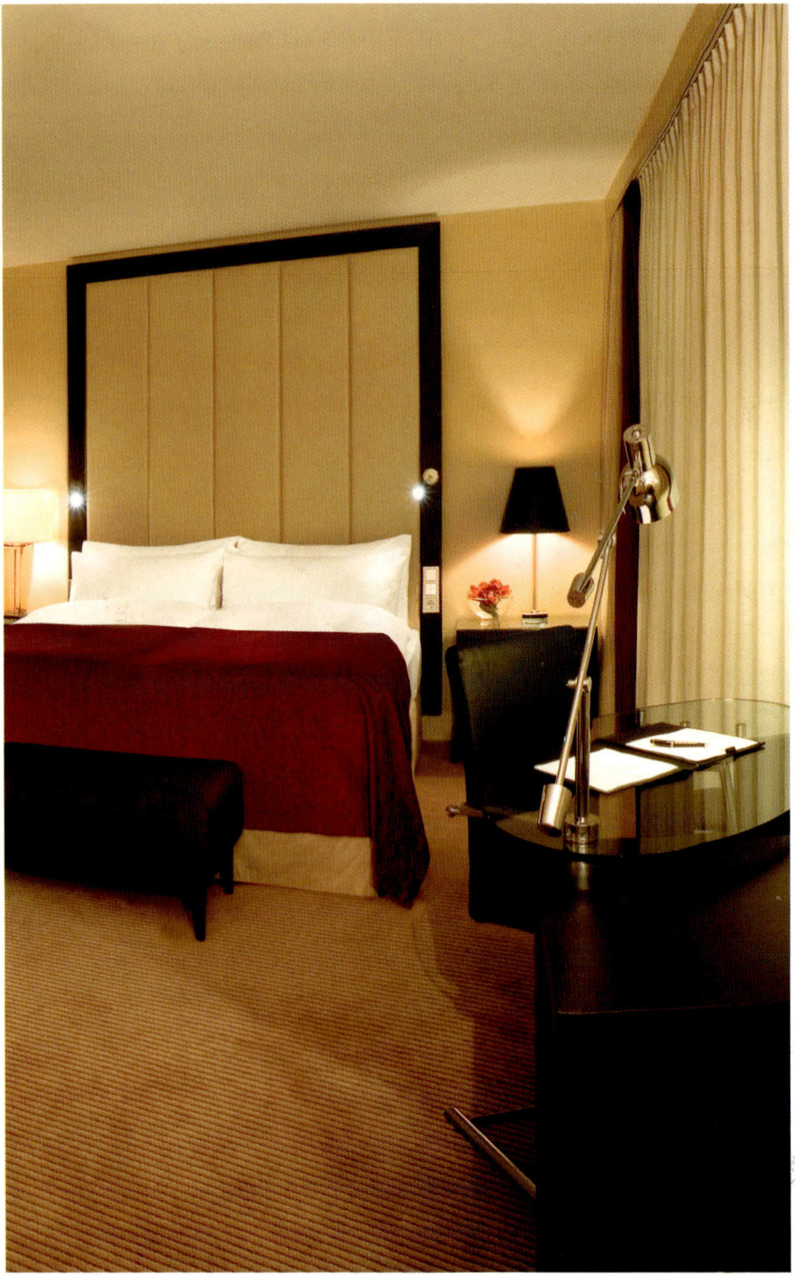

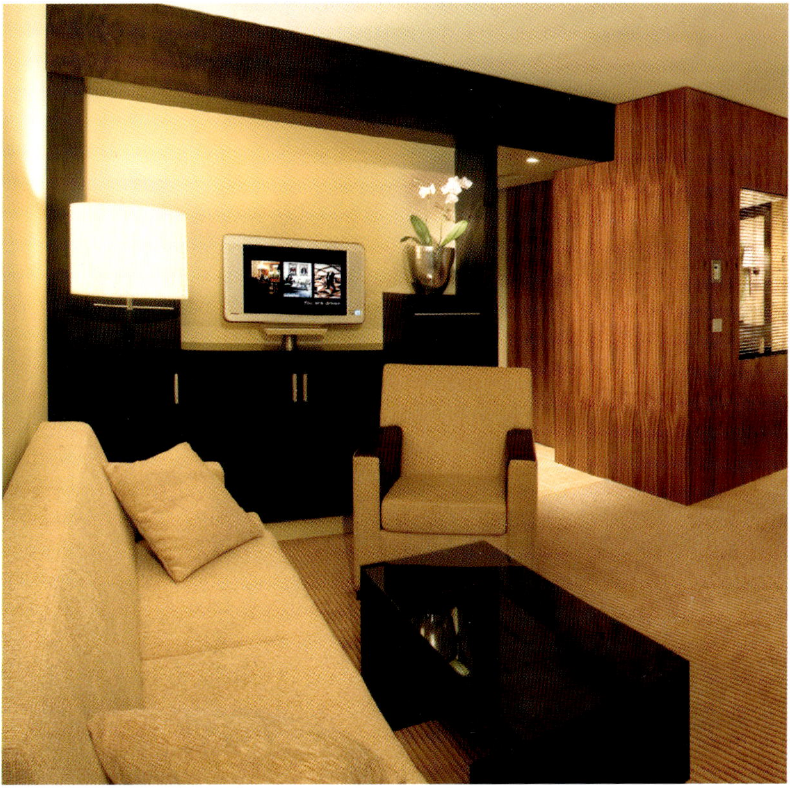

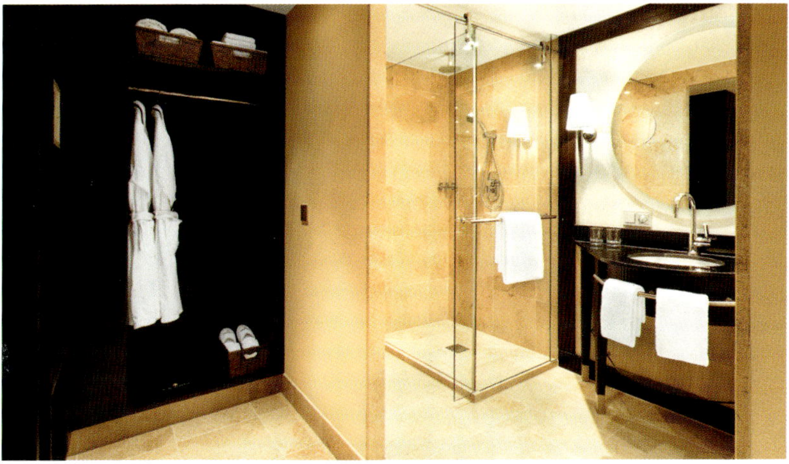

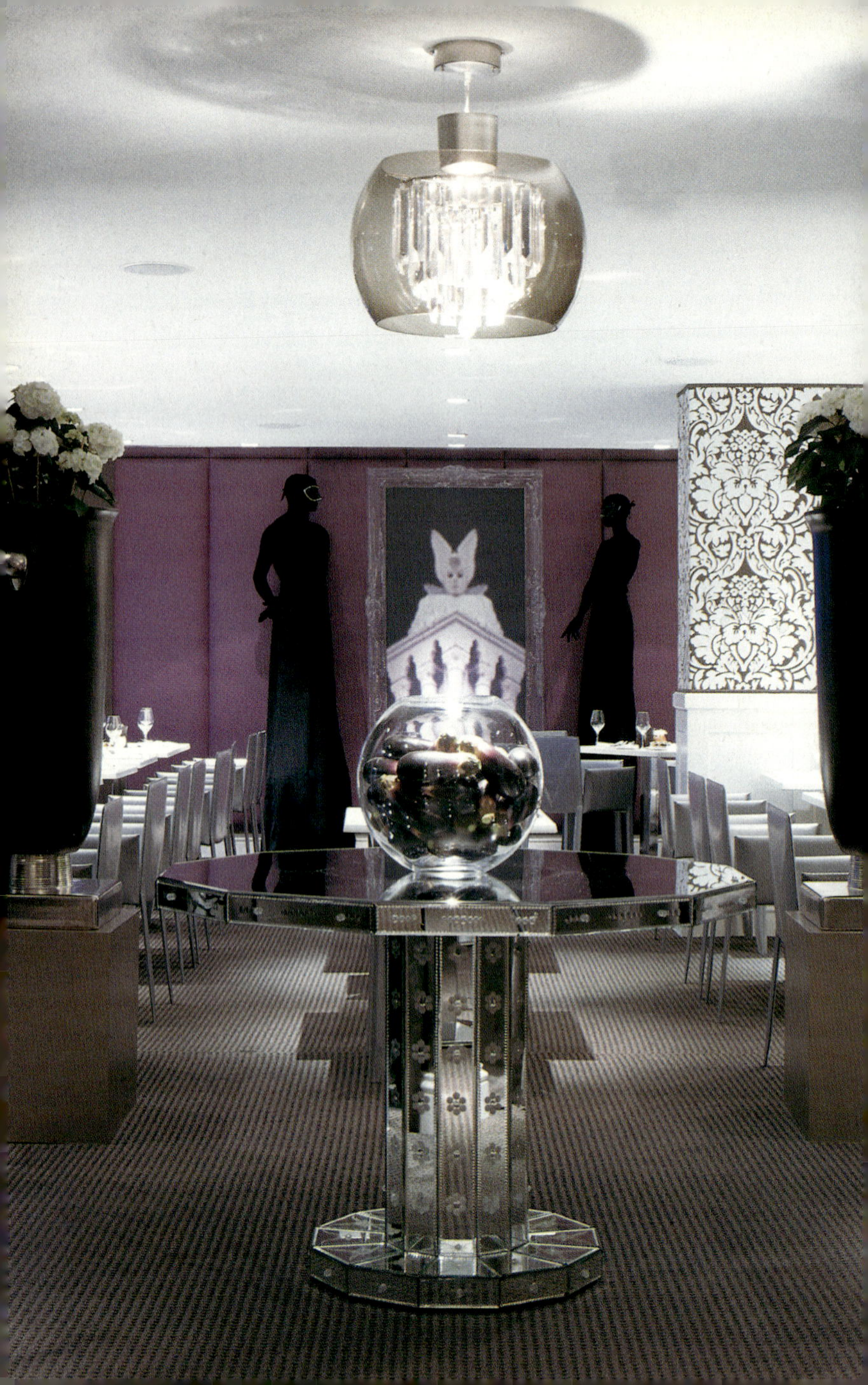

THE MANDEVILLE HOTEL
Luxury Hotel in London

Decorator: **Stephen Ryan**

Date: 2005
Address: Mandeville Place, W1U 2BE London, United Kingdom
Tel.: +44 20 7935 5599 Fax: +44 20 7935 9588
www.mandeville.co.uk
Photos: © James Balston

Location: Urban
Style: Modern regency
Rooms: 142
Special features: Flat-screen interactive LCD screens, power shower, penthouse suite, non-smoking hotel

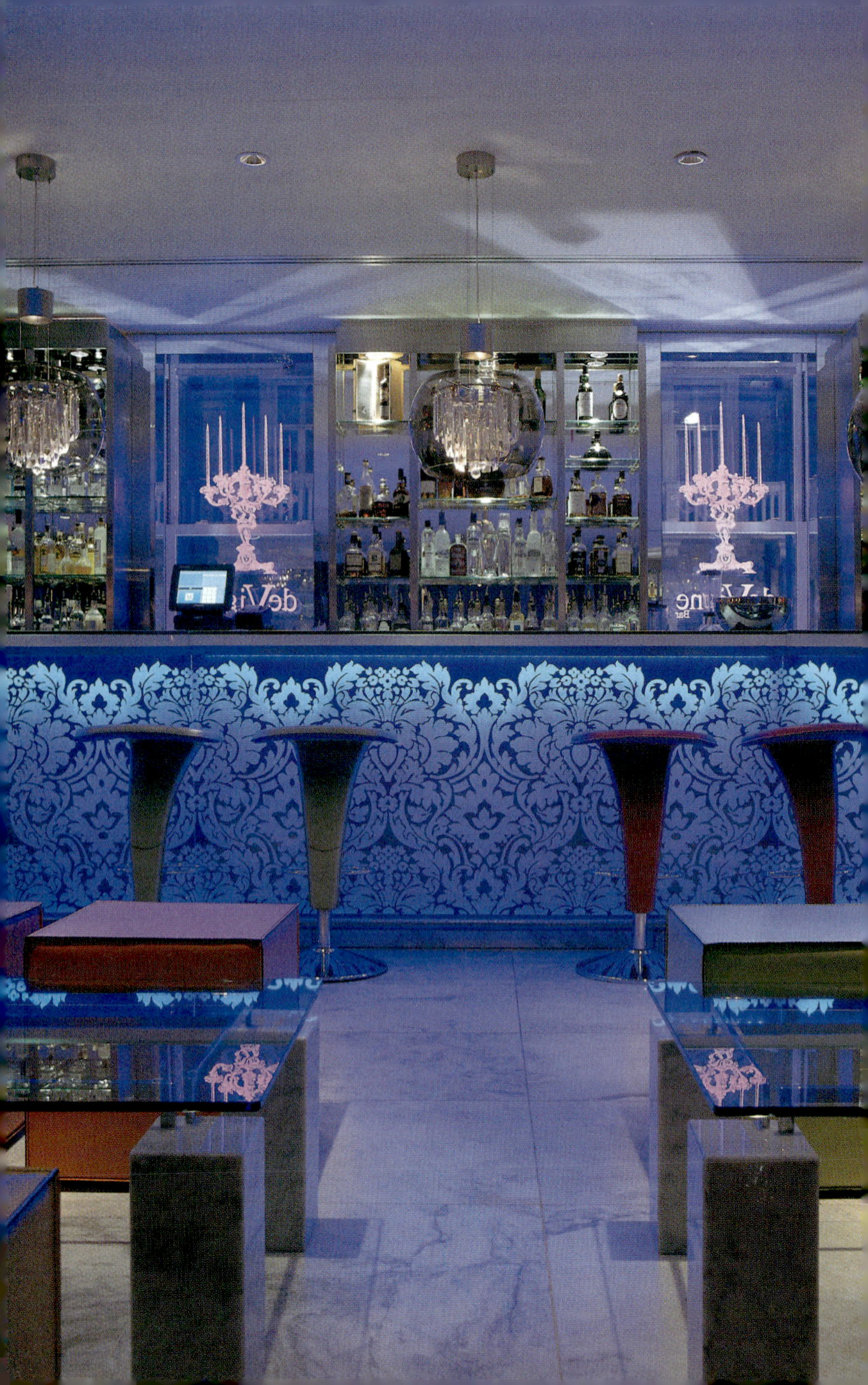

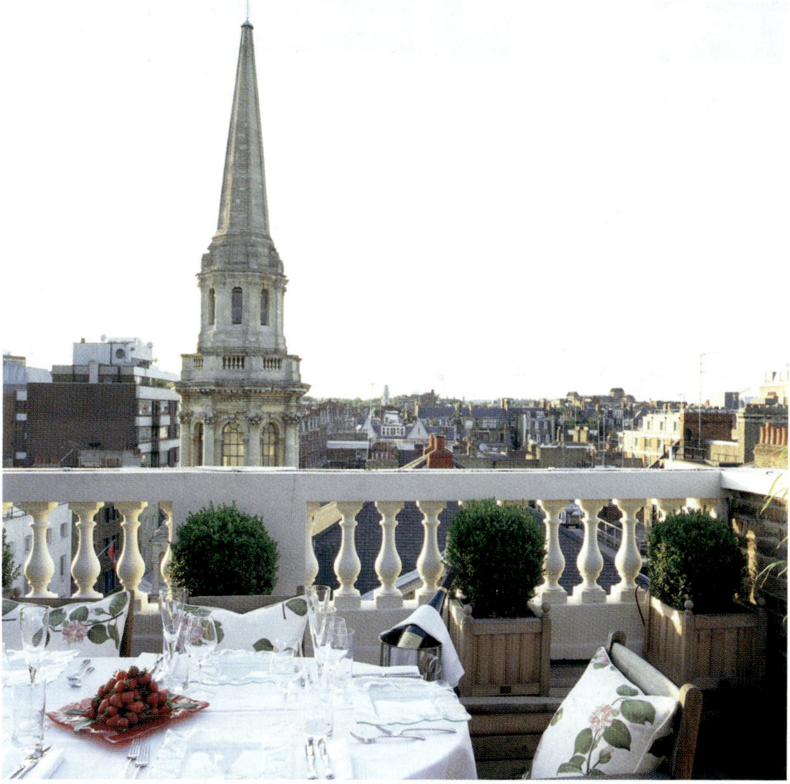

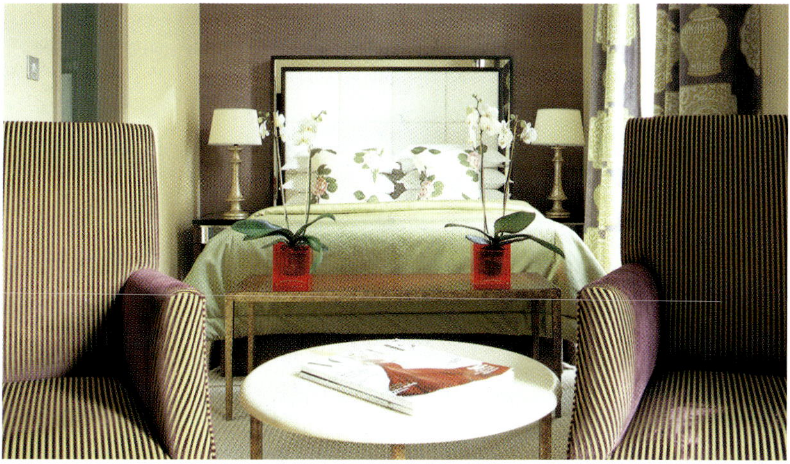

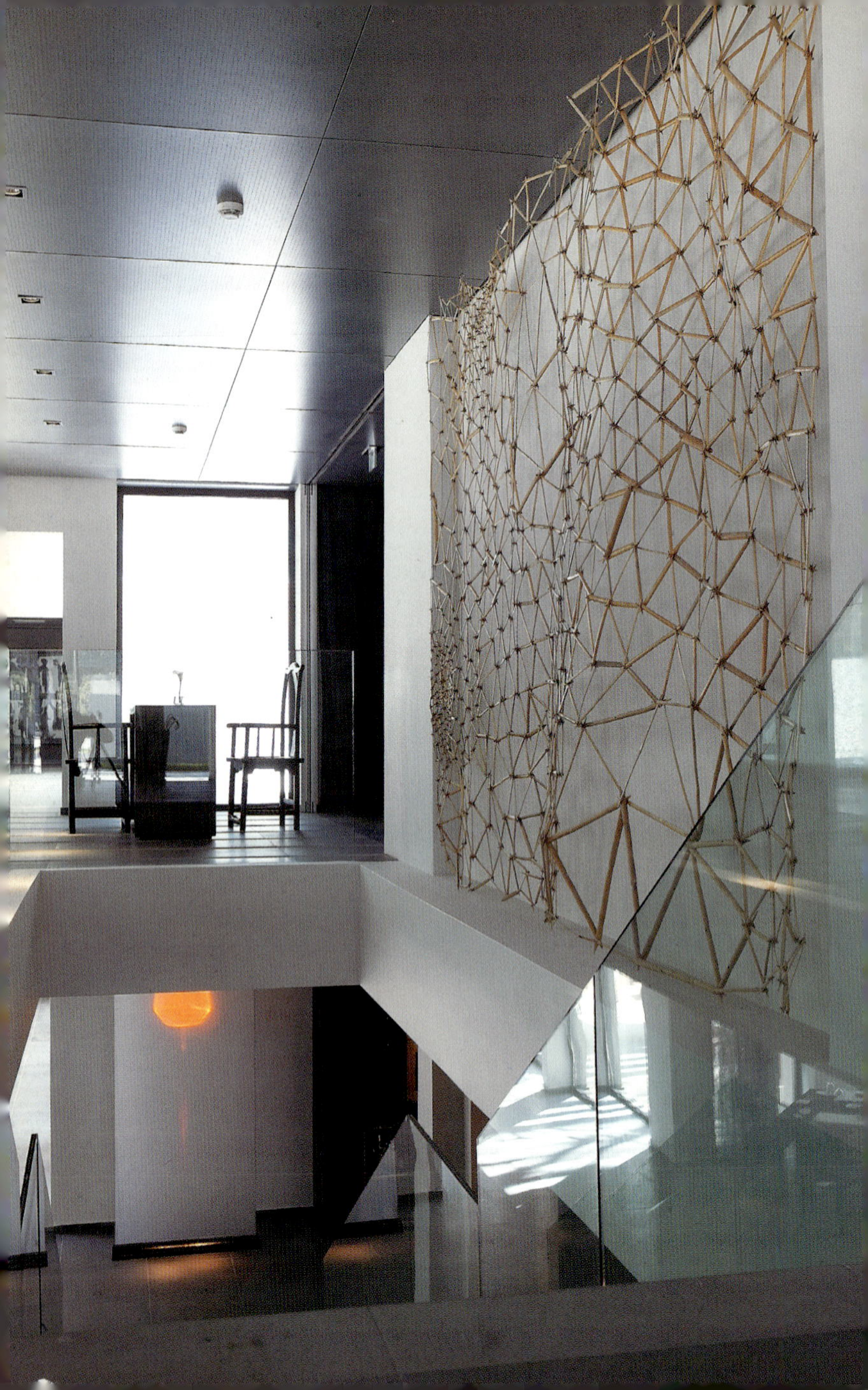

LIFE GALLERY ATHENS
Boutique Hotel

Architects: **Kline Haller & Vassillis Rodatos Architects**

Date: 2004
Address: 103 Thisseos Avenue, 14565 Ekali, Athens, Greece
Tel.: +30 210 626 0400 Fax: +30 210 622 9353
www.lux-hotels.com/gr/life-gallery
Photos: © Life Gallery Athens

Location: Urban
Style: Minimalist
Rooms: 30
Special features: Library specialized in Greek literature and ancient mythology, spa

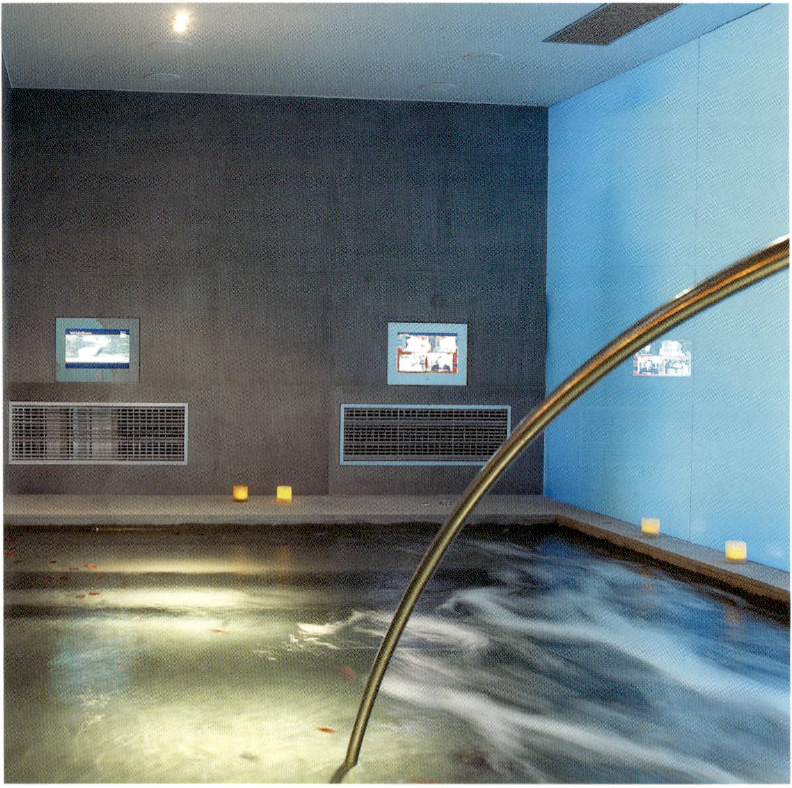

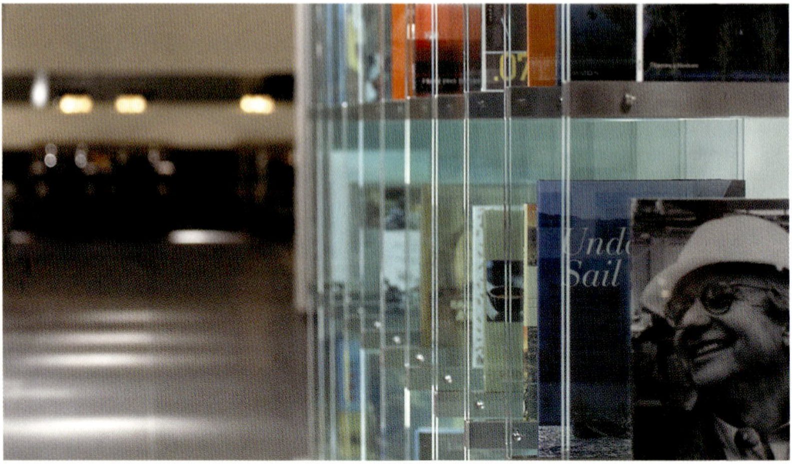

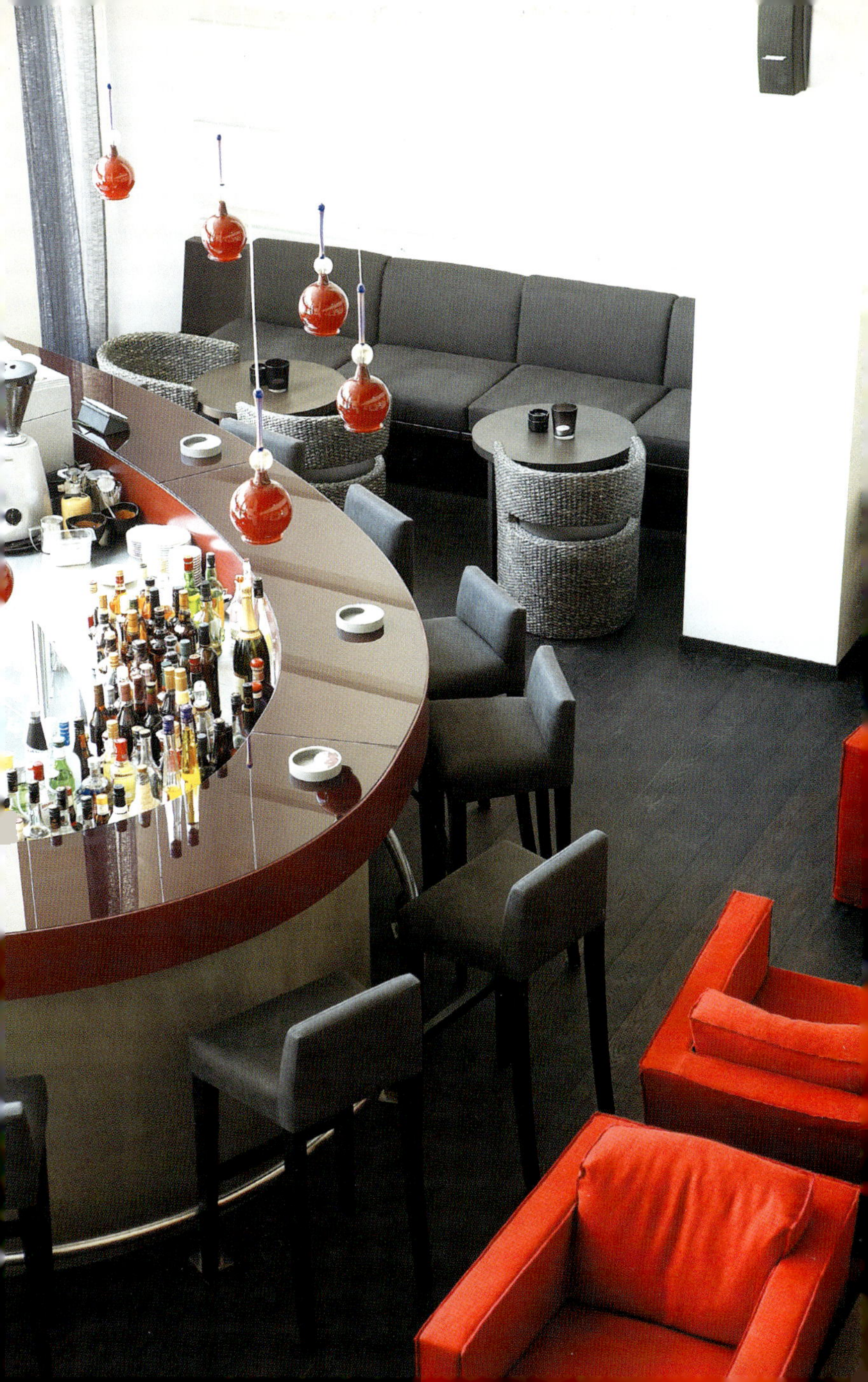

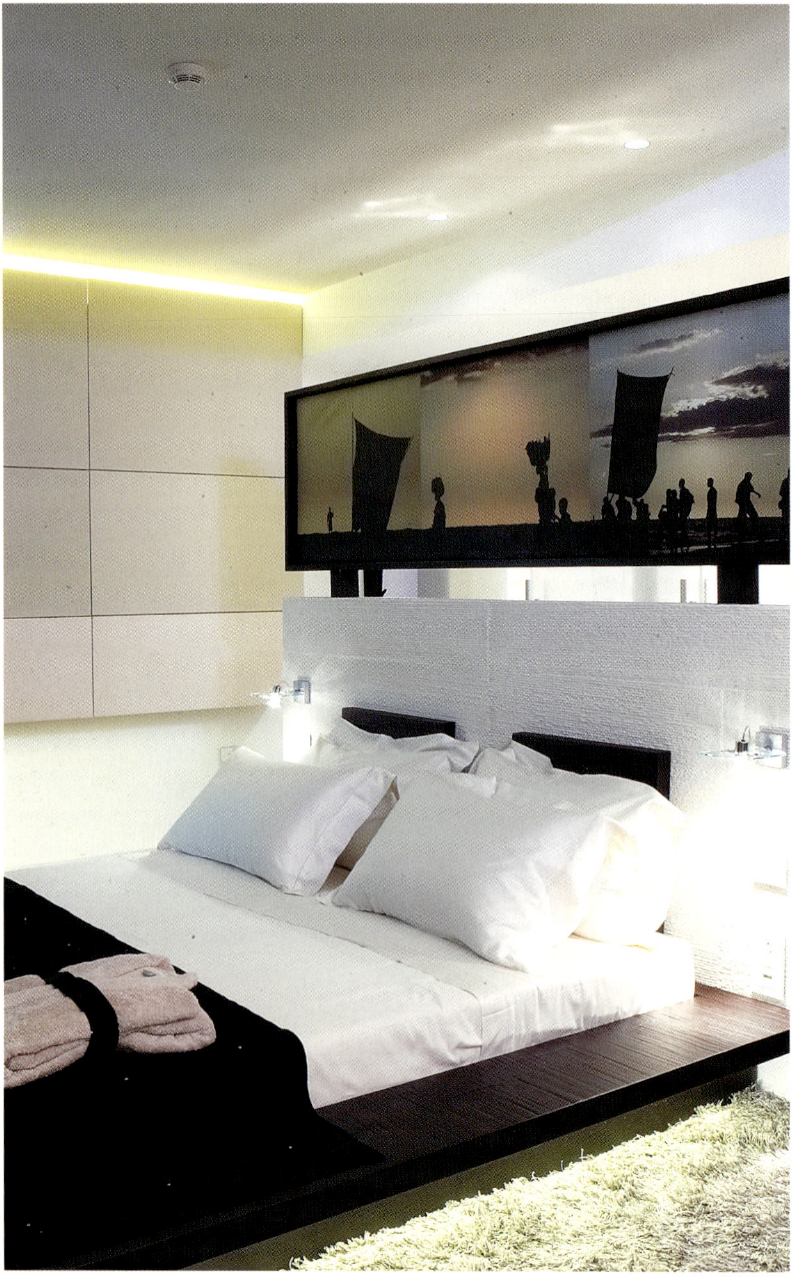

57

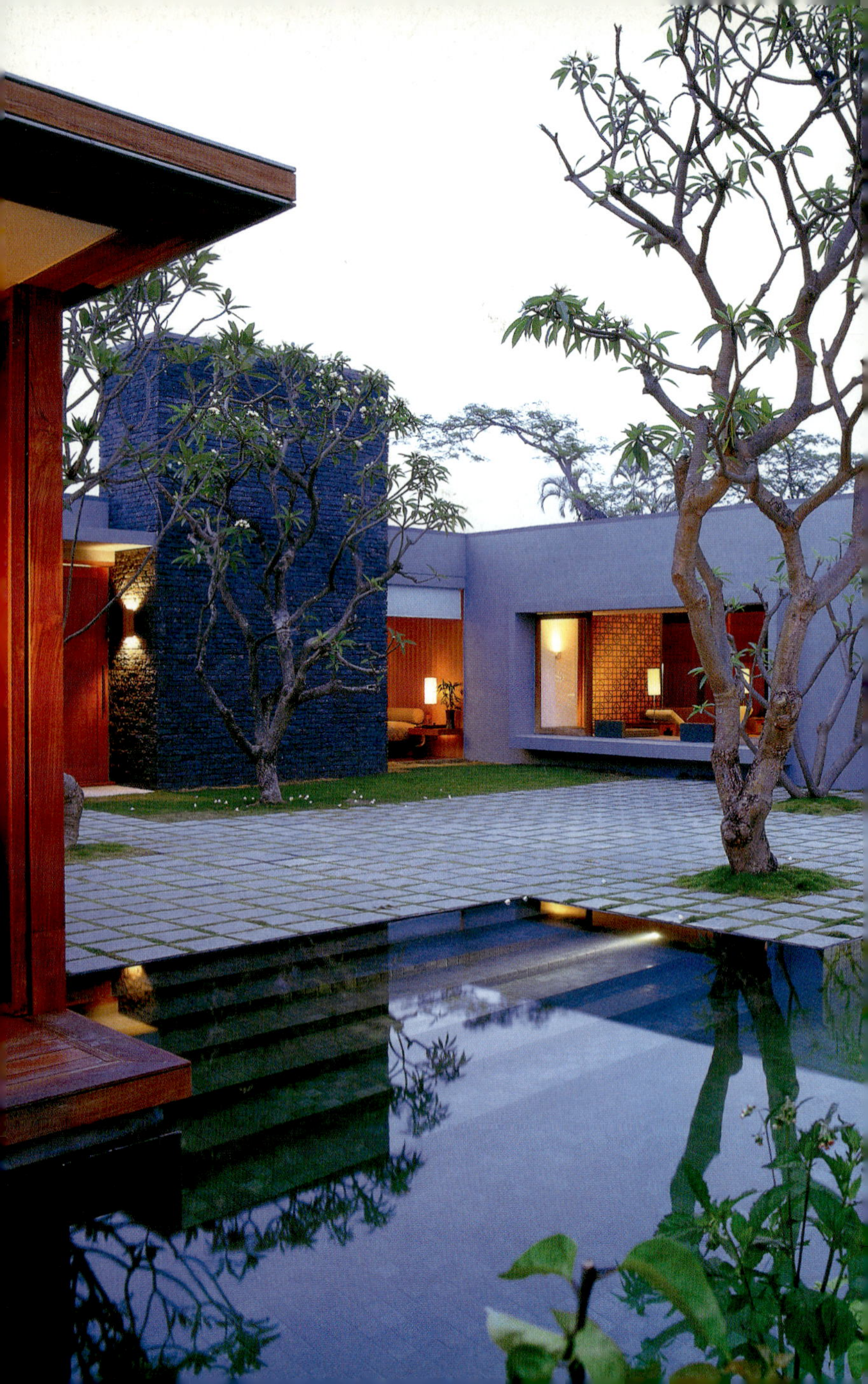

THE LALU
Ongoing Style Hotel

Architects: **Kerry Hill Architects**

Date: 2003
Address: 142 Jungshing Road, Yuchr Shiang Nantou, Taiwan
Tel.: +886 (049) 285 5311 Fax: +886 (049) 285 5312
www.thelalu.com.tw
Photos: © The Lalu

Location: Lake
Style: Minimalist
Rooms: 98
Special features: Spa, sauna, aerobic room, gym, bike rental, warm swimming pool

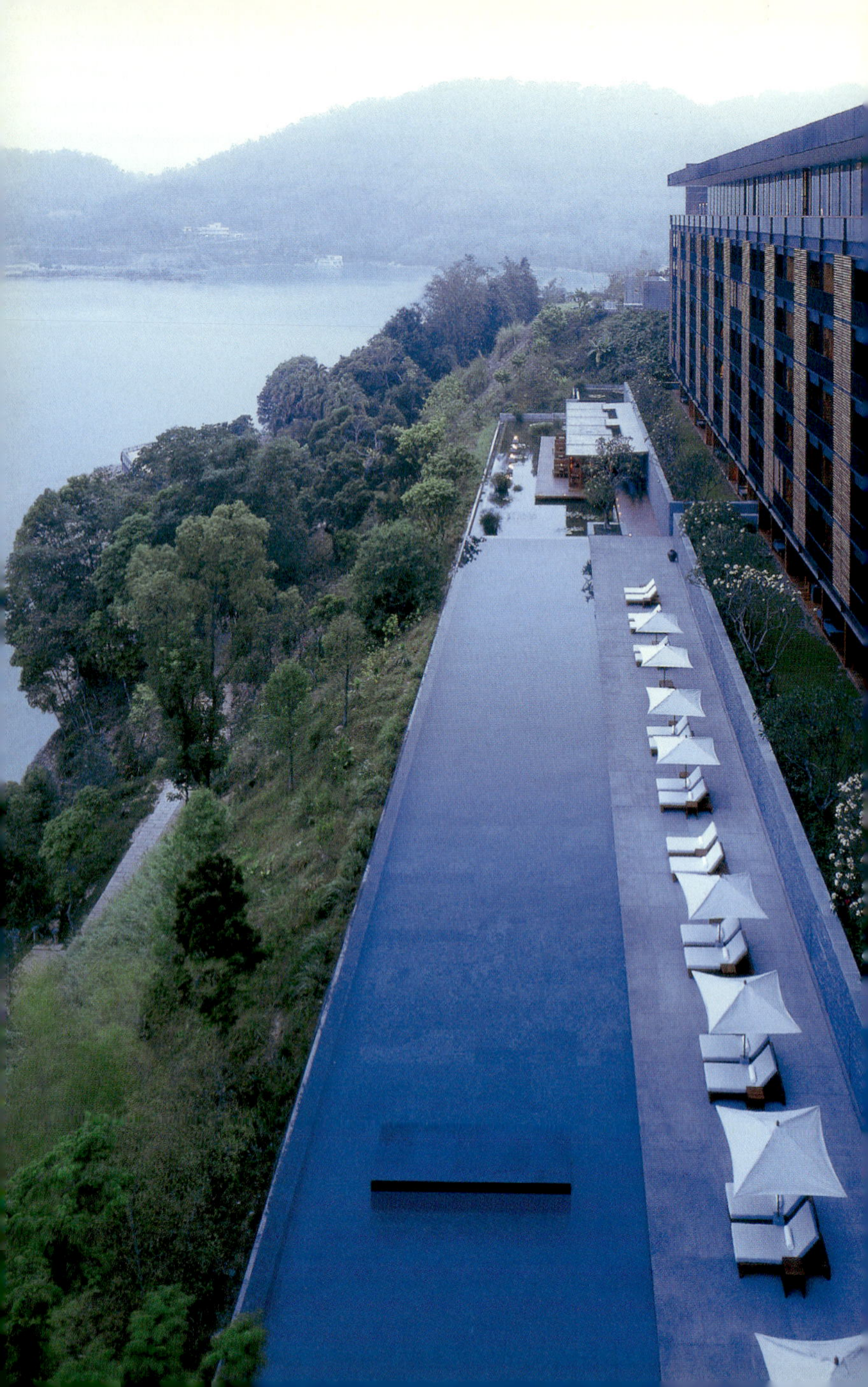

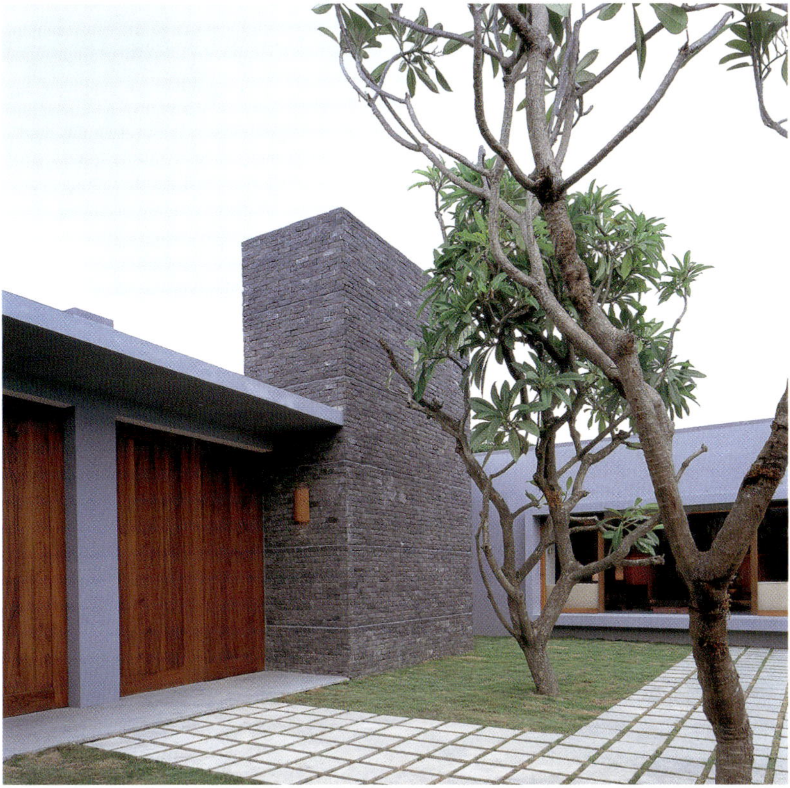

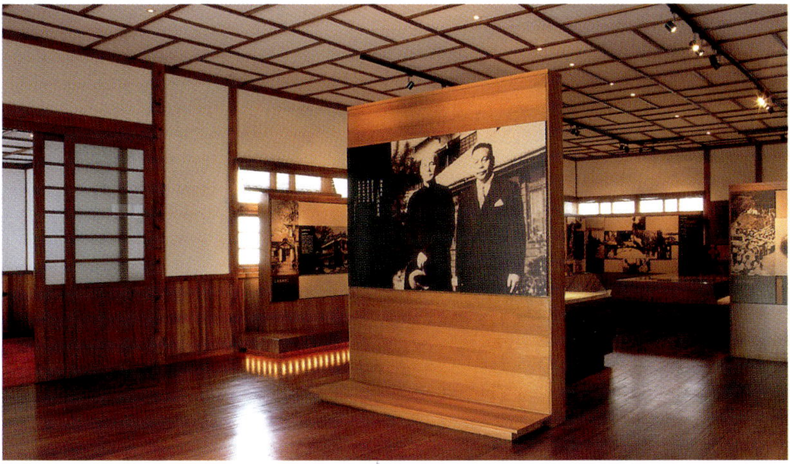

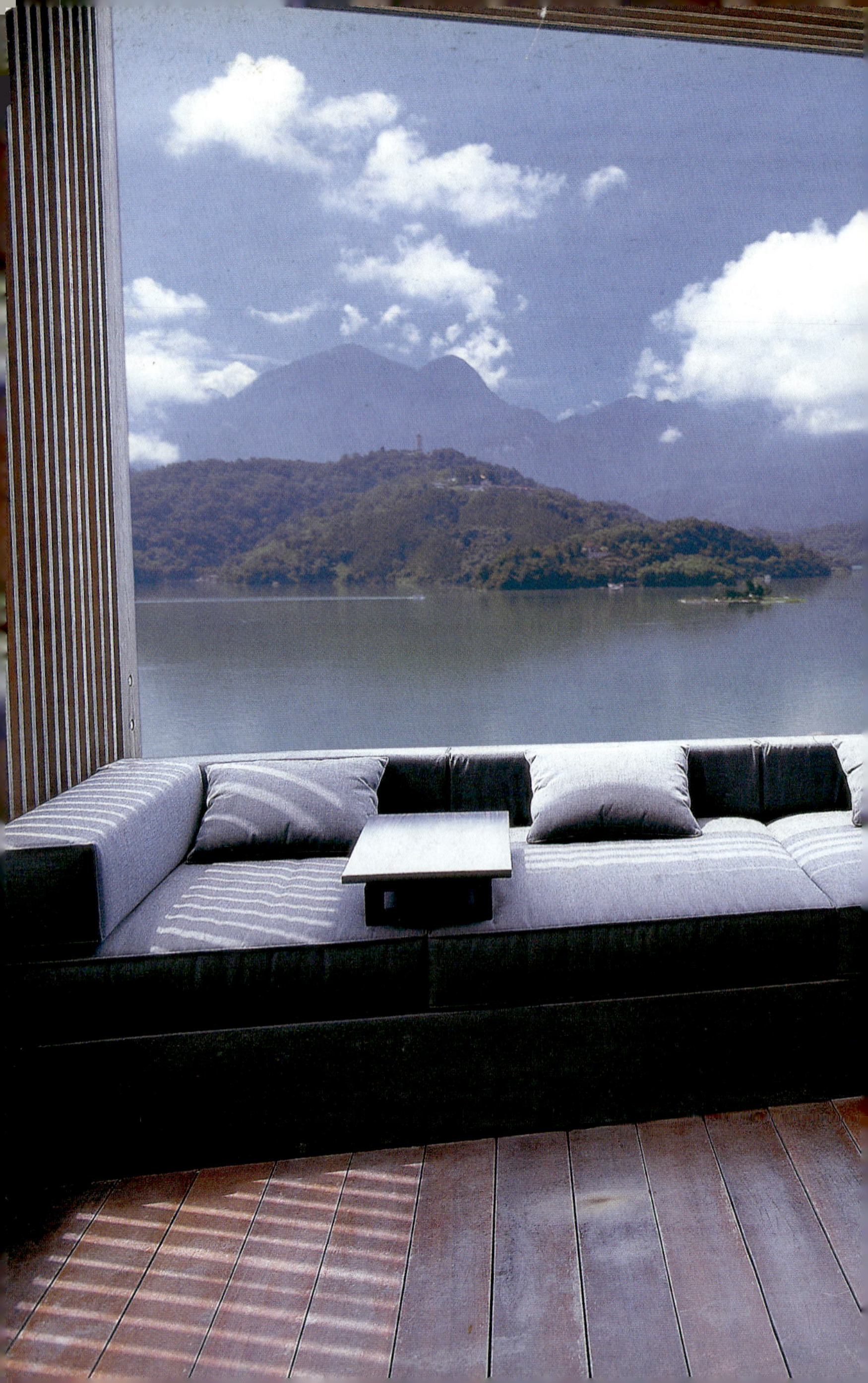

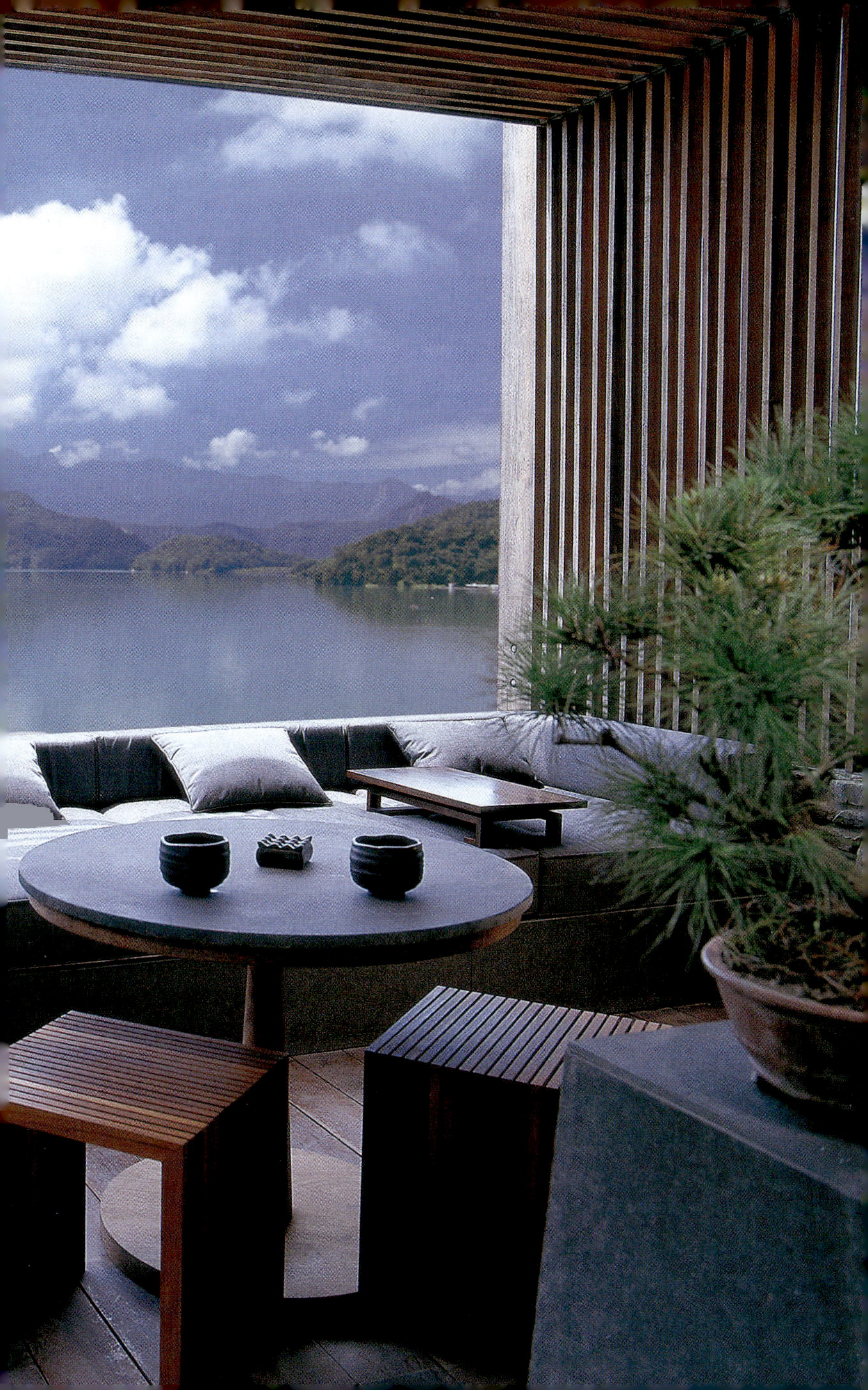

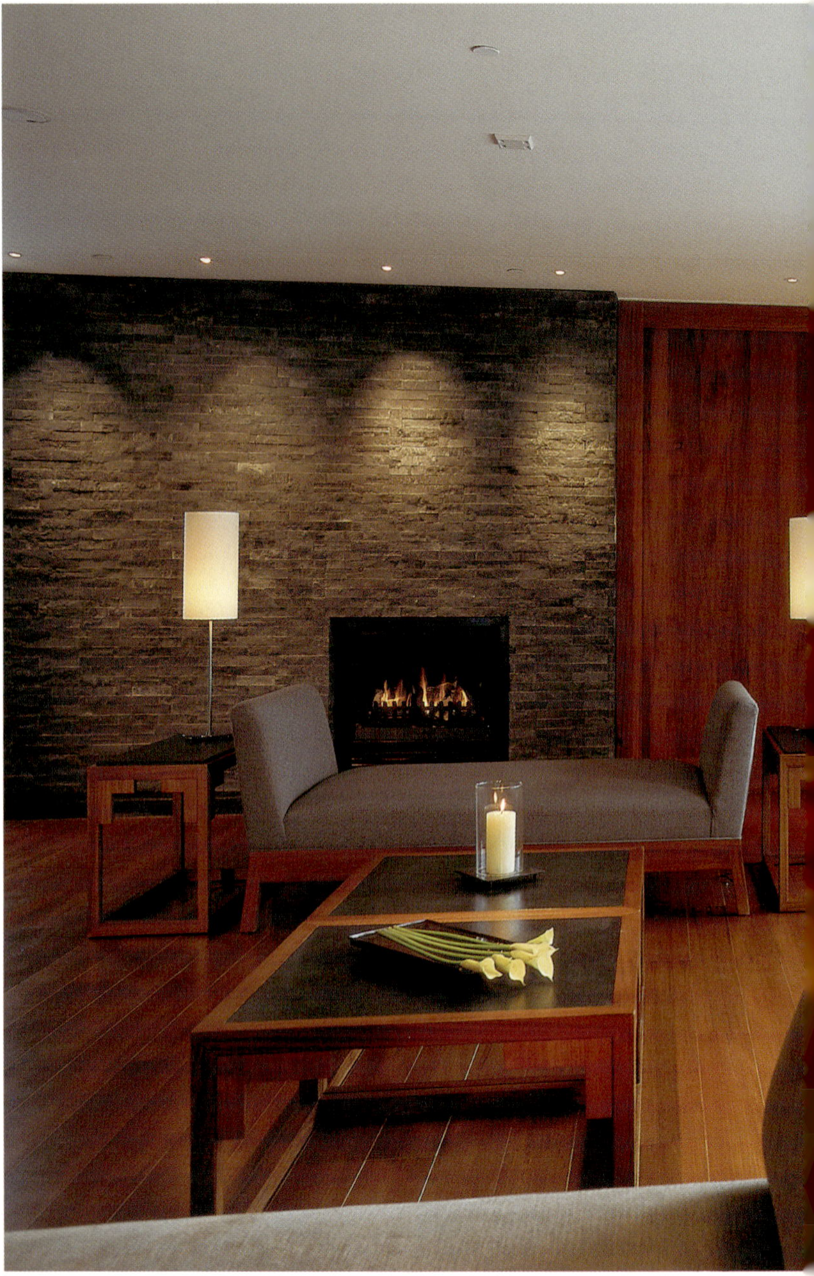

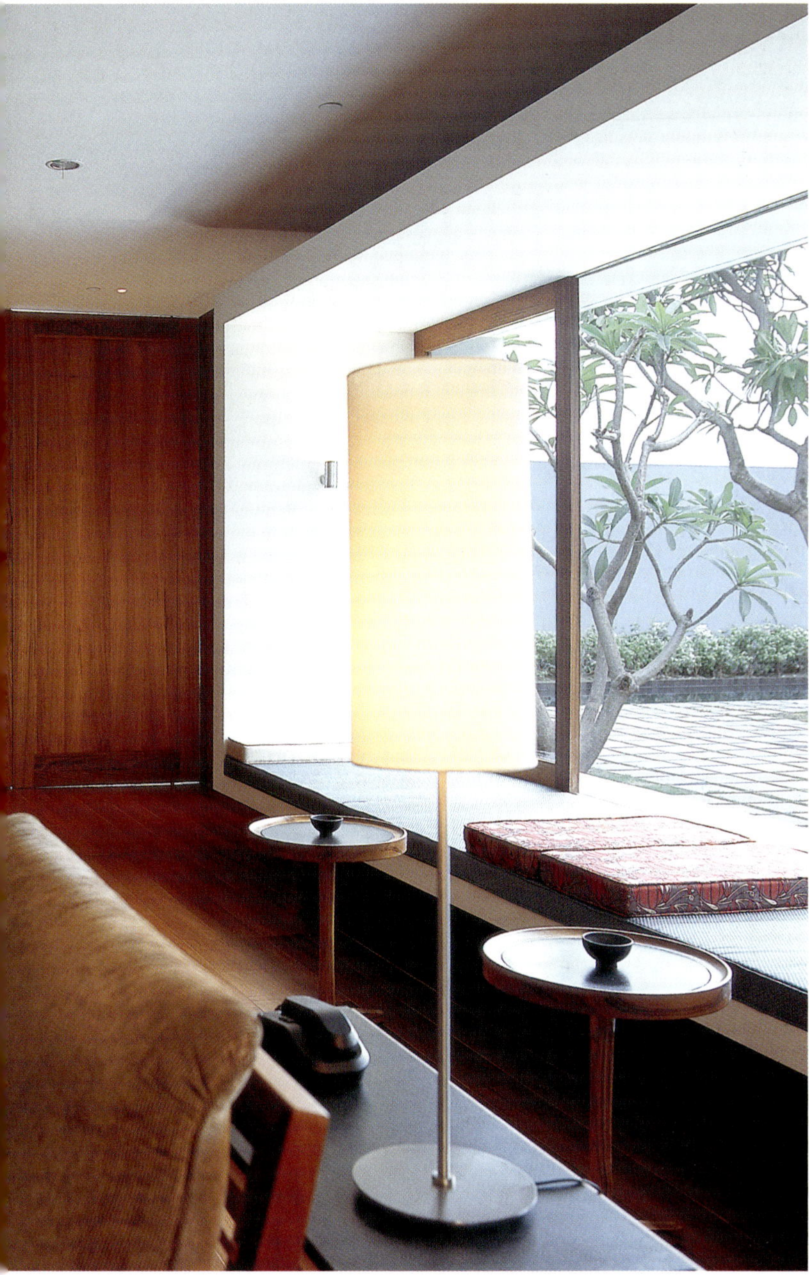

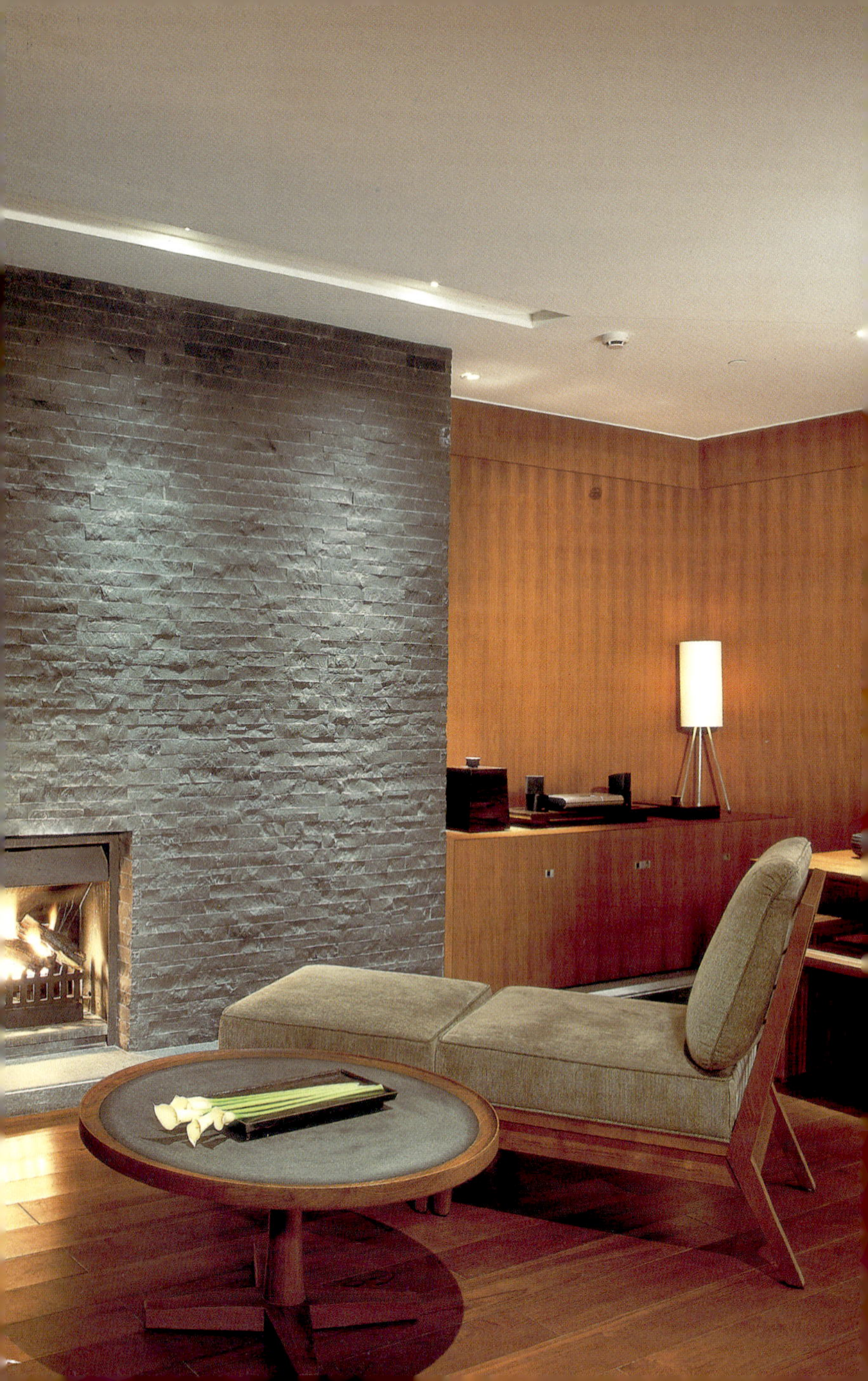

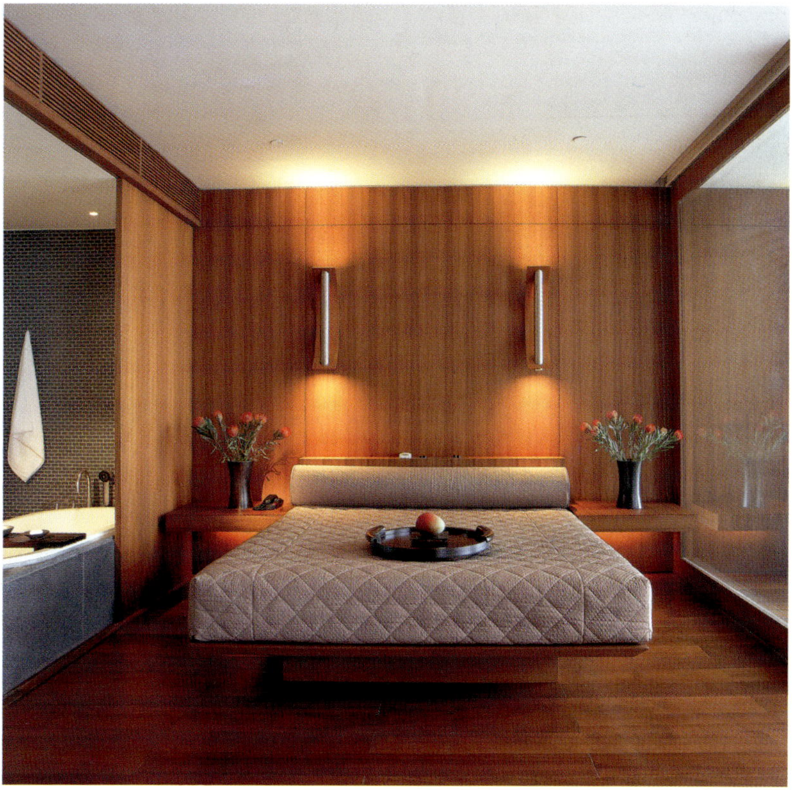

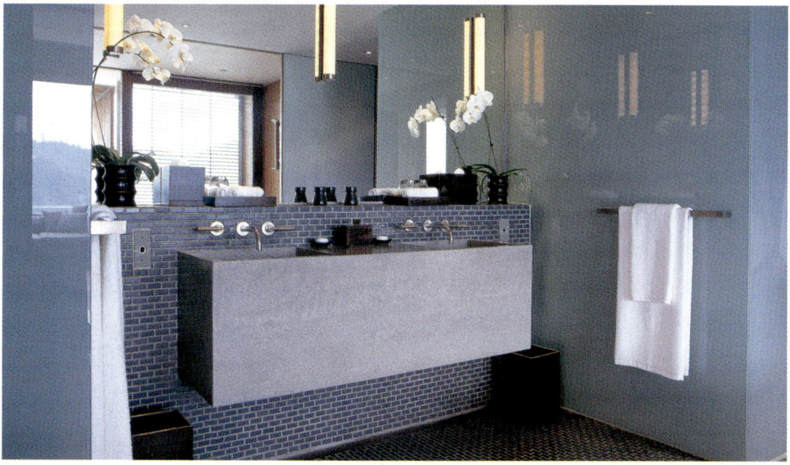

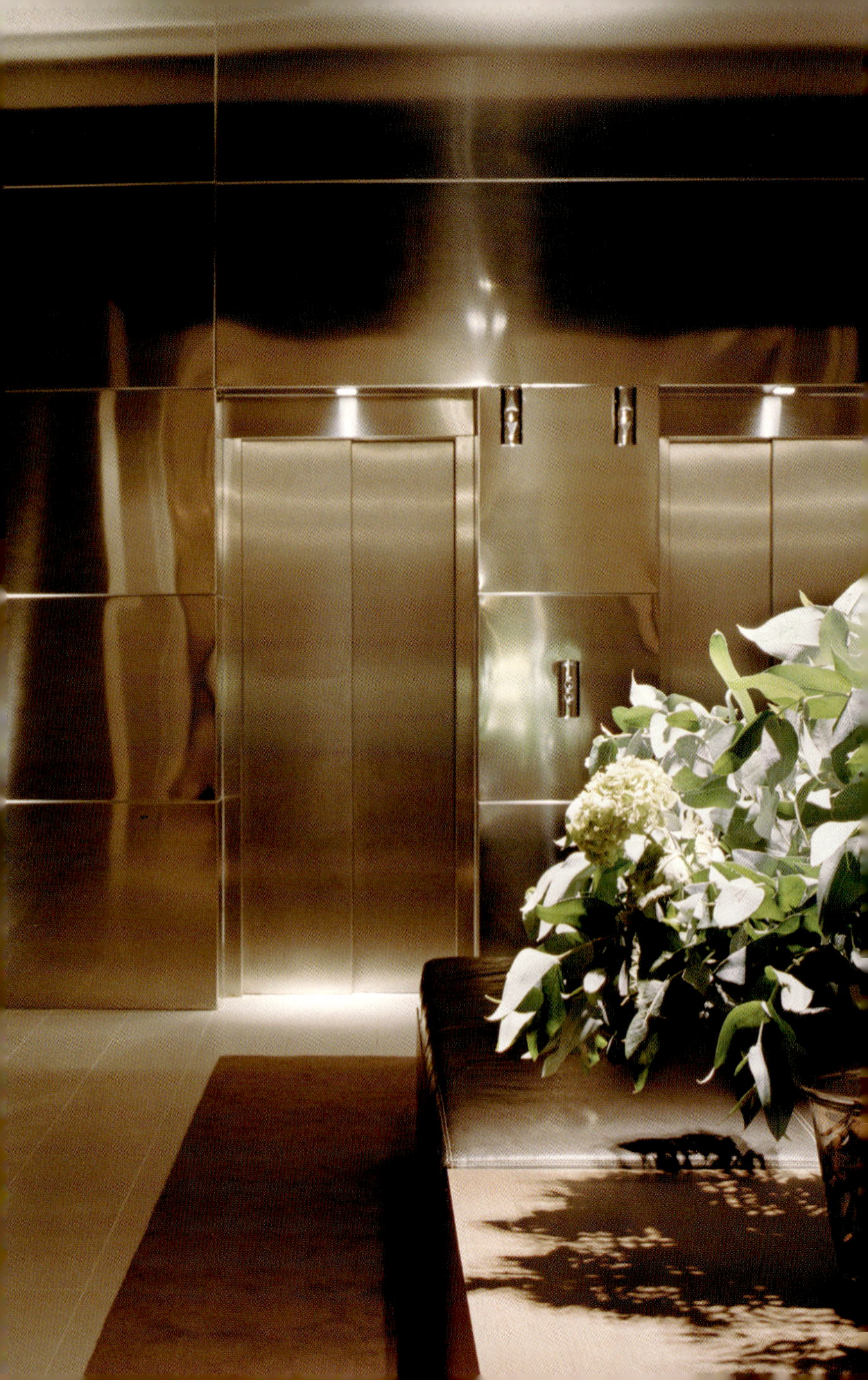

GRAND HOTEL CENTRAL
A Unique Place to Stay in a Unique City to Enjoy

Renovation: **TMA Arquitectura**
Designer: **Sandra Tarruella and Isabel López**

Date: 2005
Address: Via Laietana 30, 08003 Barcelona, Spain
Tel.: +34 932 957 900 Fax: +34 932 681 215
www.grandhotelcentral.com
Photos: © Grand Hotel Central

Location: Urban
Style: Classic contemporary
Rooms: 147
Special features: Rooftop pool and view over Barcelona, architecture library, original 1920s structure

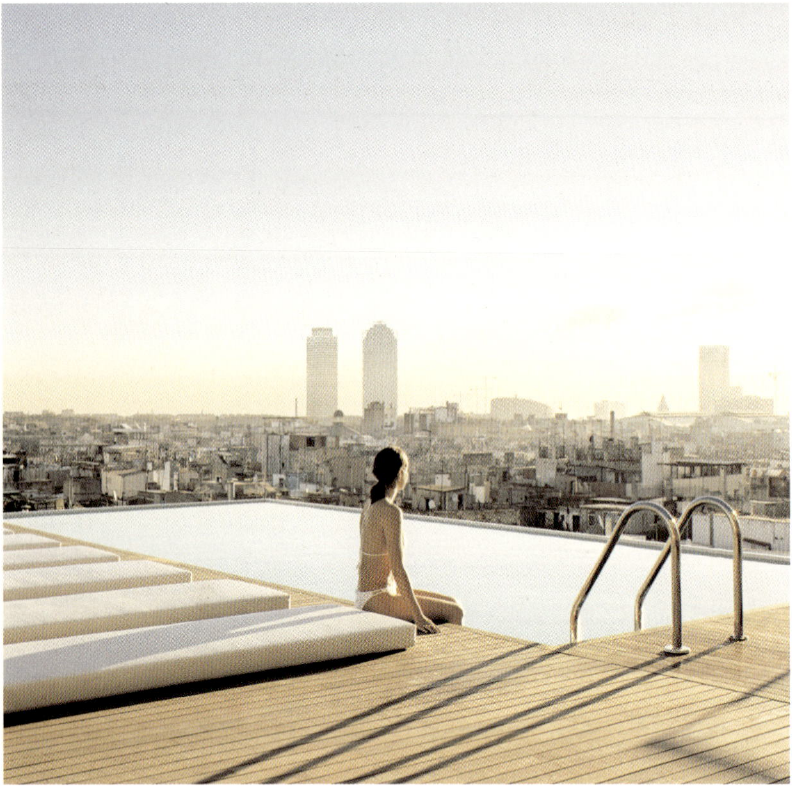

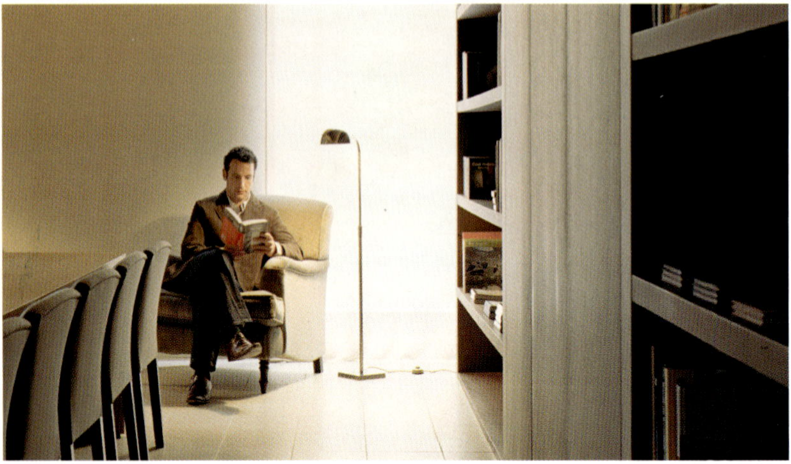

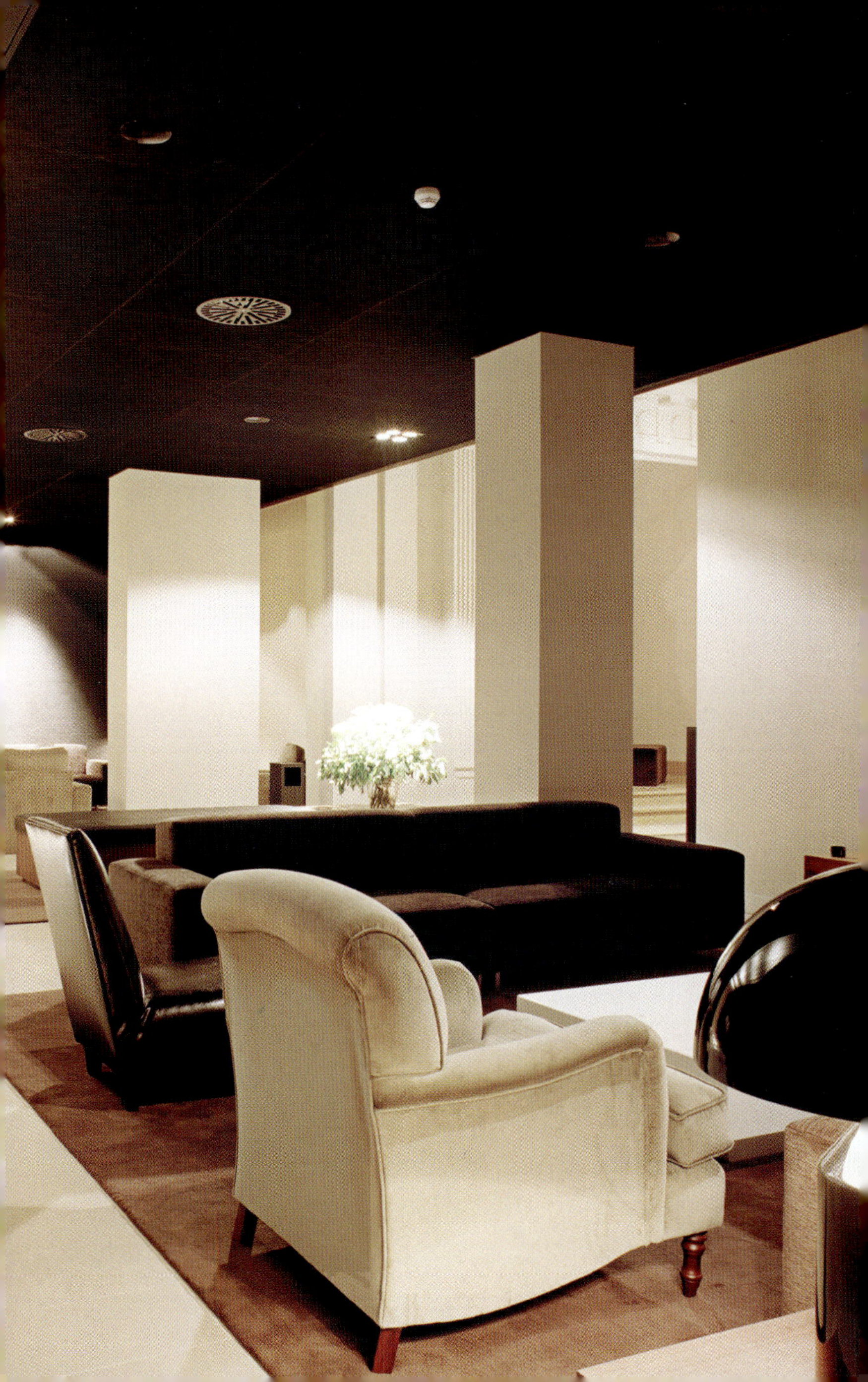

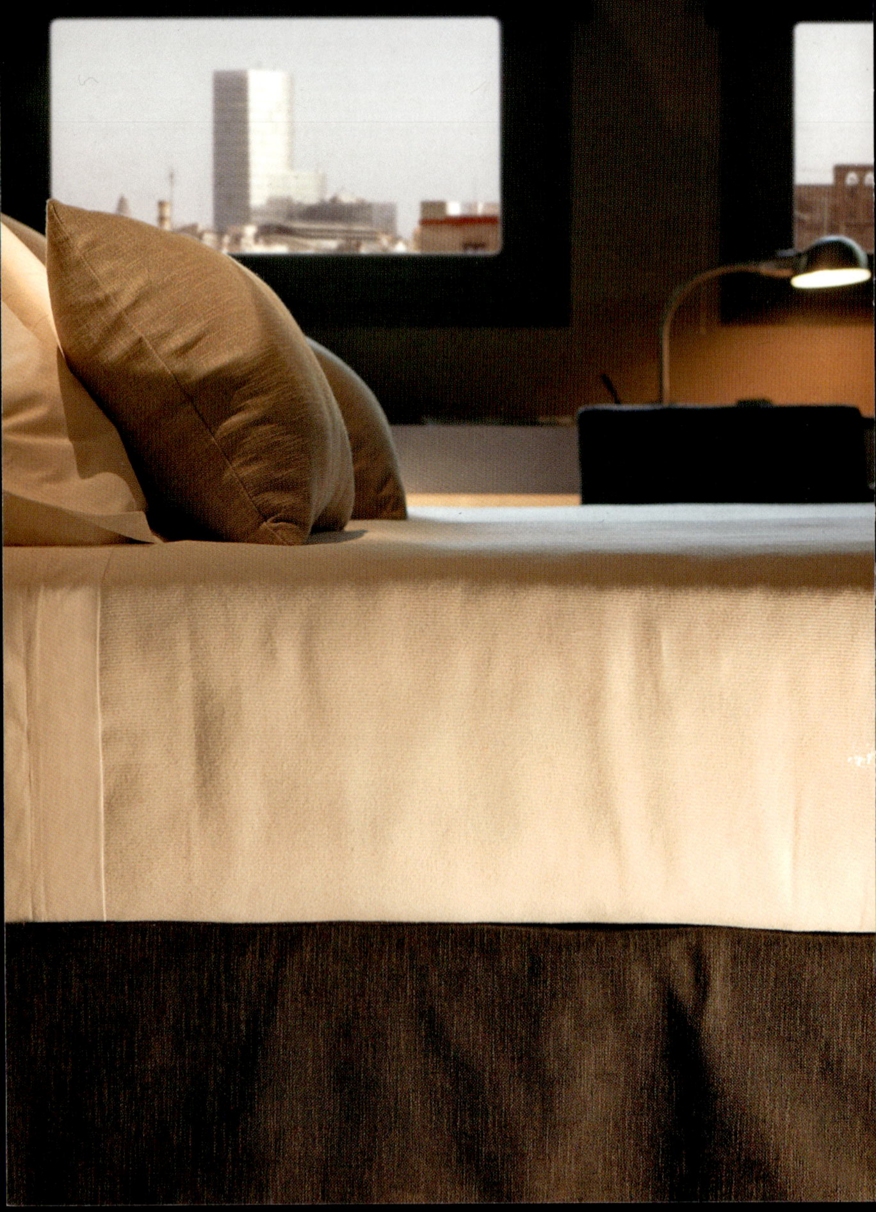

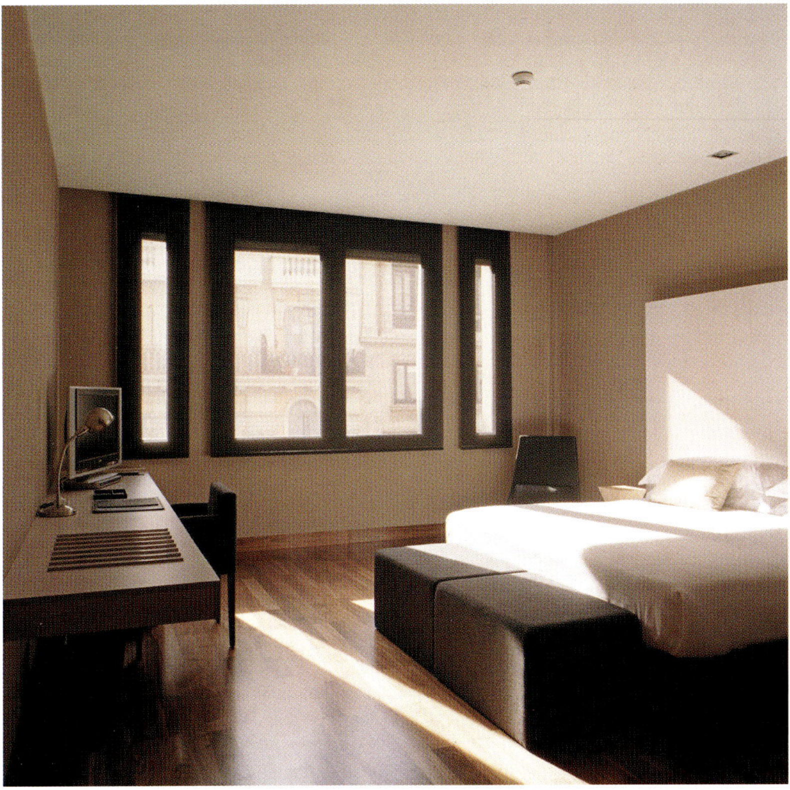

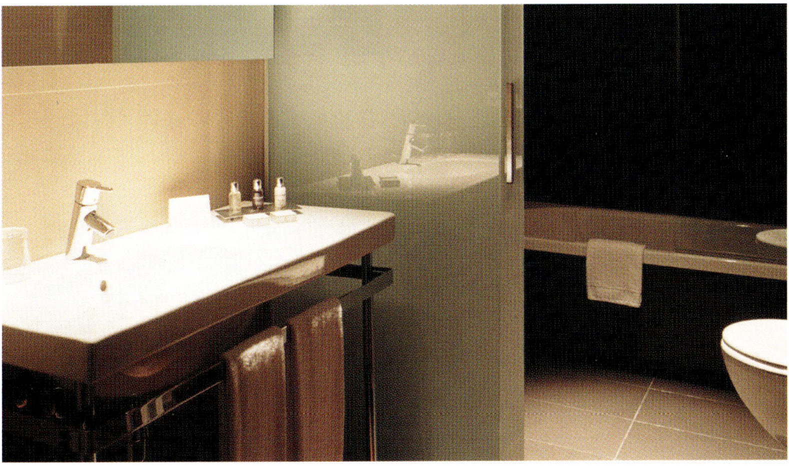

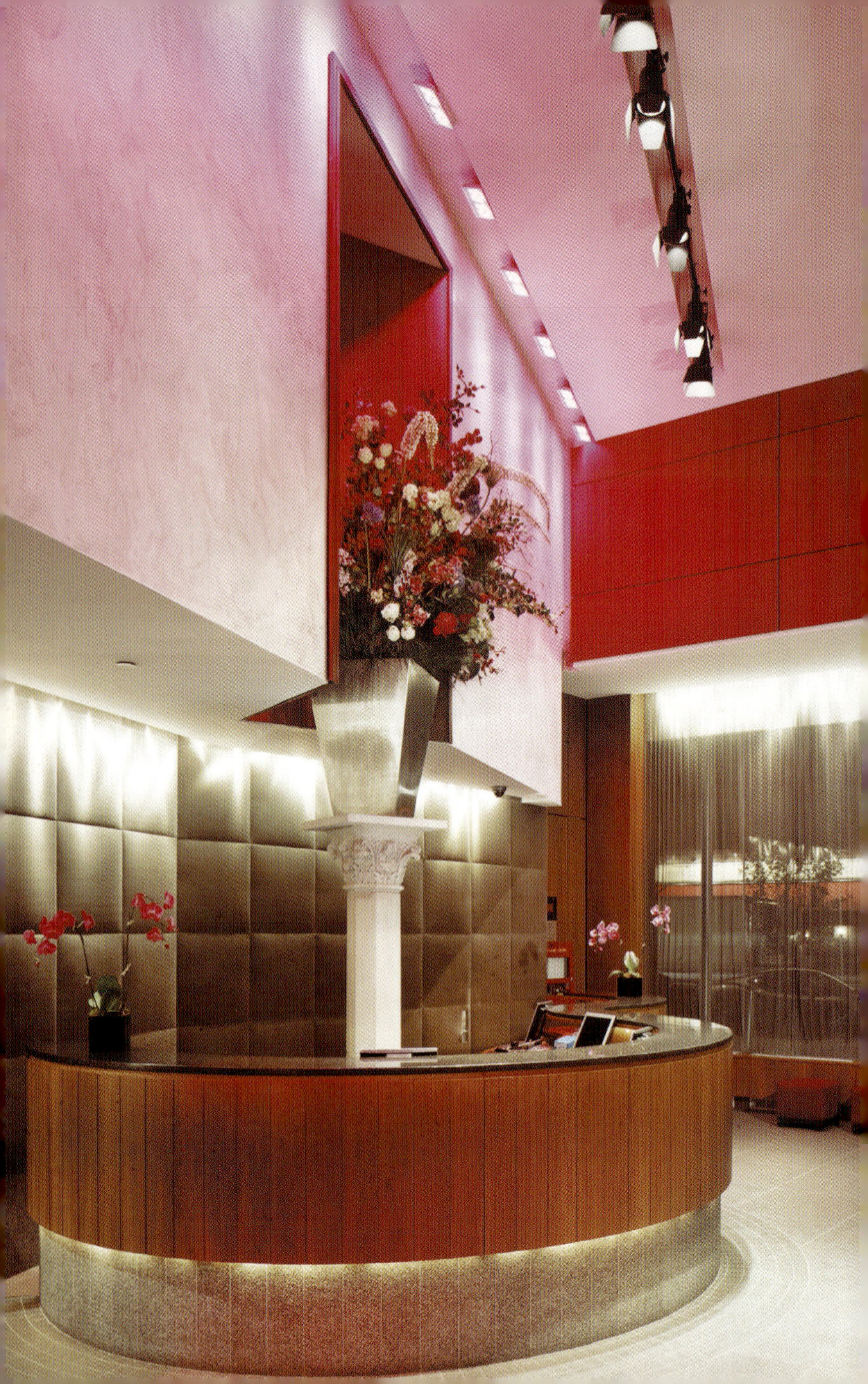

HOTEL GANSEVOORT
The First Full-Service Hotel in Manhattan's Meatpacking District

Architects: **The Stephen B Jacobs Group**

Date: 2004
Address: 18 9th Avenue (at 13th Street), New York, NY 10014, United States
Tel.: +1 212 206 6700 Fax: +1 212 255 5858
www.hotelgansevoort.com
Photos: © David Joseph

Location: Urban
Style: Contemporary hip
Rooms: 187
Special features: G Spa & Lounge, 14 m. heating outdoor glass-surrounded pool with underwater music, event loft

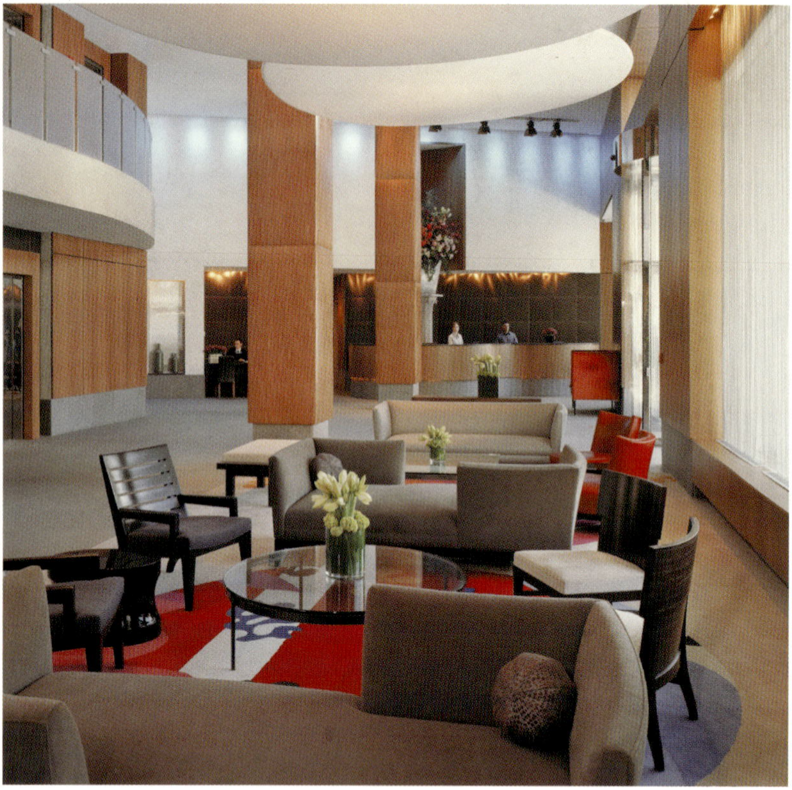

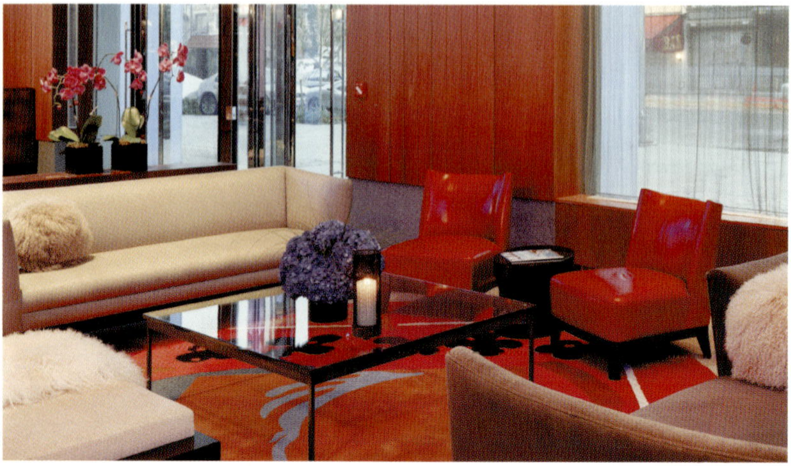

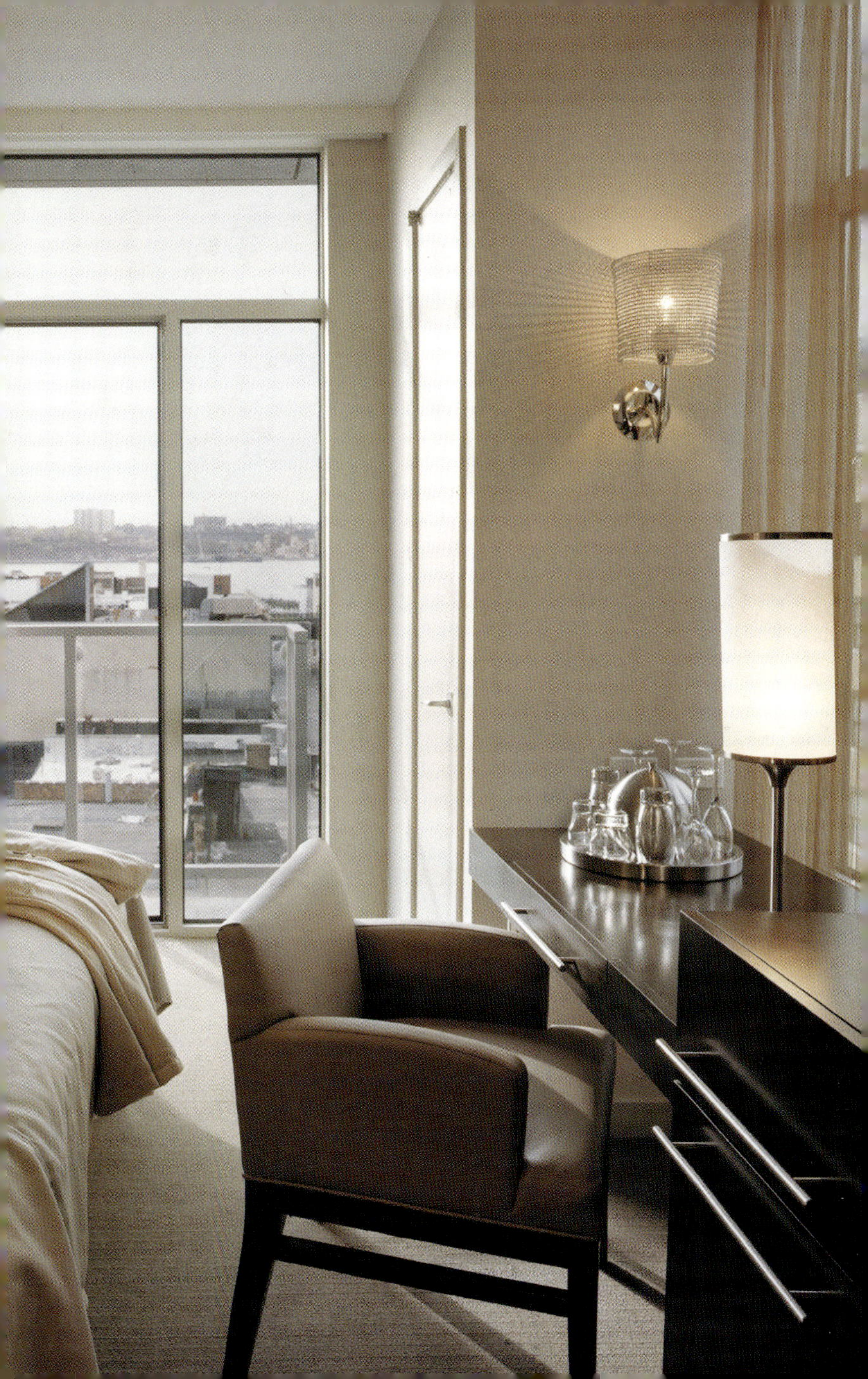

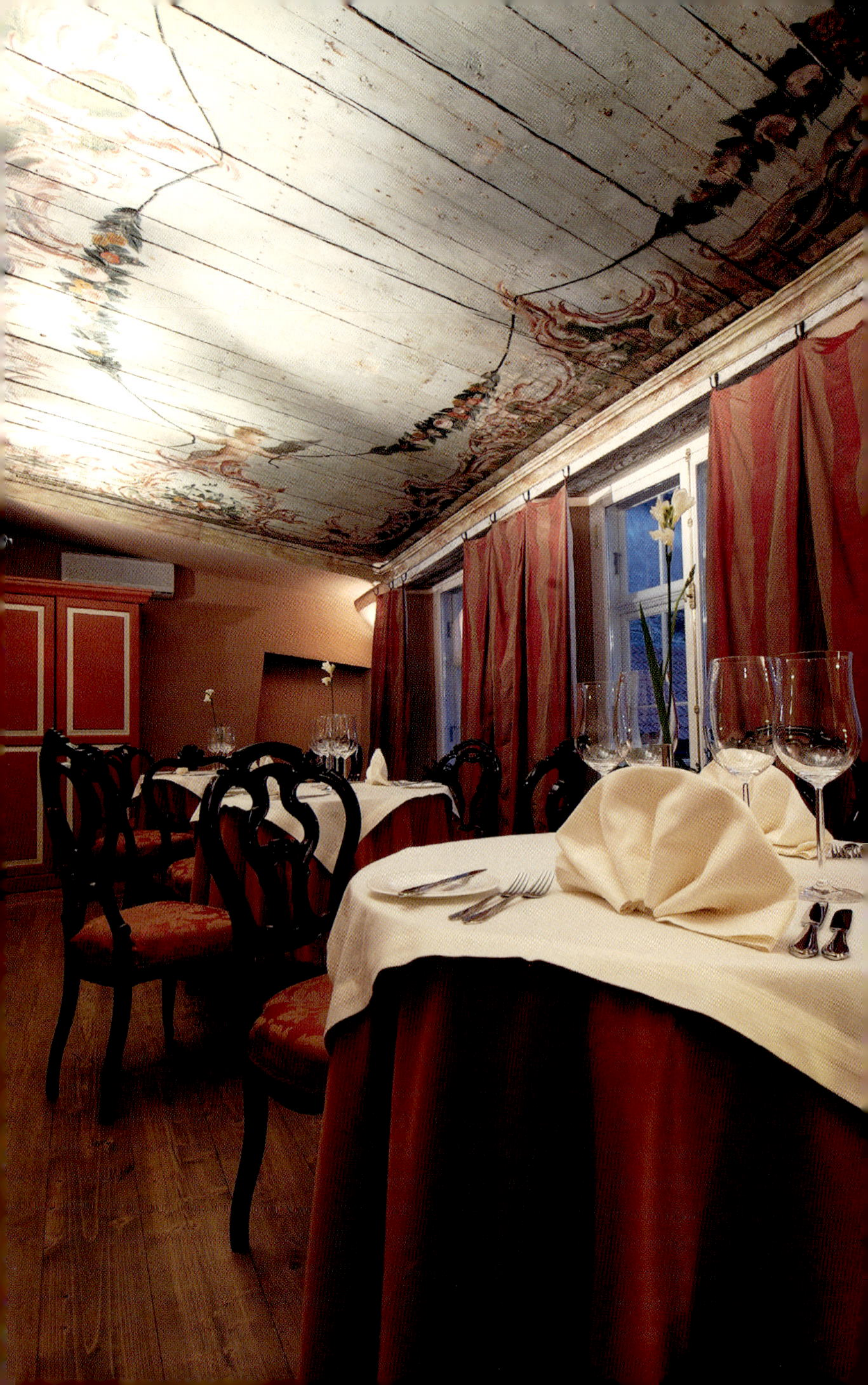

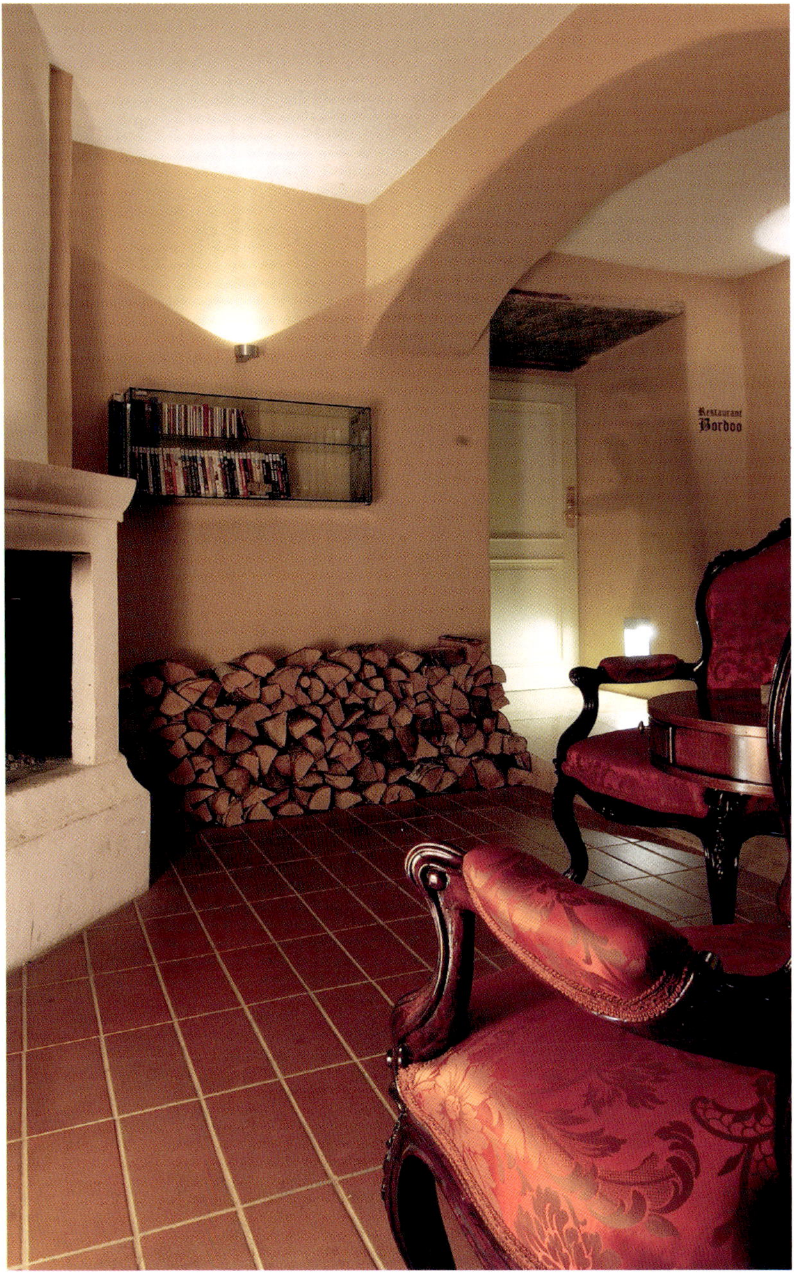
Restaurant
Bordoo

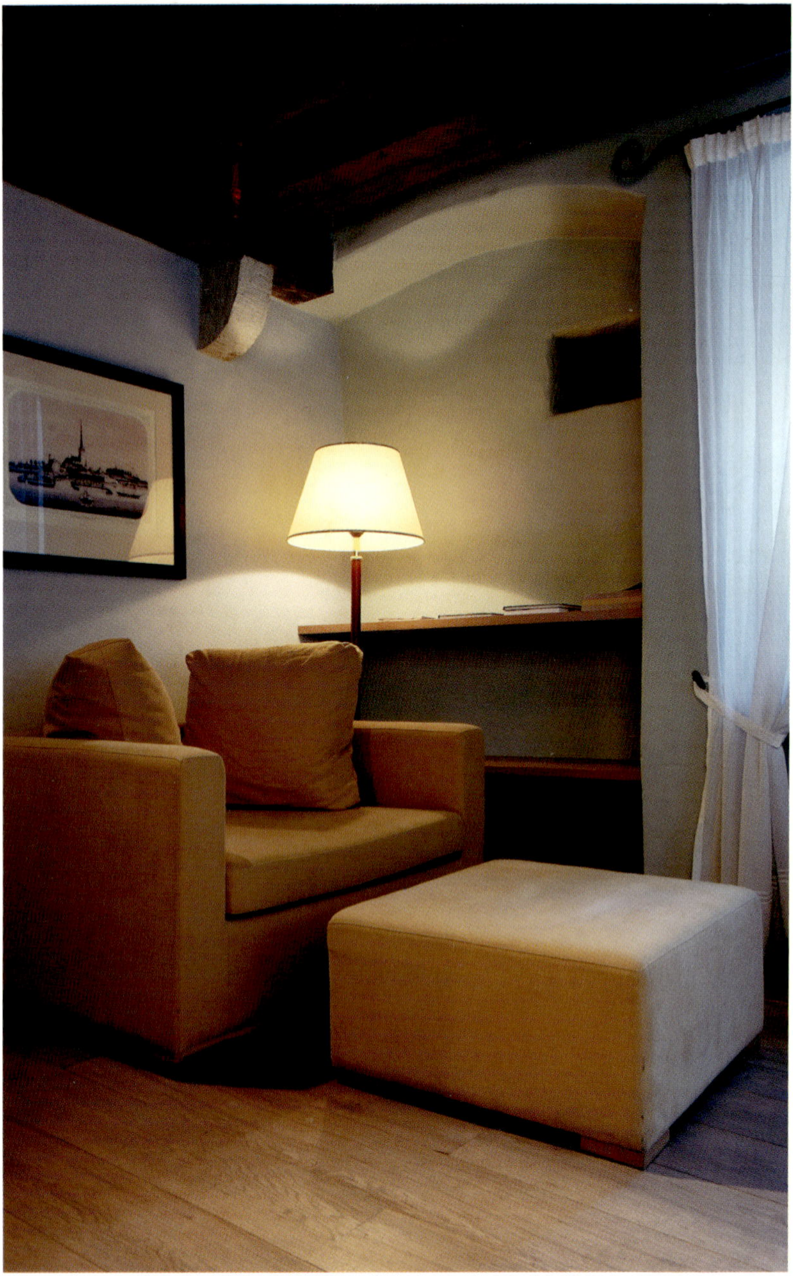

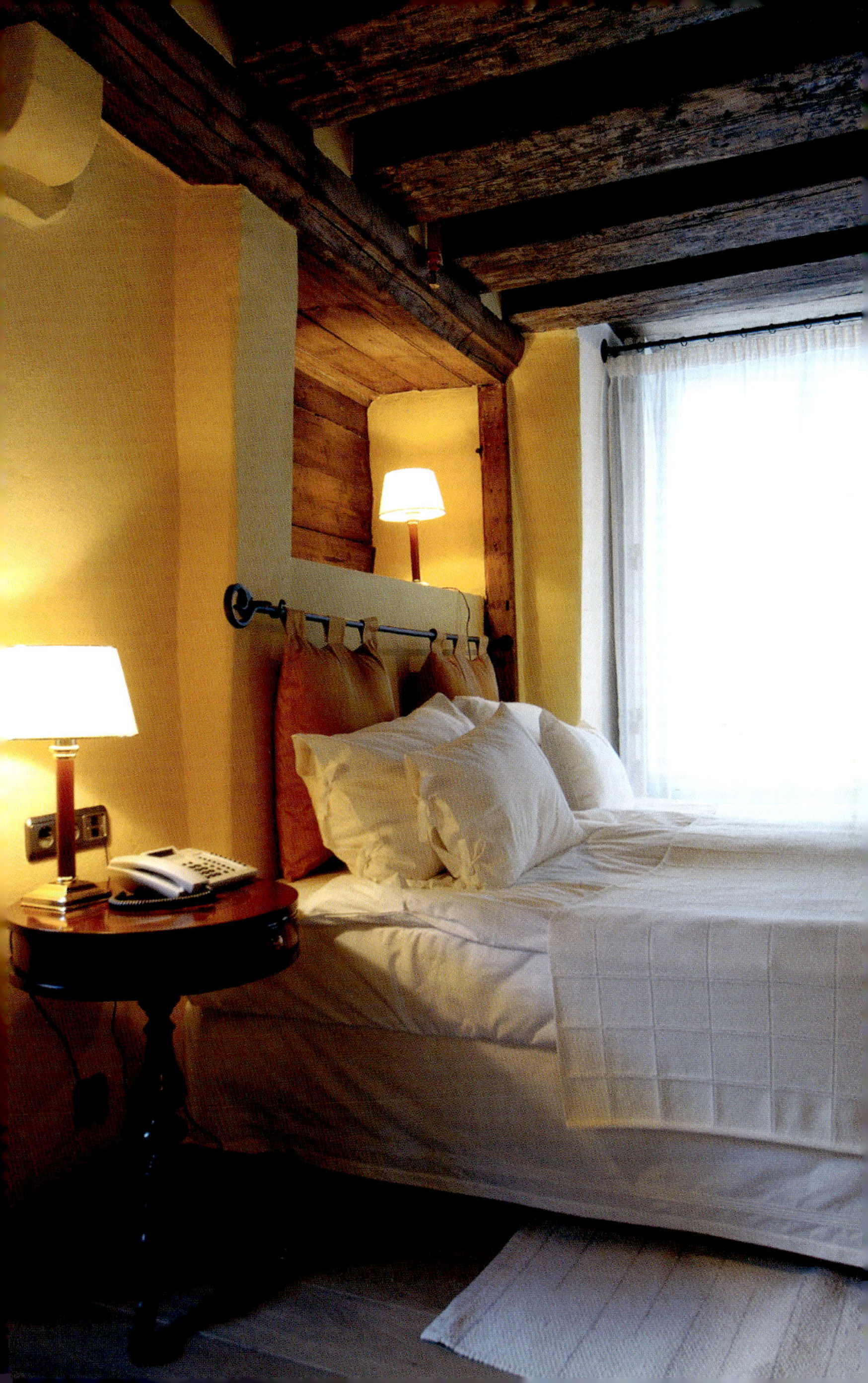

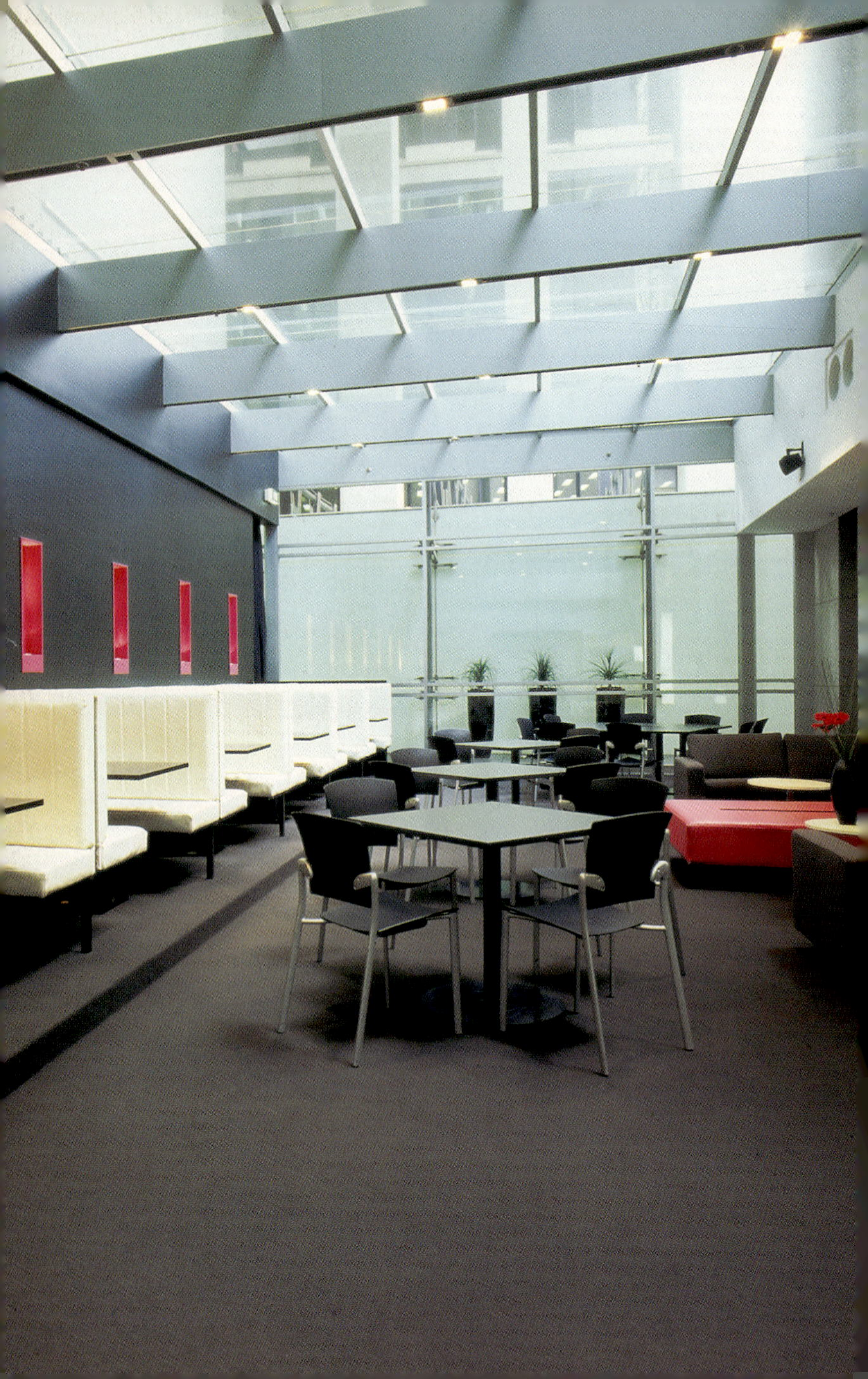

THE BLACKET
Retreat and Rejuvenate

Architect: **Edmund Thomas Blacket (1817-1883)**
Designer: **John Harrs**

Date: 2001
Address: 70 King Street, Sydney NSW 2000, Australia
Tel.: +61 2 9279 3030 Fax: +61 2 9279 3020
www.theblacket.com
Photos: © Marian Riabic

Location: Urban
Style: Contemporary design
Rooms: 42
Special features: Cool ambient in the heart of Sydney's corporate, retail and leisure

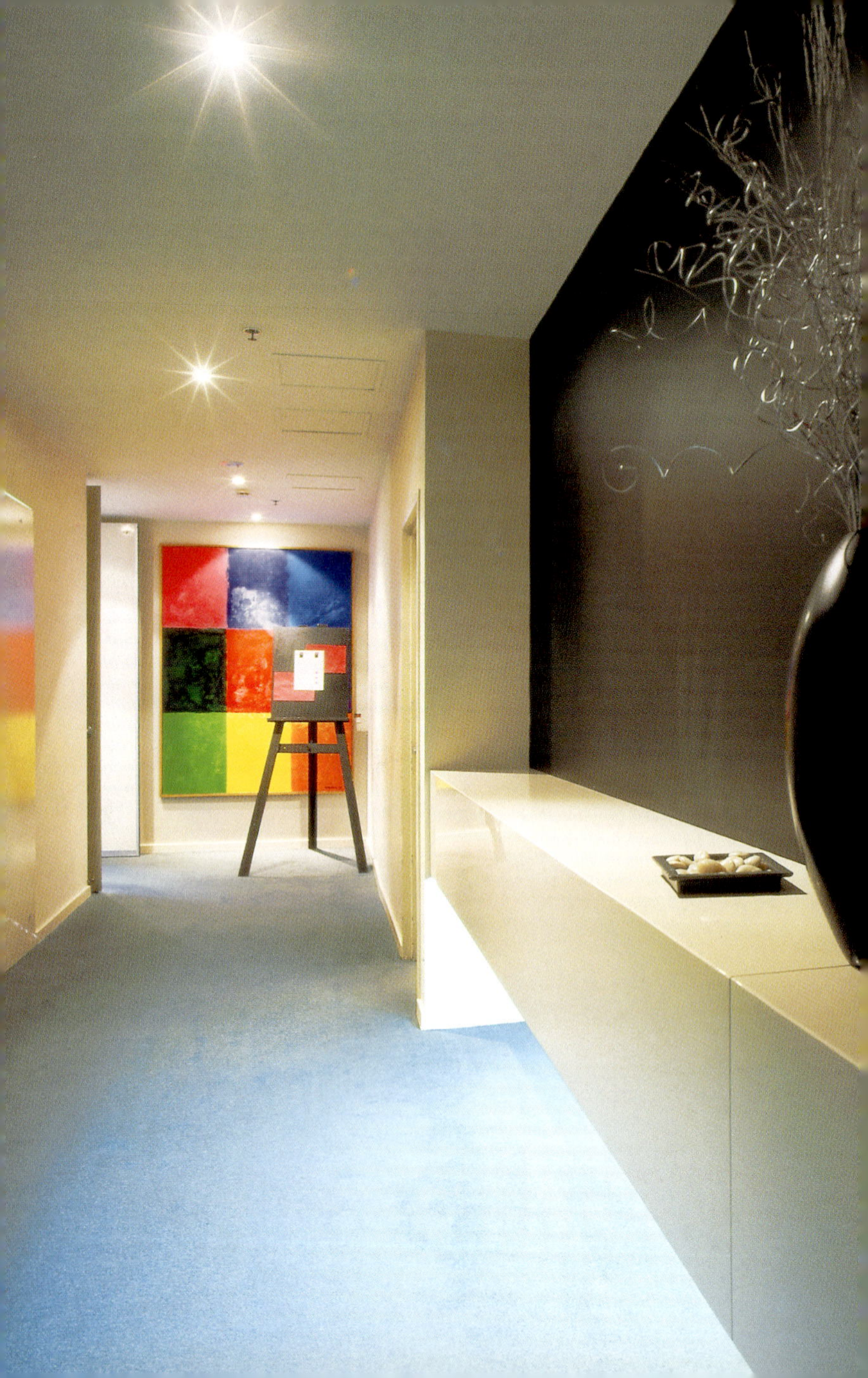

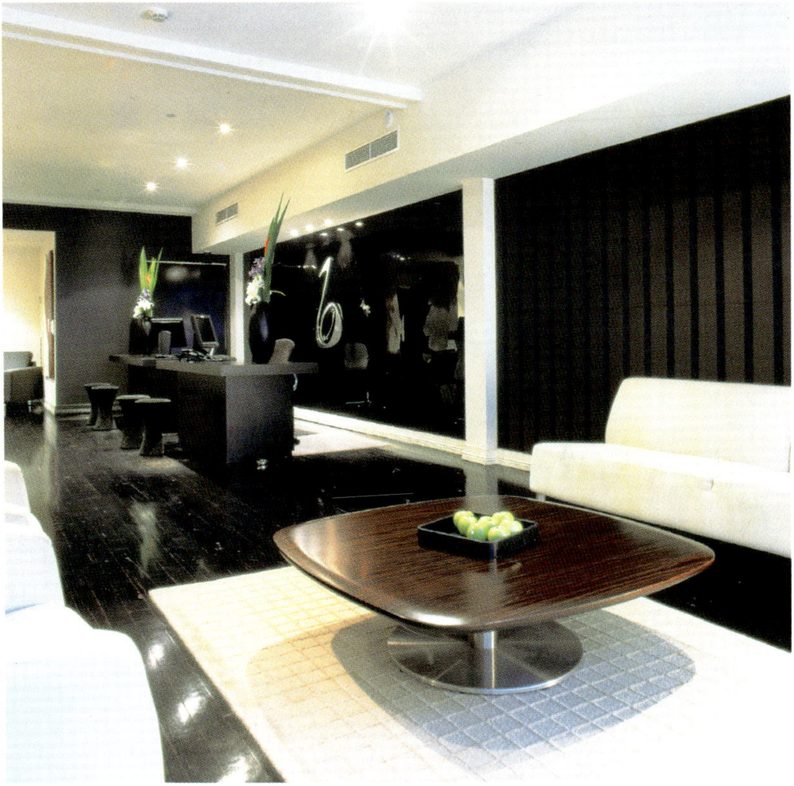

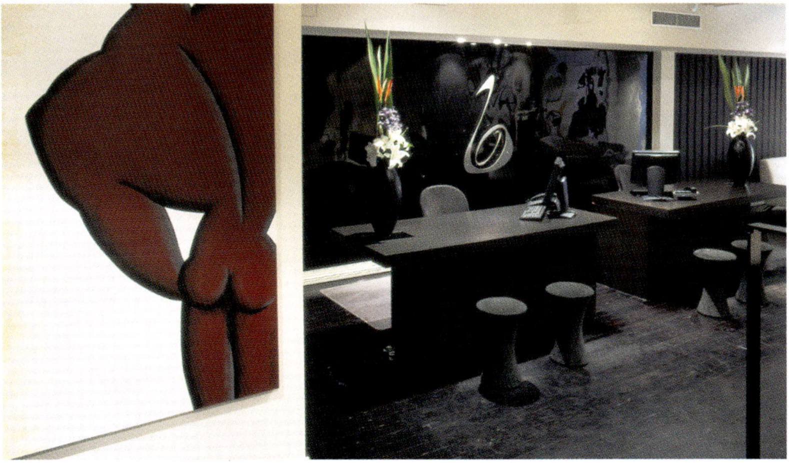

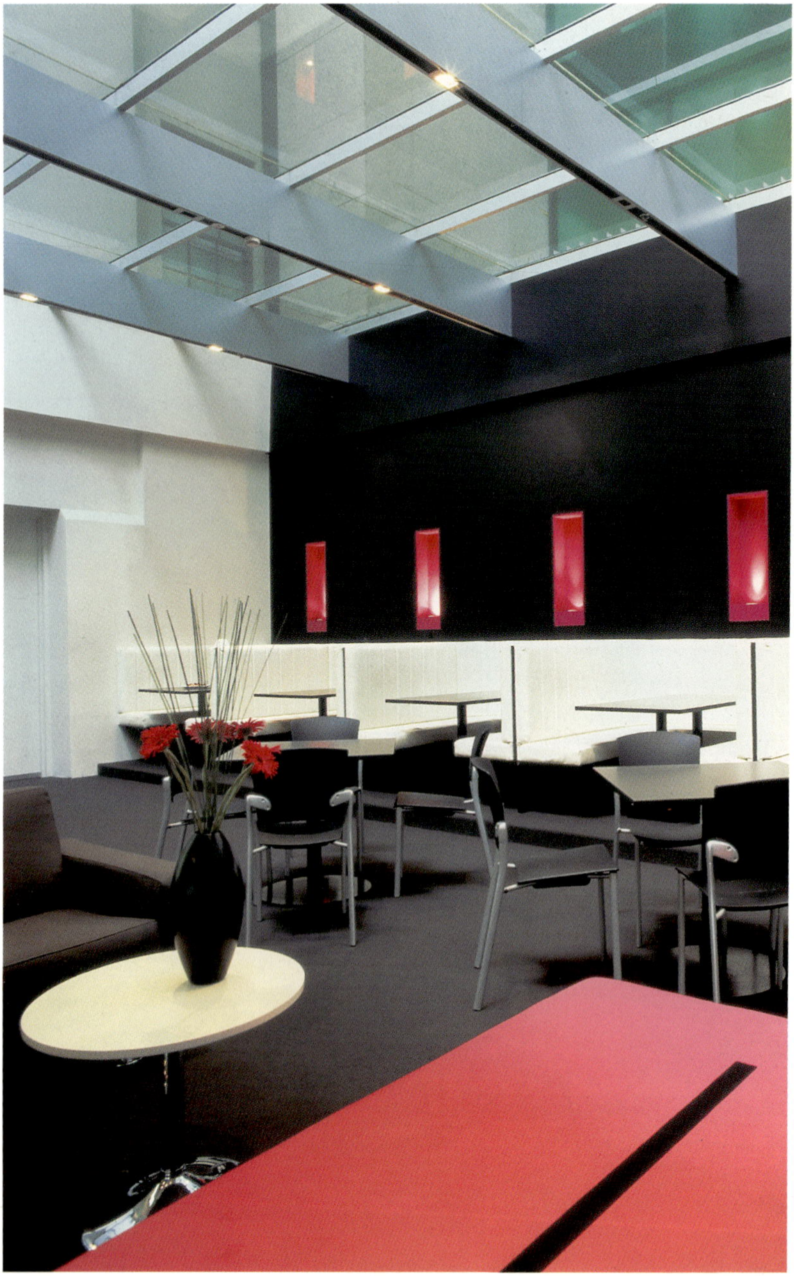

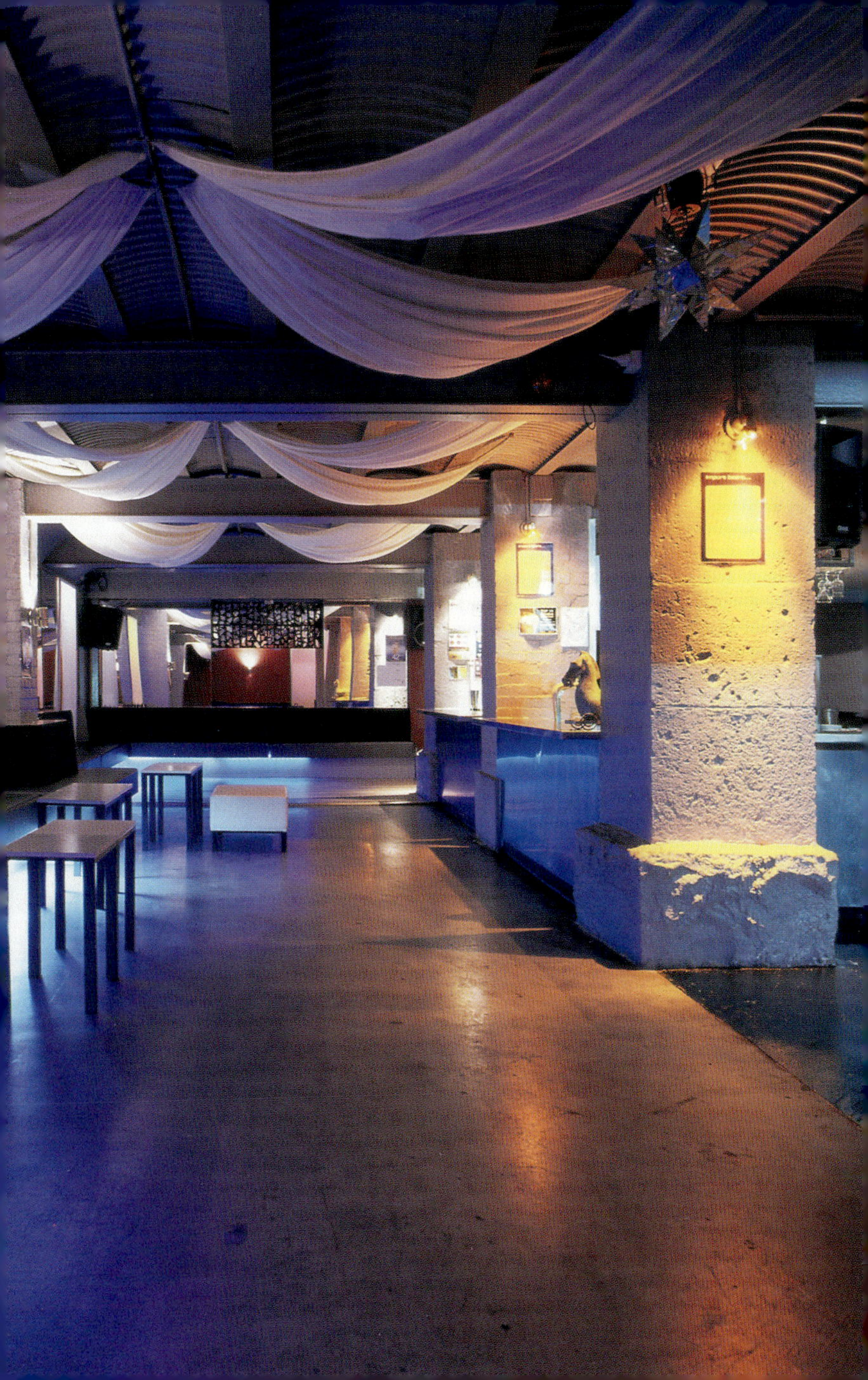

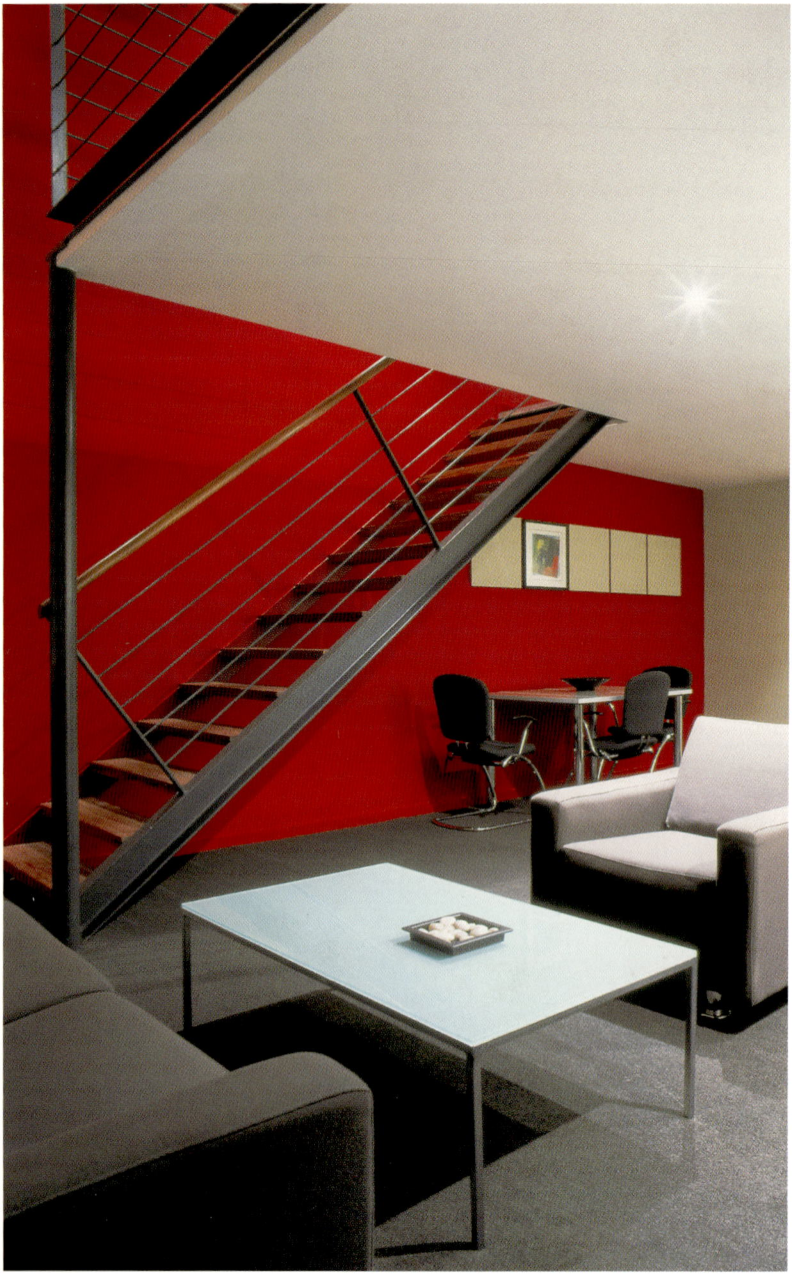

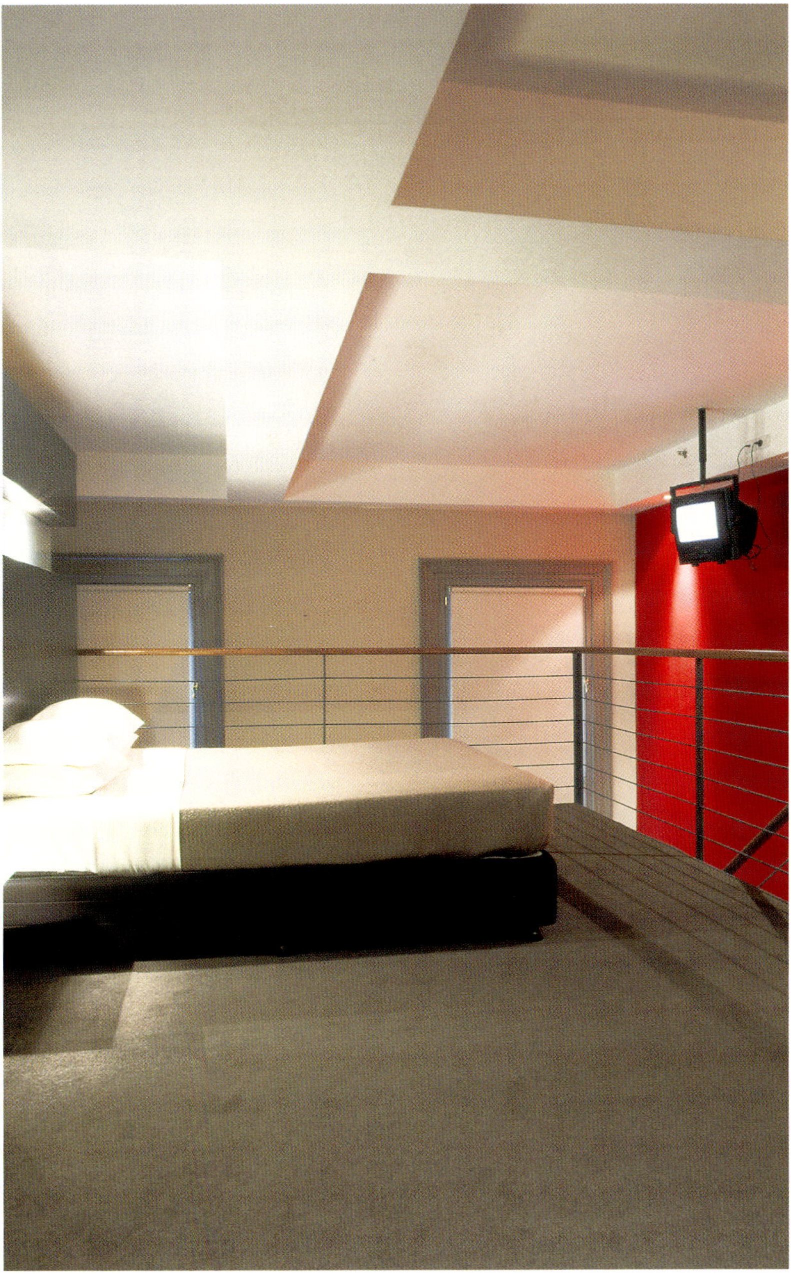

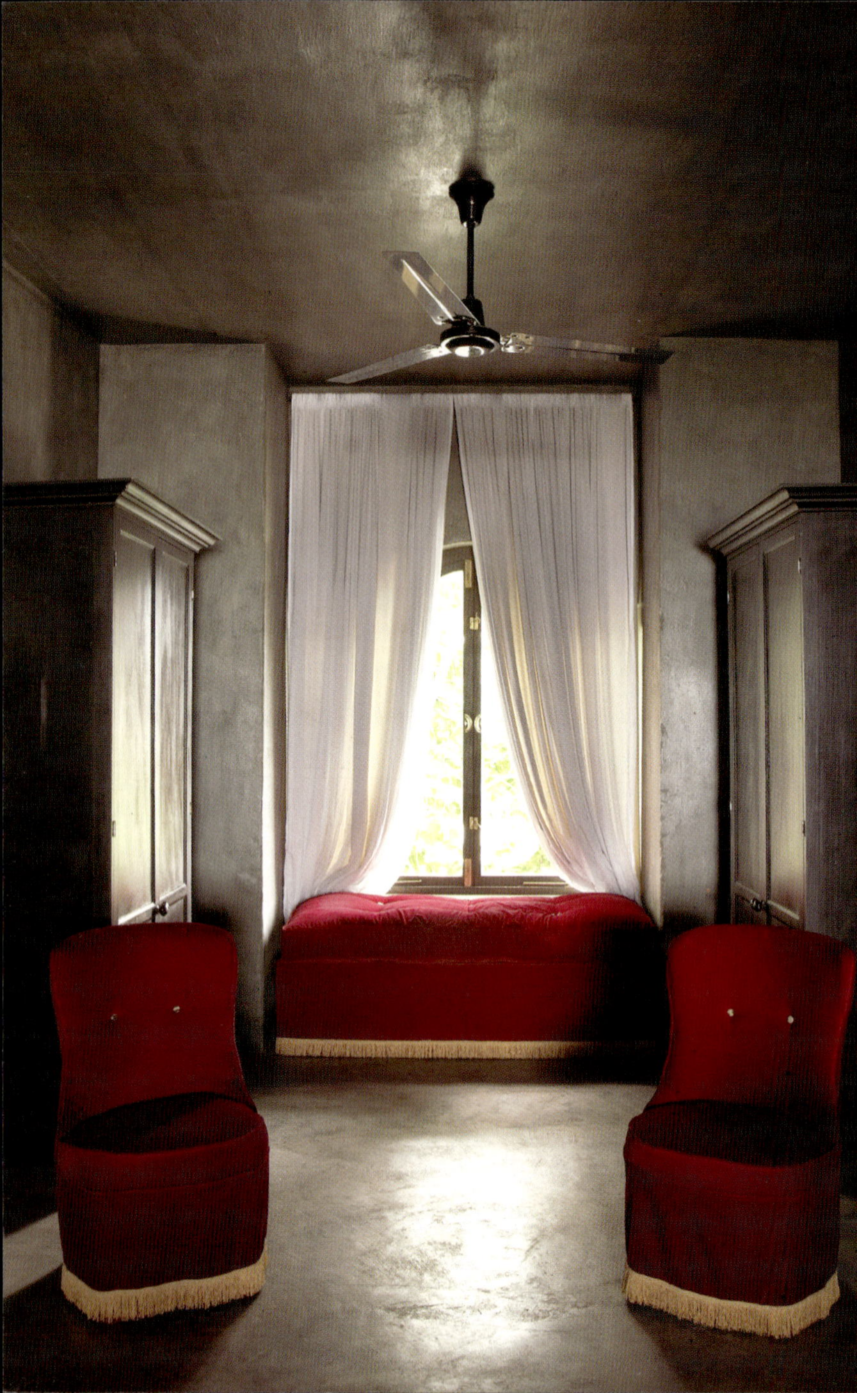

THE GRAND
Café and Rooms

Designer: **Gail Behr**

Date: 2004
Address: 27 Main Road, Plettenberg Bay, 6600 Cape Town, South Africa
Tel.: +27 44 533 3301 Fax: +27 44 533 3301
www.thegrand.co.za
Photos: © Jac de Villiers

Location: Beach
Style: Modern romantic
Rooms: 8
Special features: Café, oversized king beds, double showers, room access to pool deck

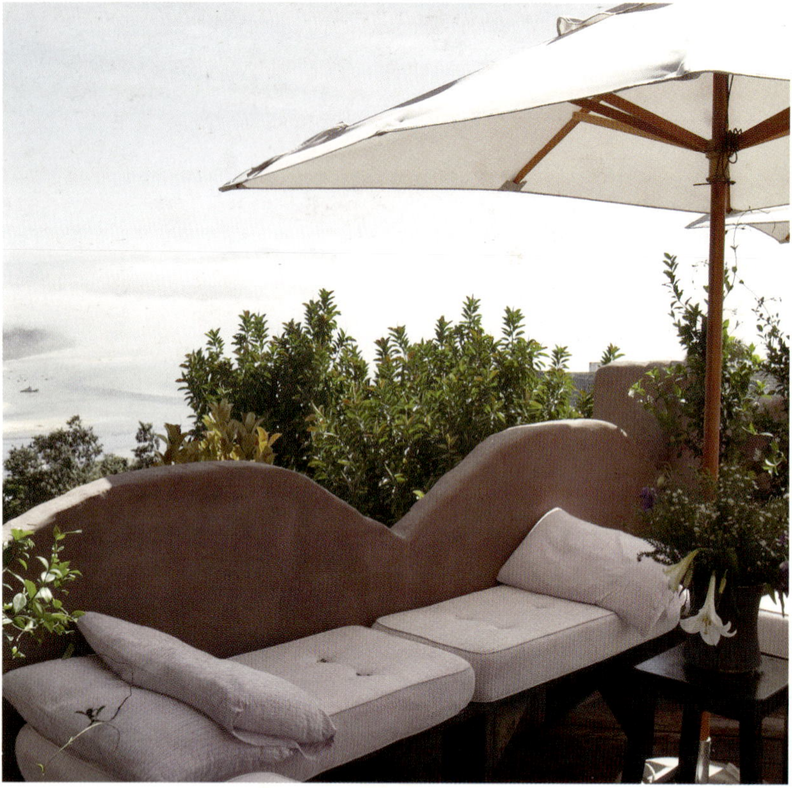

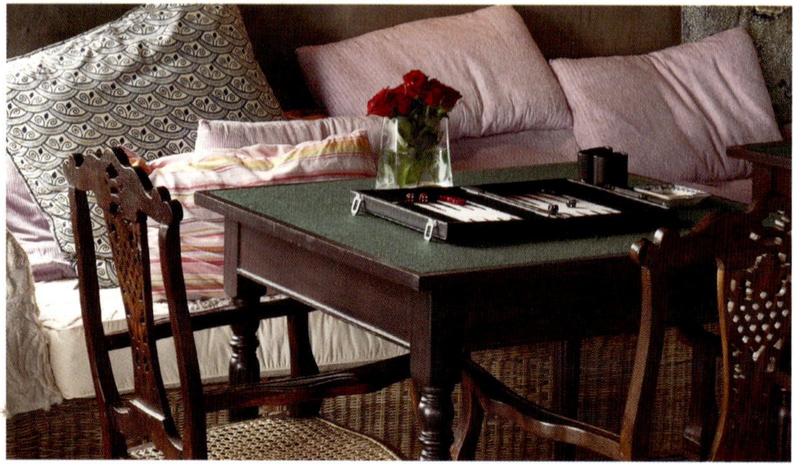

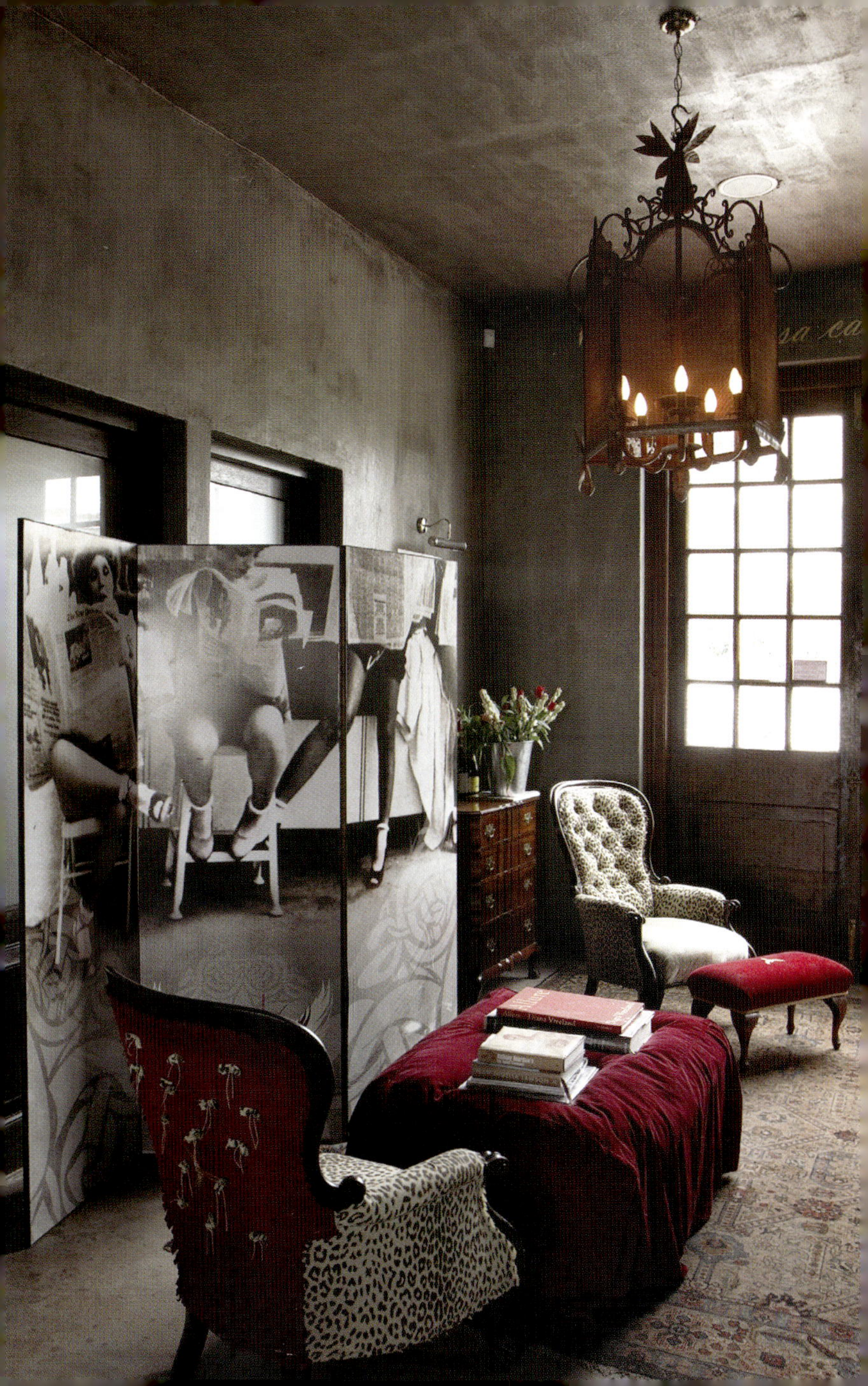

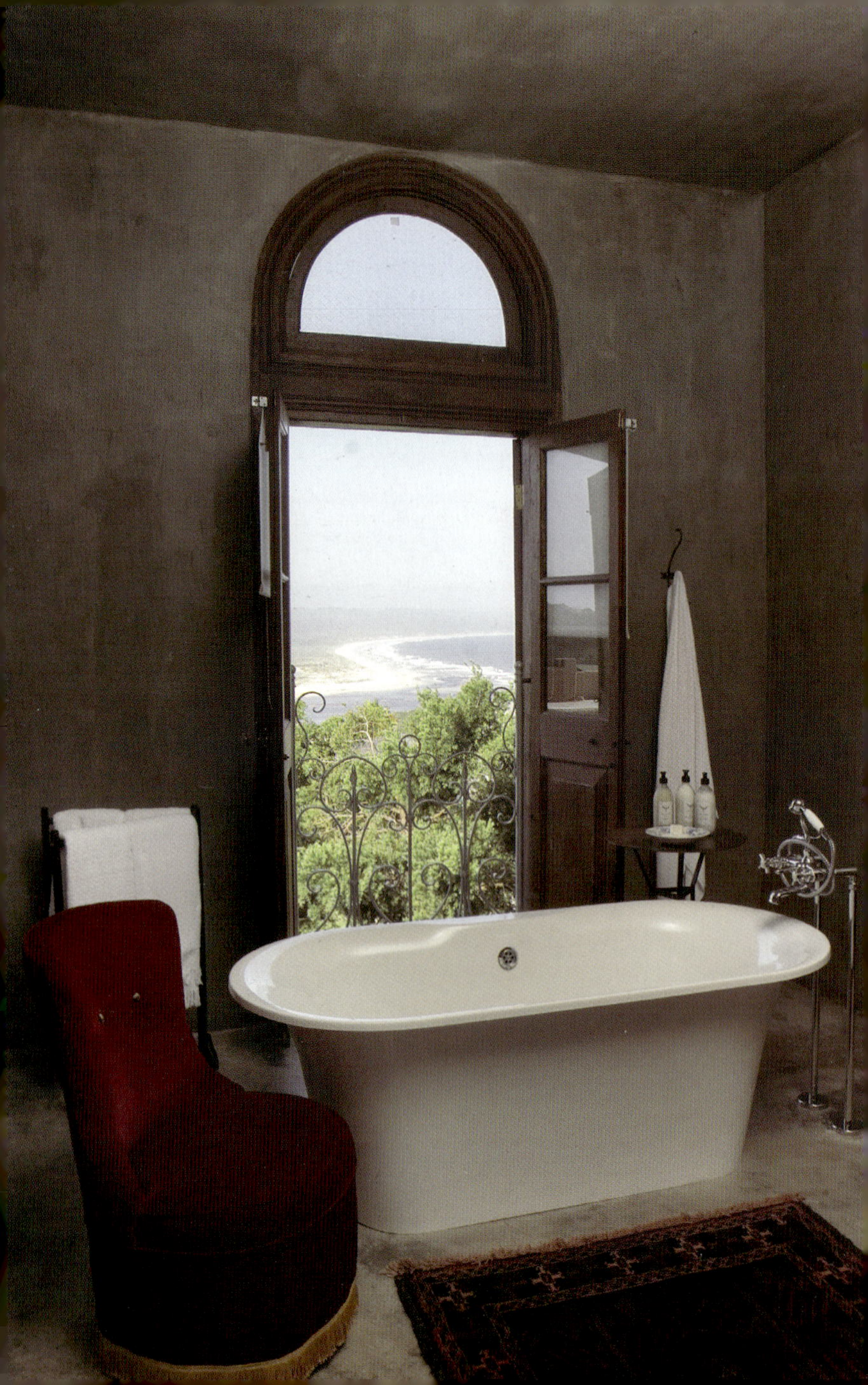

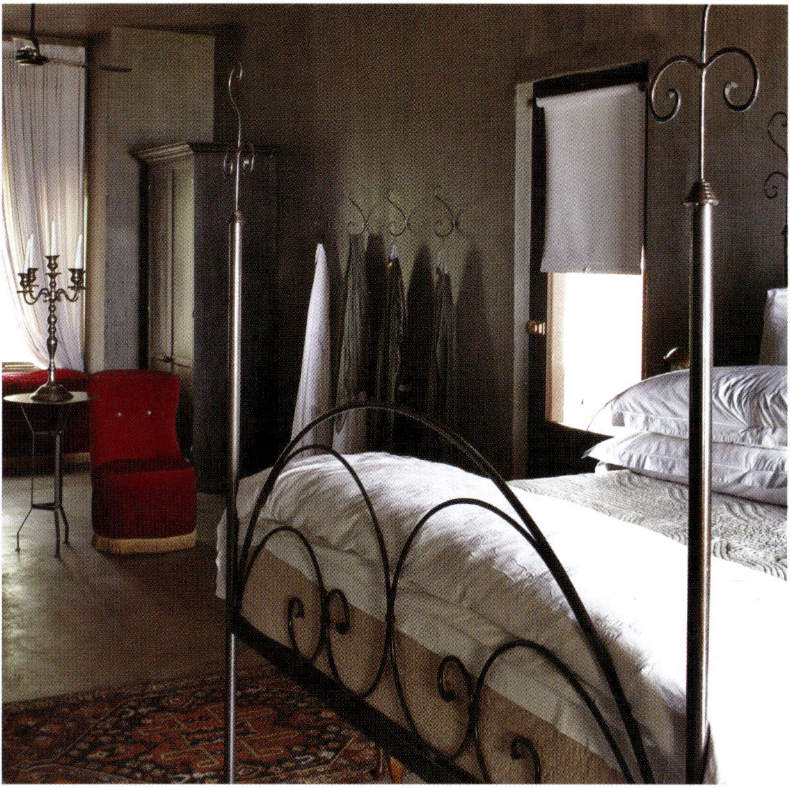

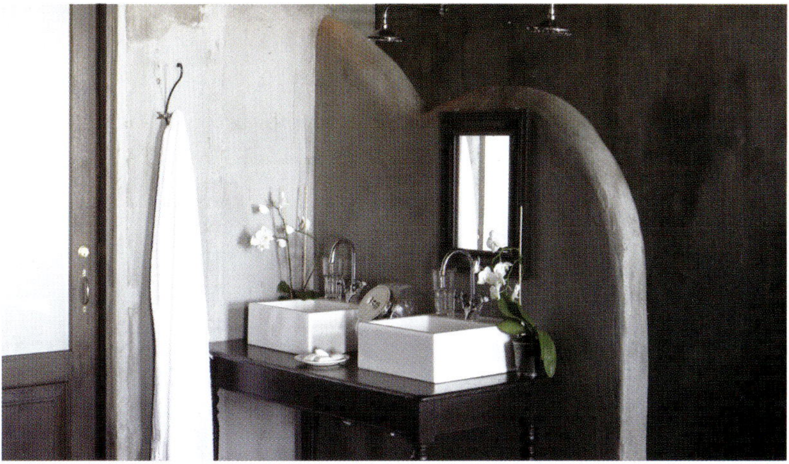

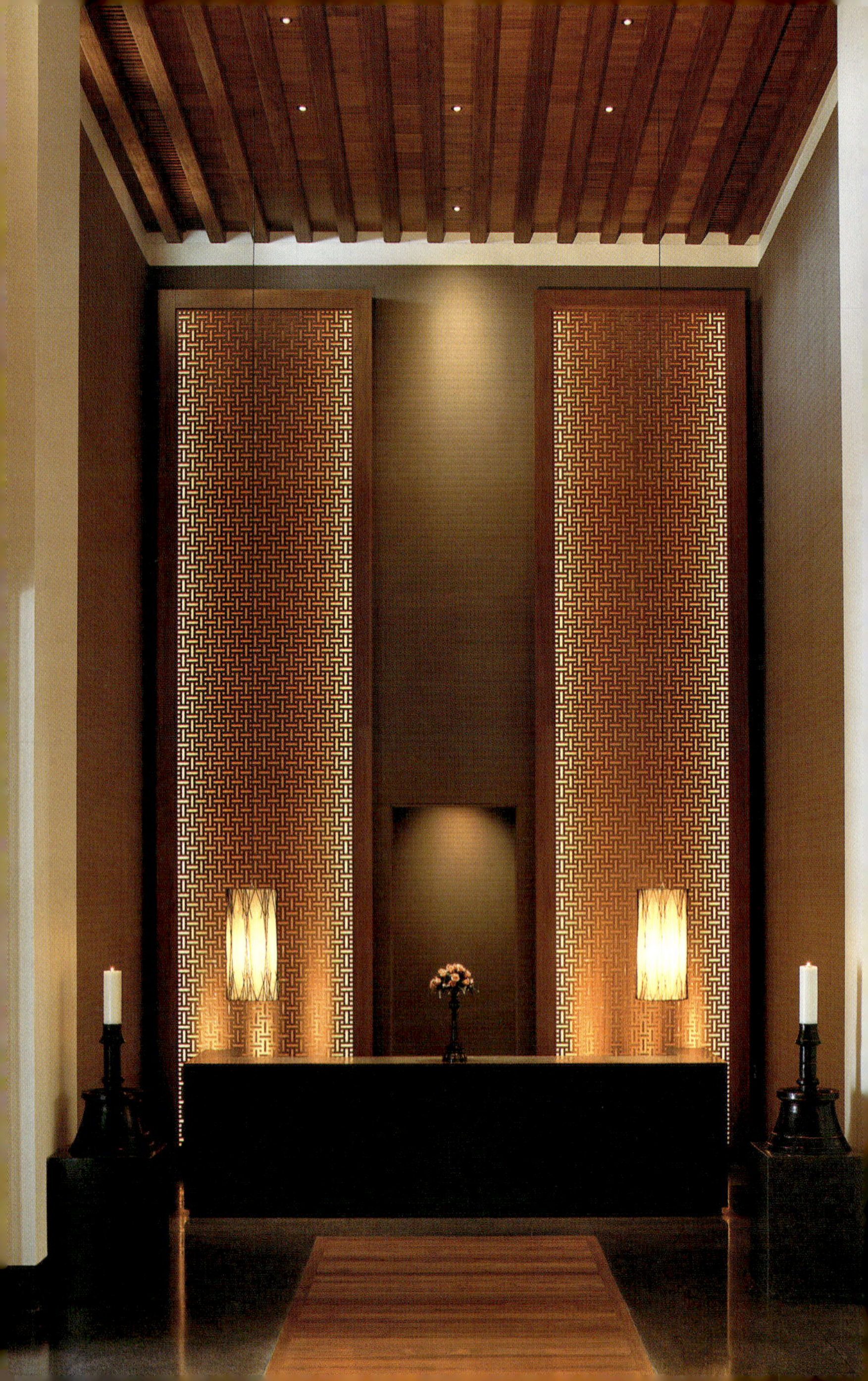

THE CHEDI MUSCAT
A Style to Remember

Architect: **Jean-Michel Gathy/Denniston International Architects & Planners**

Date: 2002
Address: North Ghubra 232, Way 3215, Street 46, 133 Muscat, Oman
Tel.: +968 24 52 44 00 Fax: +968 24 49 34 85
www.ghmhotels.com
Photos: © The Chedi Muscat

Location: Beach
Style: Traditional Omani
Rooms: 151
Special features: Mediterranean and Asian restaurant, spa, two swimming pools, poolside cabanas, tennis courts

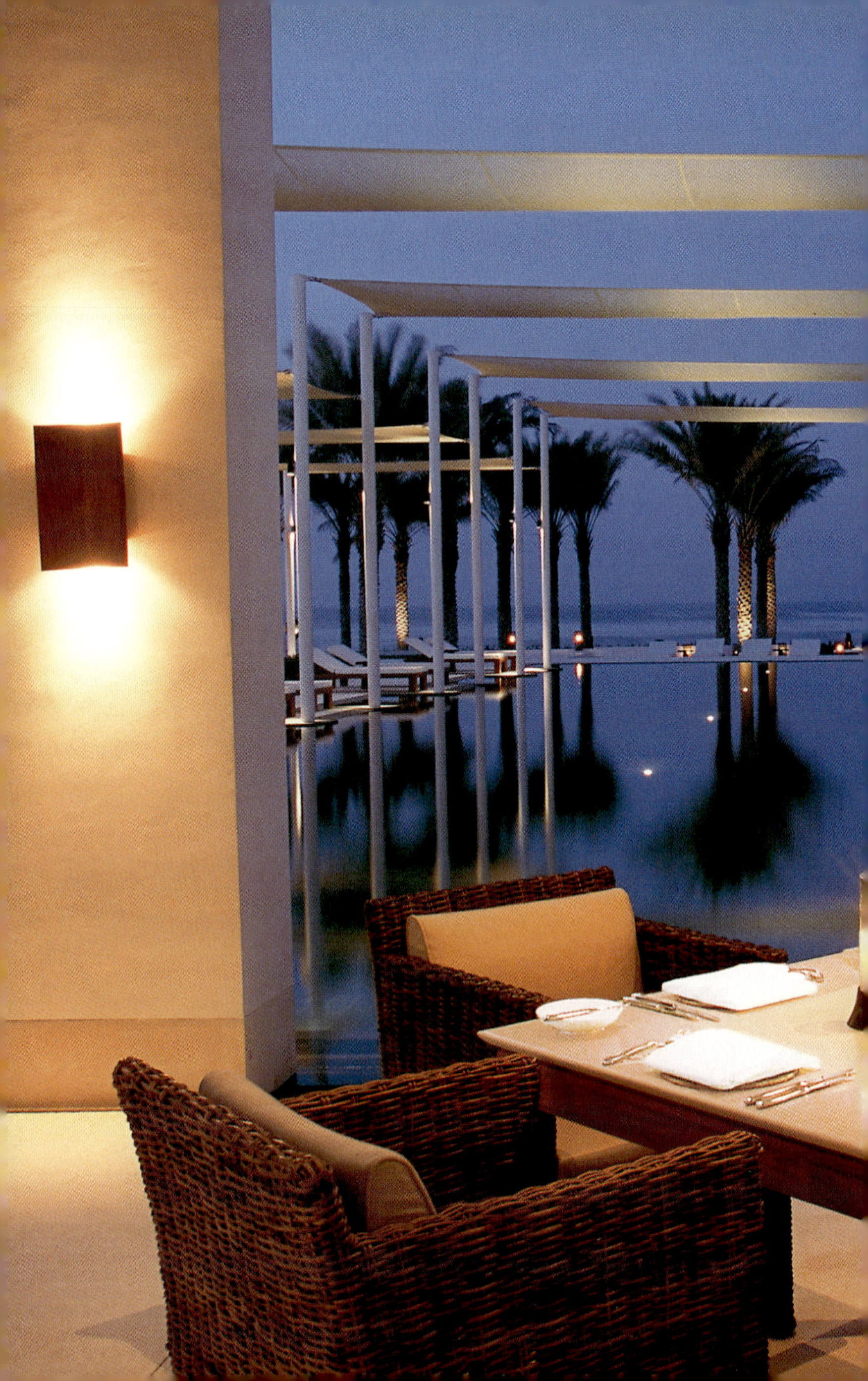

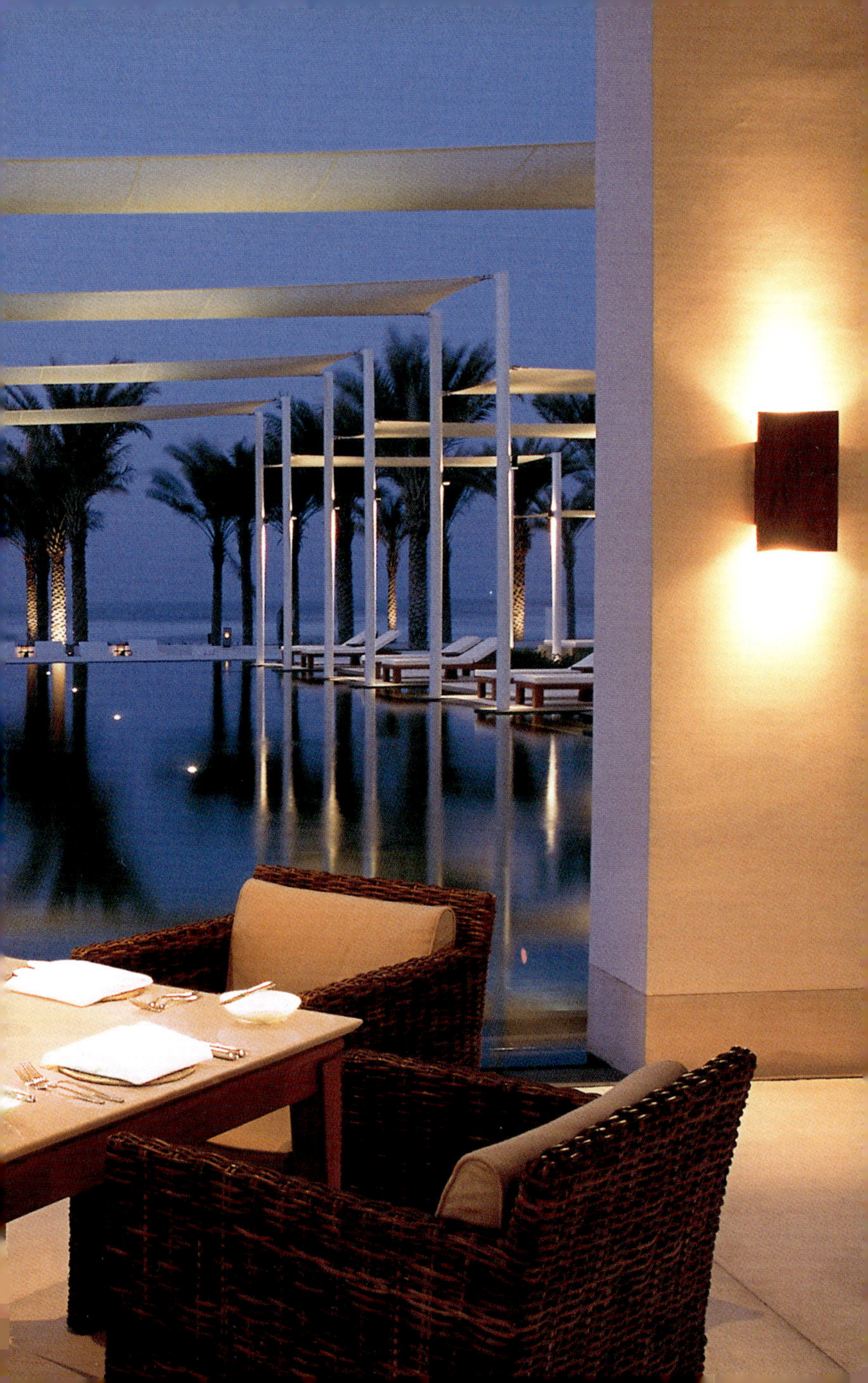

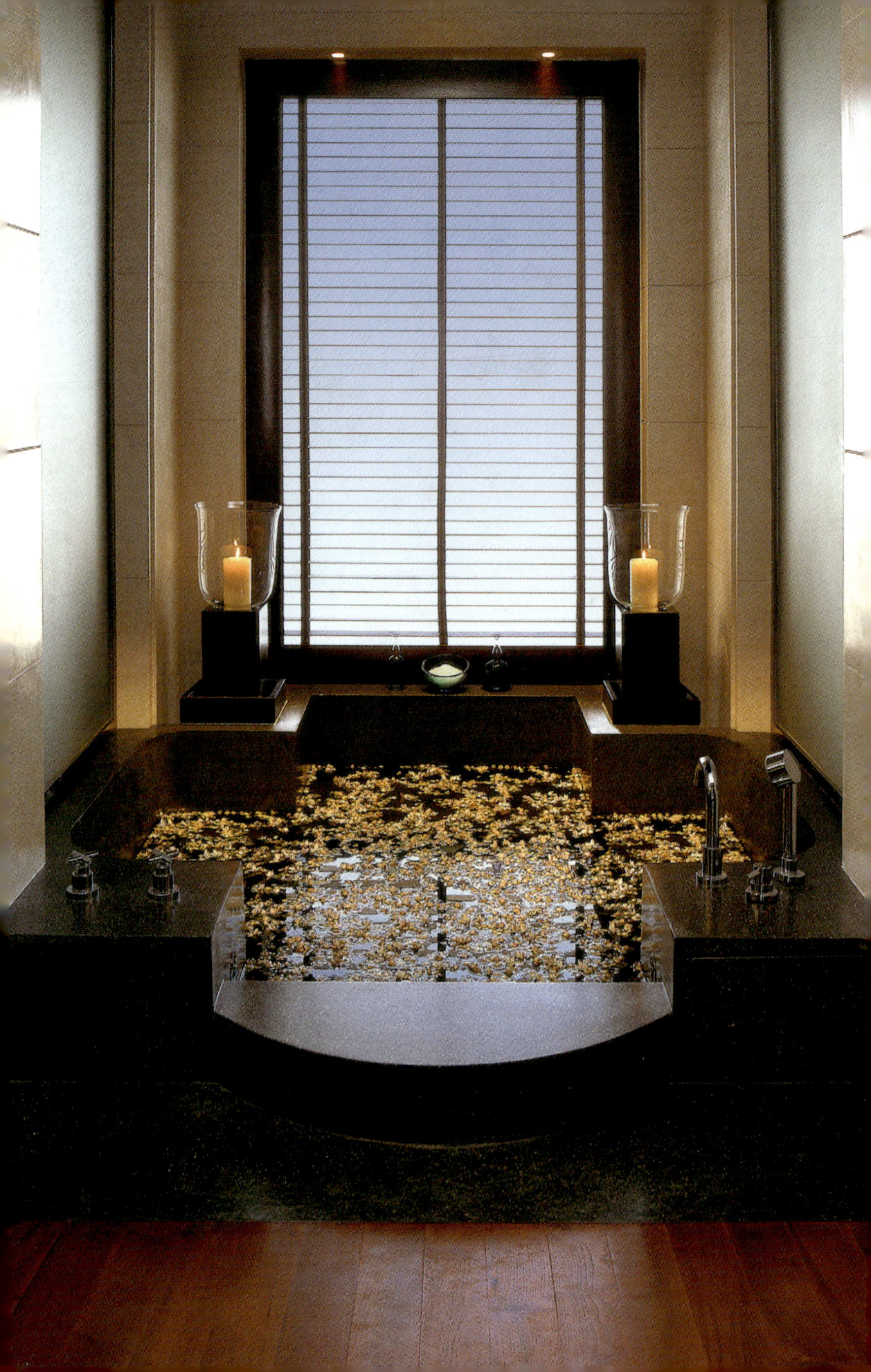

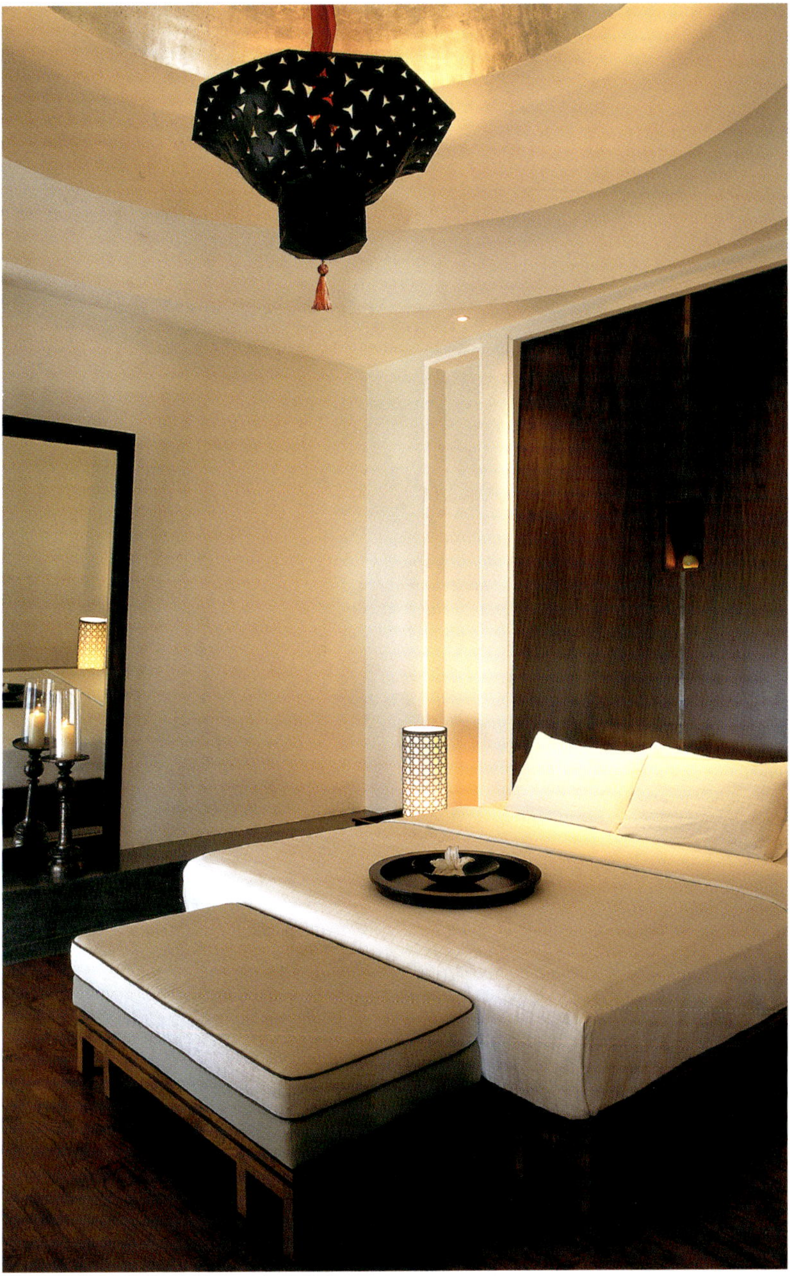

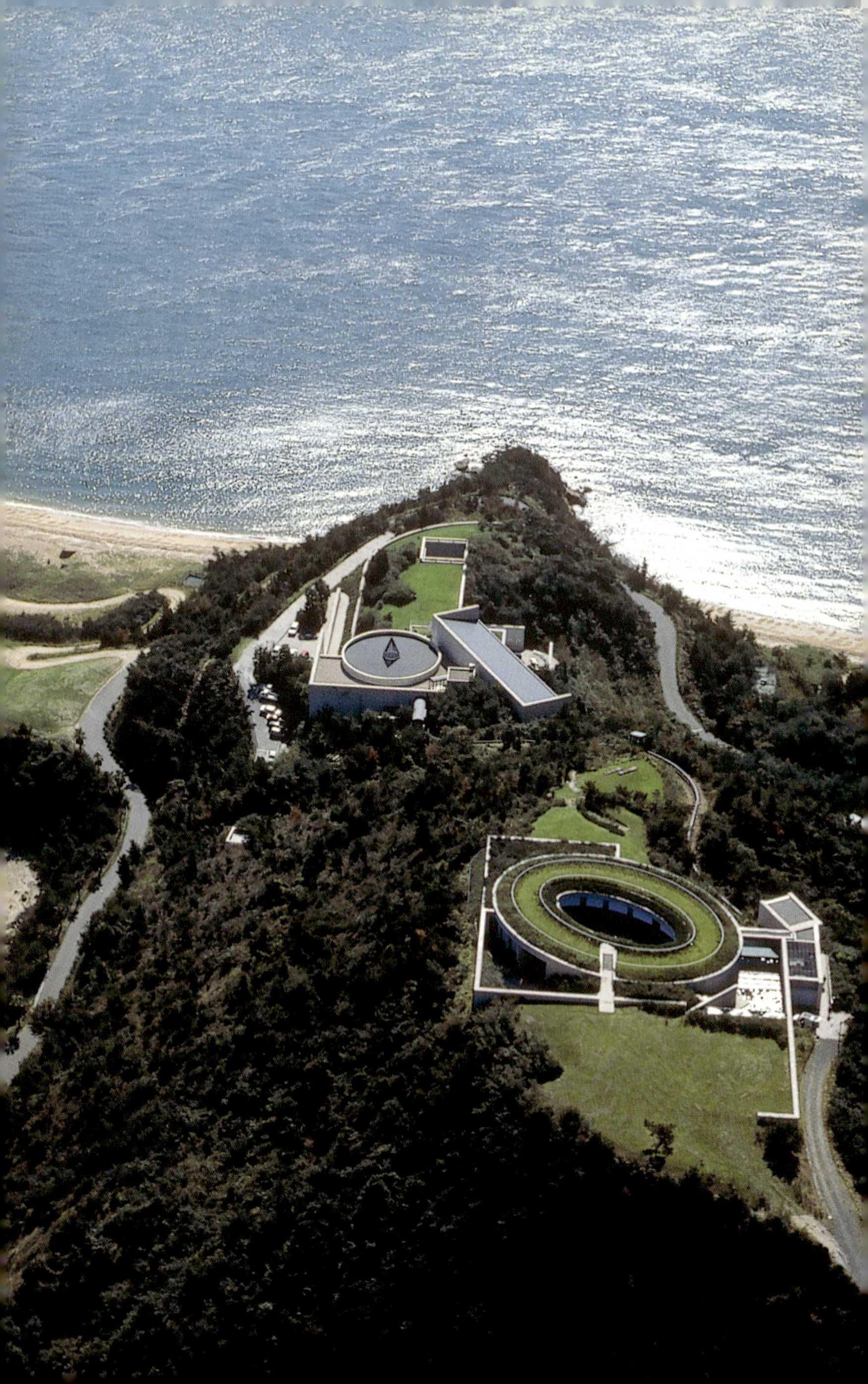

BENESSE HOUSE
Experience Living Surrounded by Art

Architect: **Tadao Ando**

Date: 1995
Address: Gotanji, Naoshima-cho, Kagawa-gun 761-3110, Kagawa, Japan
Tel.: +81 (0) 87 892 2030 Fax: +81 (0) 87 892 2259
www.naoshima-is.co.jp
Photos: © Mitsuo Matasuoka, Tomio Ohashi, Tadao Ando

Location: Beach
Style: Minimalist
Rooms: 6
Special features: Forms part of the Naoshima Contemporary Art Museum complex; artworks in each room

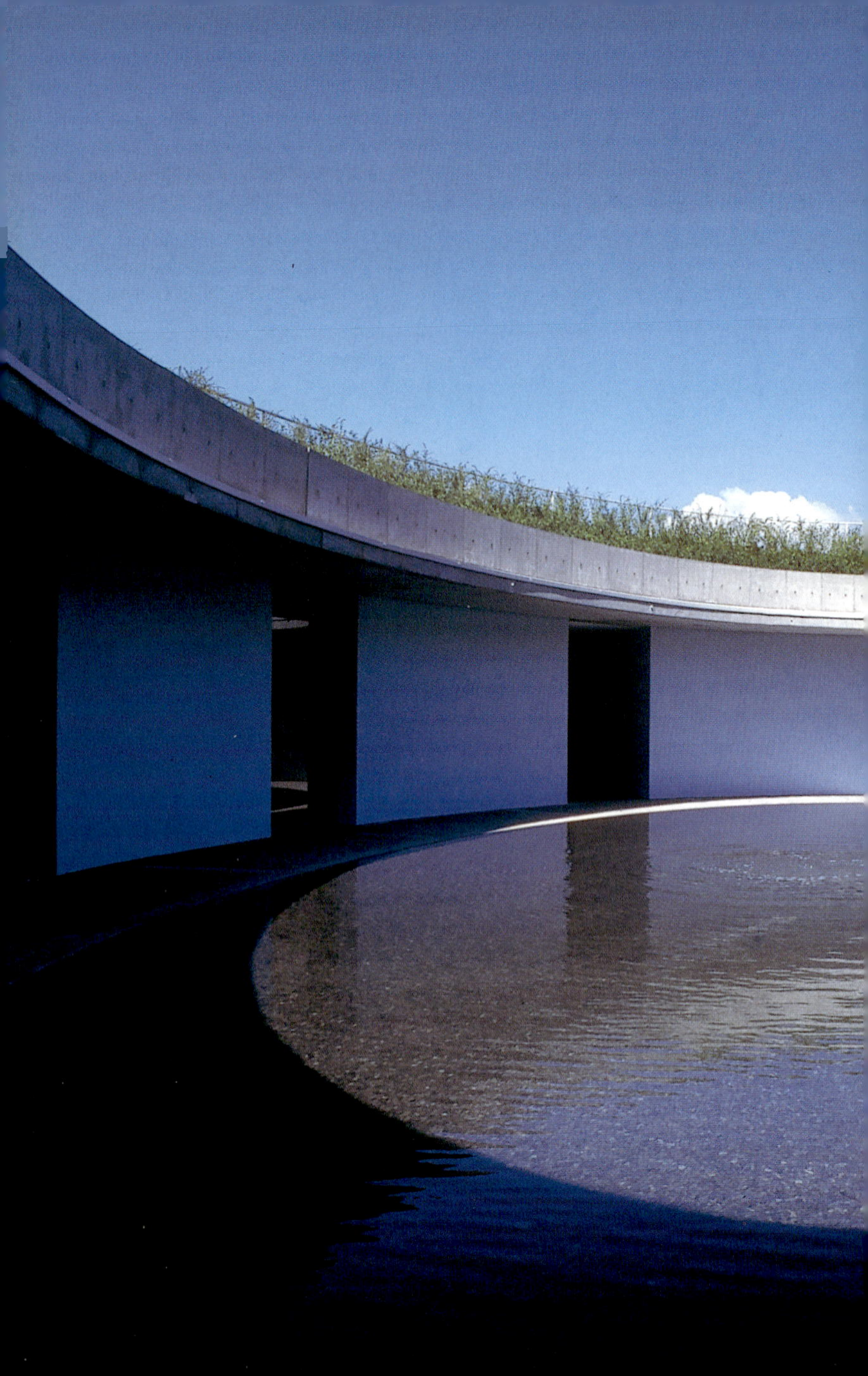

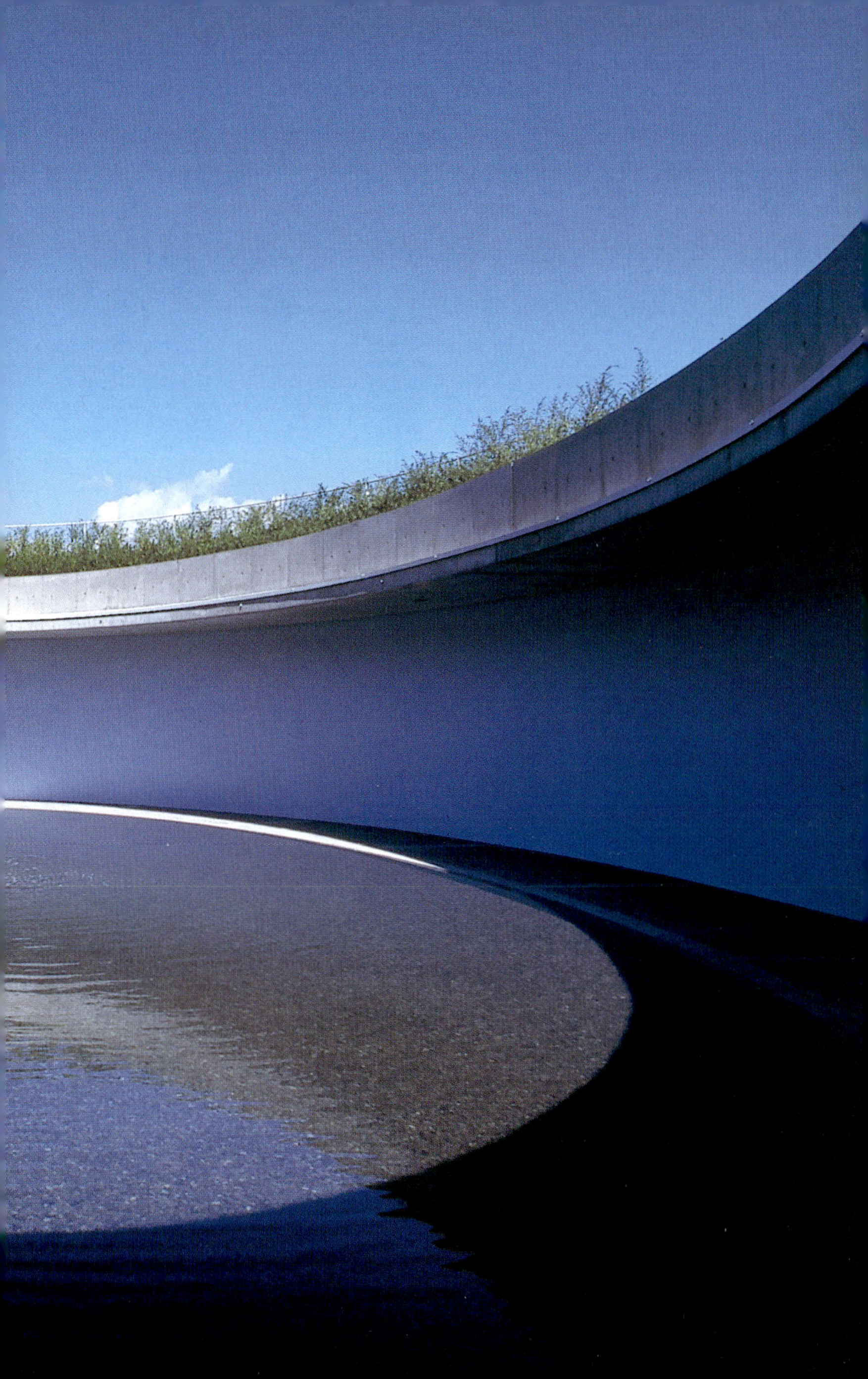

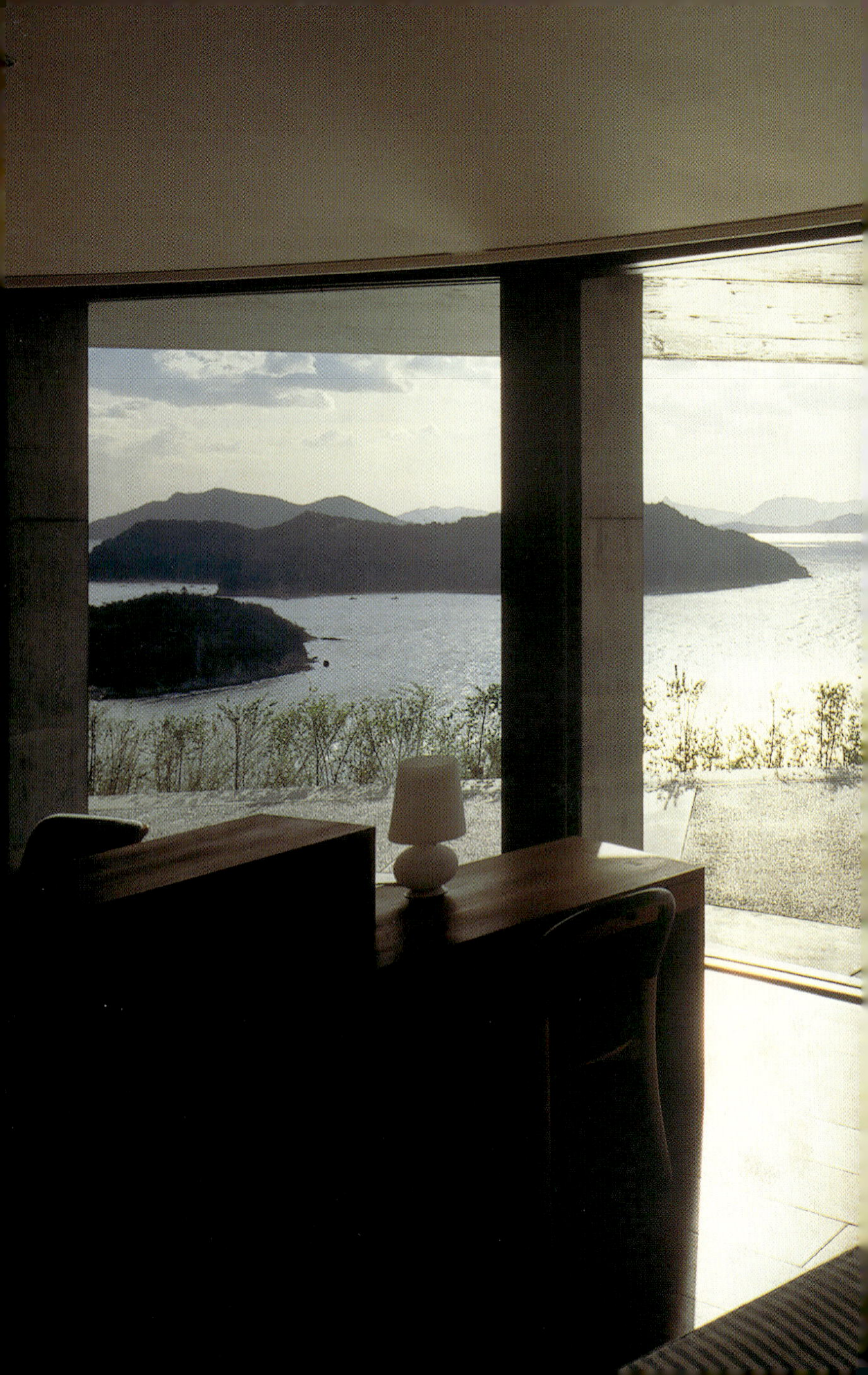

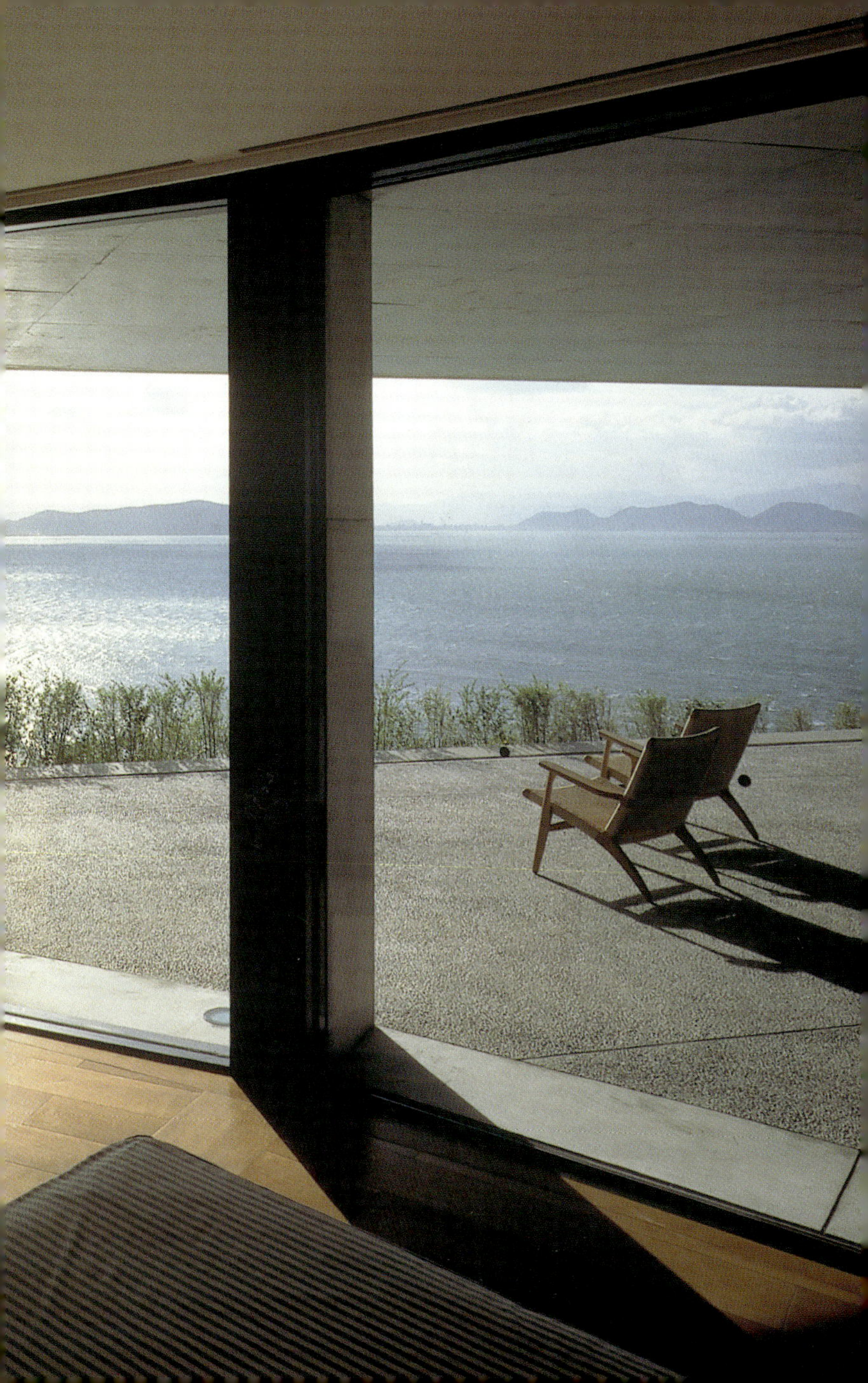

Lyall
HOTEL

Lyall
HOTEL

14

THE LYALL

Experience the Lifestyle

Architects: Bruce Henderson Architects

Date: 2002
Address: 14 Murphy St, South Yarra, Victoria 3141, Melbourne, Australia
Tel.: +61 3 9868 8222 Fax: +61 3 9820 1724
www.thelyall.com
Photos: © The Lyall

Location: Urban
Style: Contemporary in a French-renaissance style
Rooms: 40
Special features: Gymnasium opened 24 hours; tranquil place in the middle of a busy city

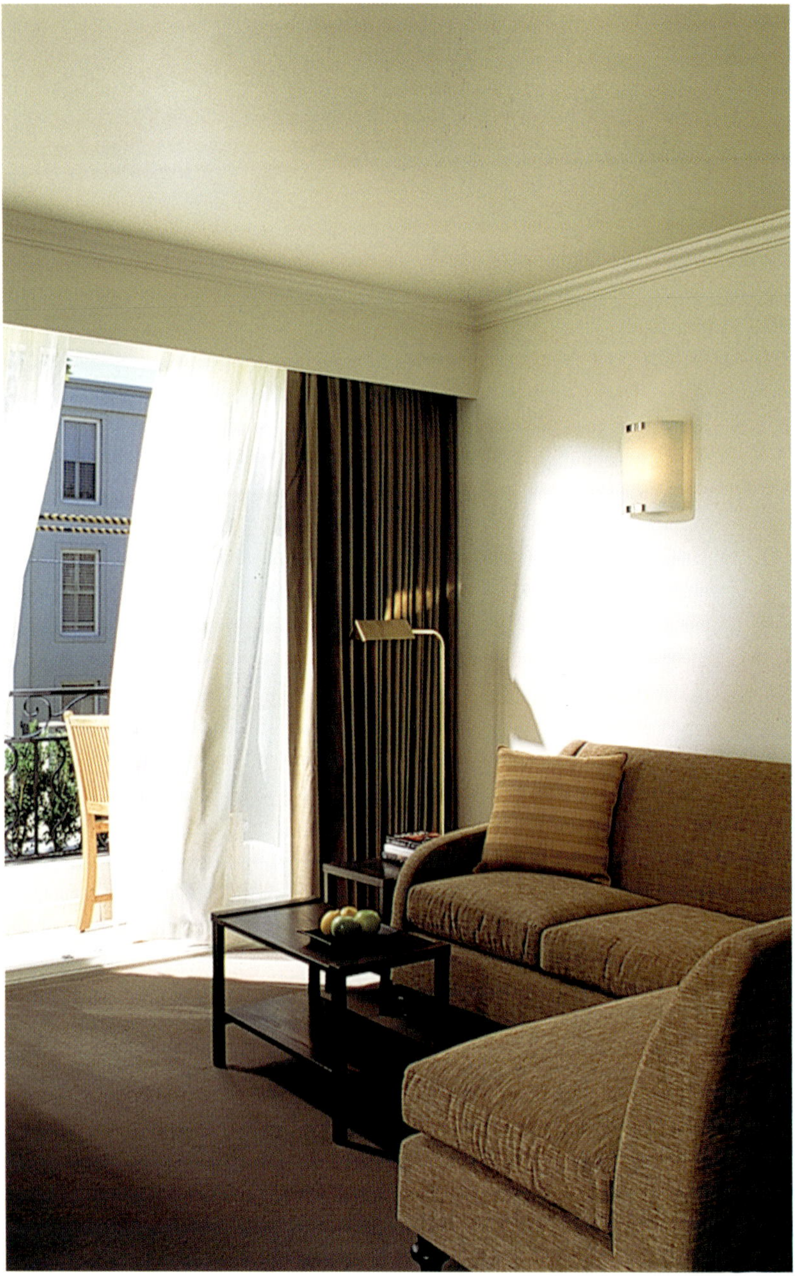

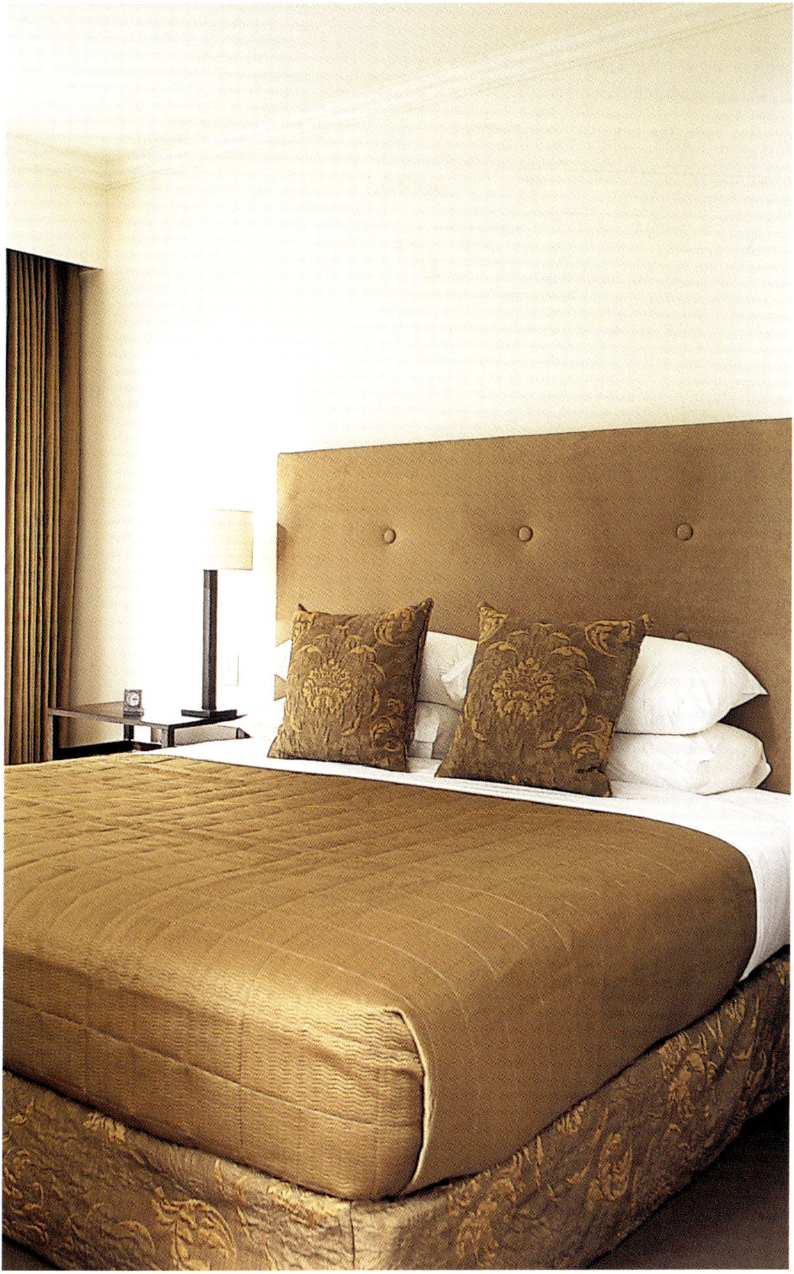

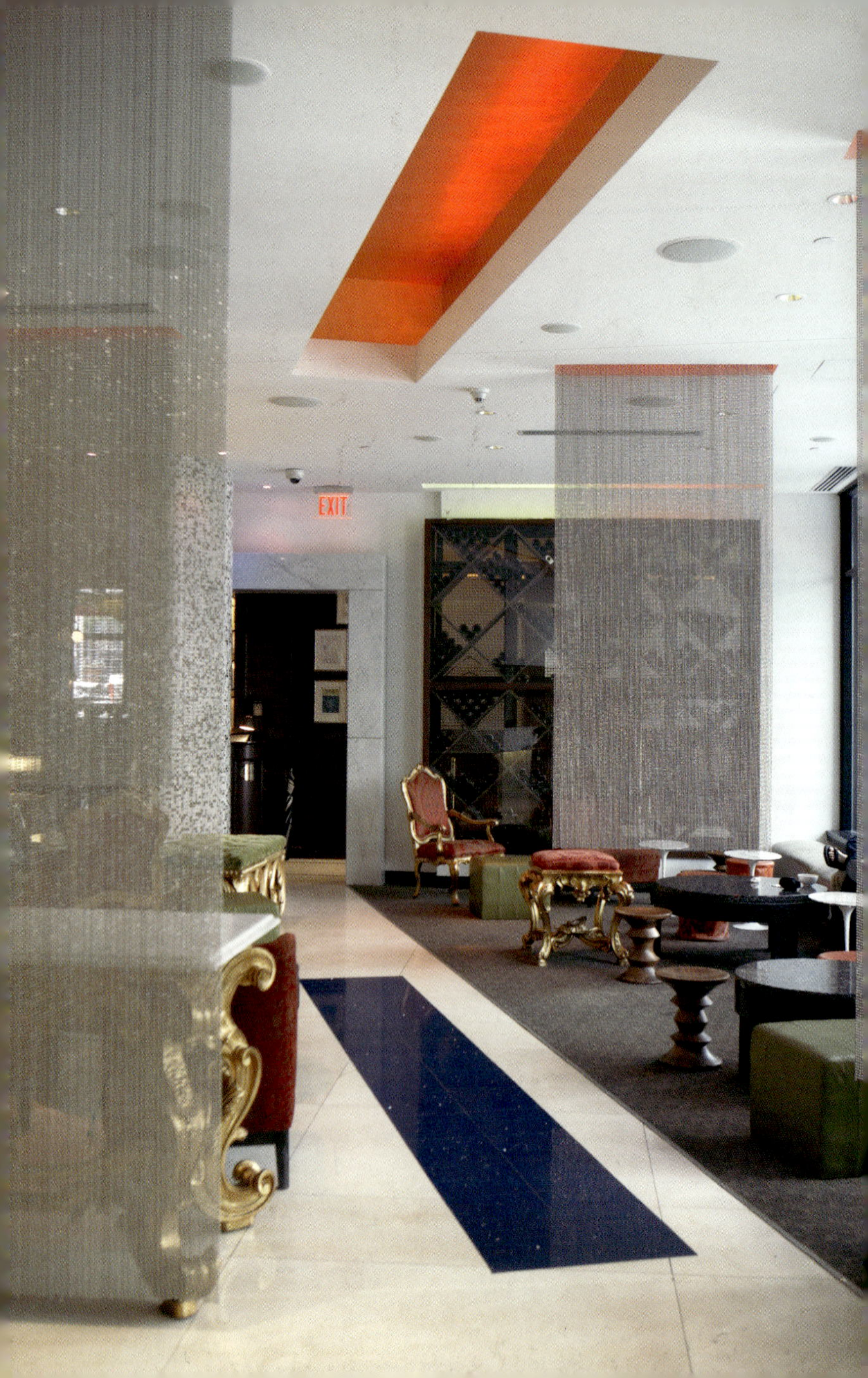
EXIT

OPUS HOTEL
Redefine the Boutique Hotel Experience

Architects: Paul Merrick Architects

Date: 2002
Address: 322 Davie Street, British Columbia V6B 5Z6, Vancouver, Canada
Tel.: +1 604 642 6787 Fax: +1 604 642 6780
www.opushotel.com
Photos: © Rob Melnychuk

Location: Urban
Style: Contemporary hip
Rooms: 97
Special features: Personalized rooms, heated bathroom floors, L'Occitane bath products, oxygen "shots"

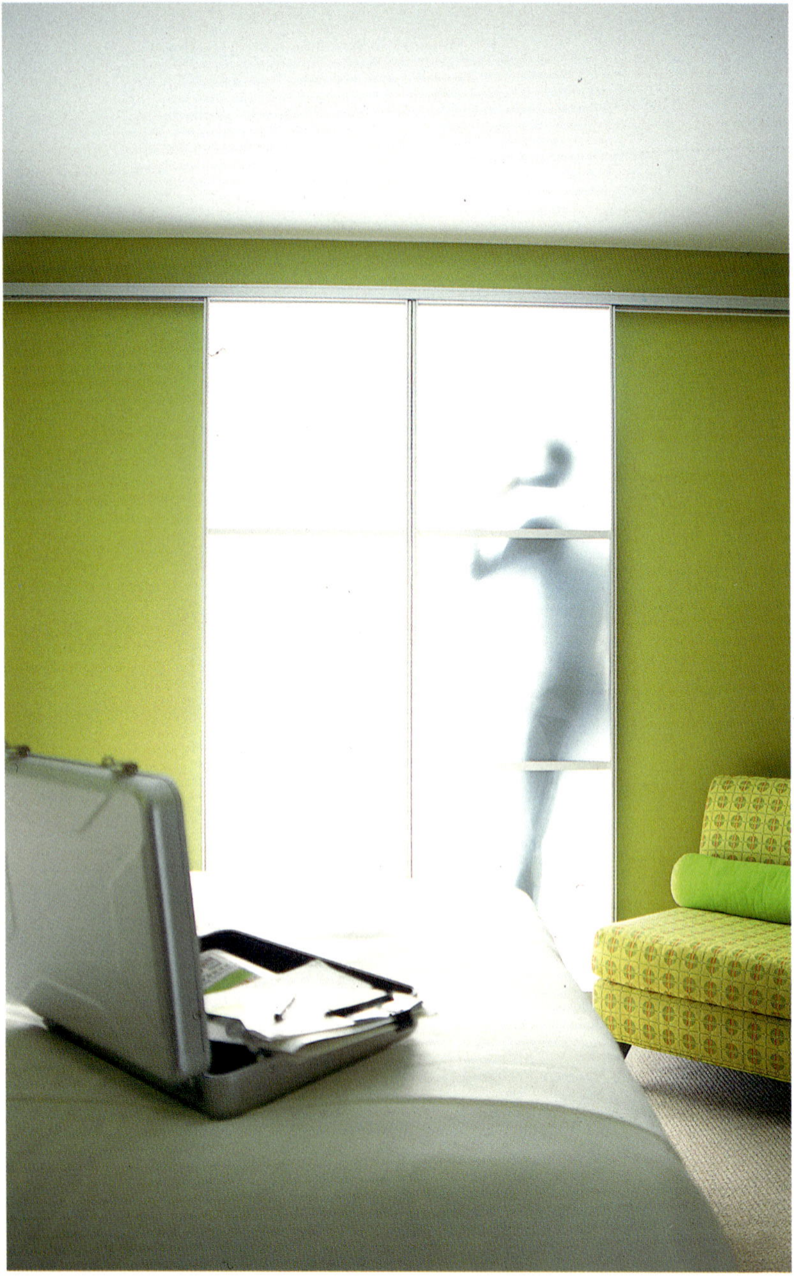

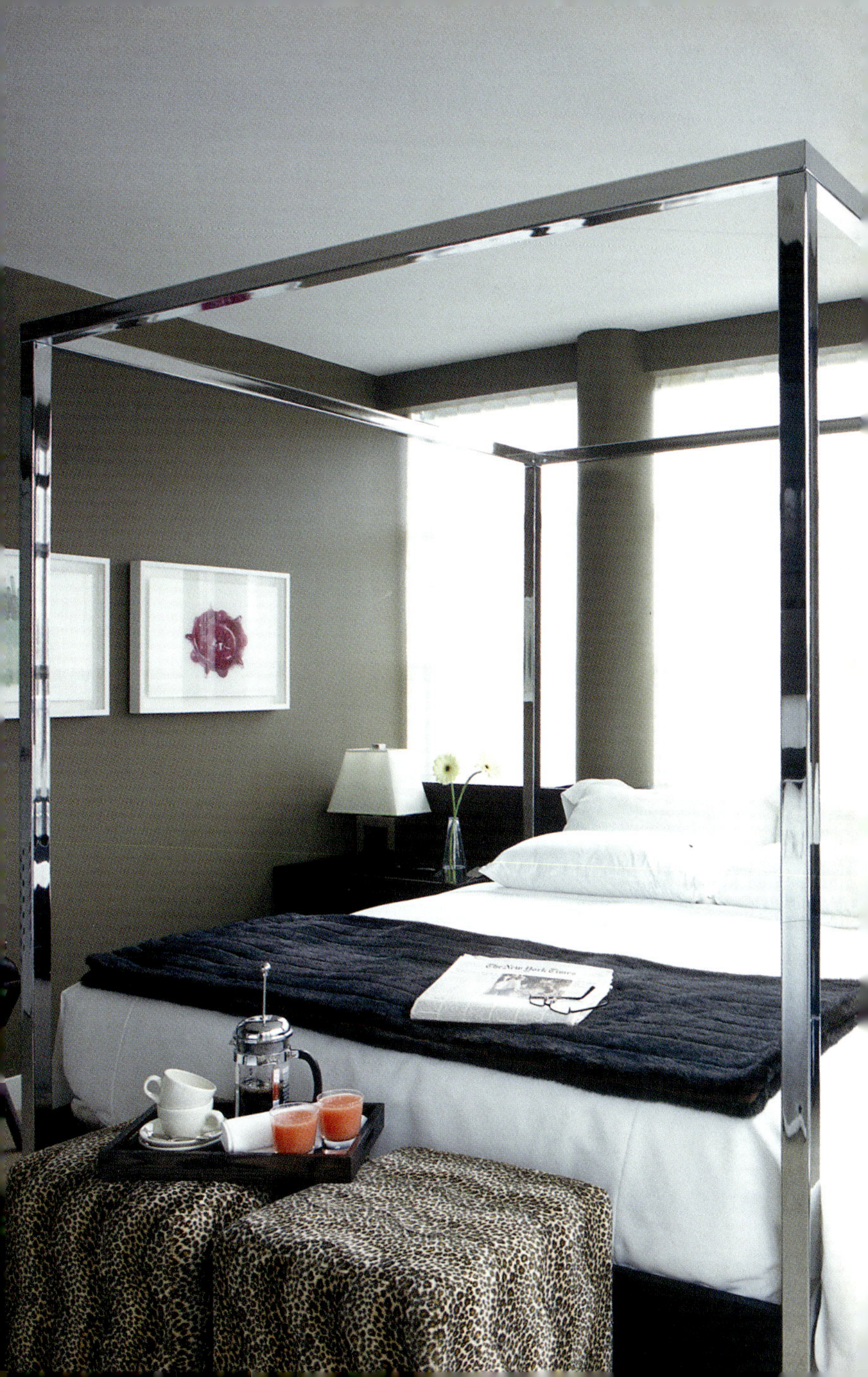
The New York Times

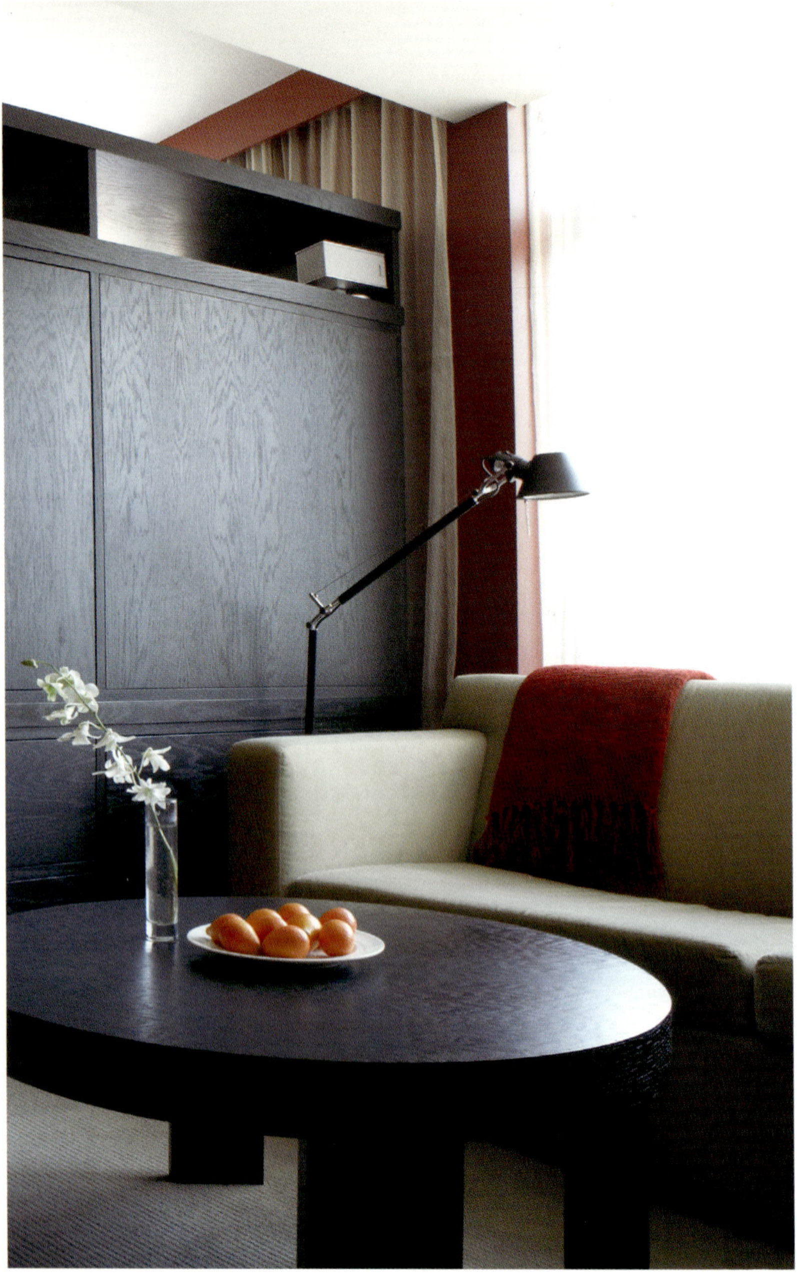

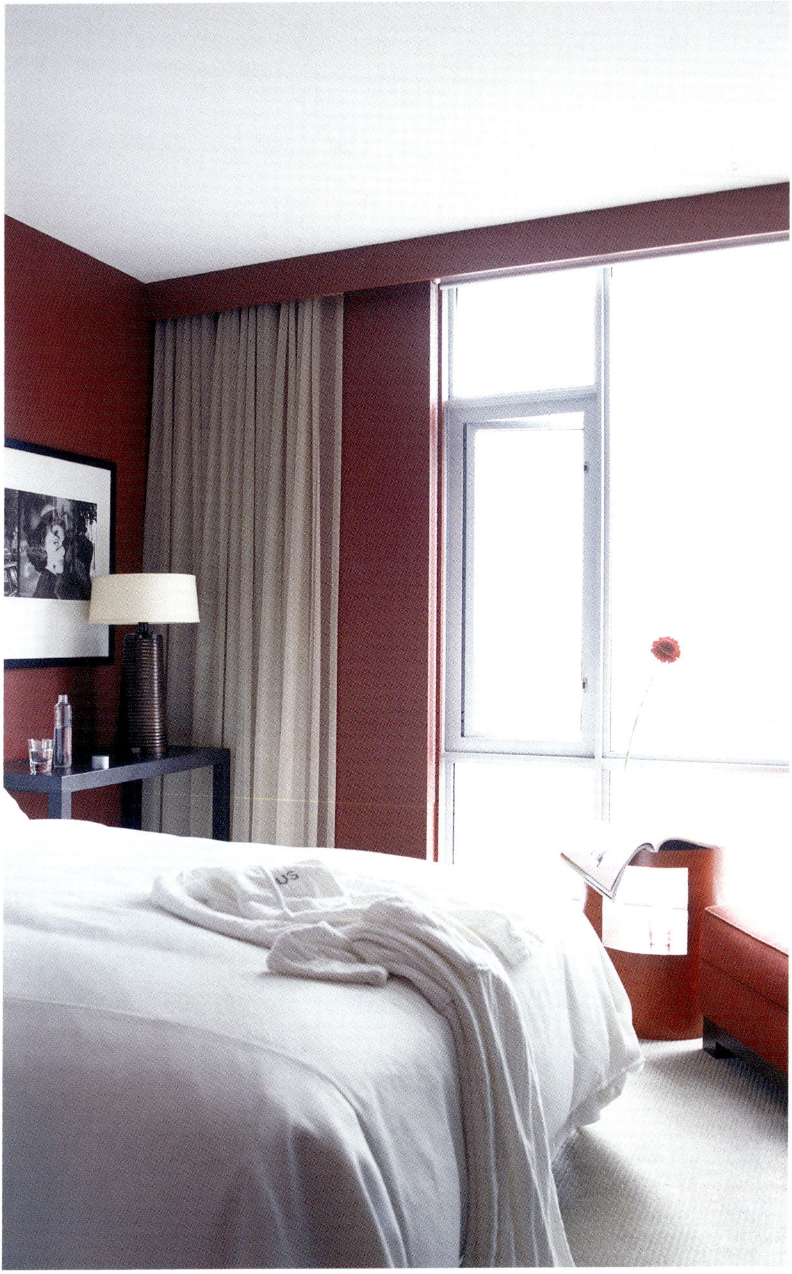

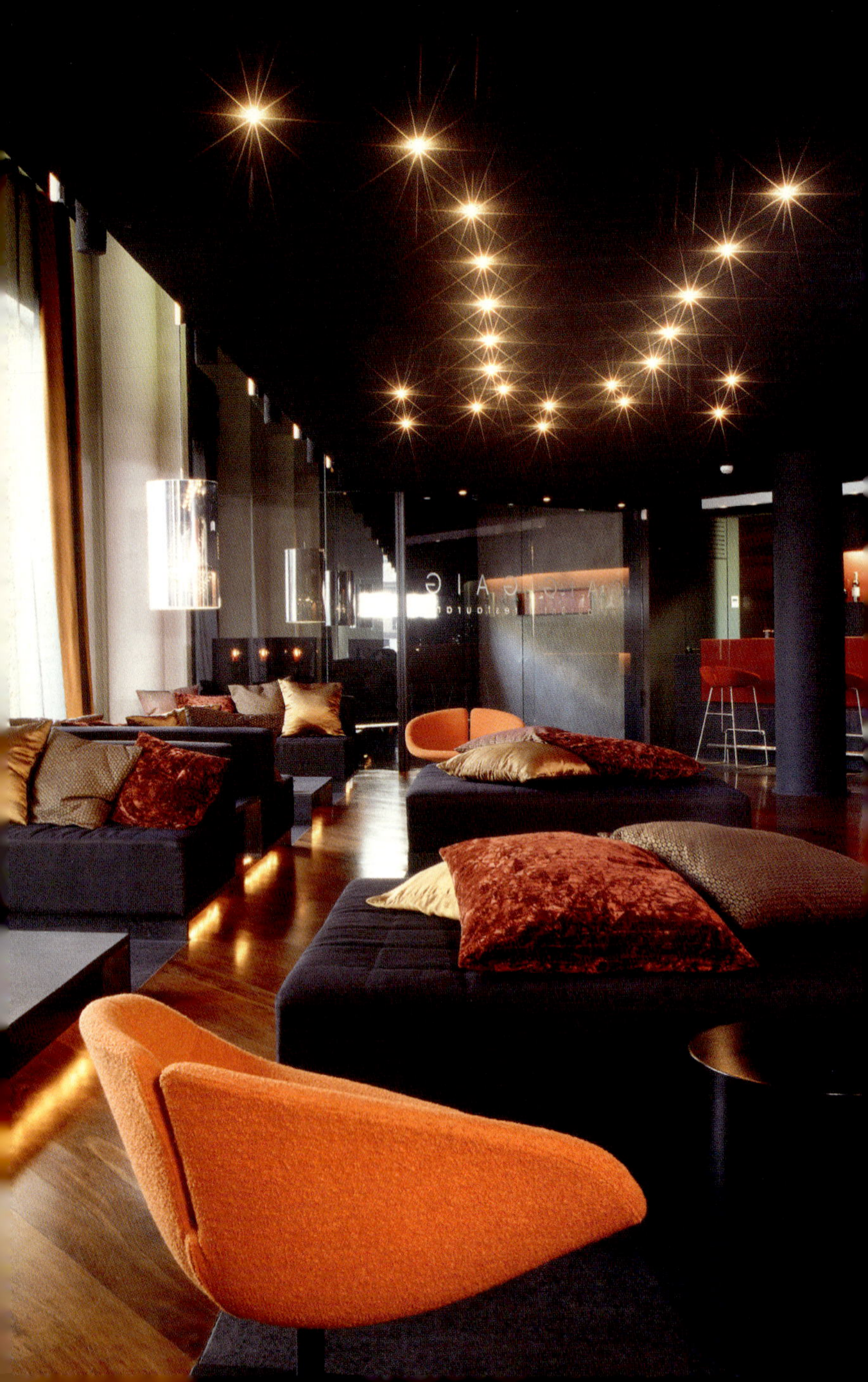

CRAM L'HOTEL
Above All... It's Expectation

Architects: **GCA Arquitectes Associats**
Collaborators: **Beatriz Cosials, Francisco de Paz**

Date: 2004
Address: Aribau 54, 08011 Barcelona, Spain
Tel.: +34 932 167 700 Fax: +34 932 167 707
www.hotelcram.com
Photos: © Jordi Miralles

Location: Urban
Style: Modern luxury
Rooms: 67
Special features: Bars, restaurant, conference rooms, swimming pool

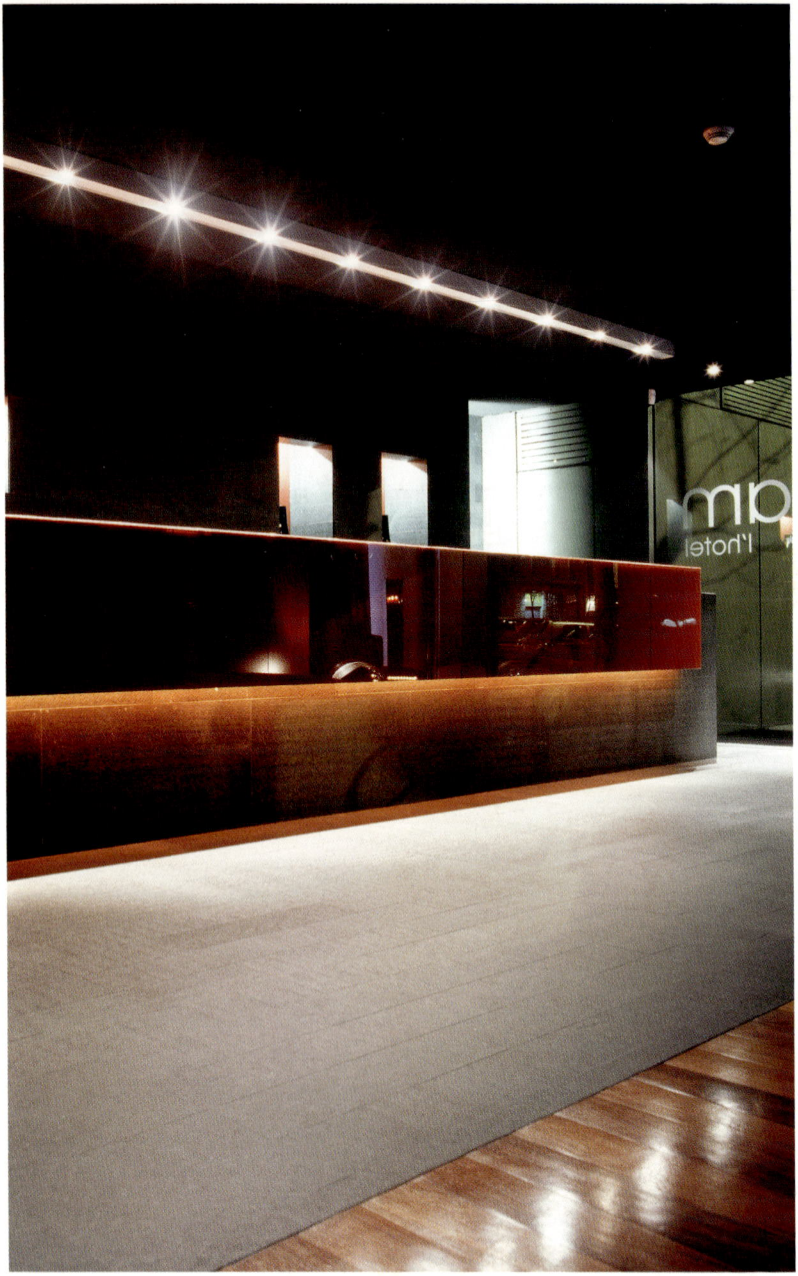

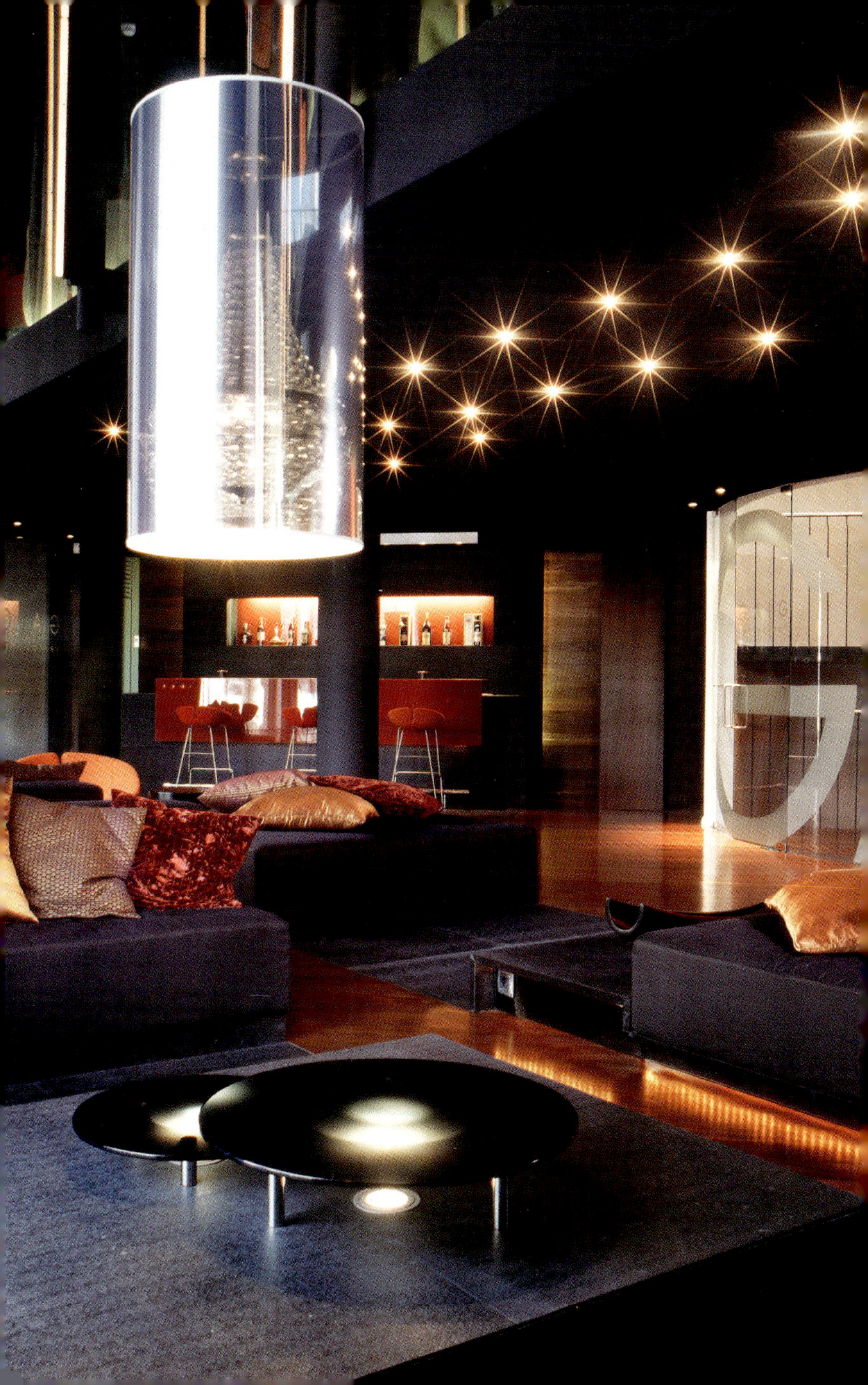

1. Room
2. Hall
3. Patio
4. Stairs
5. Office

Type plan

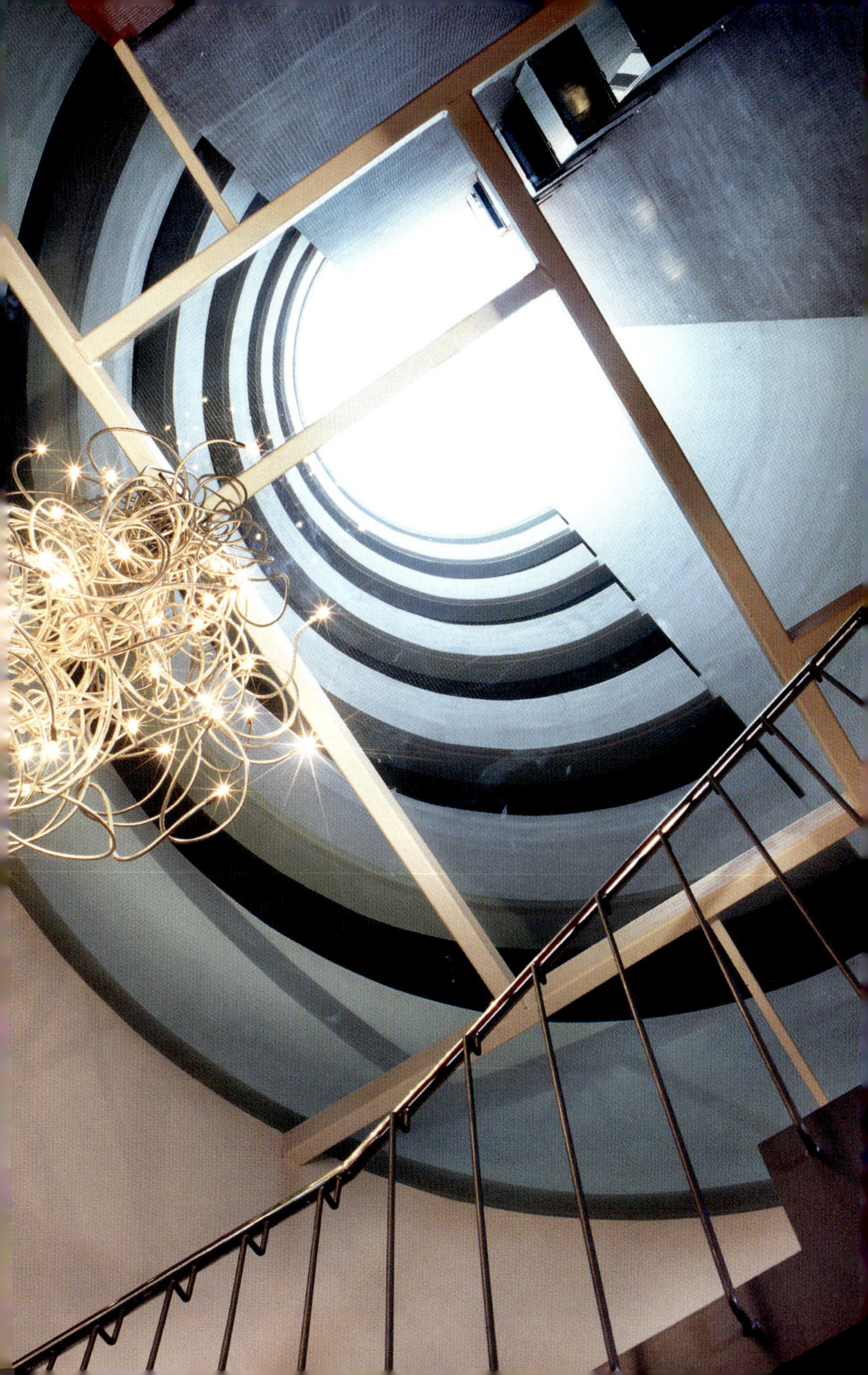

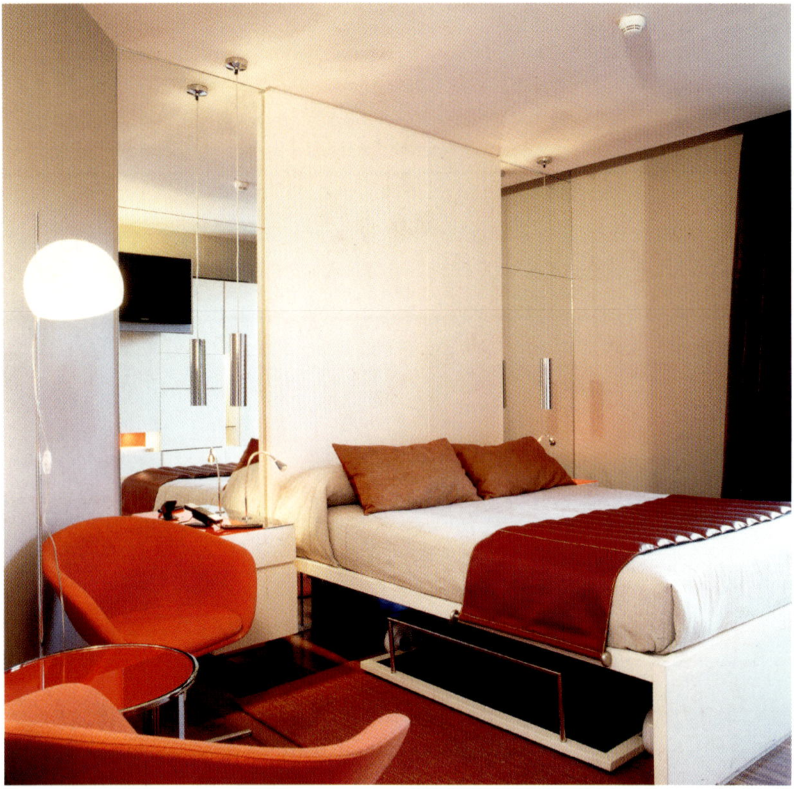

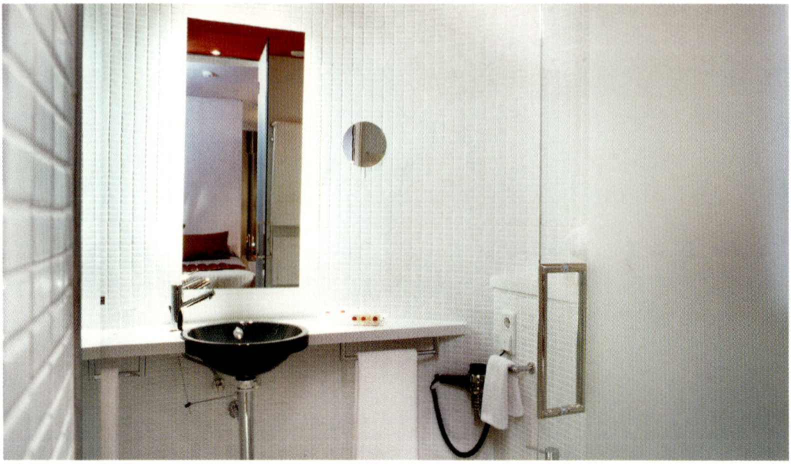

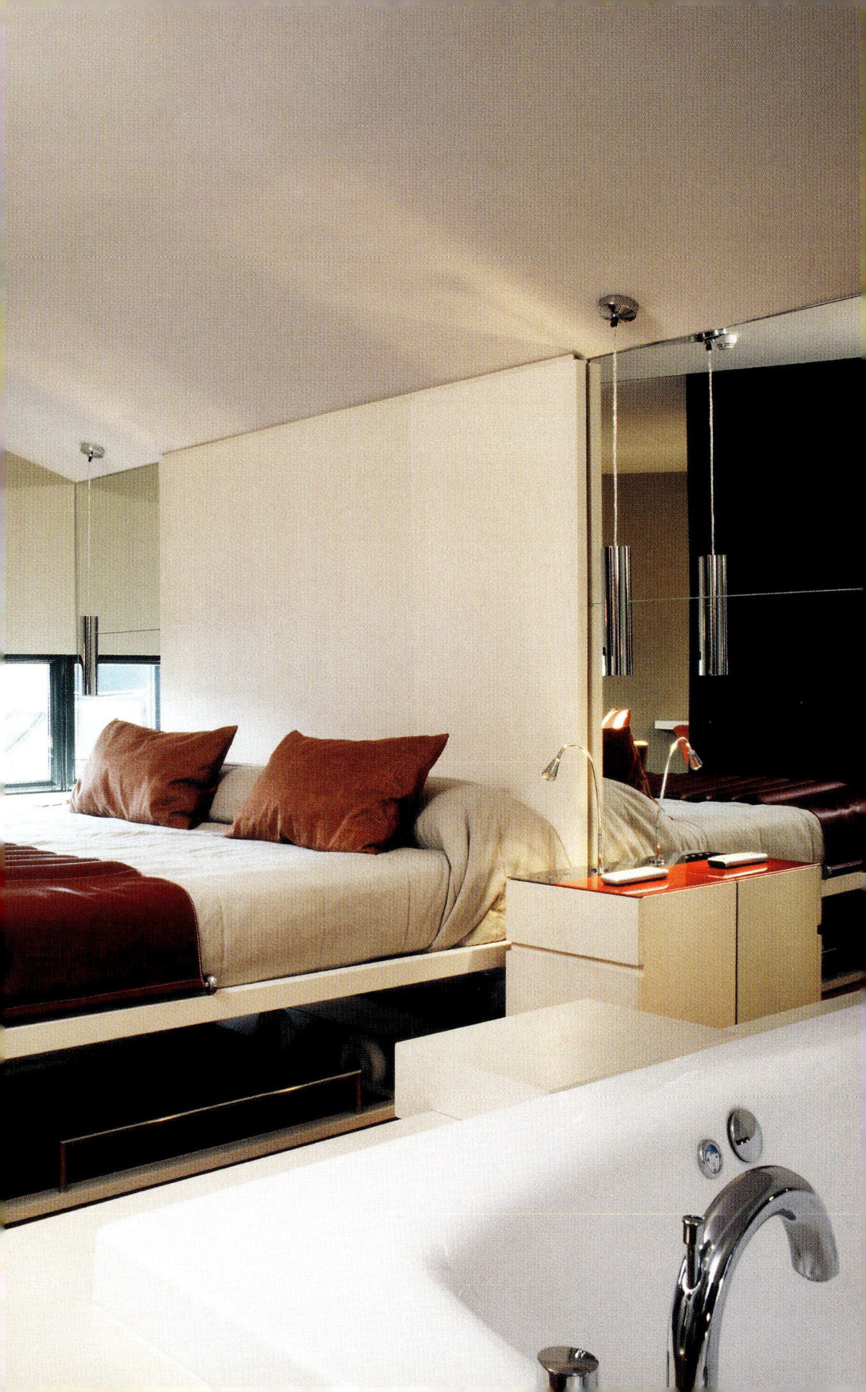

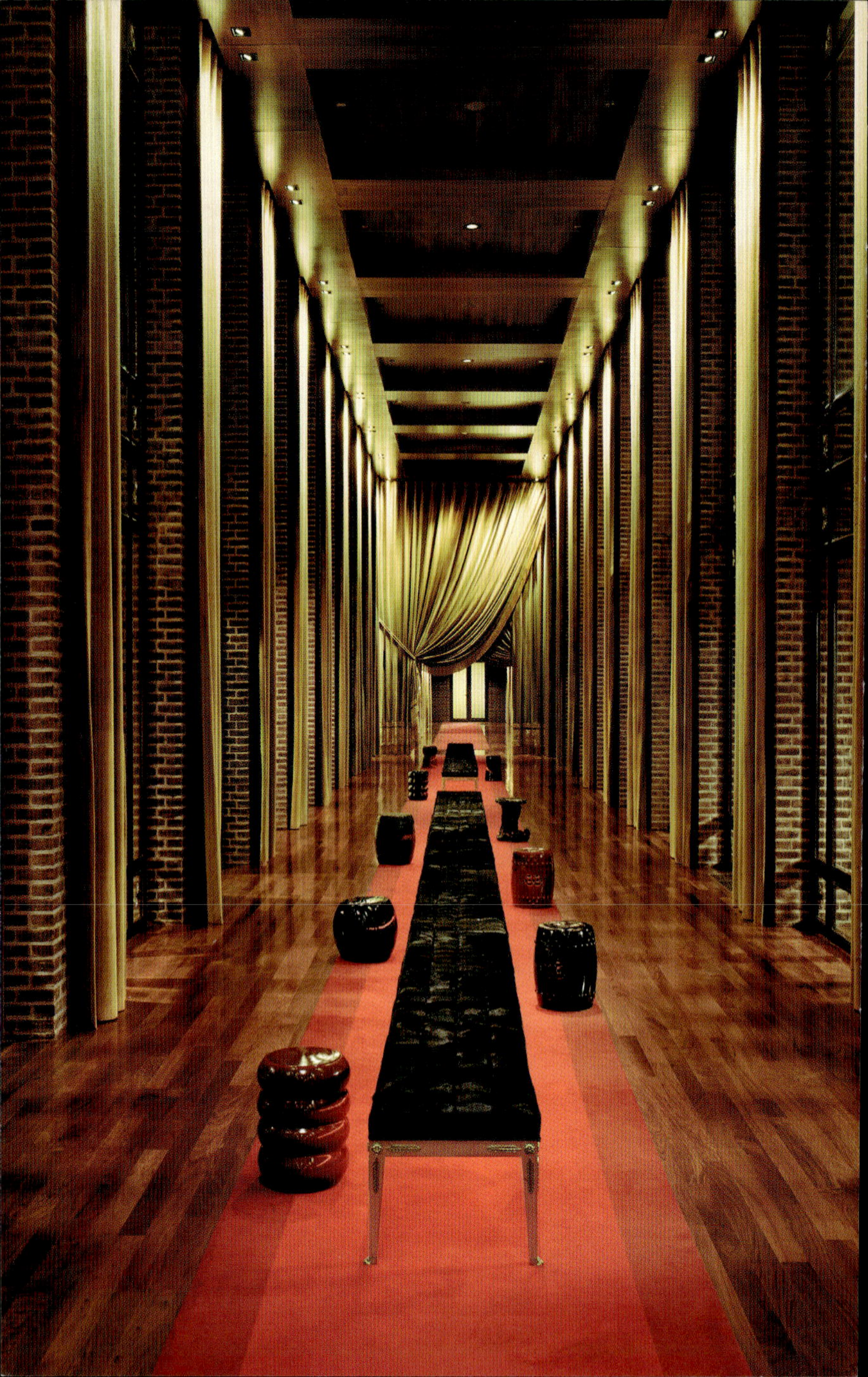

FAENA HOTEL & UNIVERSE

An Experience You Won't Forget

Architect: **Philippe Starck**

Date: 2004
Address: Martha Salotti 445, Dique 2, Puerto Madero Este, Buenos Aires, Argentina
Tel.: +54 11 4010 9000 Fax: +54 11 4010 9001
www.faenahotelanduniverse.com
Photos: © Nikolas Koenig

Location: Urban
Style: Modern romantic
Rooms: 83
Special features: Boutique, library lounge, pool bar

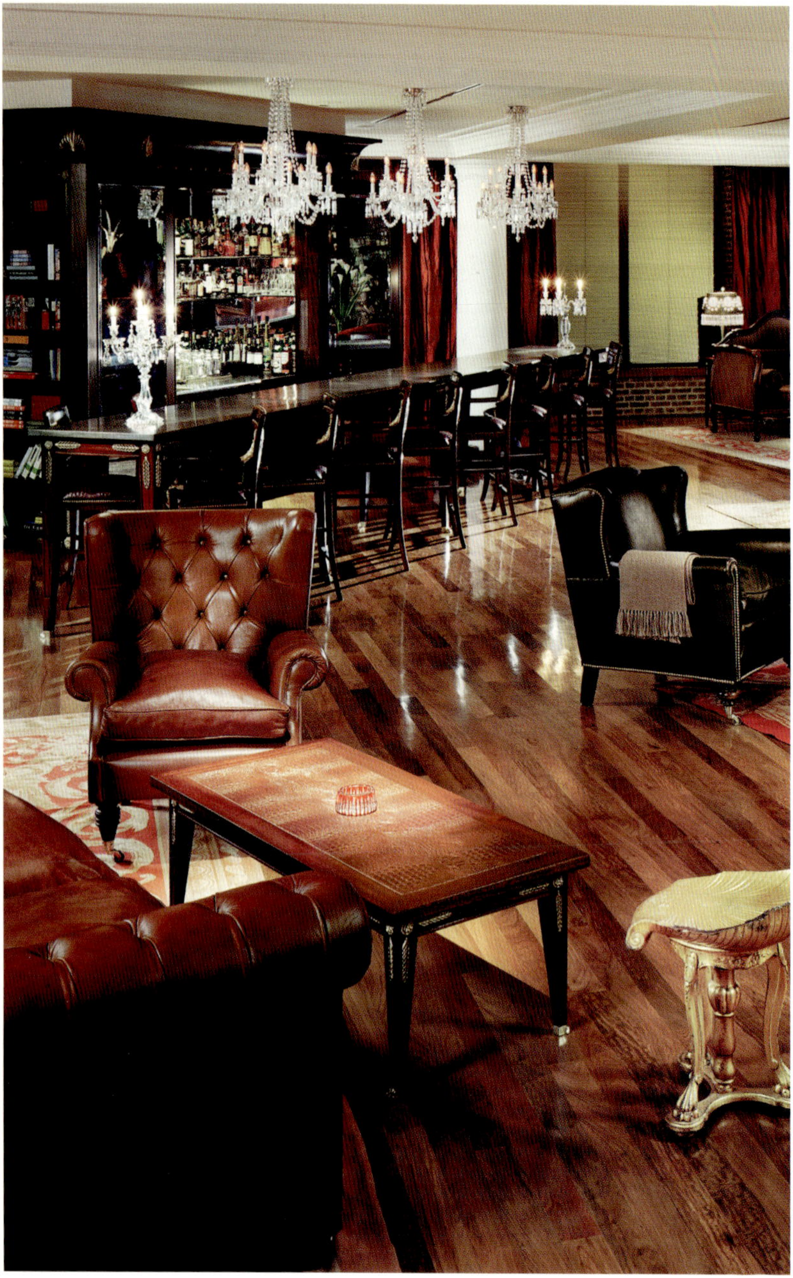

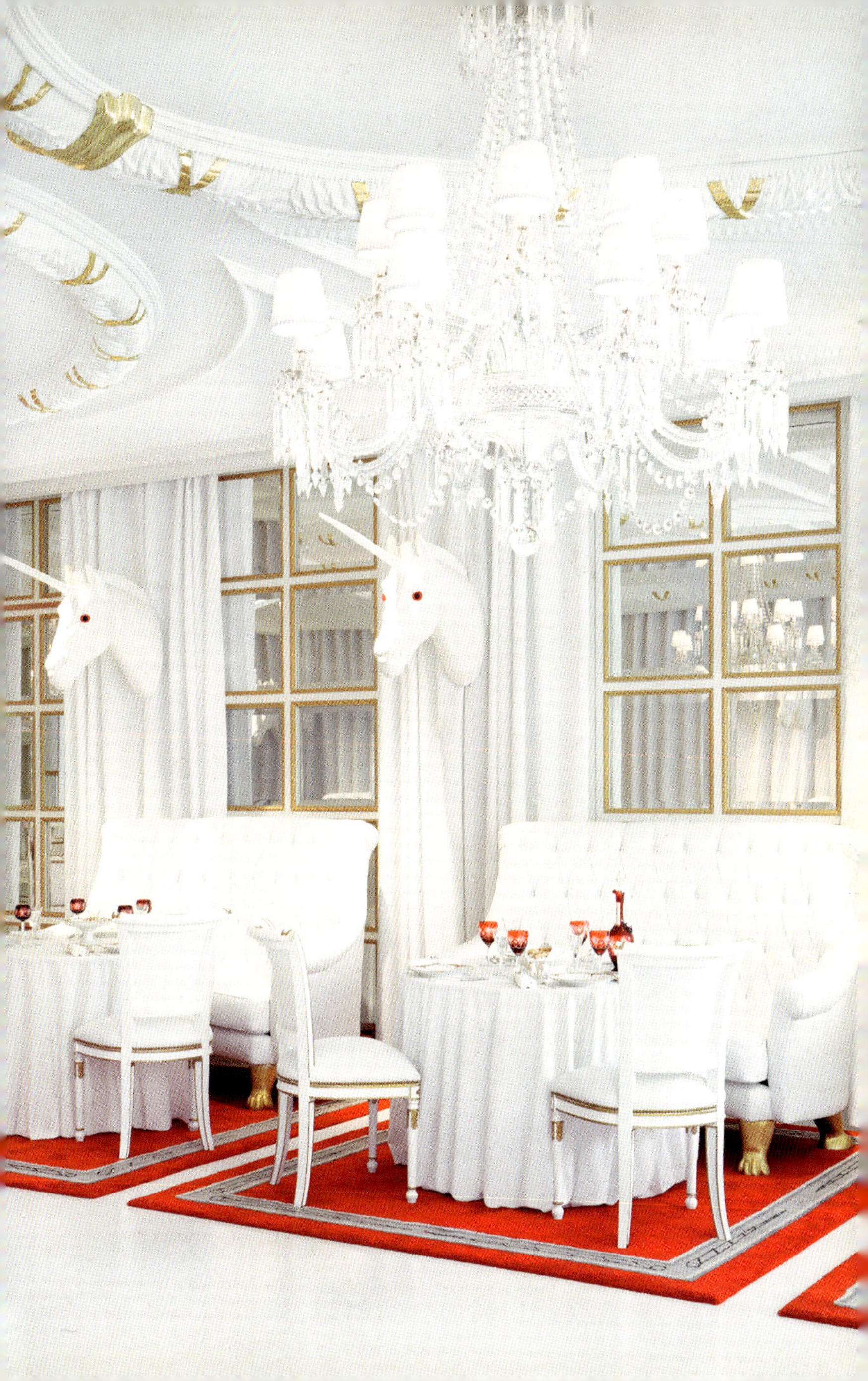

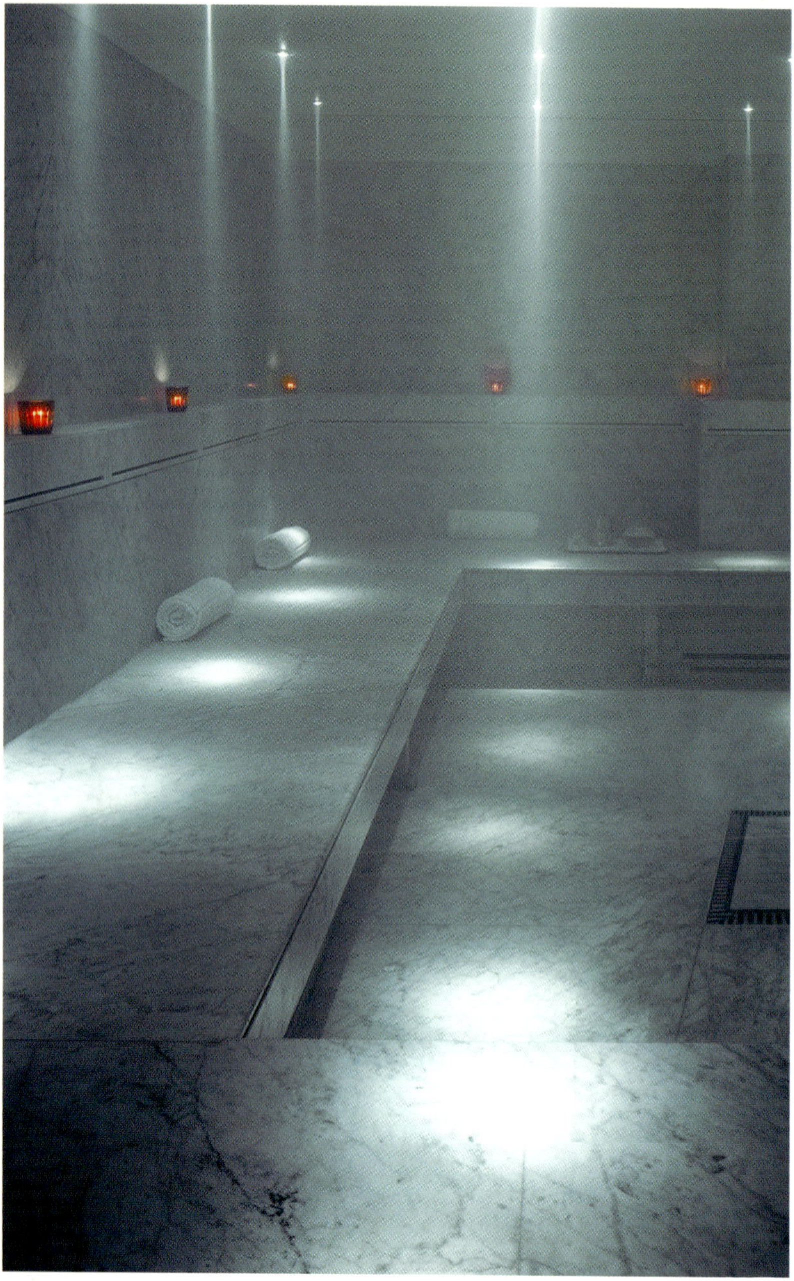

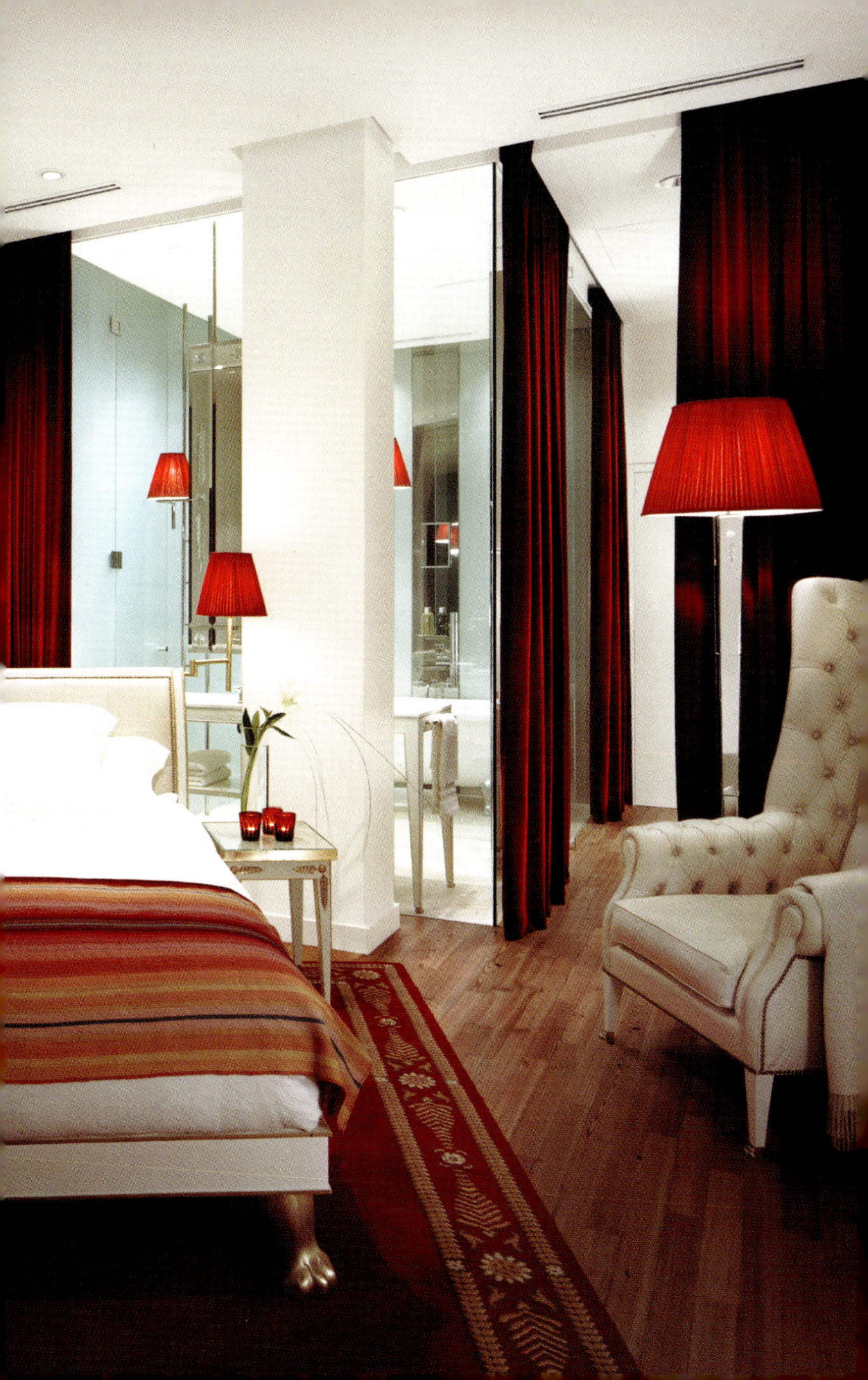

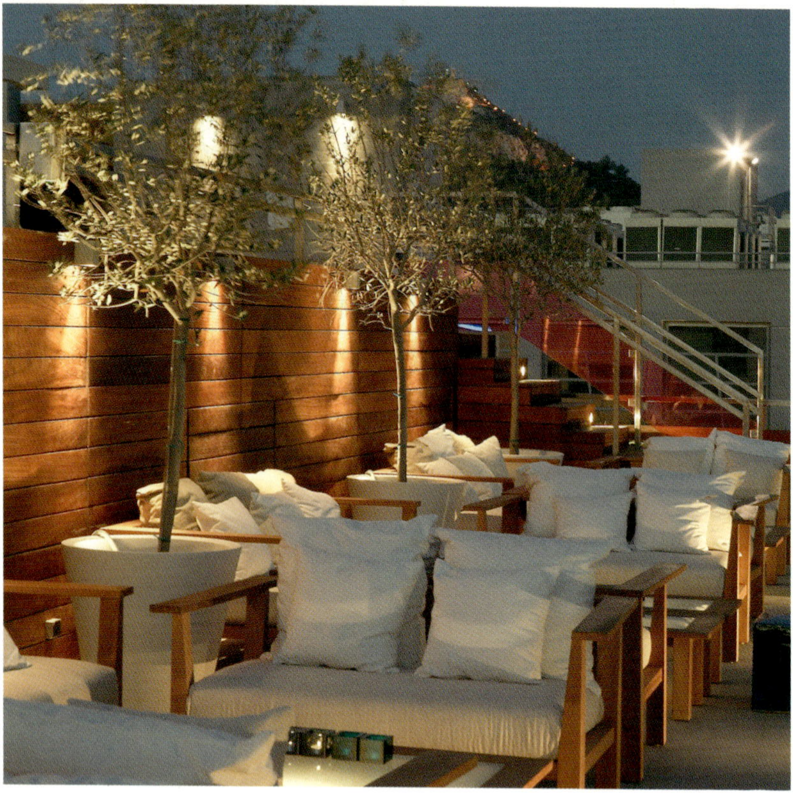

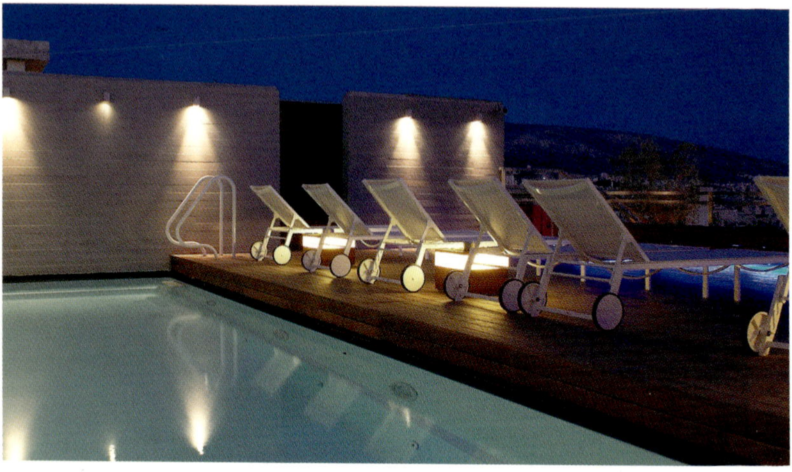

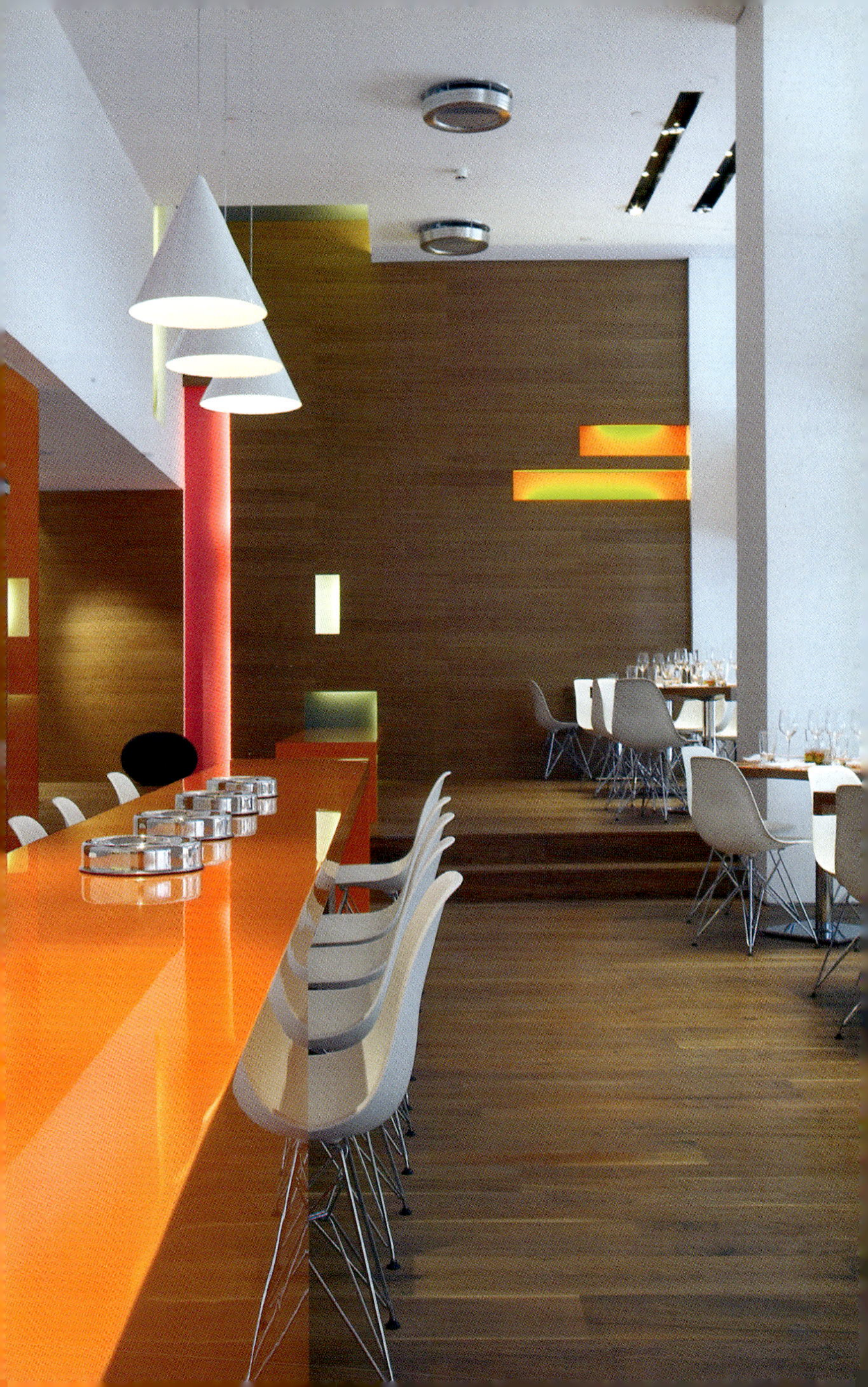

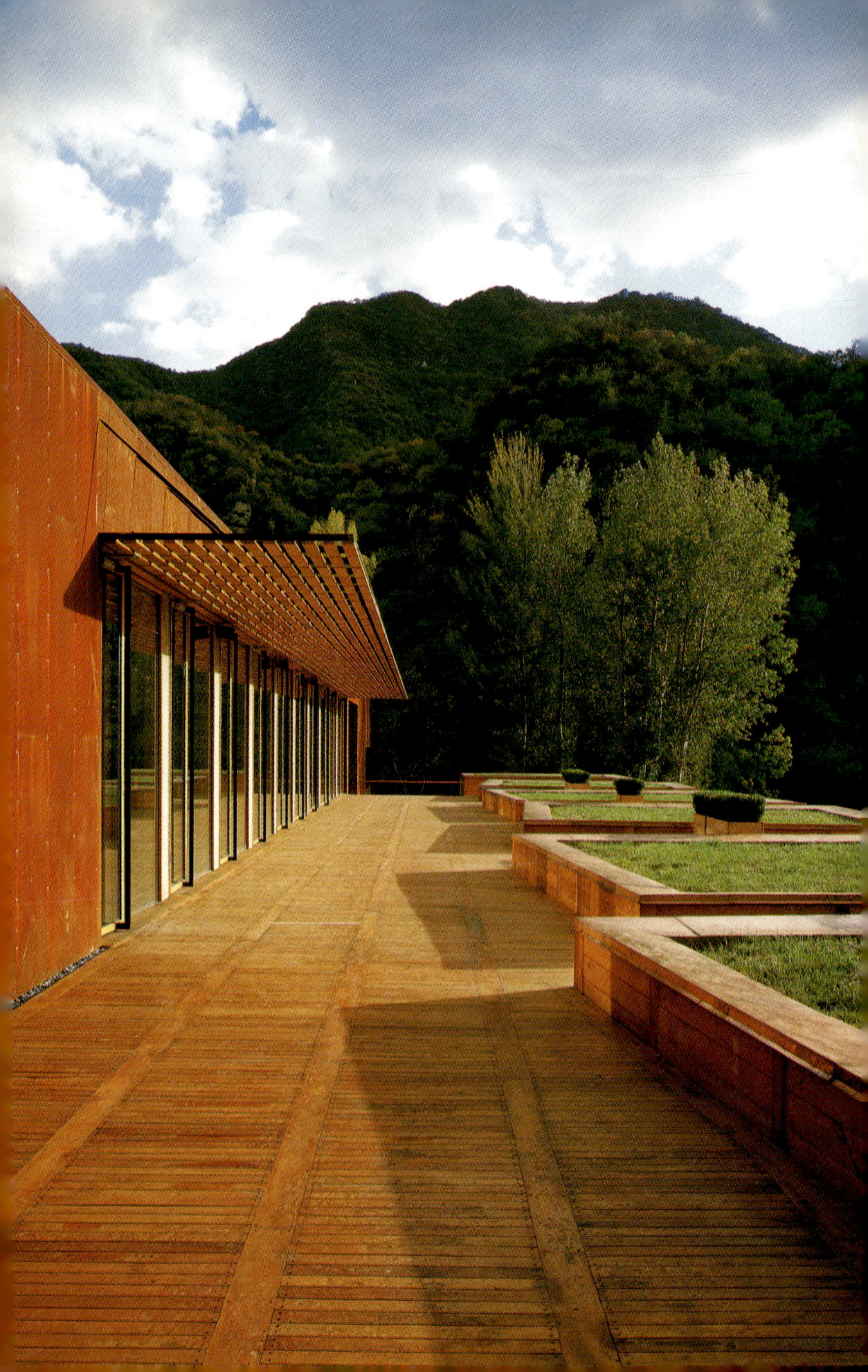

THE COMMUNE BY THE GREAT WALL
A New Architectural Wonder of China

Architects: **Gary Chang, Shigeru Ban, Cui Kai, Rocco Yim, Chien Hsueh-Yi, Antonio Ochoa-Piccardo, Kengo Kuma, Kanika R'kul, Kay Ngee Tan, Nobuaki Furuya, Seung H-Sang, Yung Ho Chang**

Date: 2002
Address: Exit at Shuiguan, Badaling Highway, Beijing, China
Tel.: +86 10 8118 1888 Fax: +86 10 8118 1866
www.commune.com.cn
Photos: © Satoshi Asakawa, Ma Xiaochun

Location: Mountain
Style: Contemporary rustic
Rooms: 59 villas and 1 clubhouse; 4 to 6 bedrooms at each house
Special features: The Commune by the Great Wall is a private collection of contemporary architecture designed by 12 Asian affluent architects; one of the coolest hotels in the world

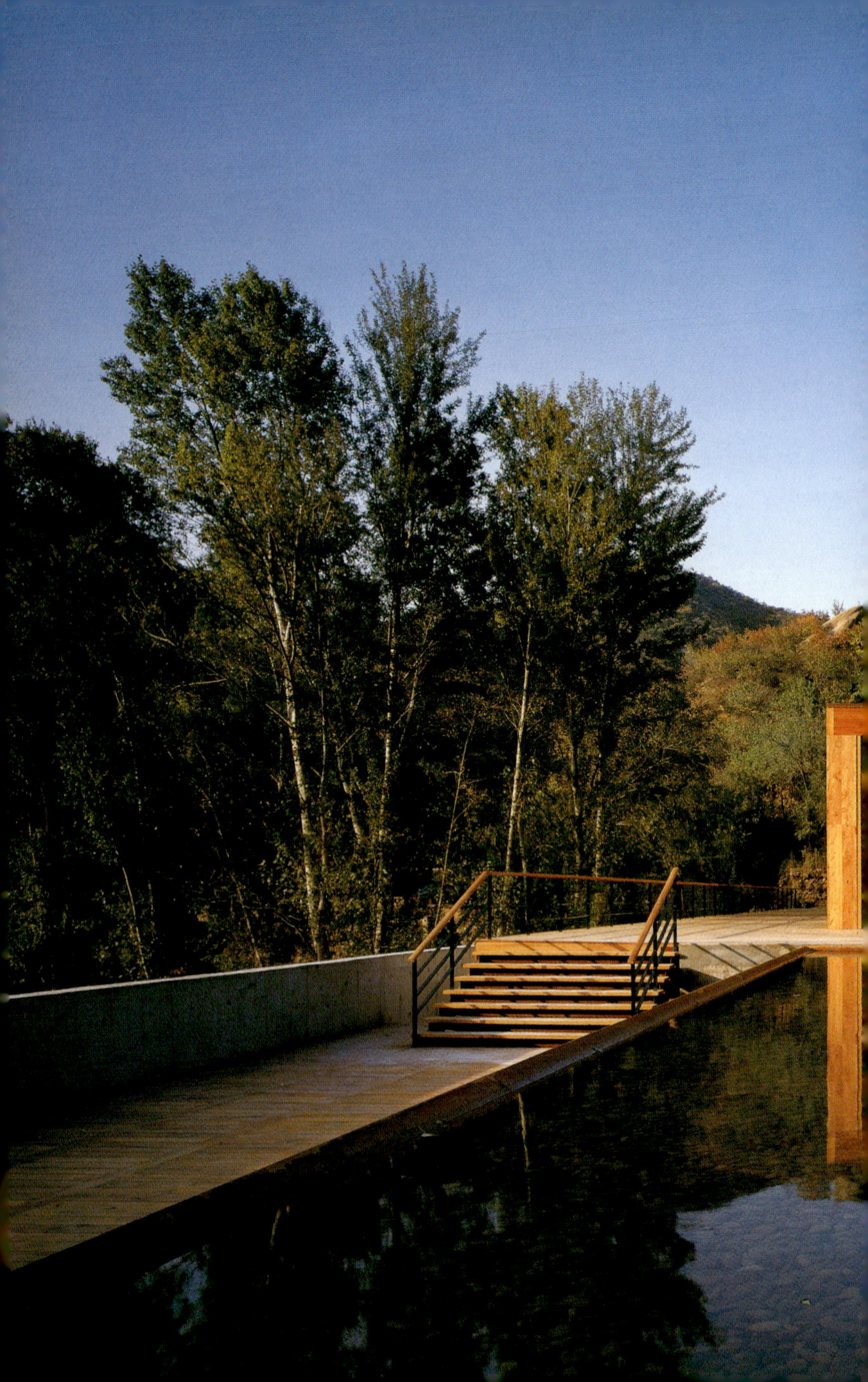

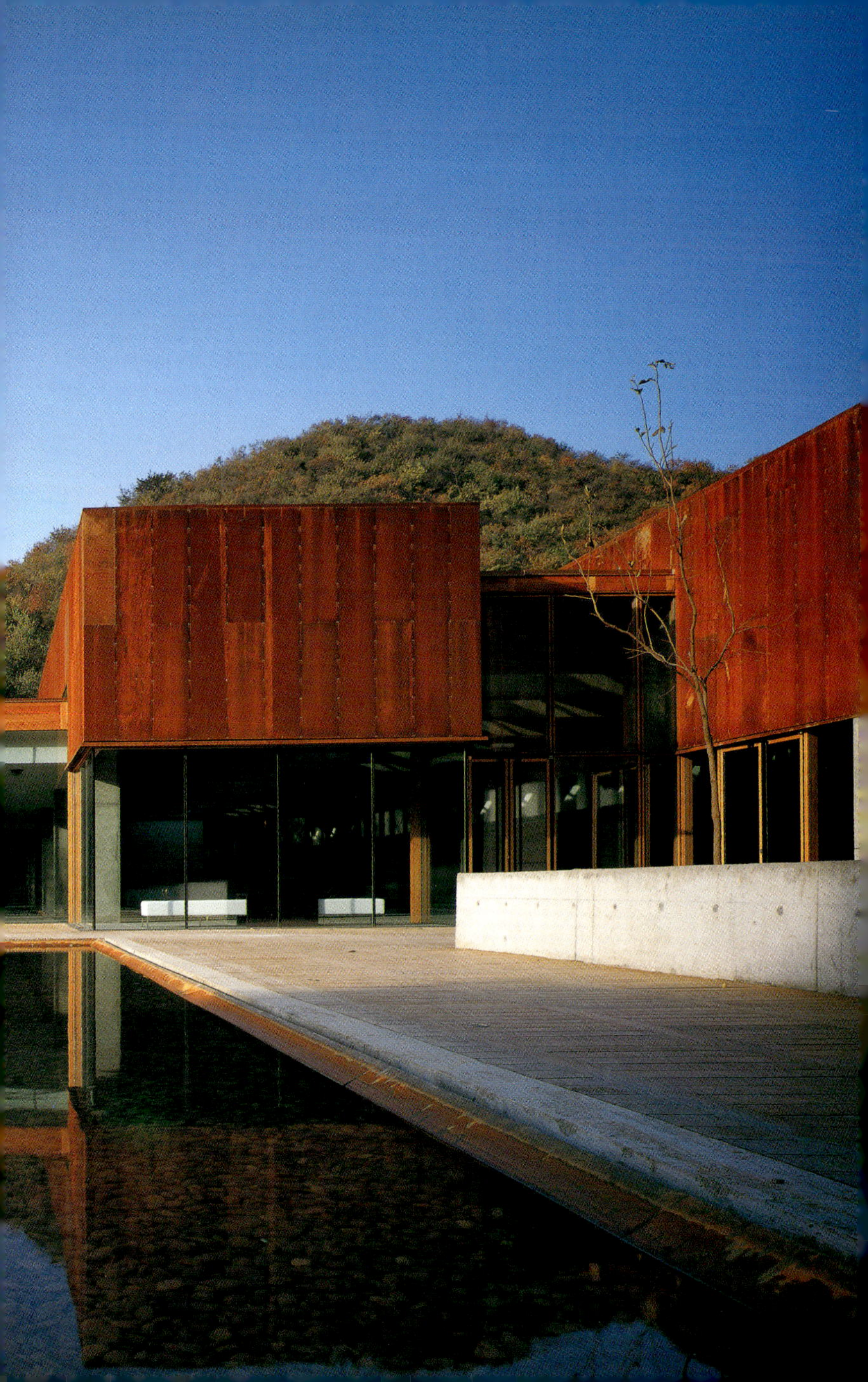

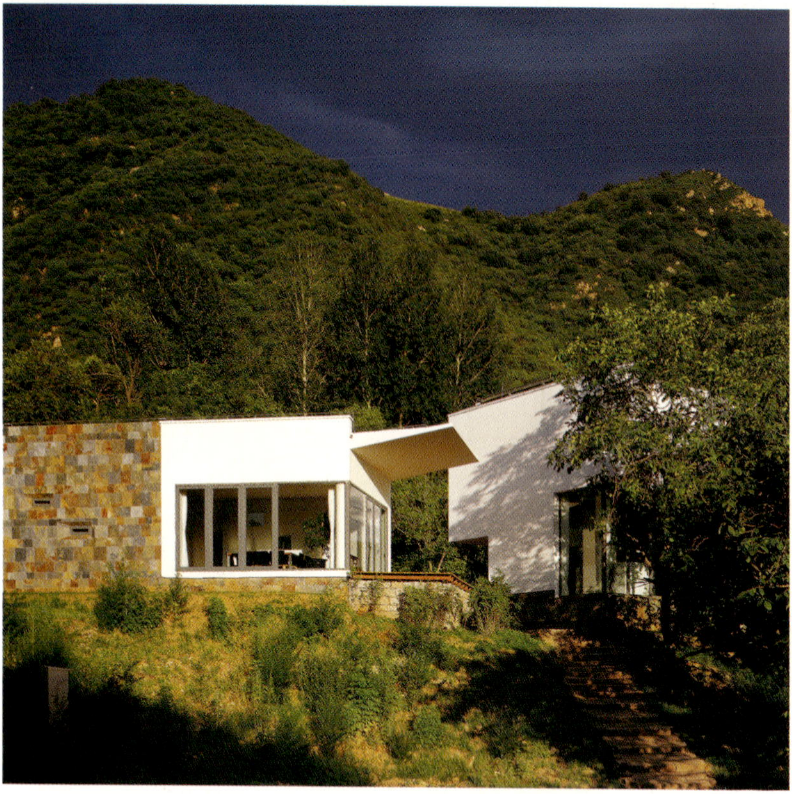

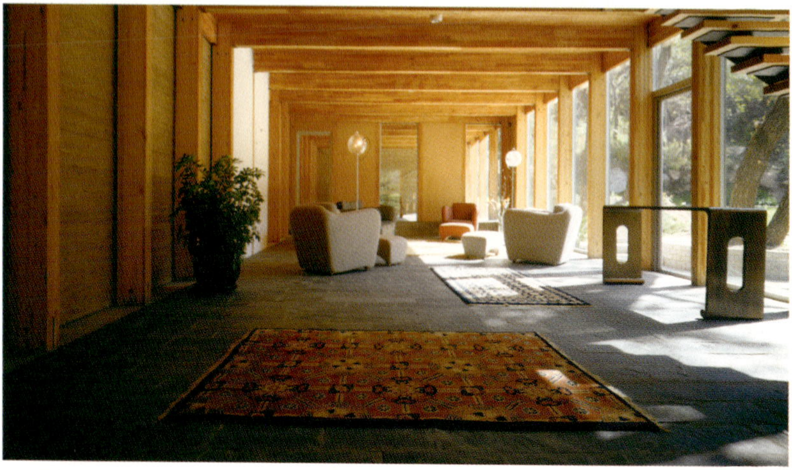

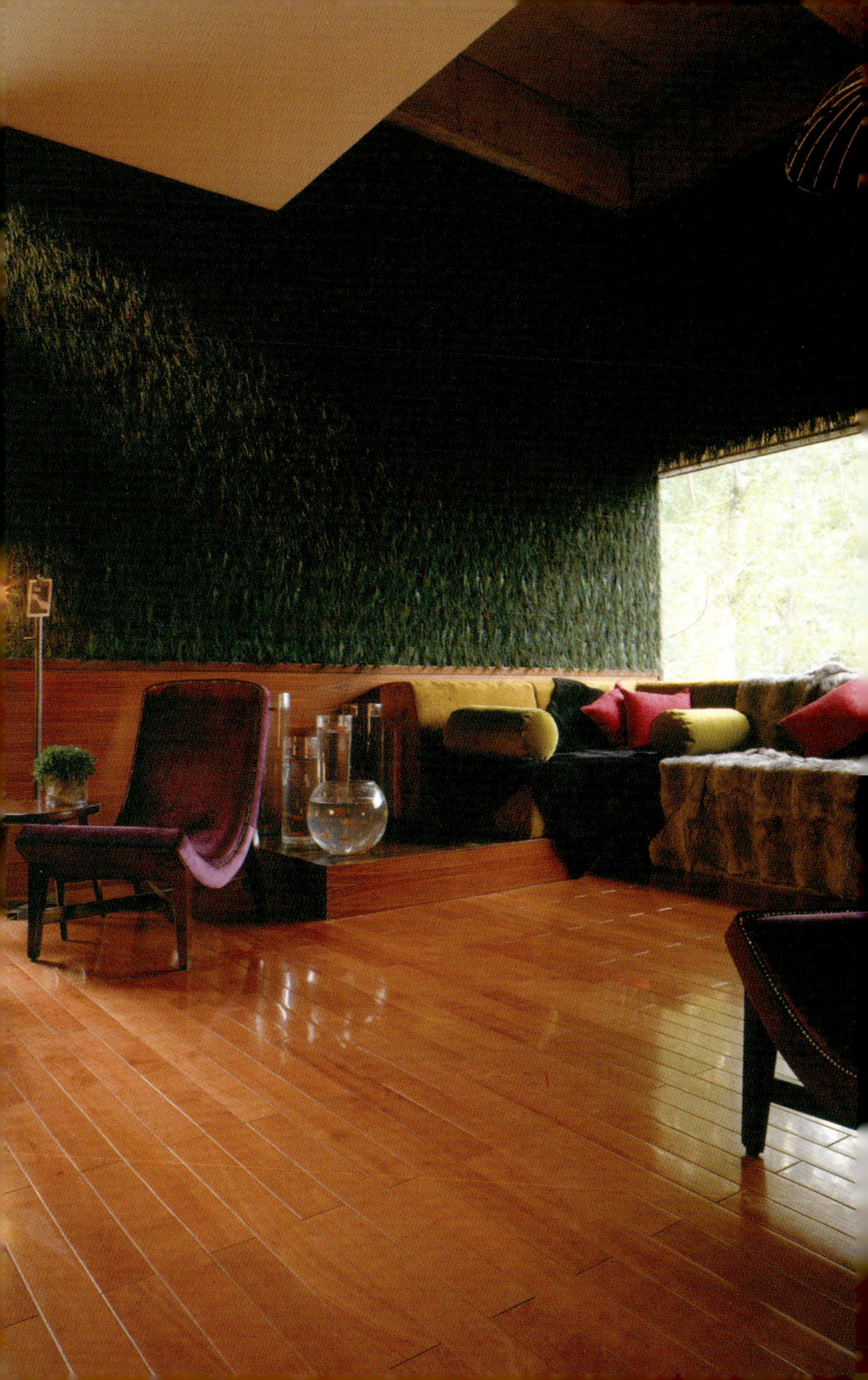

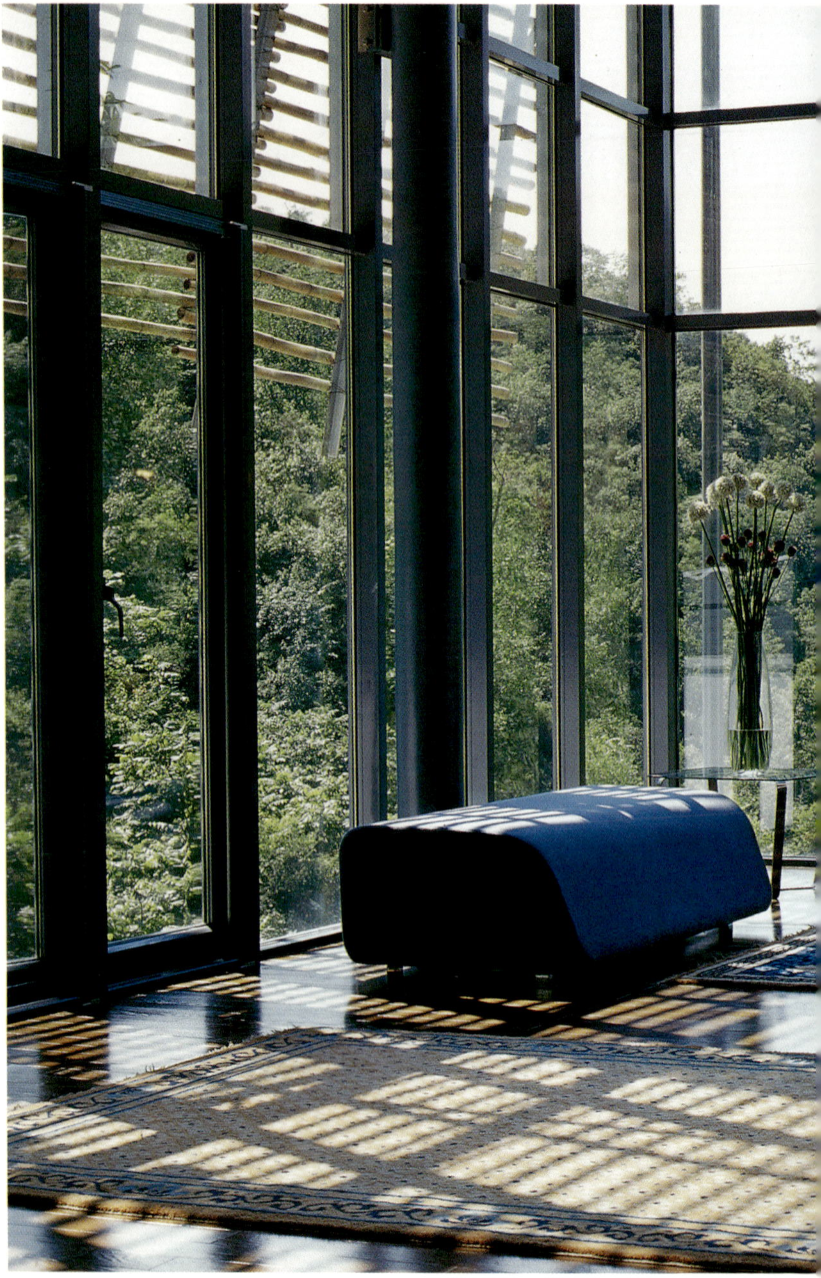

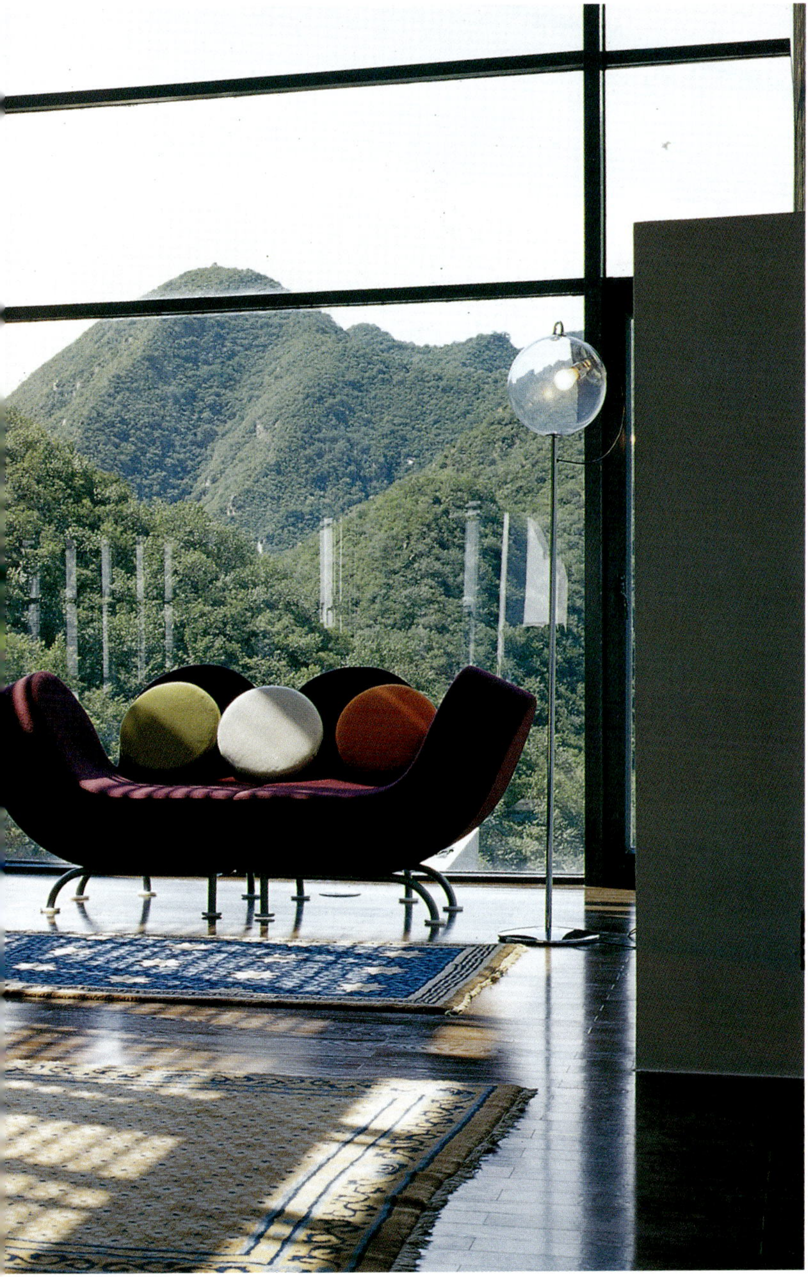

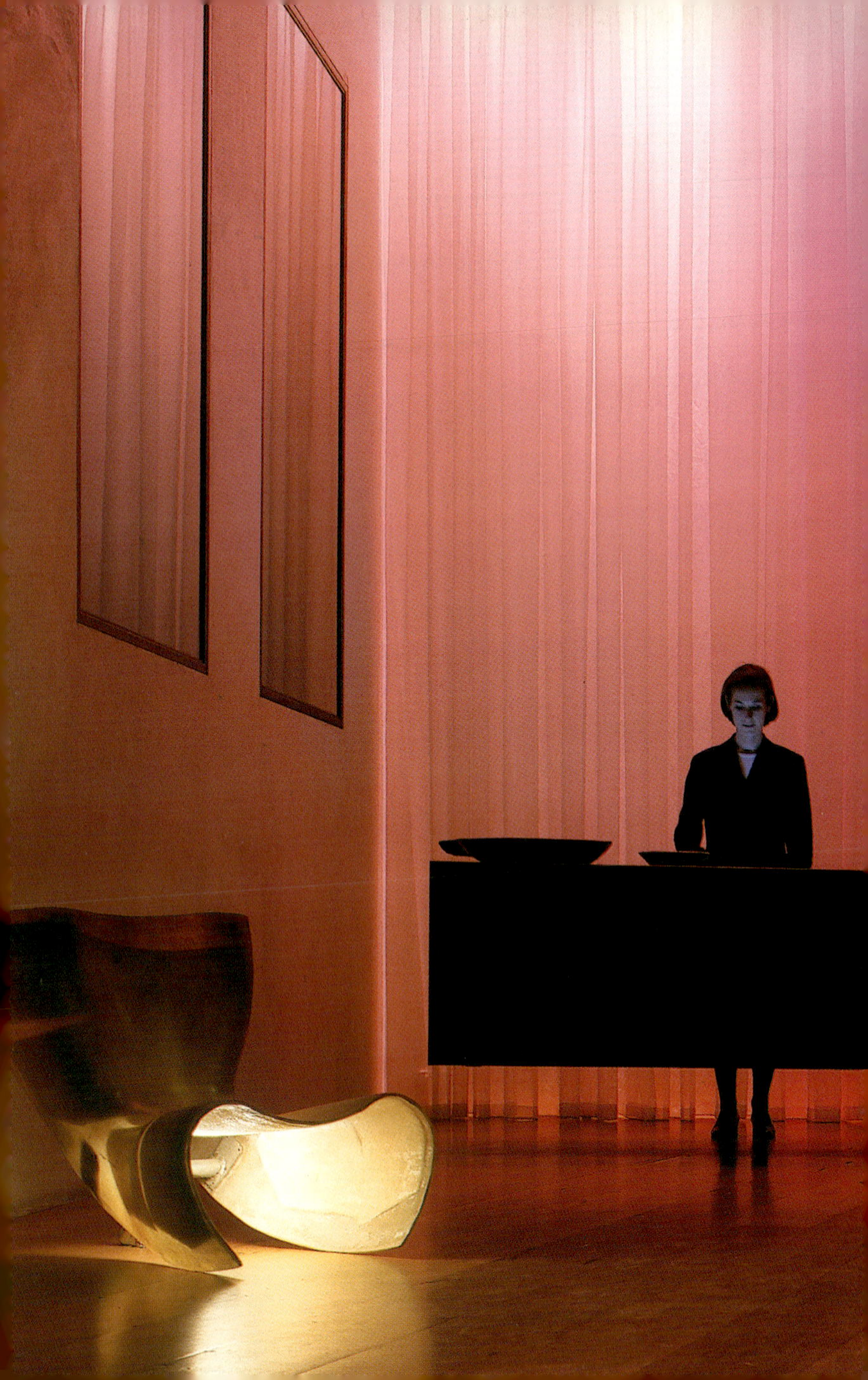

THE PRINCE
An Oasis of Luxe

Architects: **Allan Powell Architects**
Interior designer: **Paul Hecker**

Date: 1999
Address: 2 Acland Street, St. Kilda, Victoria 3182, Melbourne, Australia
Tel.: +61 3 9536 1111 Fax: +61 3 9536 1100
www.theprince.com.au
Photos: © Earl Carter

Location: Beach
Style: Contemporary design
Rooms: 40
Special features: Bar, bakery, restaurant, open-air pool, car park

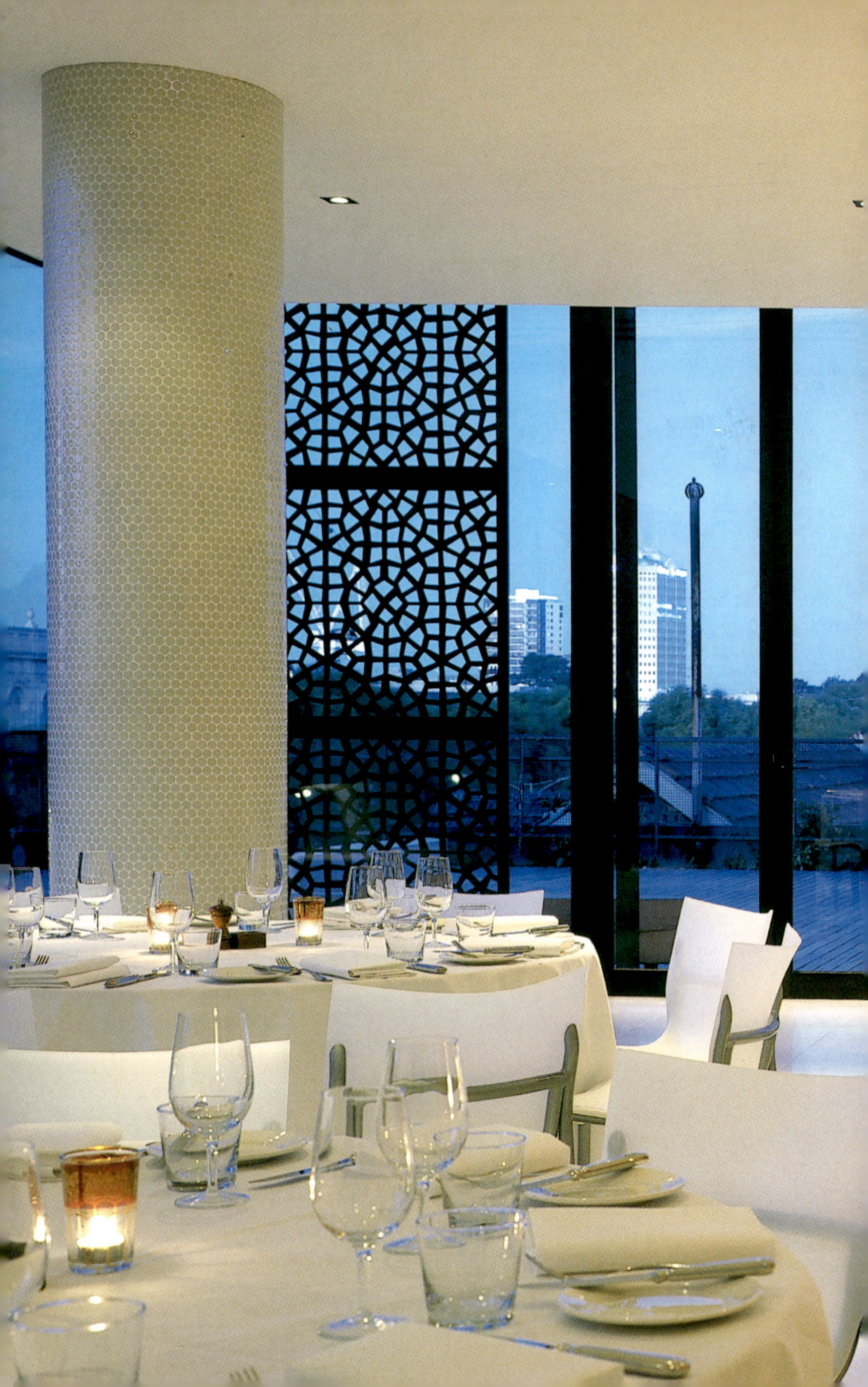

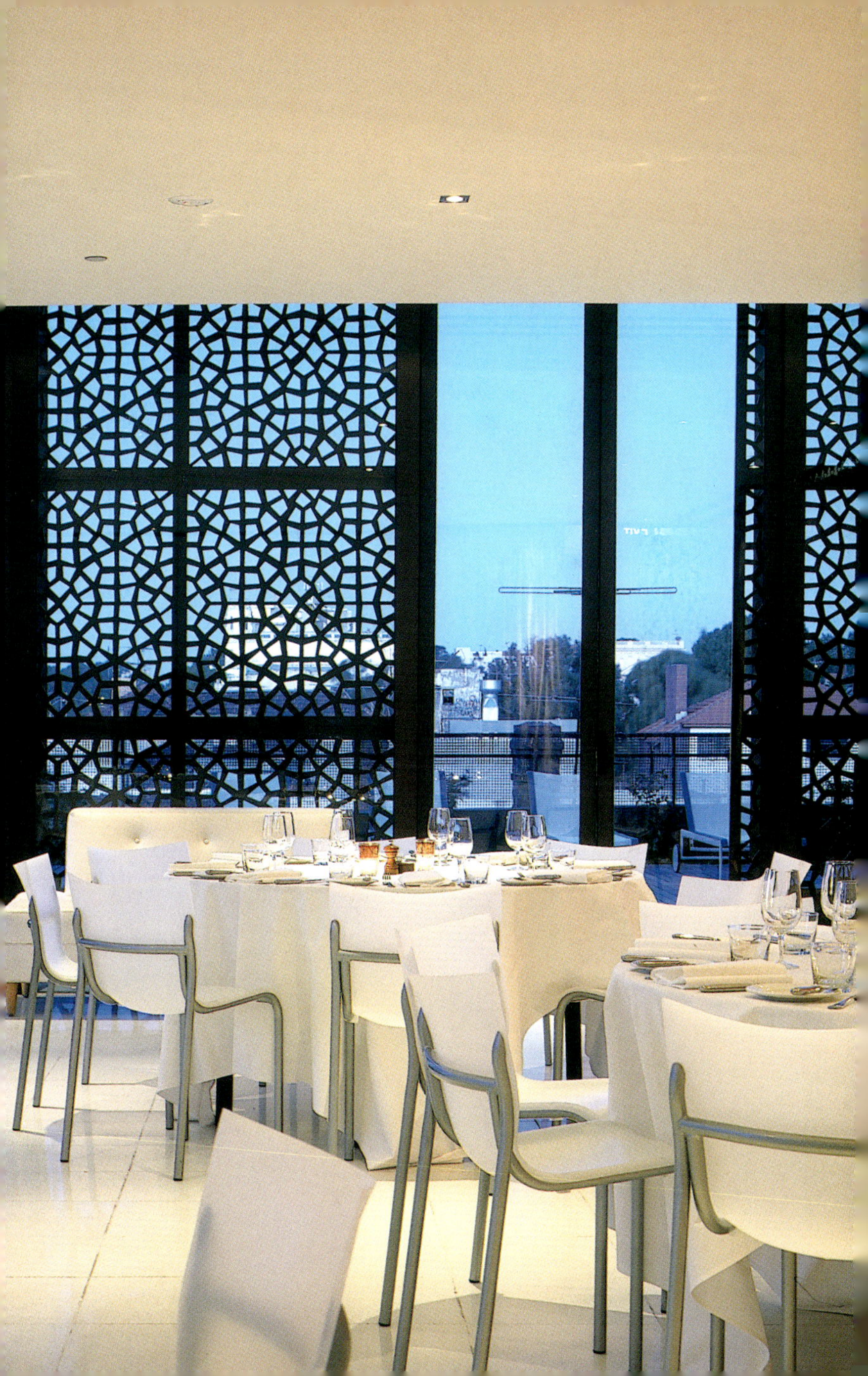

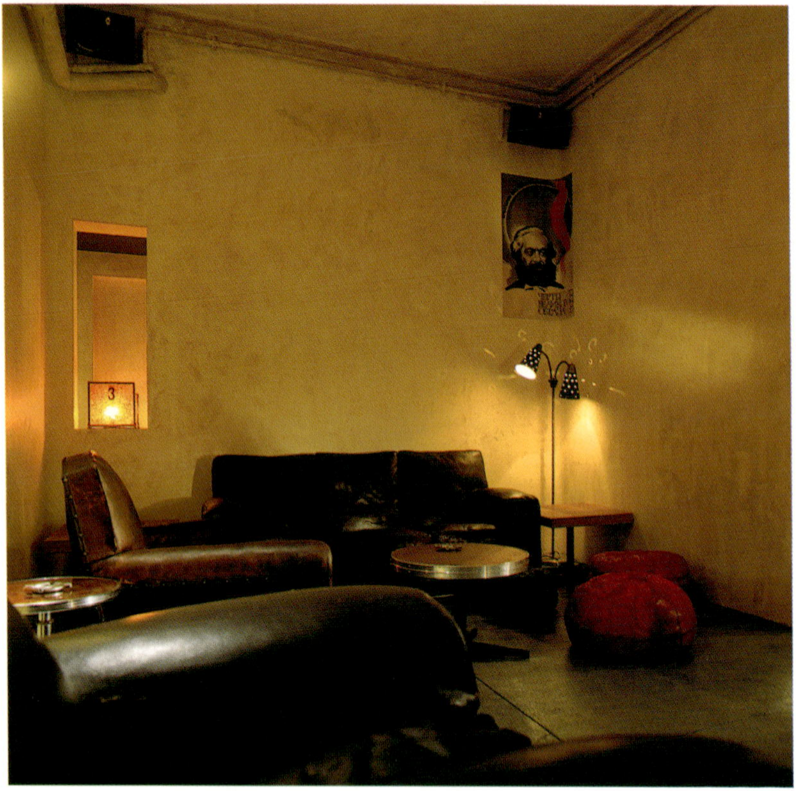

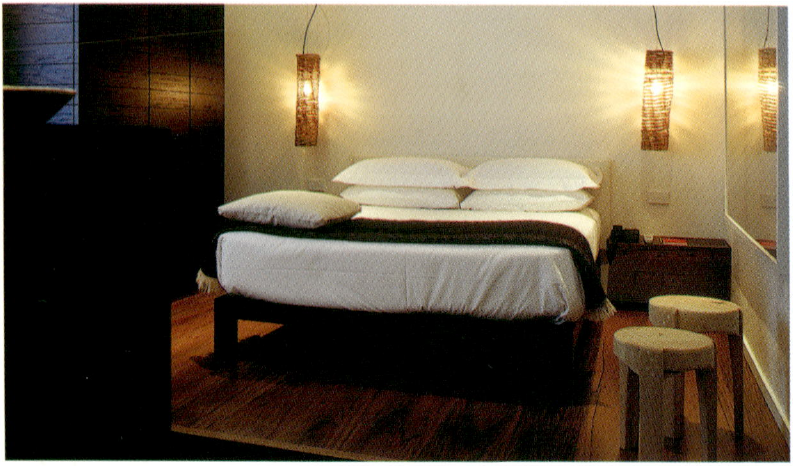

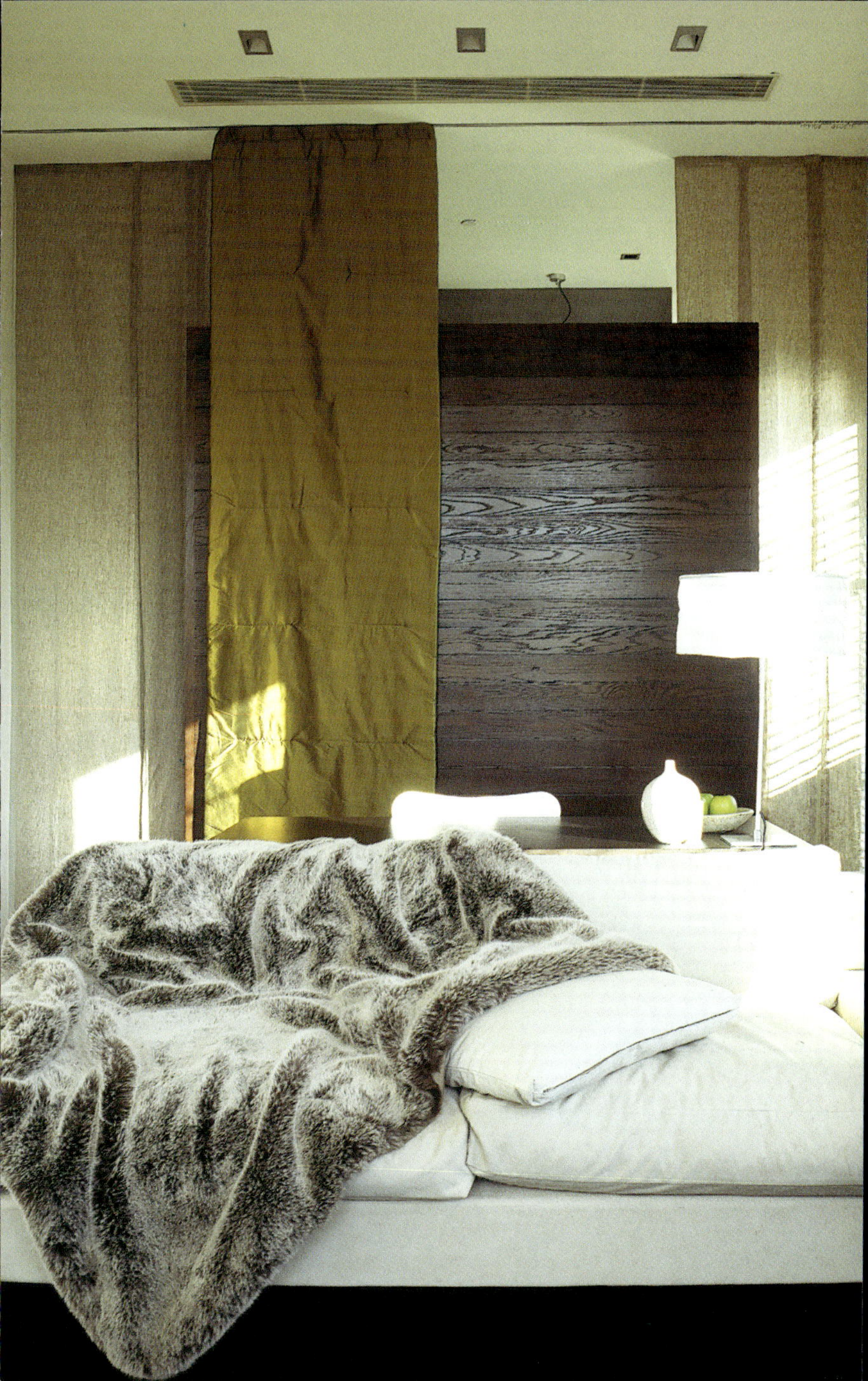

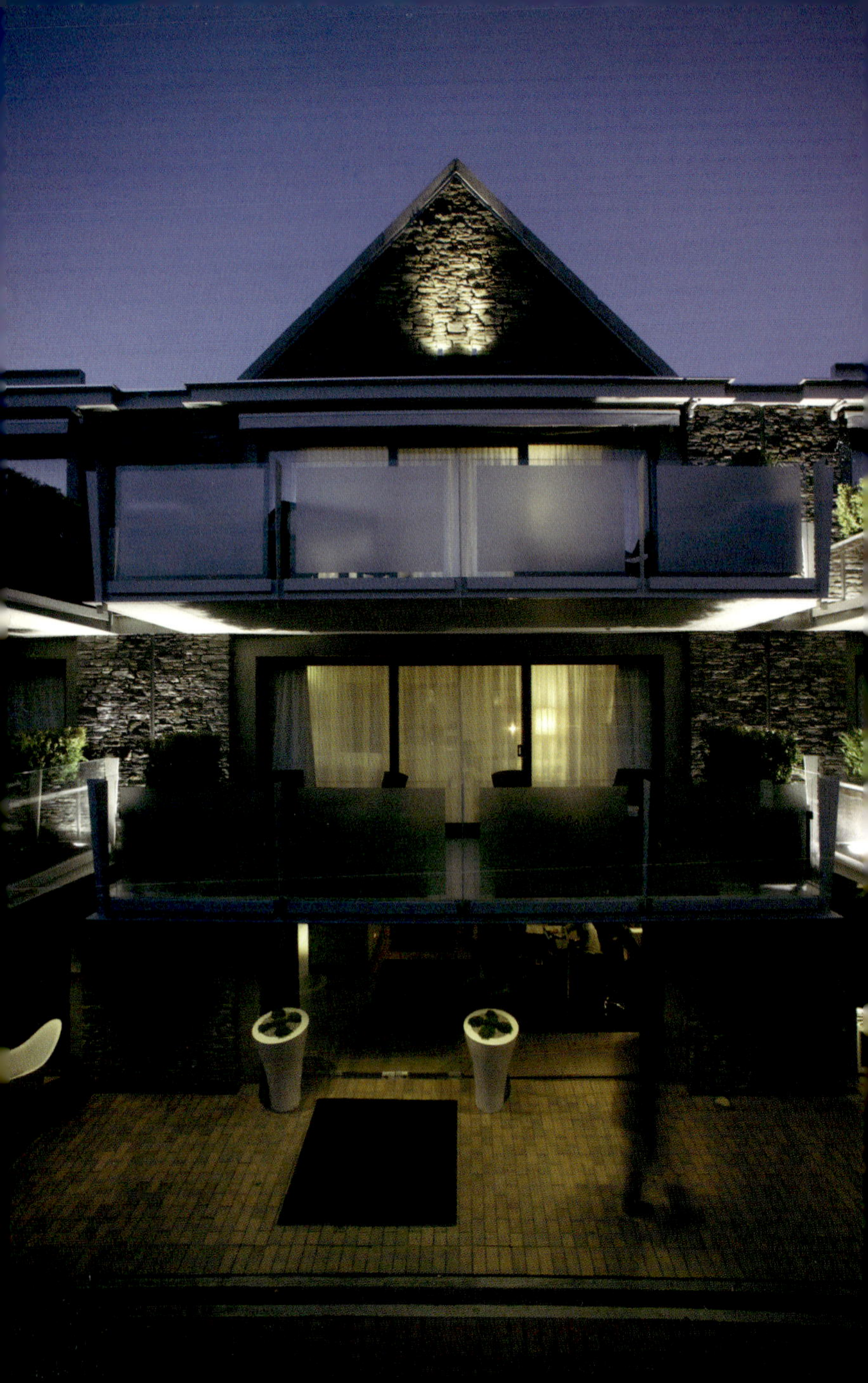

THE SPIRE QUEENSTOWN
Ten Carefully Calibrated Suites

Architect: Martin Hughes Architecture Interiors

Date: 2005
Address: Church Lane, PO Box 1129, 9197 Queenstown, New Zealand
Tel.: +64 3 441 0004 Fax: +64 3 441 0003
www.thespirehotels.com
Photos: © The Spire

Location: Countryside
Style: Contemporary cool
Rooms: 10 suites
Special features: Interactive multimedia system, Wi-Fi network, 42-inch plasma TV, large covered balcony, boardroom

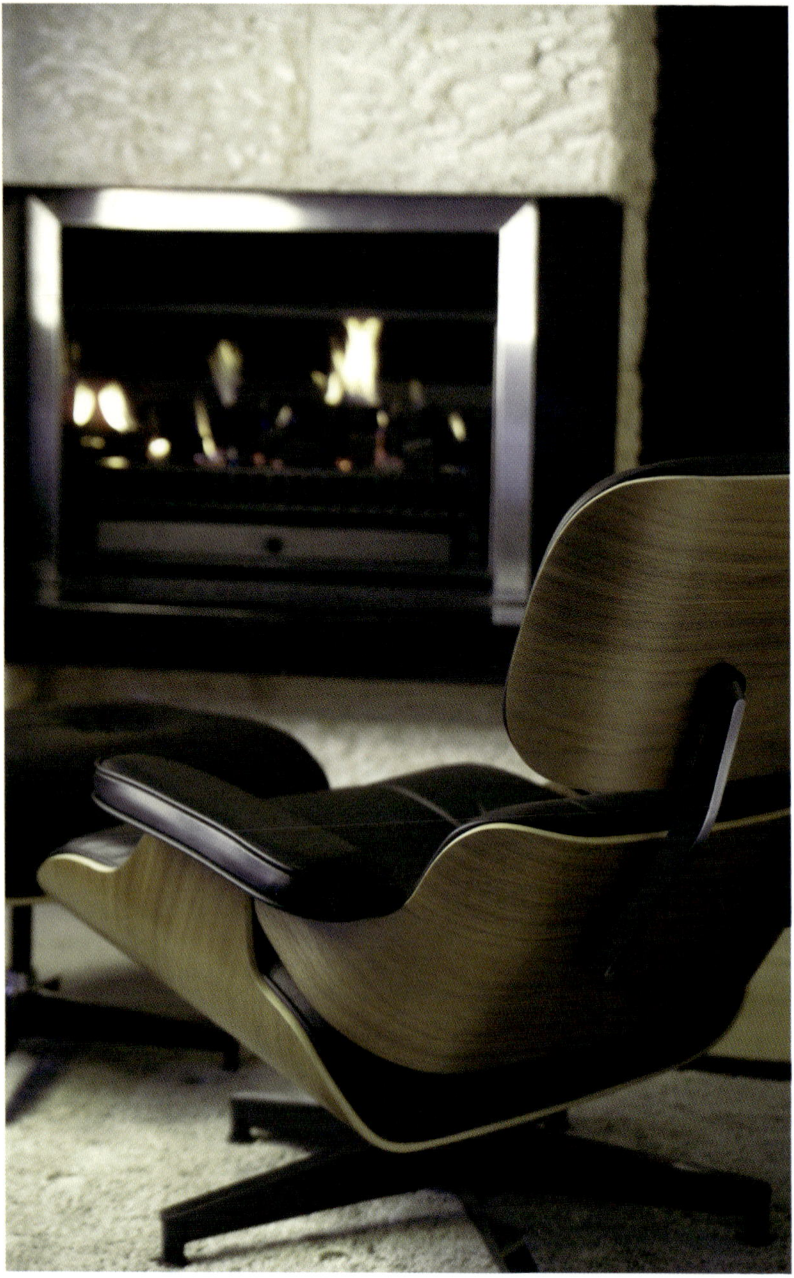

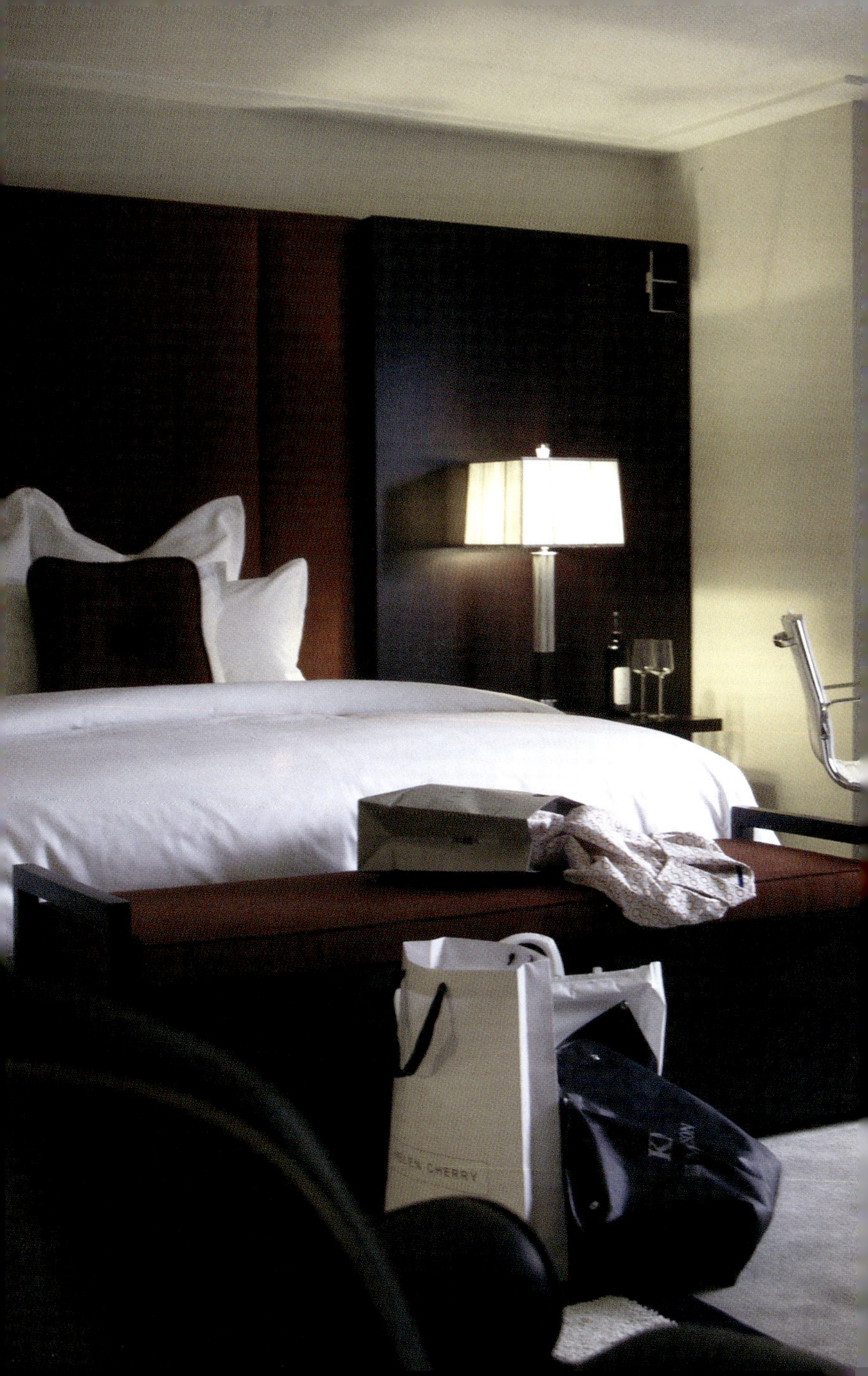

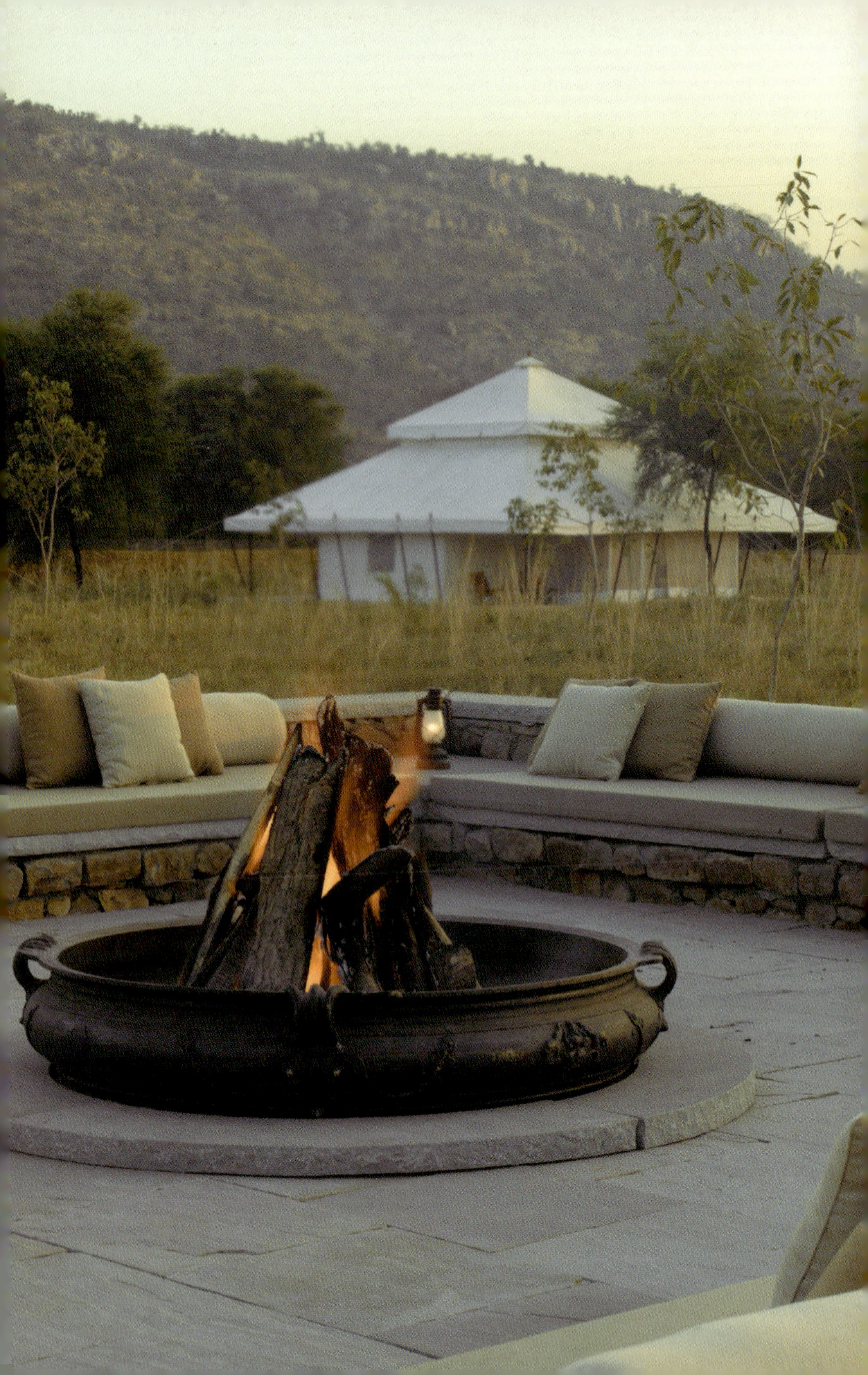

AMAN I KHAS
The Call of the Wild

Architect: **Jean-Michel Gathy/Denniston International Architects & Planners**

Date: 2003
Address: Ranthambhore National Park, Rajasthan, India
Tel.: +91 7462 252052 Fax: +91 7462 252178
www.amanresorts.com
Photos: © Amanresorts

Location: Countryside
Style: Inspired by the bygone era of local traveling tents
Rooms: 10 tents
Special features: Open seven months a year, from October until the end of April, which coincides with the season for Ranthambhore National Park

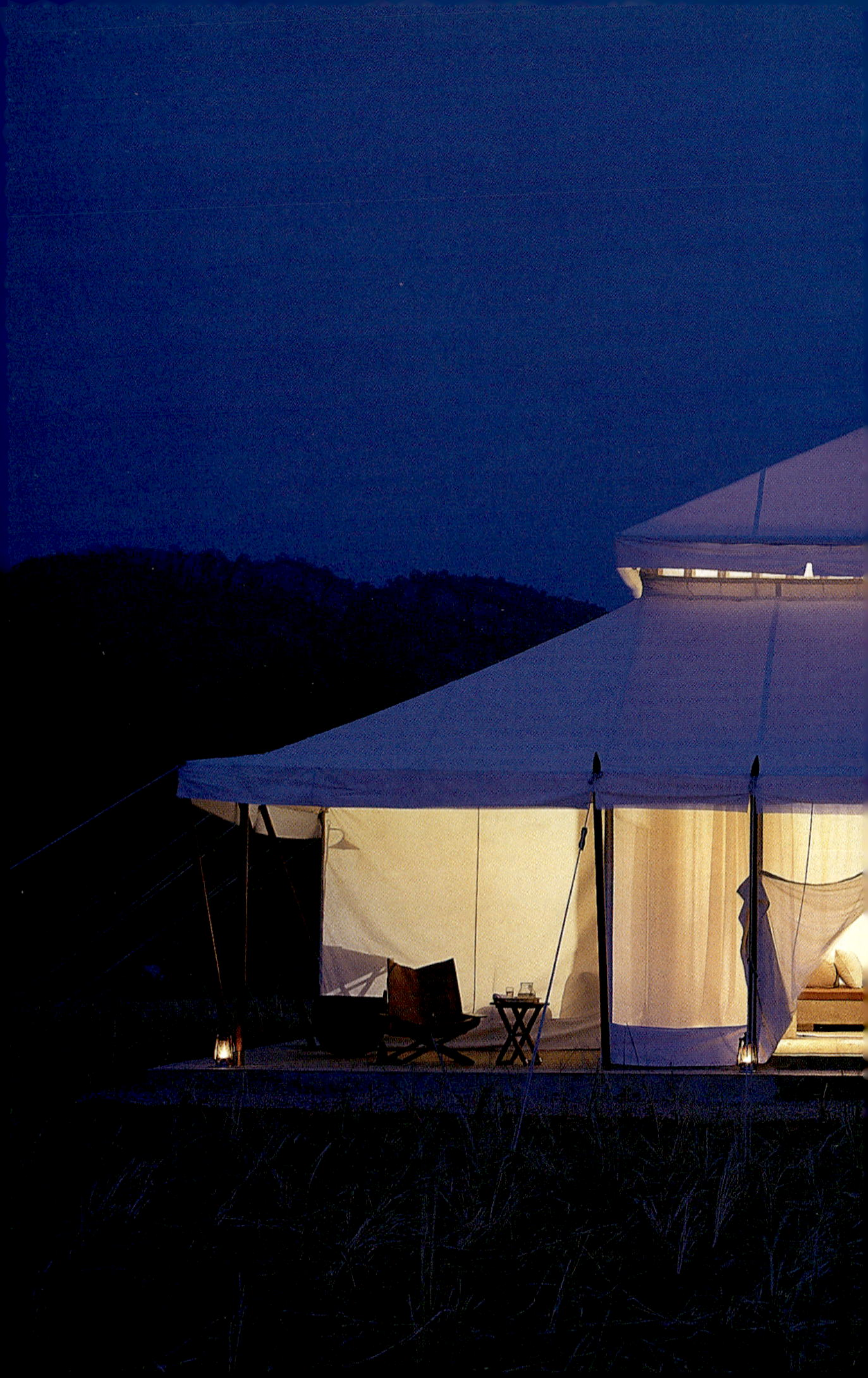

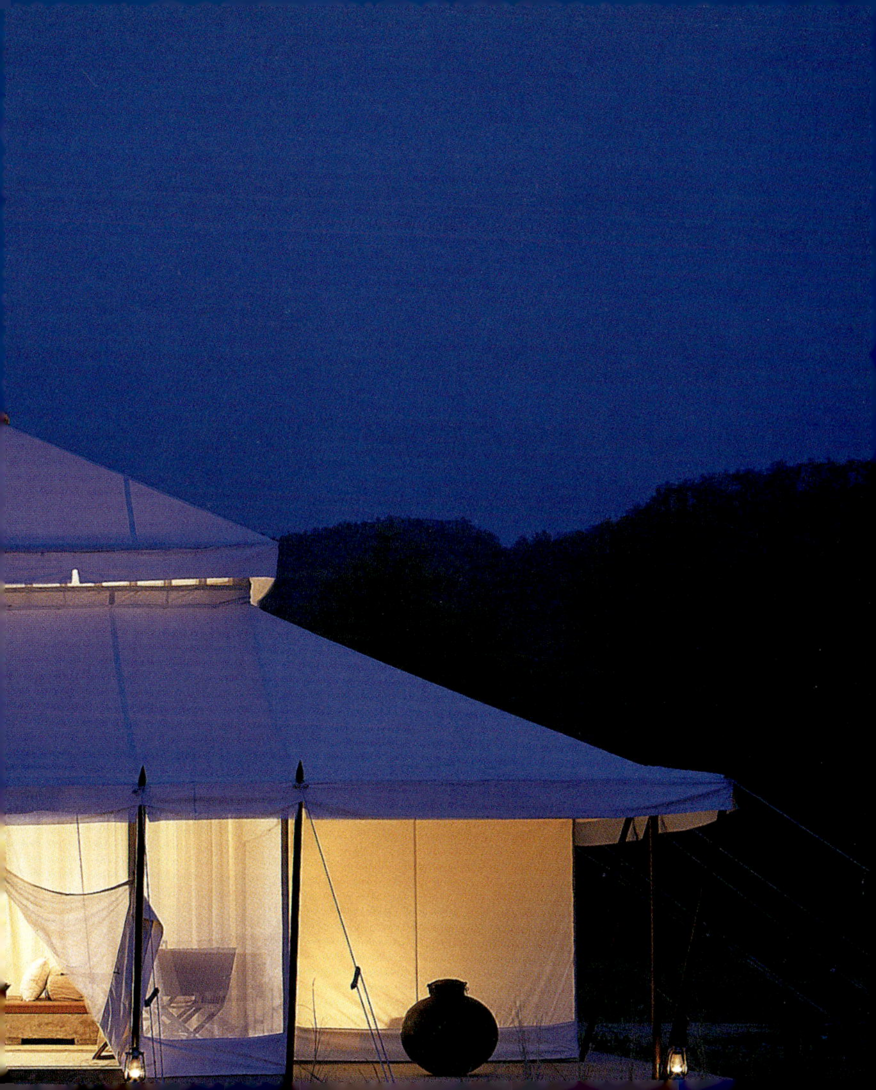

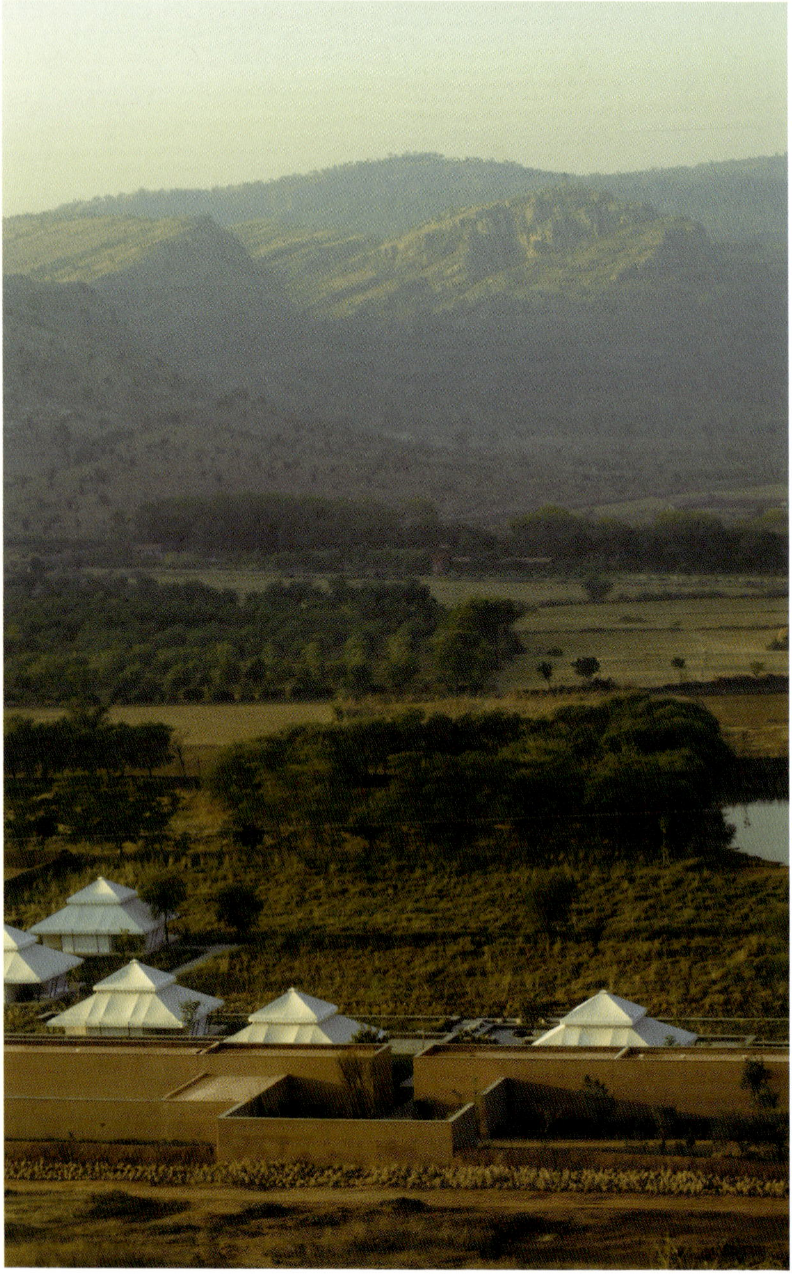

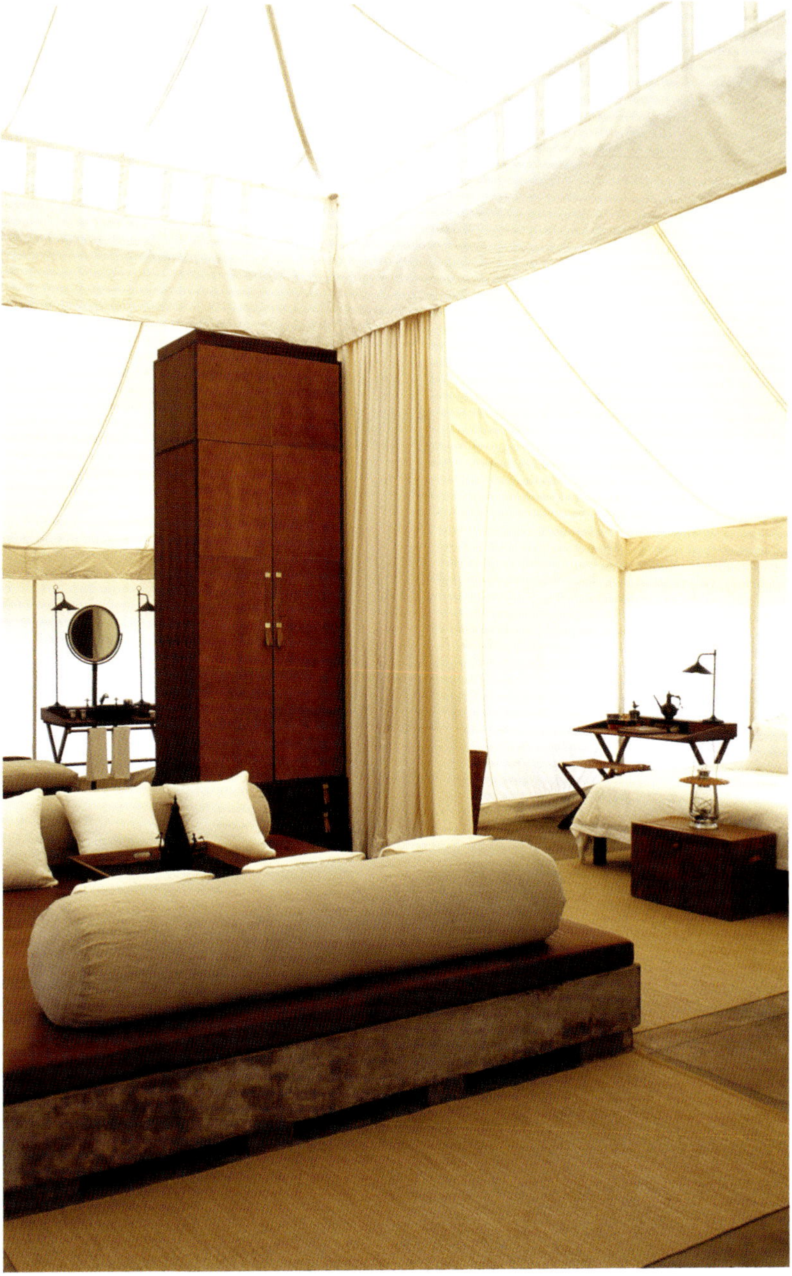

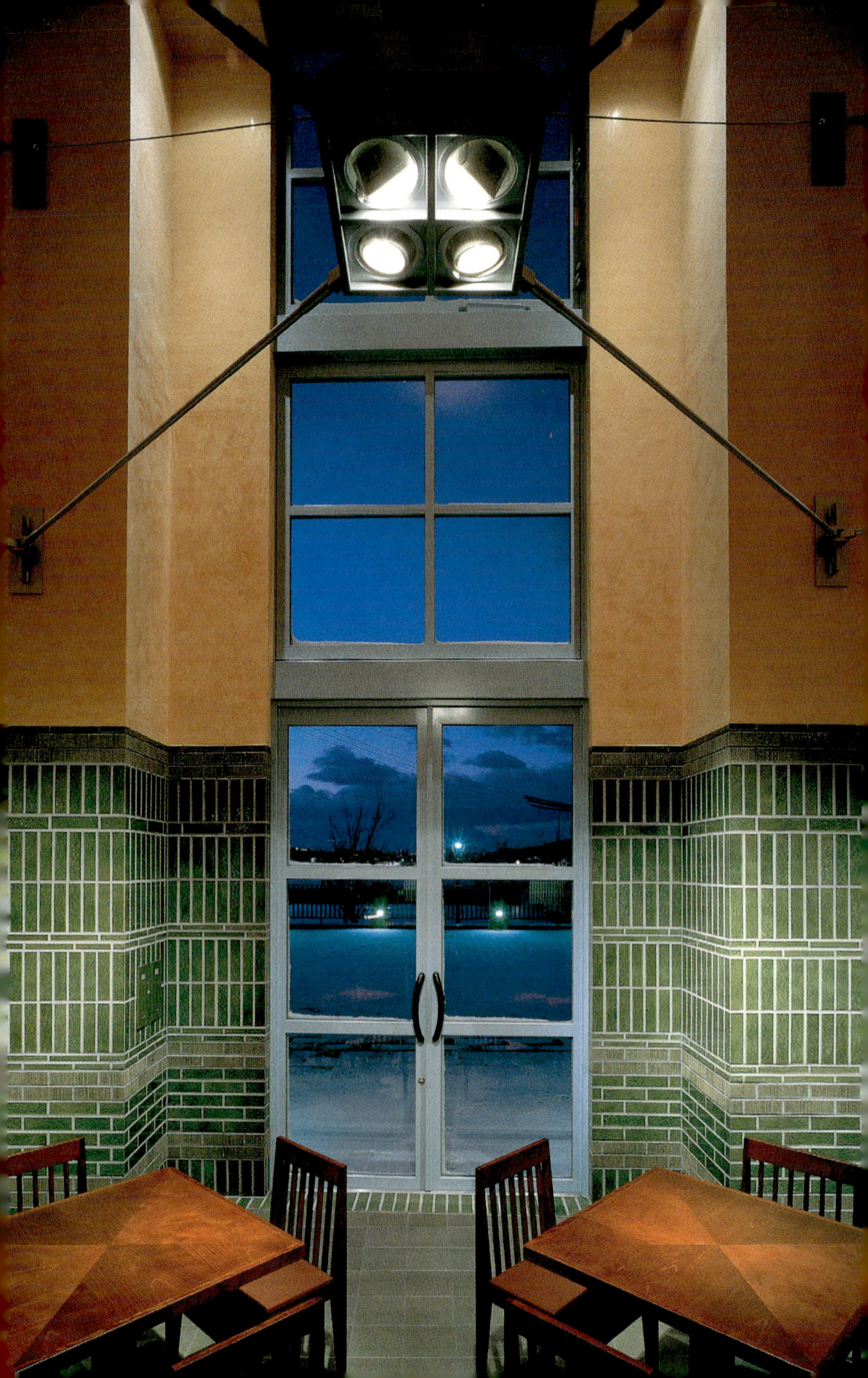

MOJIKO HOTEL
Japanese Style Ryokan

Architect: **Aldo Rossi**

Date: 1998
Address: 9-11 Minatomachi, Moji Ku, Kitakyushu, Fukuoka, Japan
Tel.: +81 (0) 93 321 1111 Fax: +81 (0) 93 321 7111
www.mojiko-hotel.com
Photos: © Shigeru Uchida

Location: Urban/beach
Style: International
Rooms: 134
Special features: Fantastic views over the city and sea

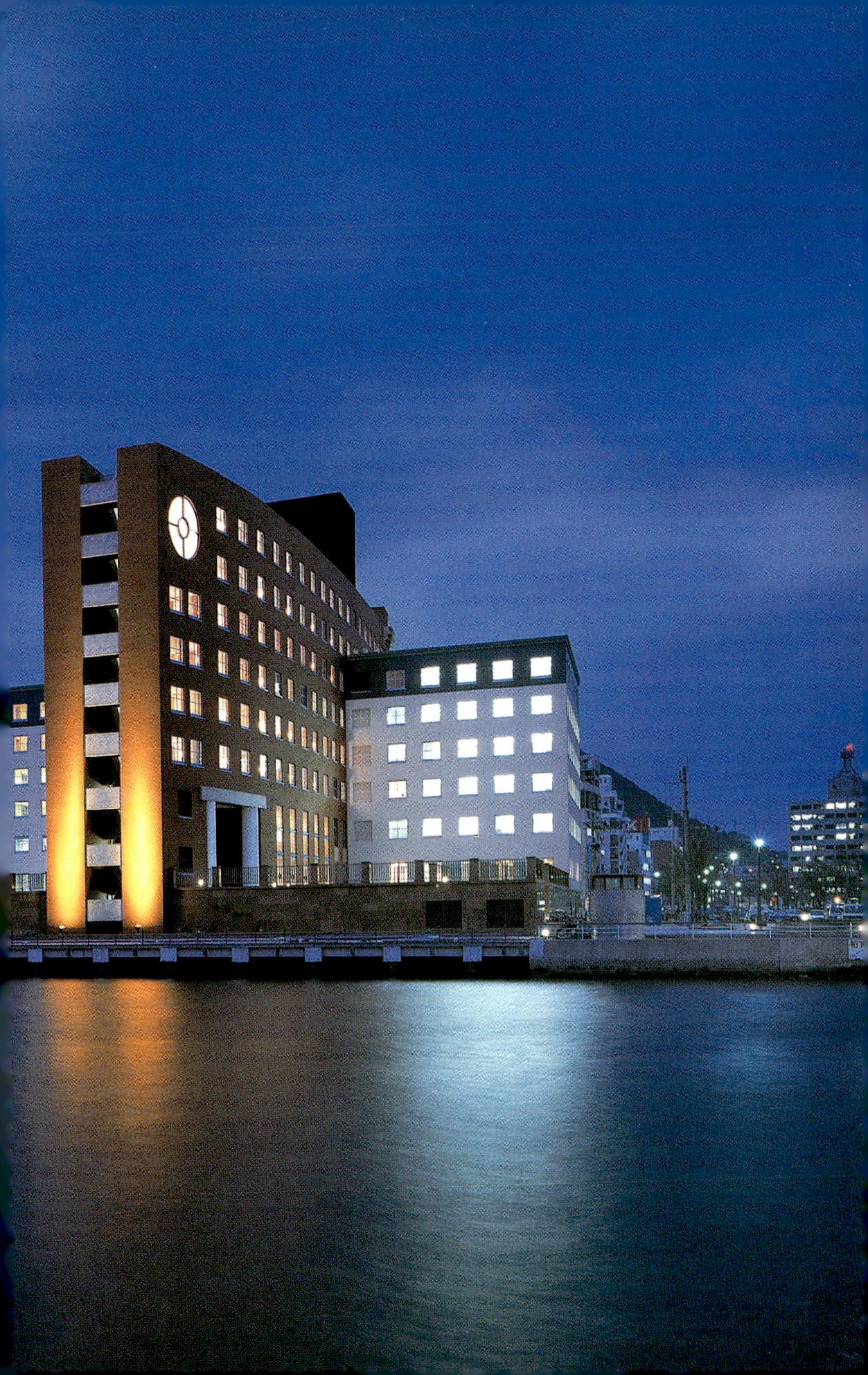

Architect's sketch of the hotel

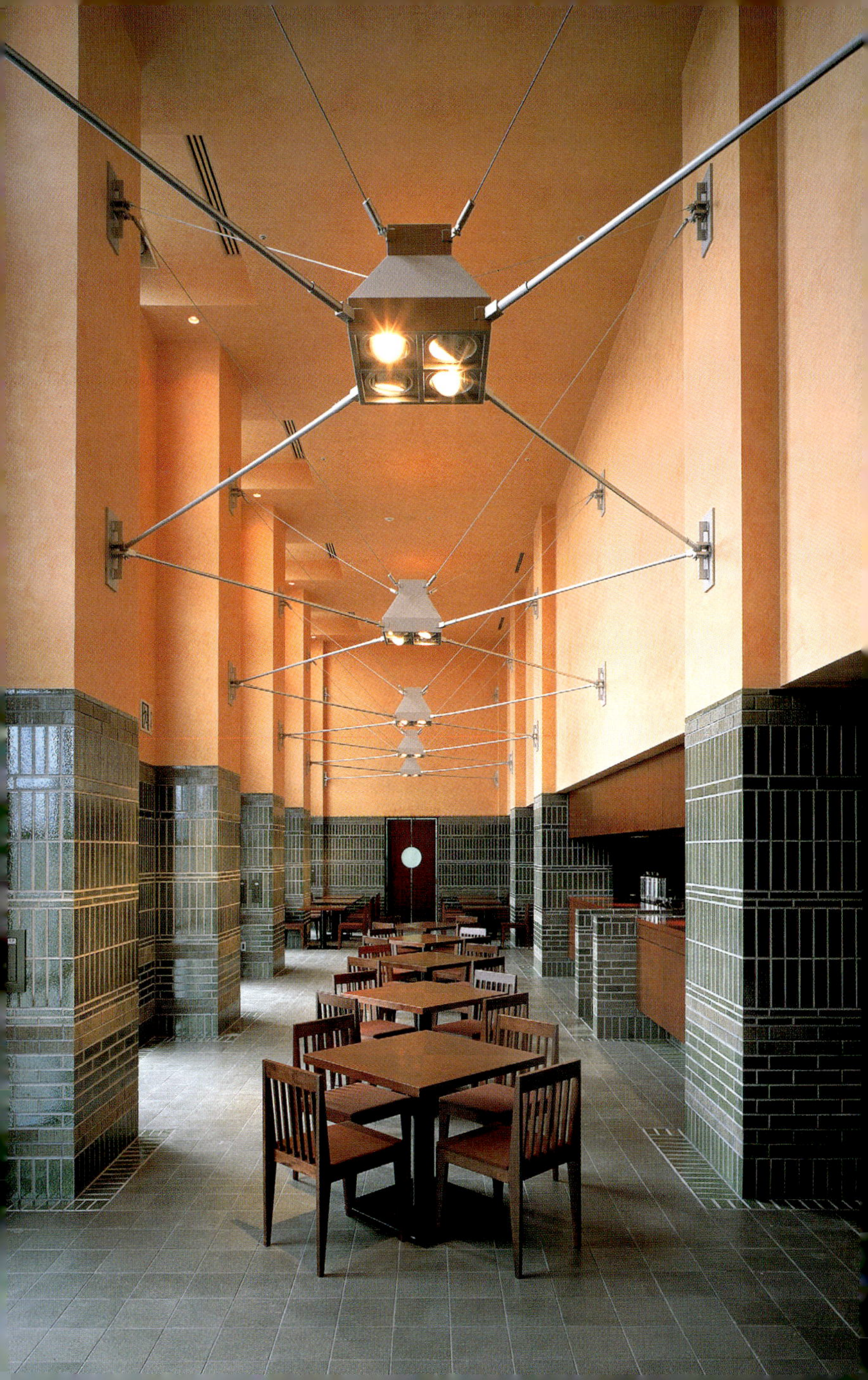

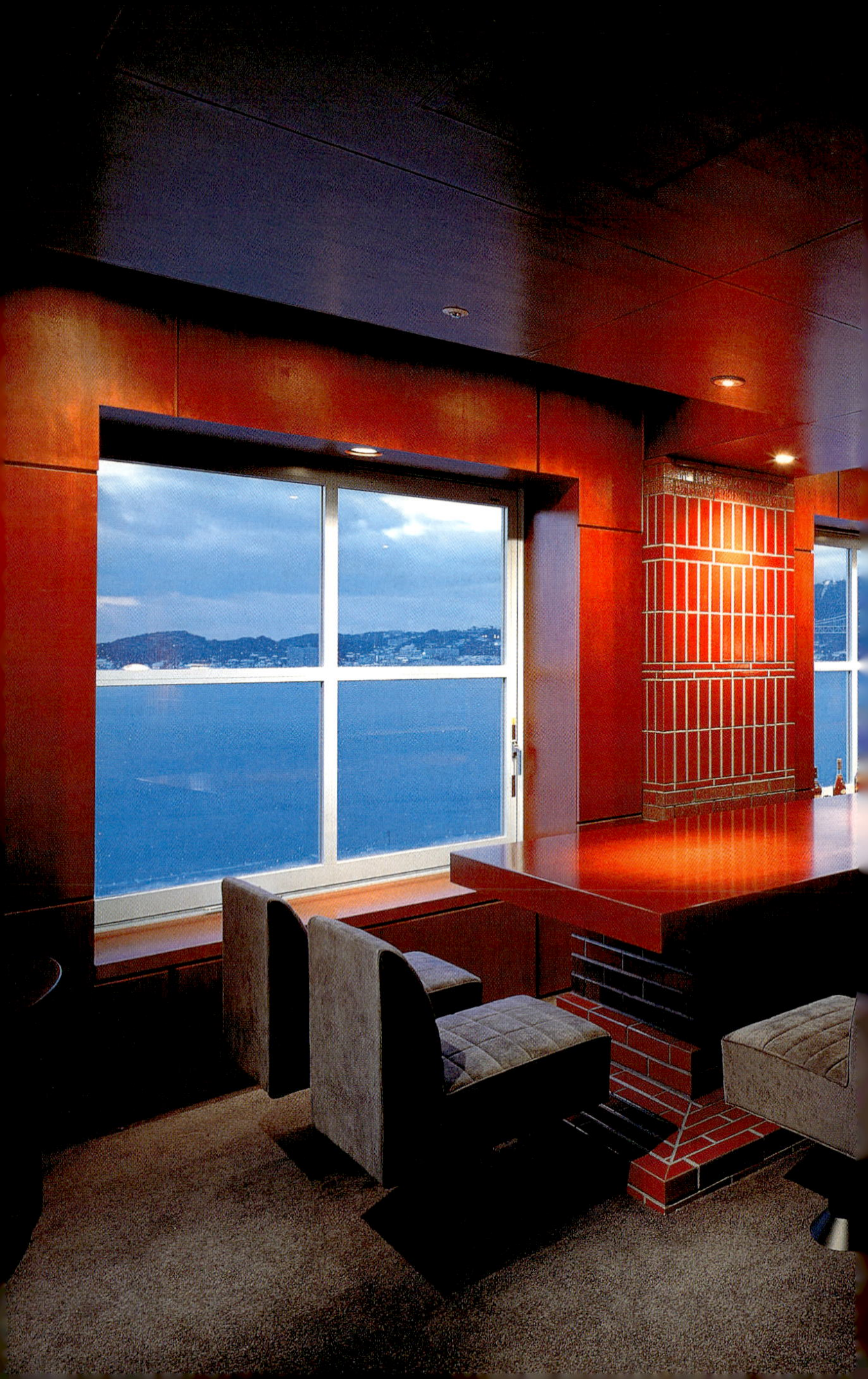

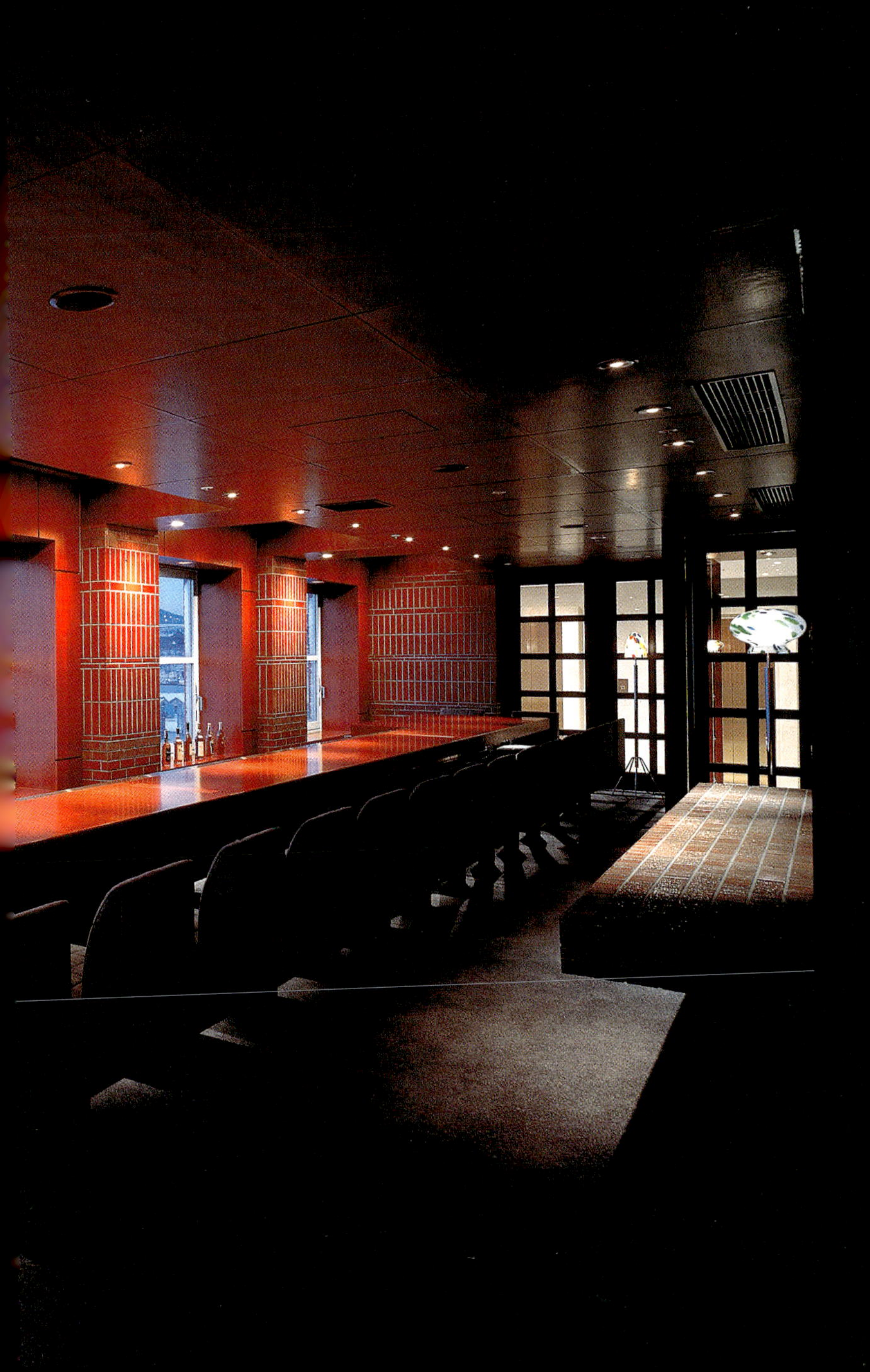

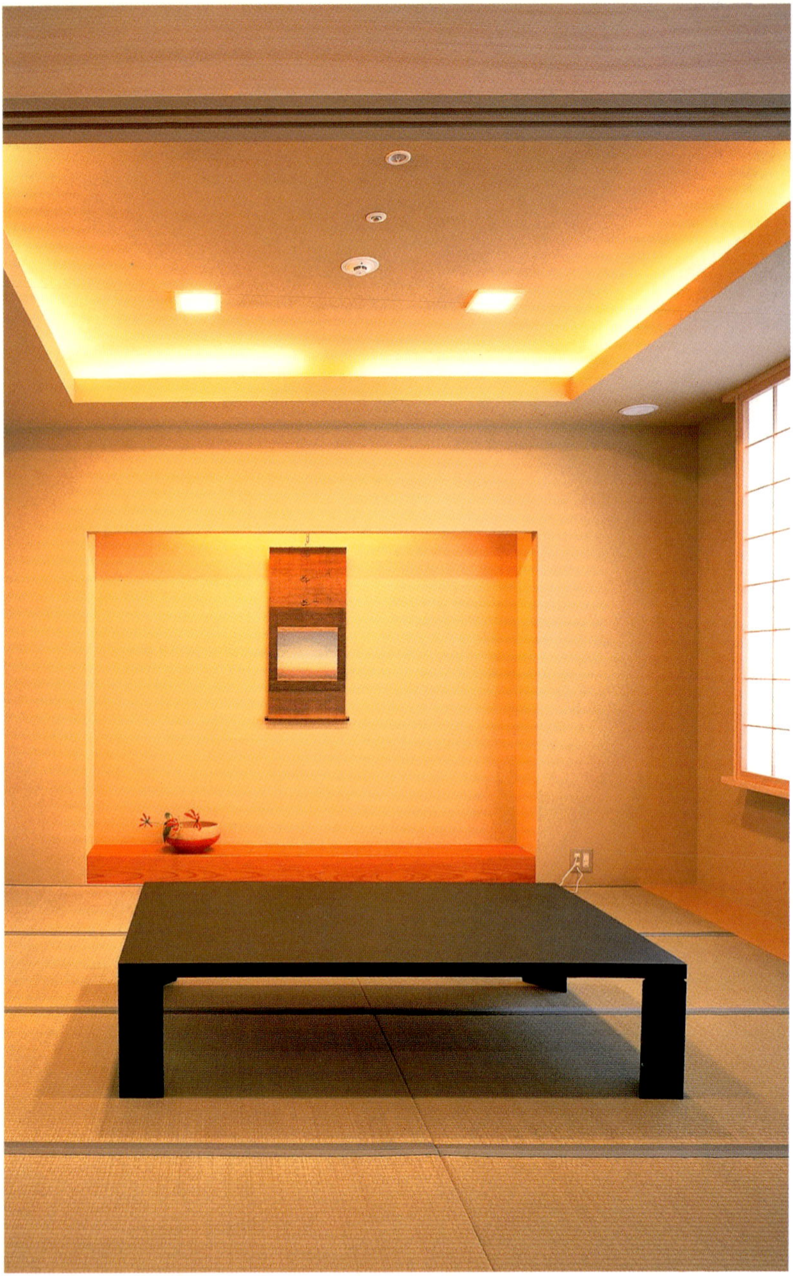

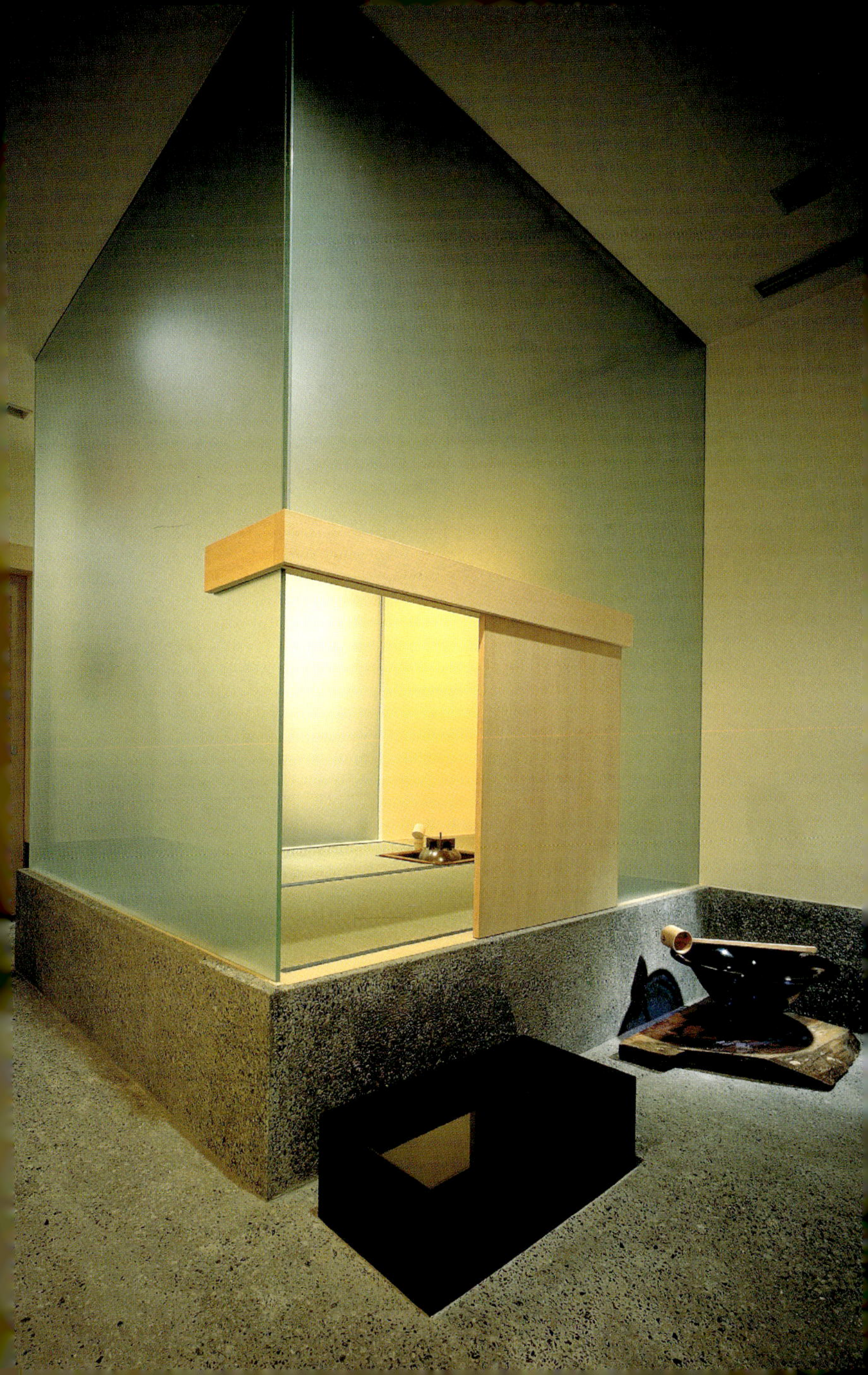

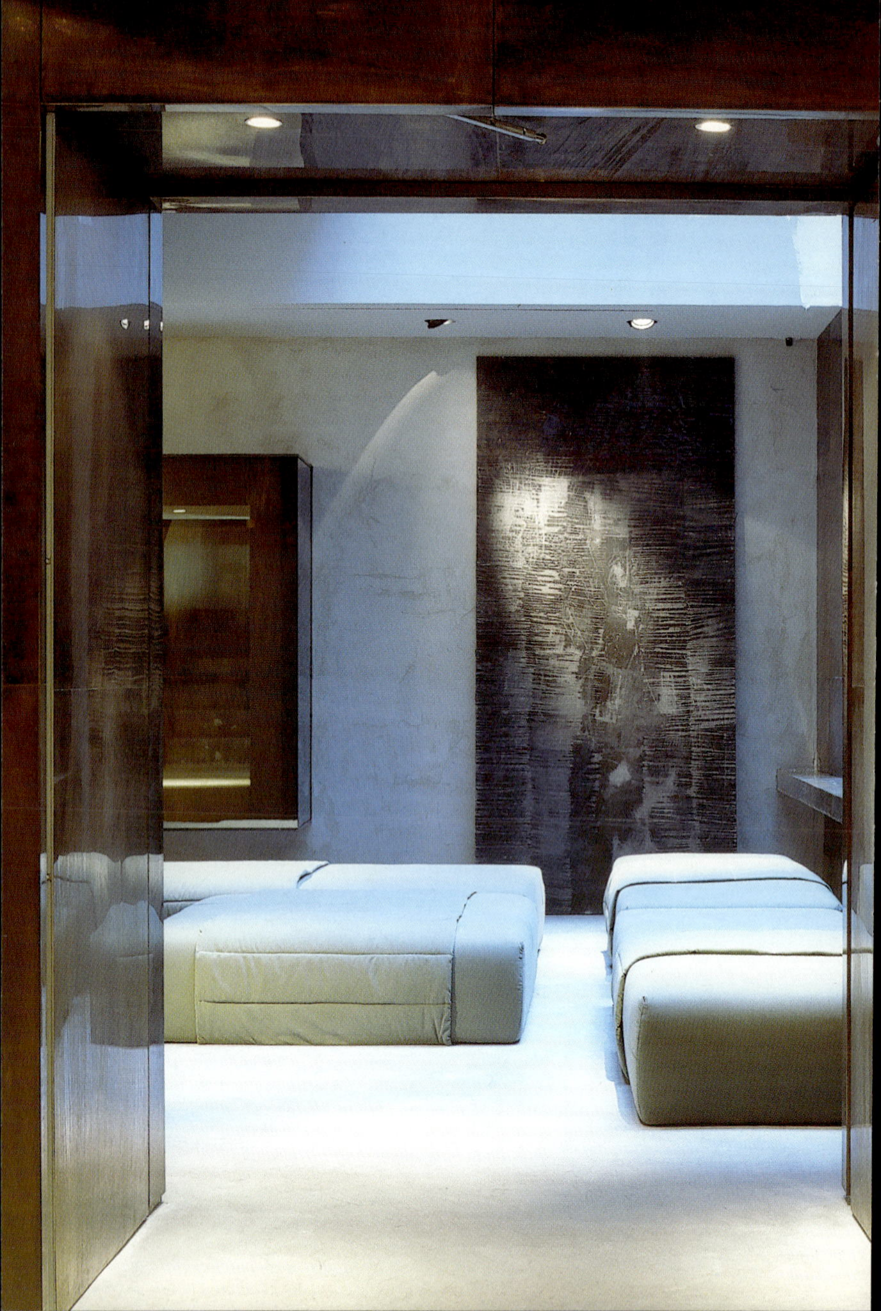

STRAF HOTEL
Italian Design Hotel

Architect: **Vincenzo de Cotiis**

Date: 2003
Address: Via San Raffaele 3, 20121 Milan, Italy
Tel.: +39 02 805 081 Fax: +39 02 890 952 94
www.straf.it
Photos: © Yael Pincus

Location: Urban
Style: Contemporary classic
Rooms: 64
Special features: Spa, pool, bar and restaurant all day

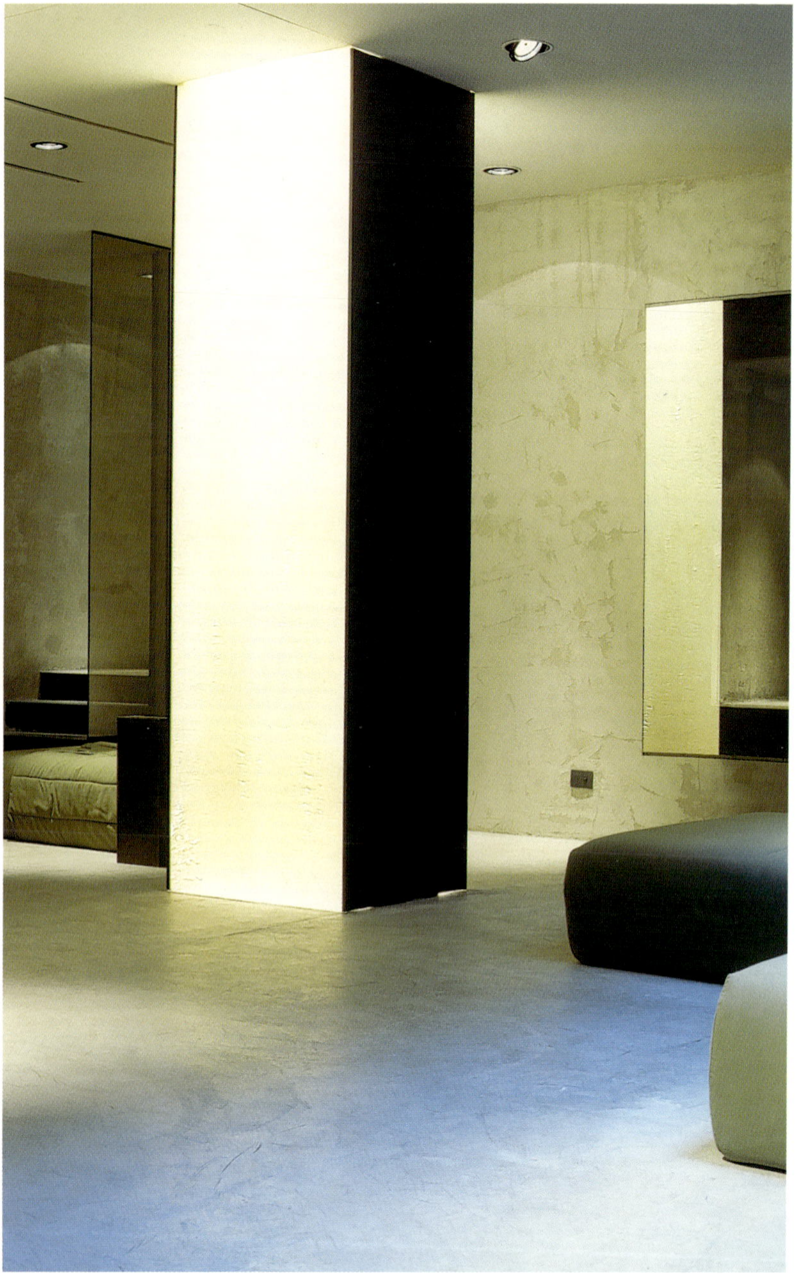

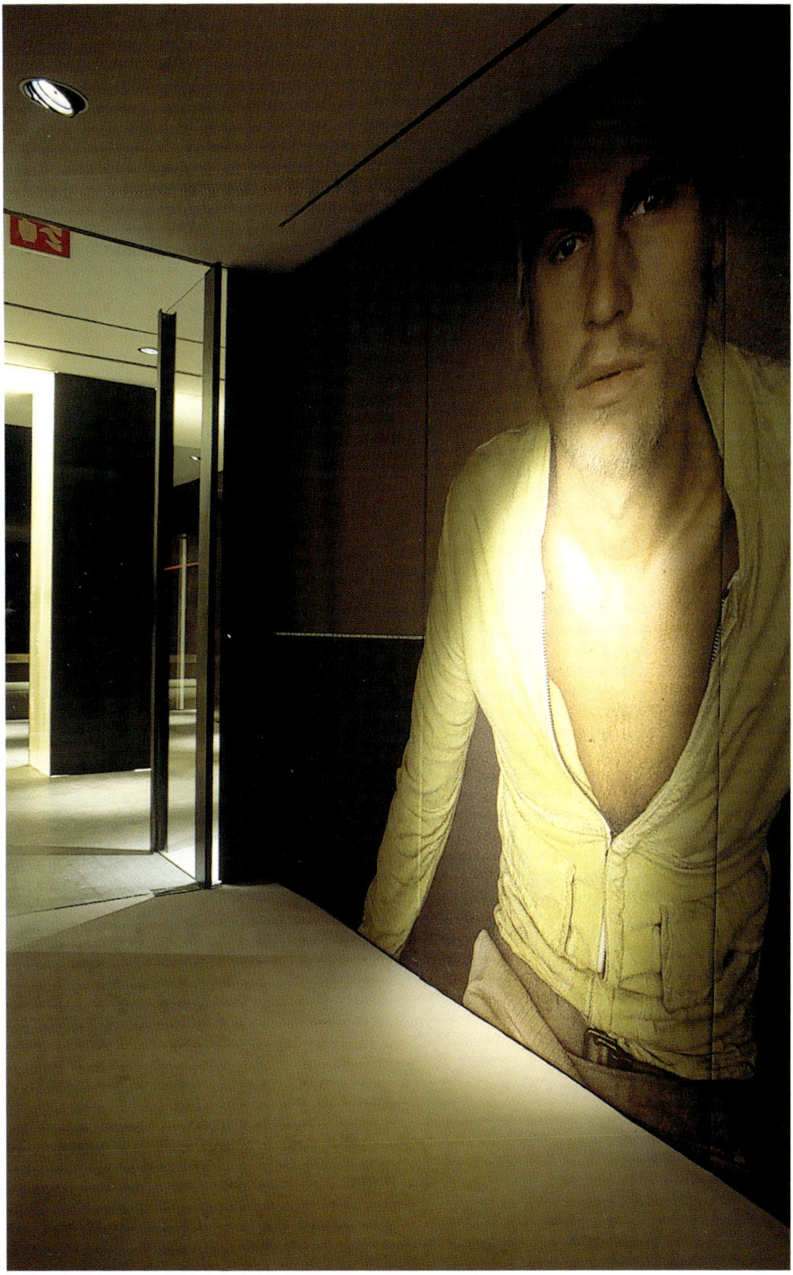

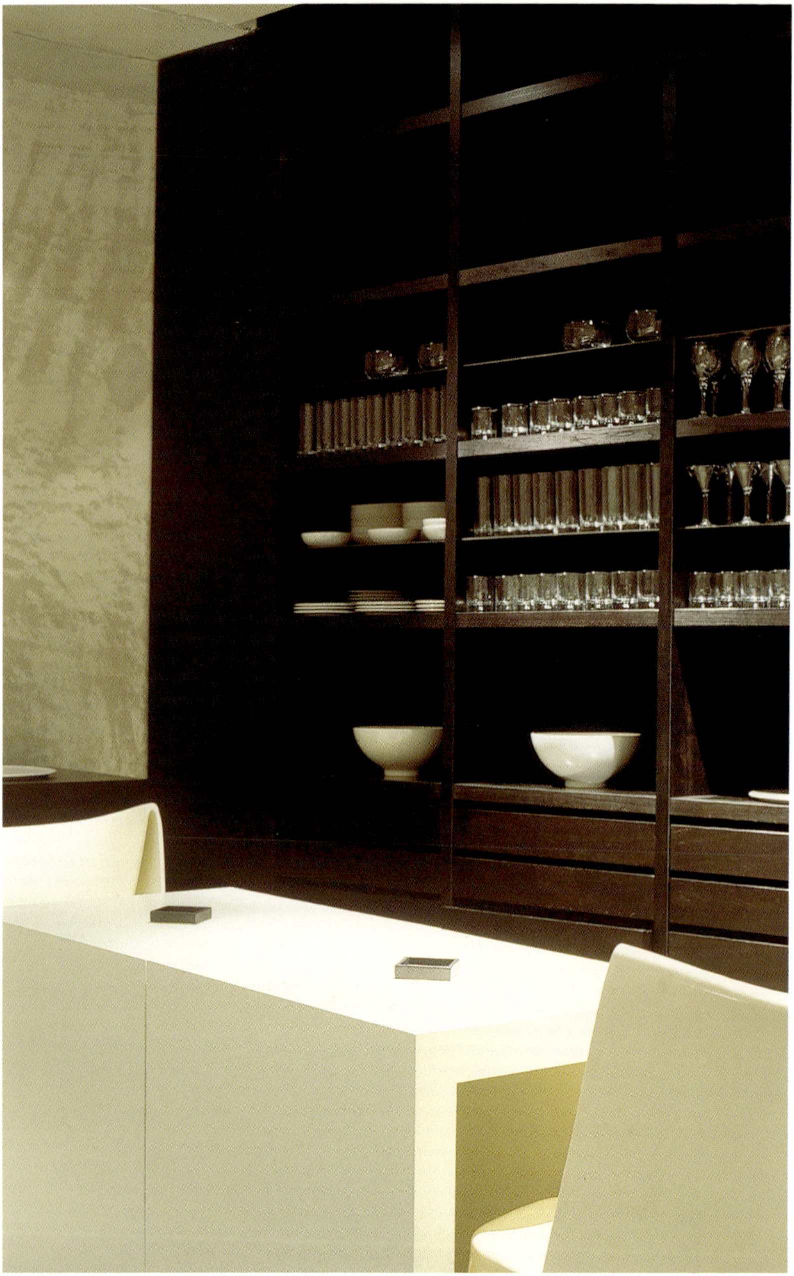

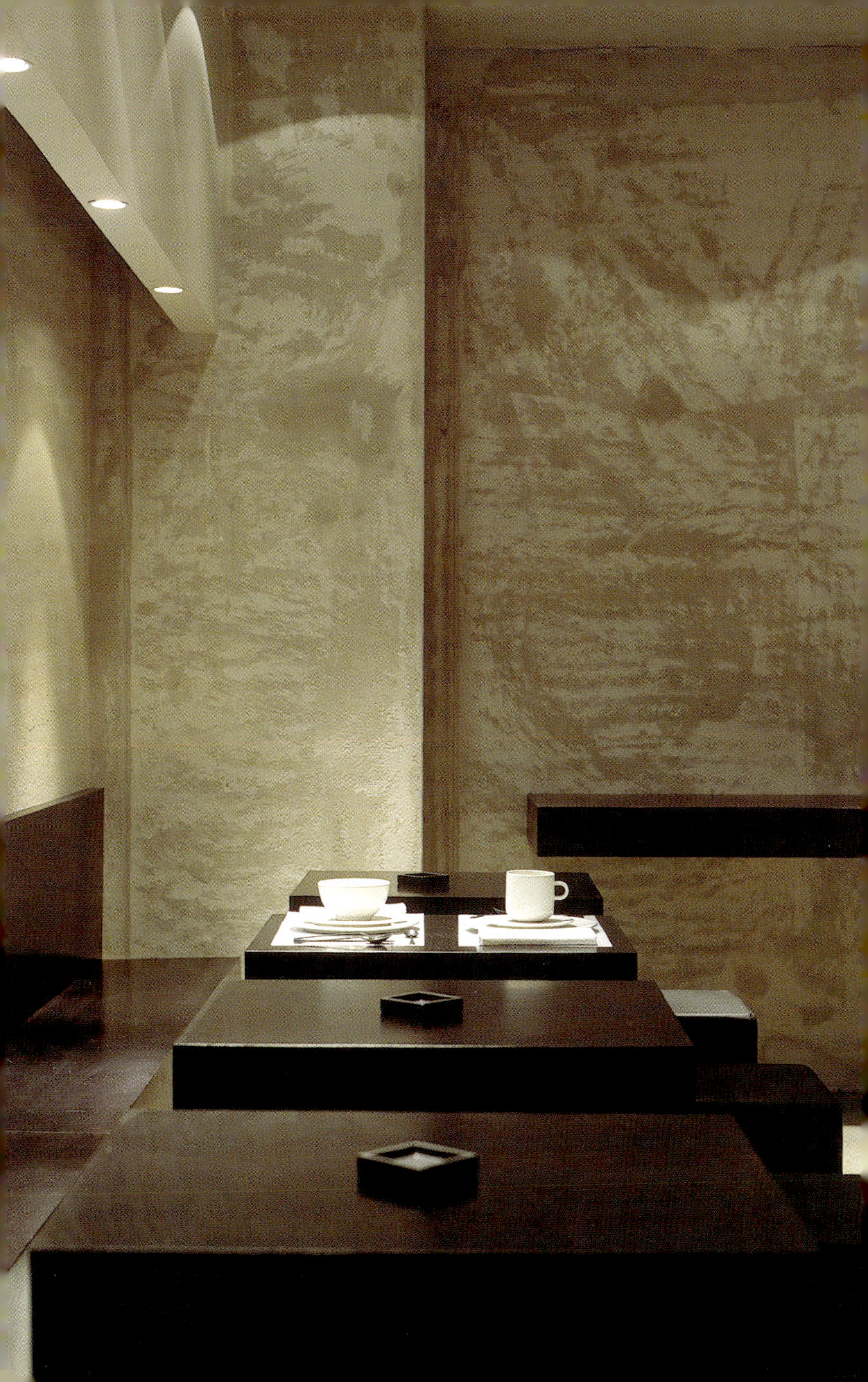

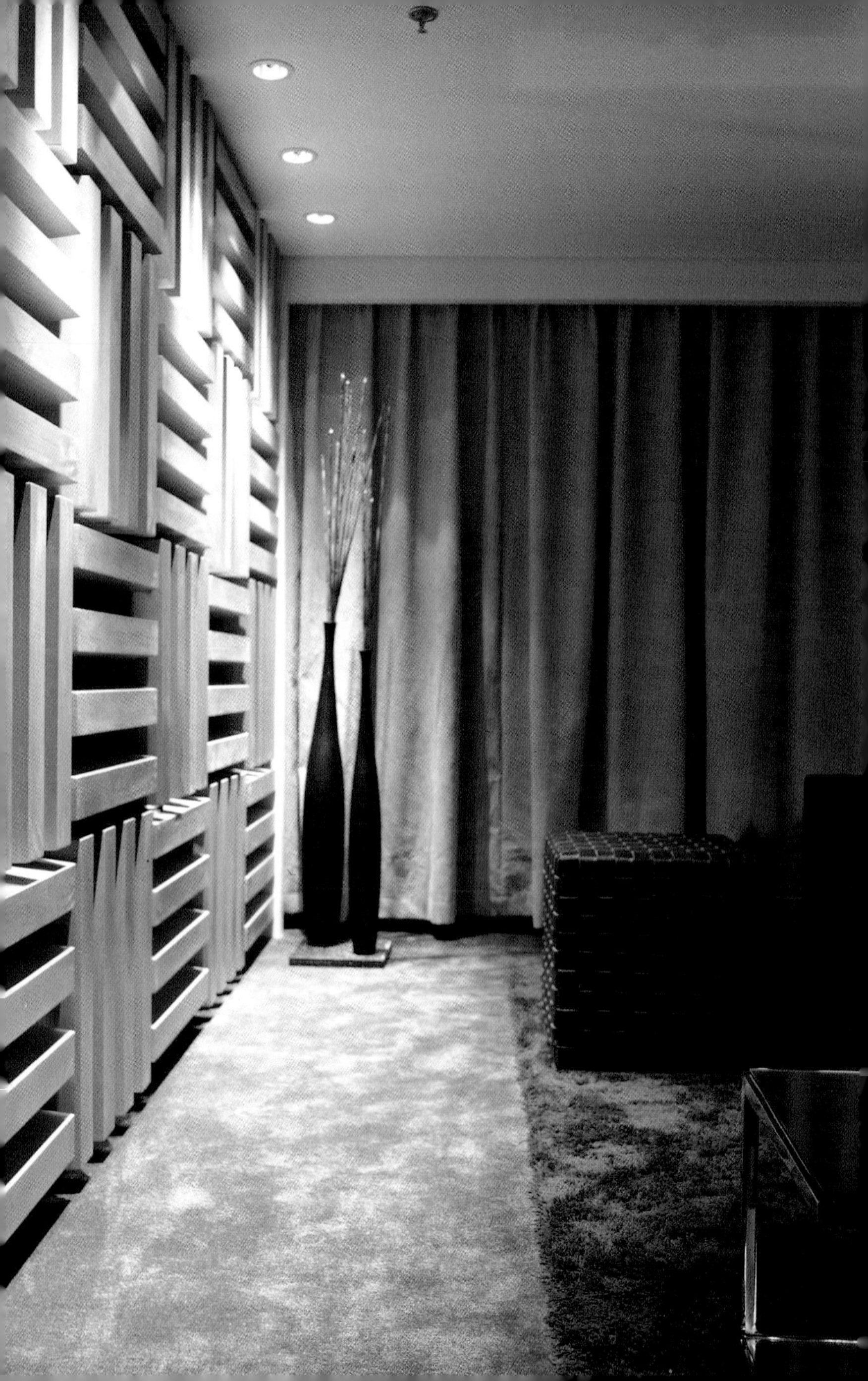

F1 KASSEL GRIMM RESORT
A Fairy Tale Hotel

Architects: **MoHen Design International**

Date: 2005
Address: 1 South Ande Road, Anting New Town, Shanghai 201805, China
Tel.: +86 21 6123 1919
Photos: © Maoder Chou/MoHen Design International

Location: Urban
Style: High-tech
Rooms: 160
Special features: Specialty hotel served for the F1 car racing players, LED lighting, high-tech multimedia

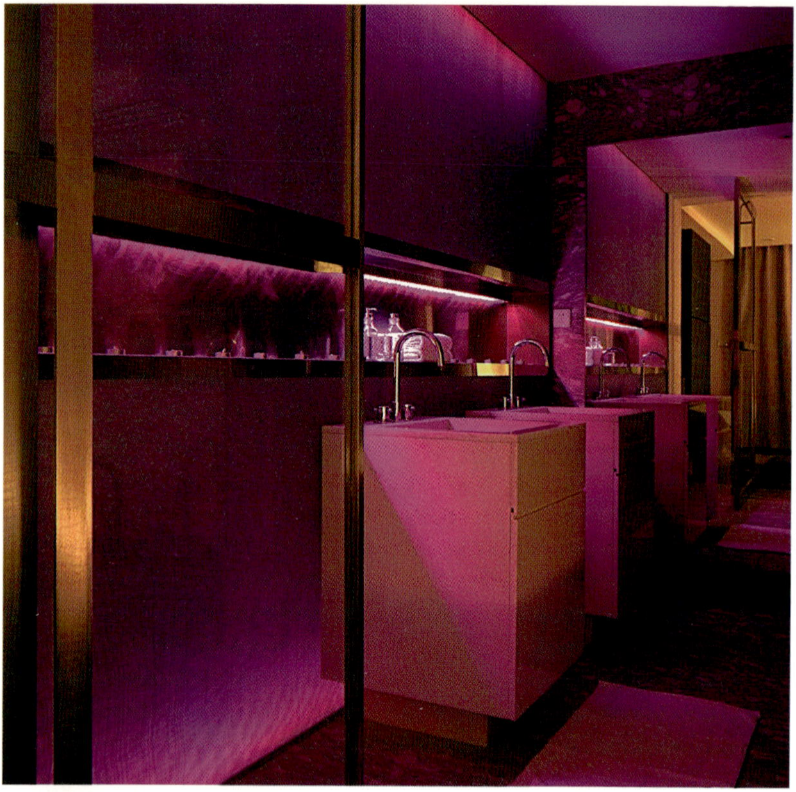

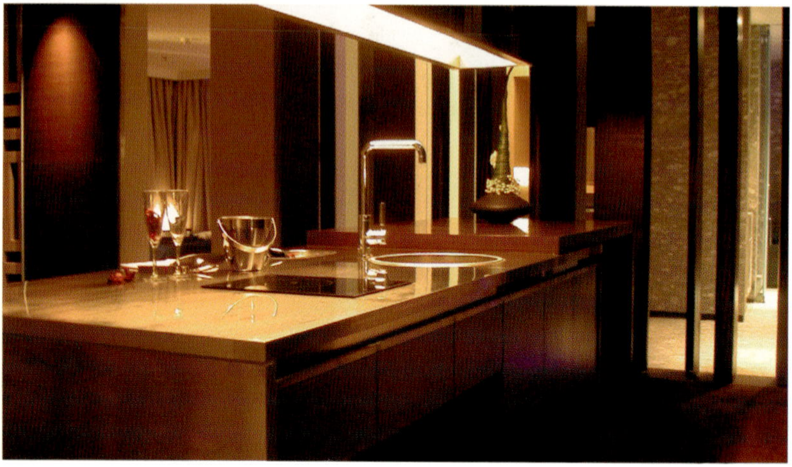

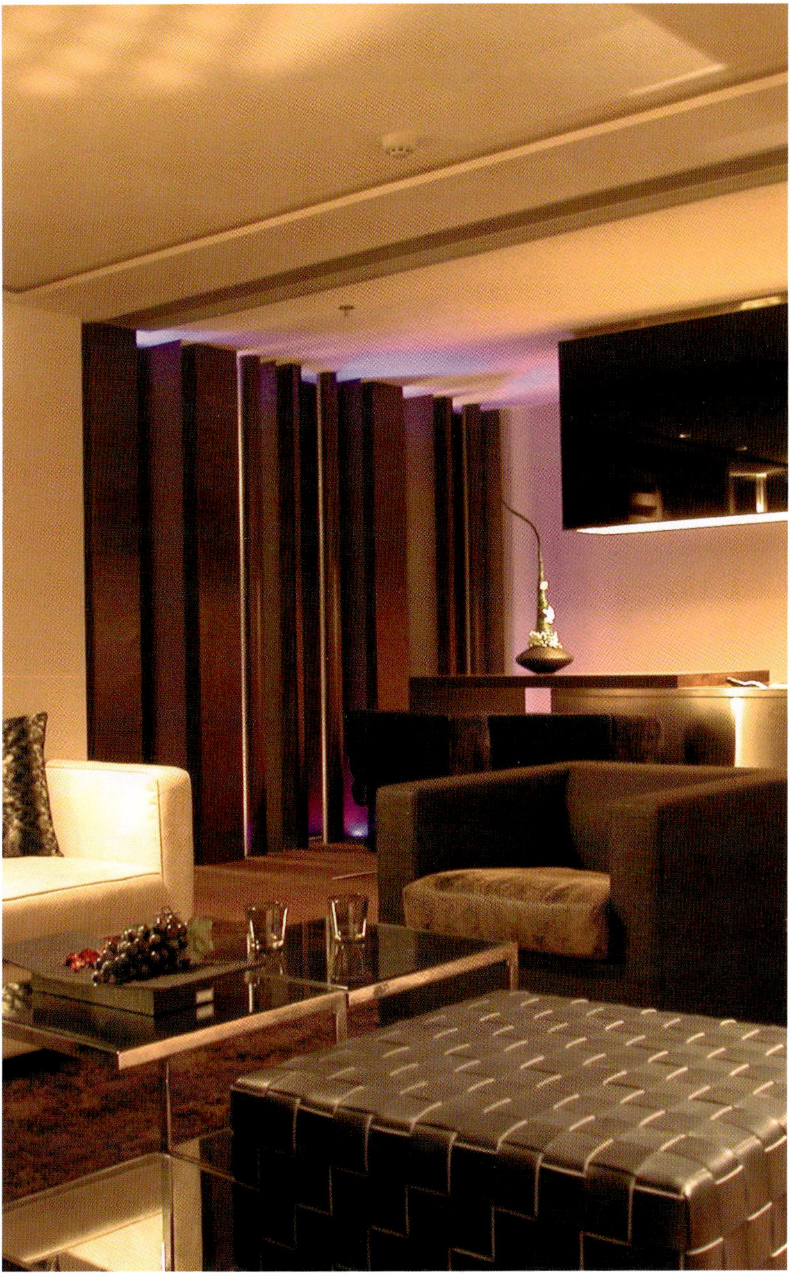

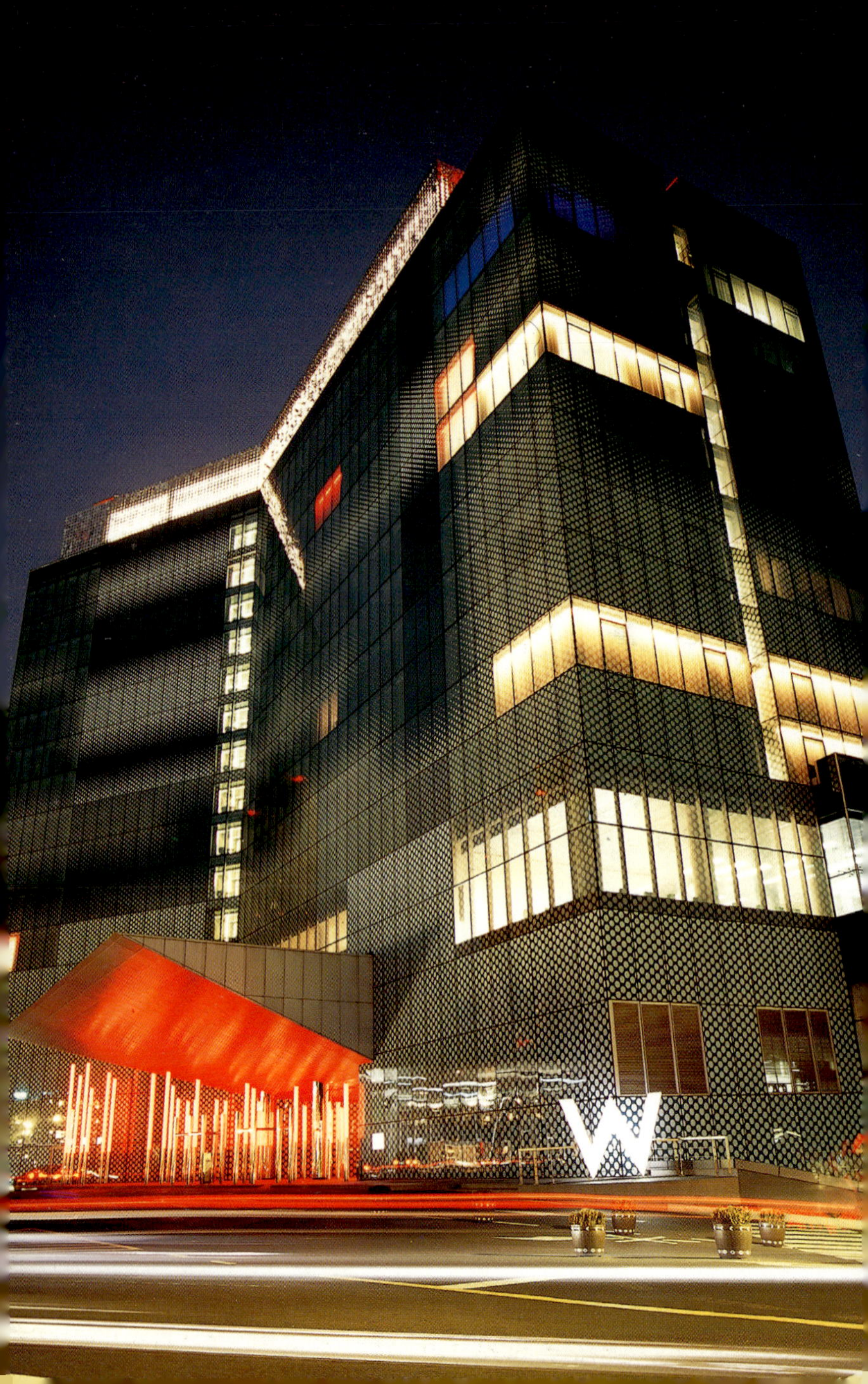
W

W SEOUL WALKERHILL
Stimulate Your Senses

Architects: **Studio Gaia**

Date: 2004
Address: 21 Kwangjang Dong, Kwangjin Gu, Seoul 143708, South Korea
Tel.: +82 2 465 2222 Fax: +82 2 450 4989
www.whotels.com/seoul
Photos: © W Seoul Walkerhill, Studio Gaia

Location: Urban
Style: Contemporary Asian
Rooms: 253
Special features: Boutique, hair salon, indoor pool

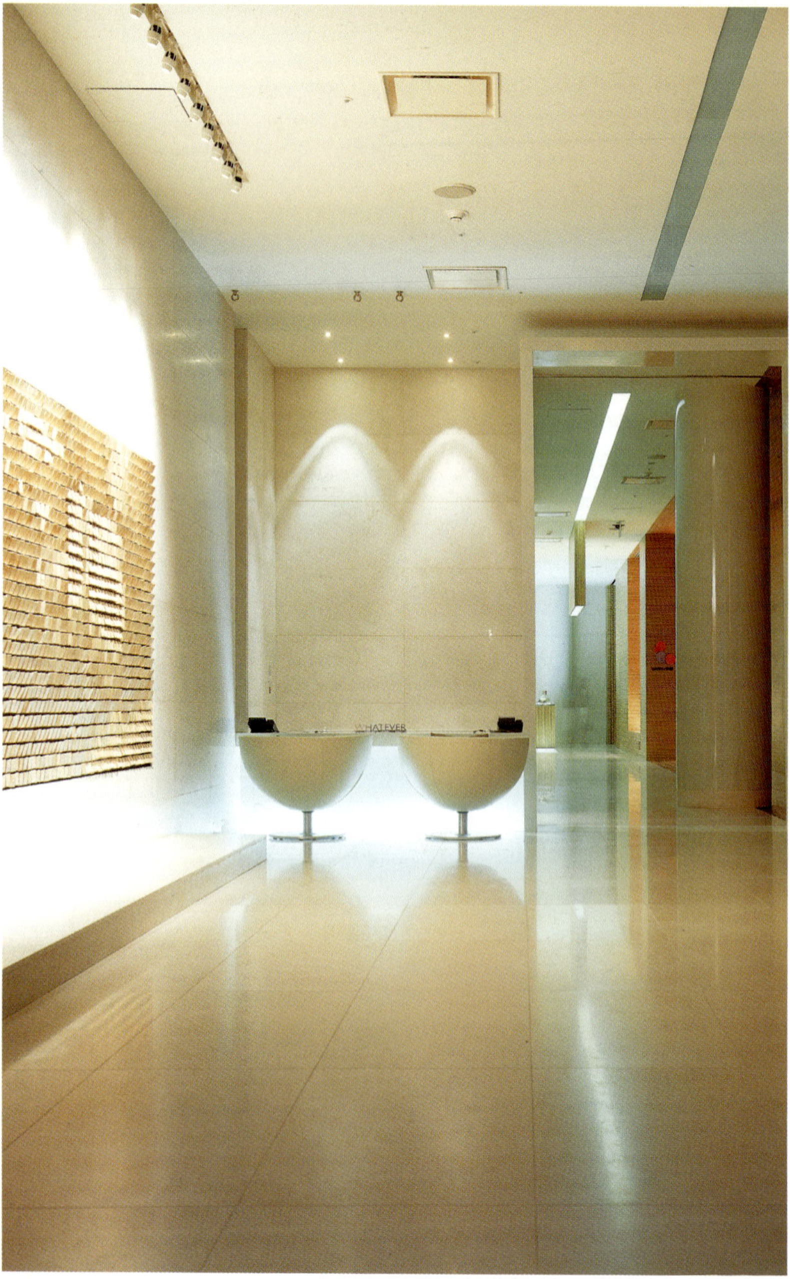
WHATEVER

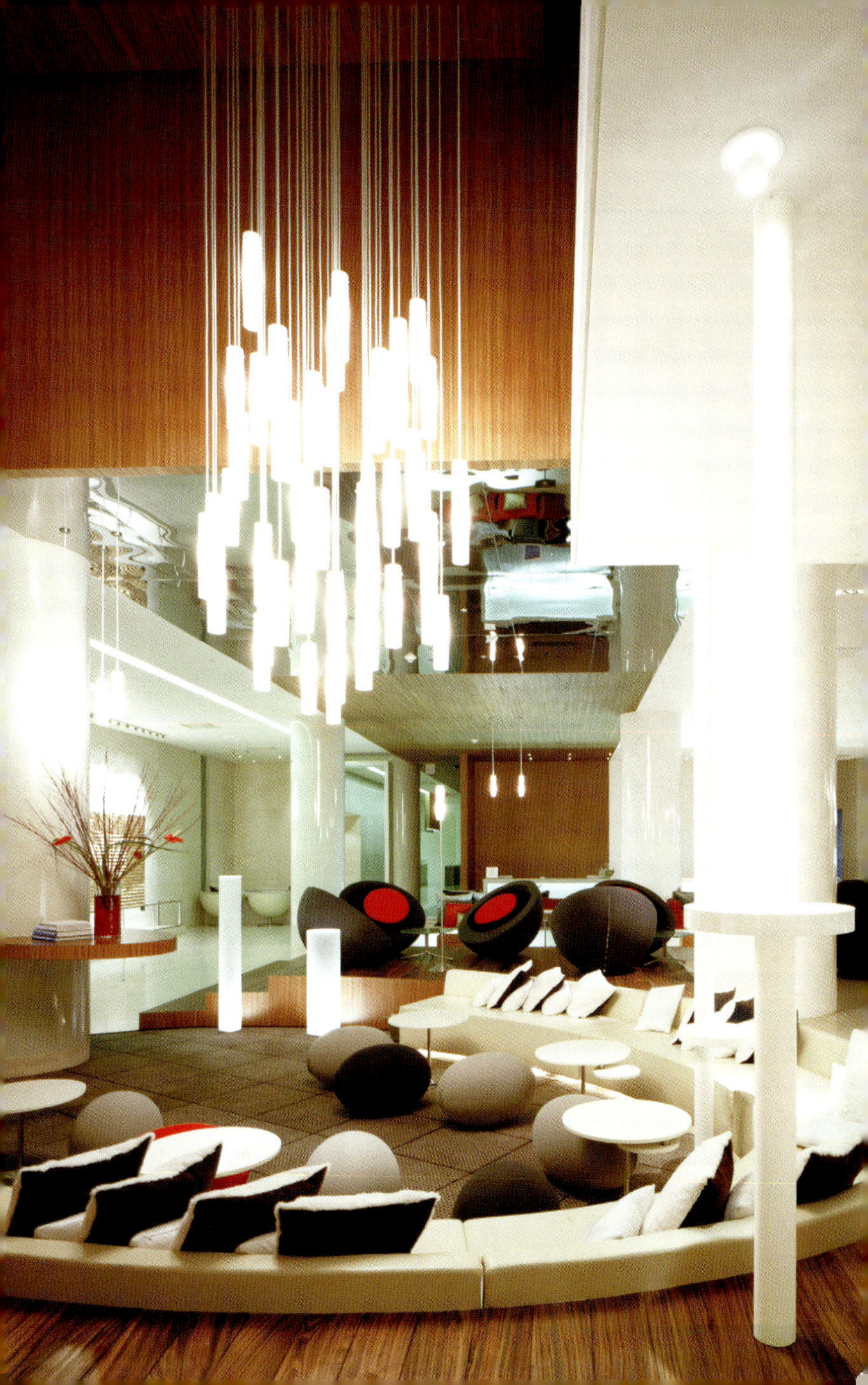

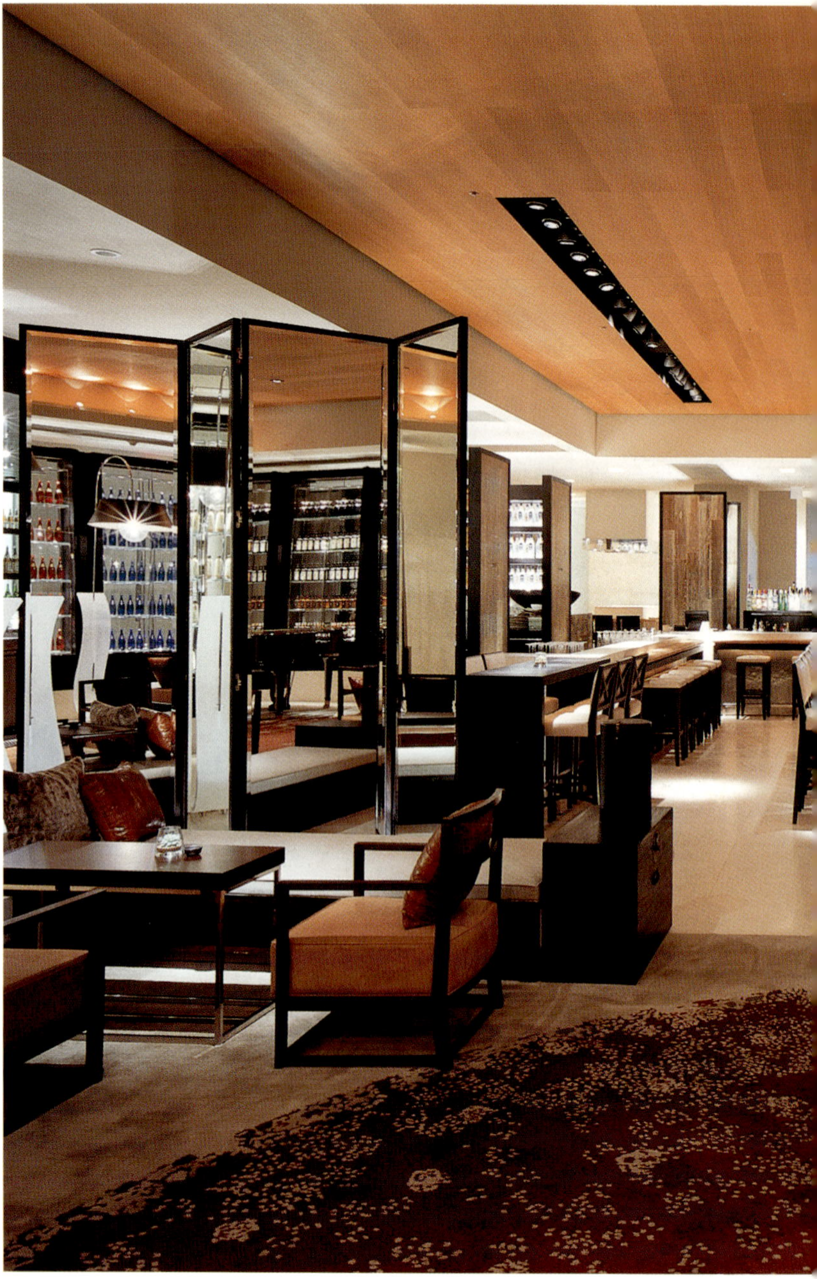

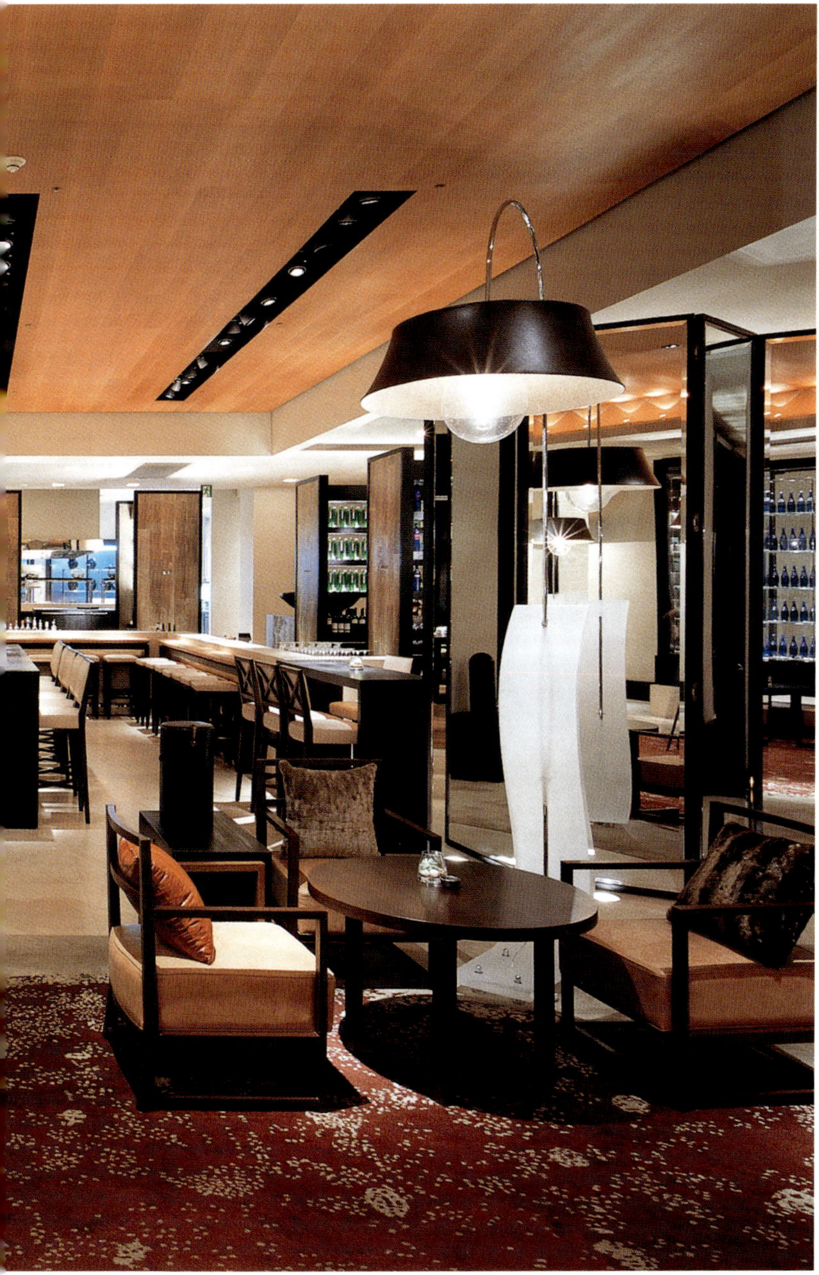

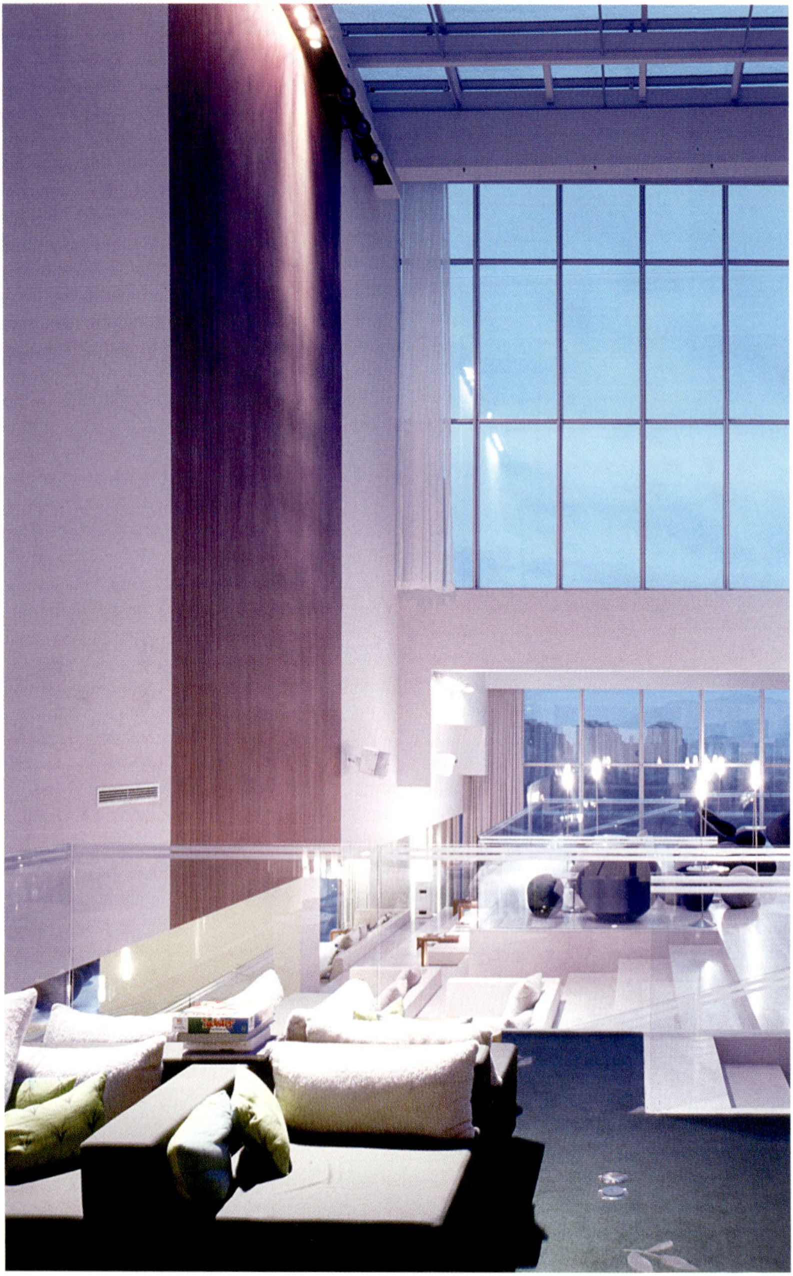

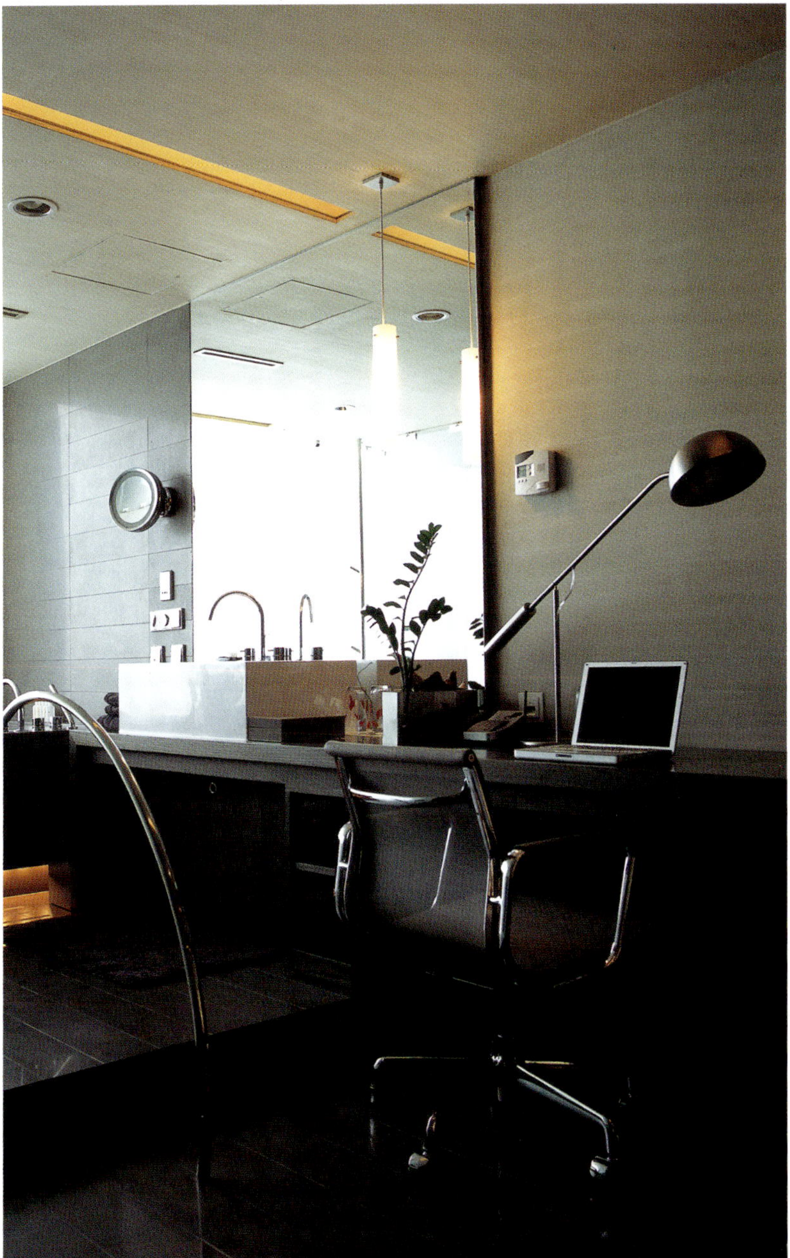

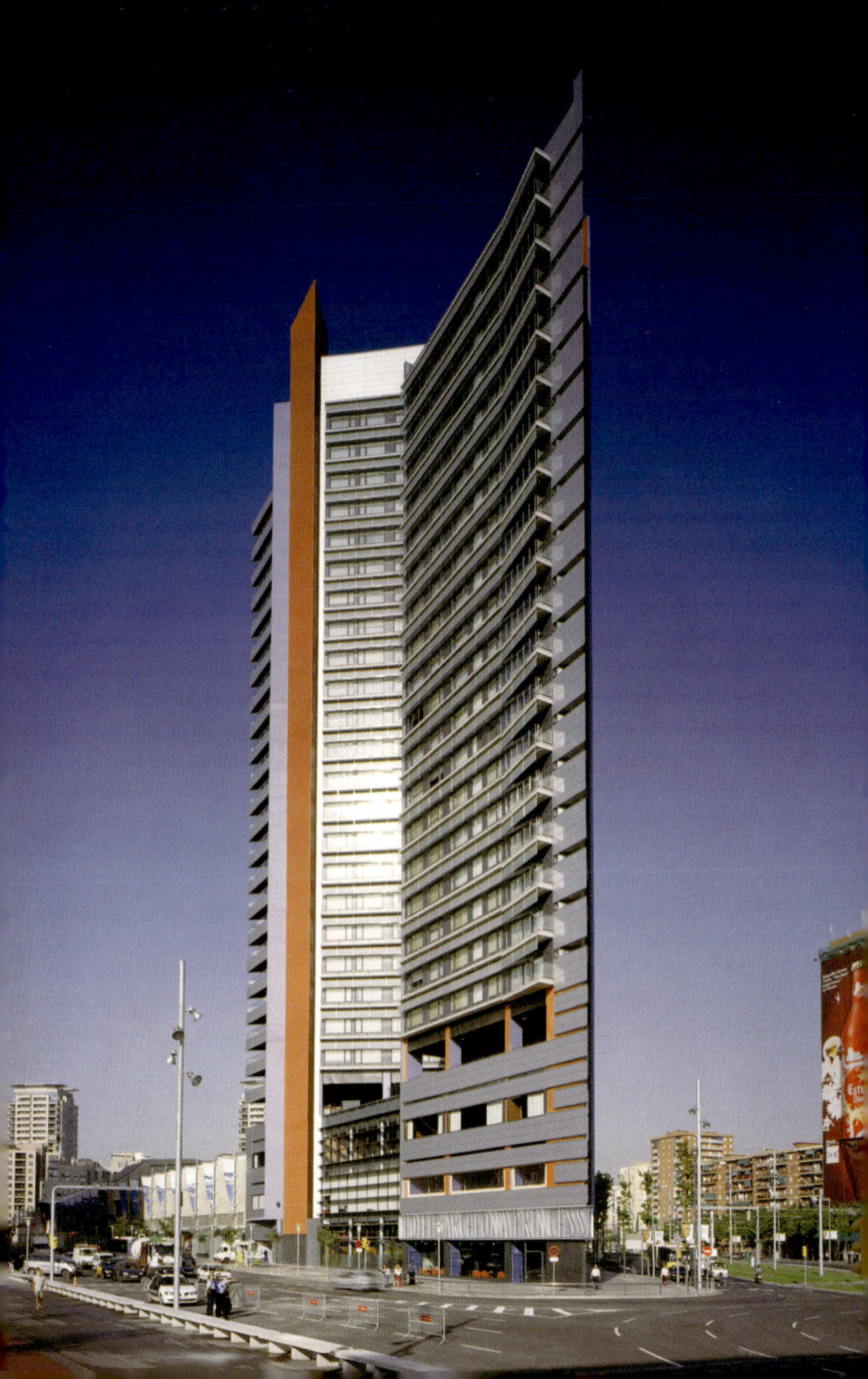

HOTEL BARCELONA PRINCESS
A New Concept for the Business

Architect: **Oscar Tusquets Blanca**

Date: 2004
Address: Avda. Diagonal 1, 08019 Barcelona, Spain
Tel.: +34 933 561 000 Fax: +34 933 561 022
www.hotelbarcelonaprincess.com
Photos: © Gunnar Knetchel, Rafael Vargas

Location: Urban
Style: Contemporary avant-garde
Rooms: 366
Special features: Bars, restaurants, conference rooms, spa, gym, swimming pools, roof terrace

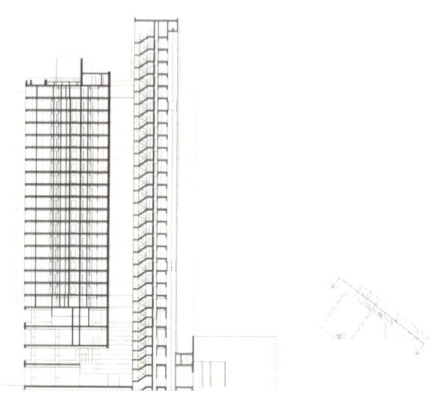

Cross section | Shows the more than 30 story building

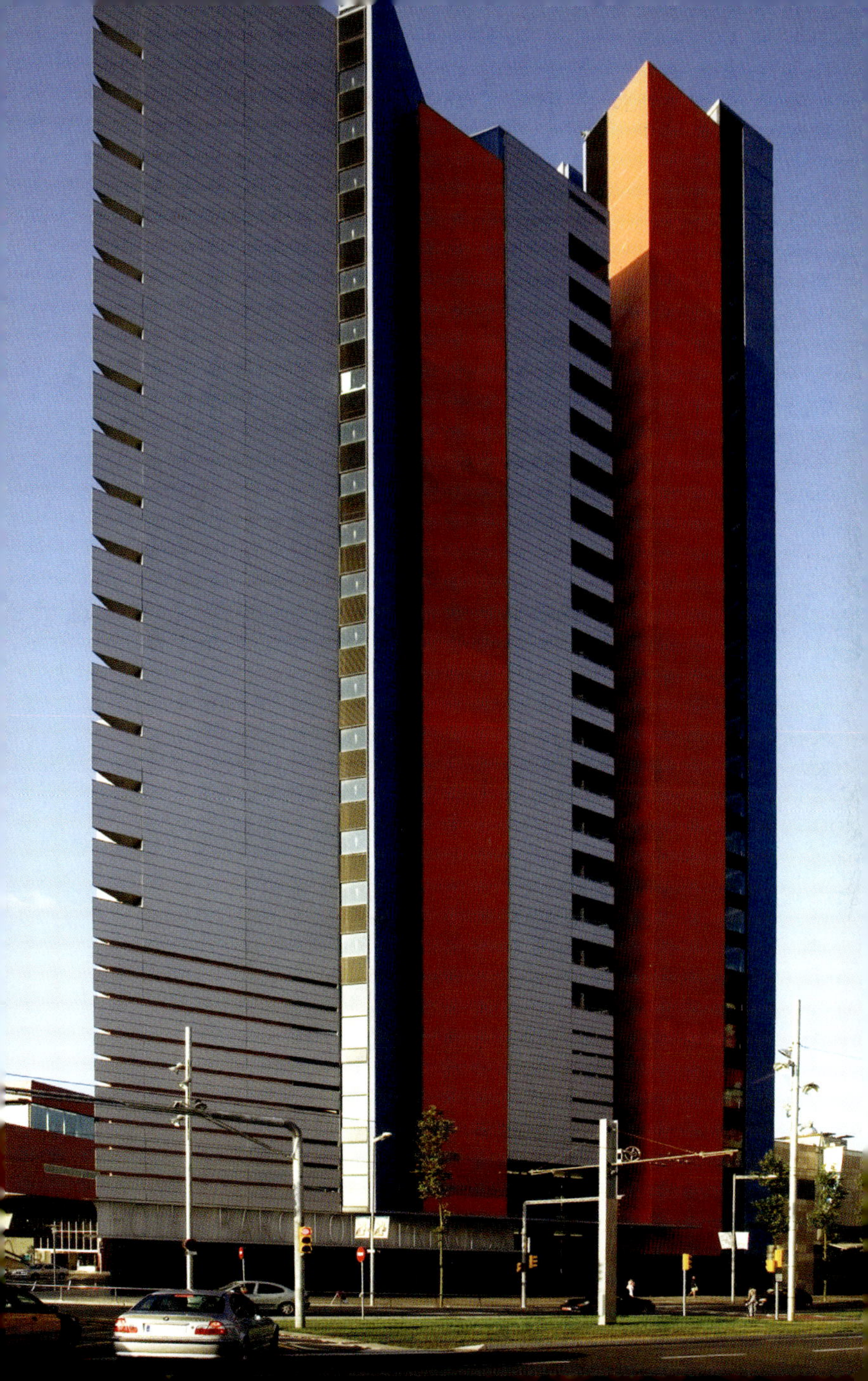

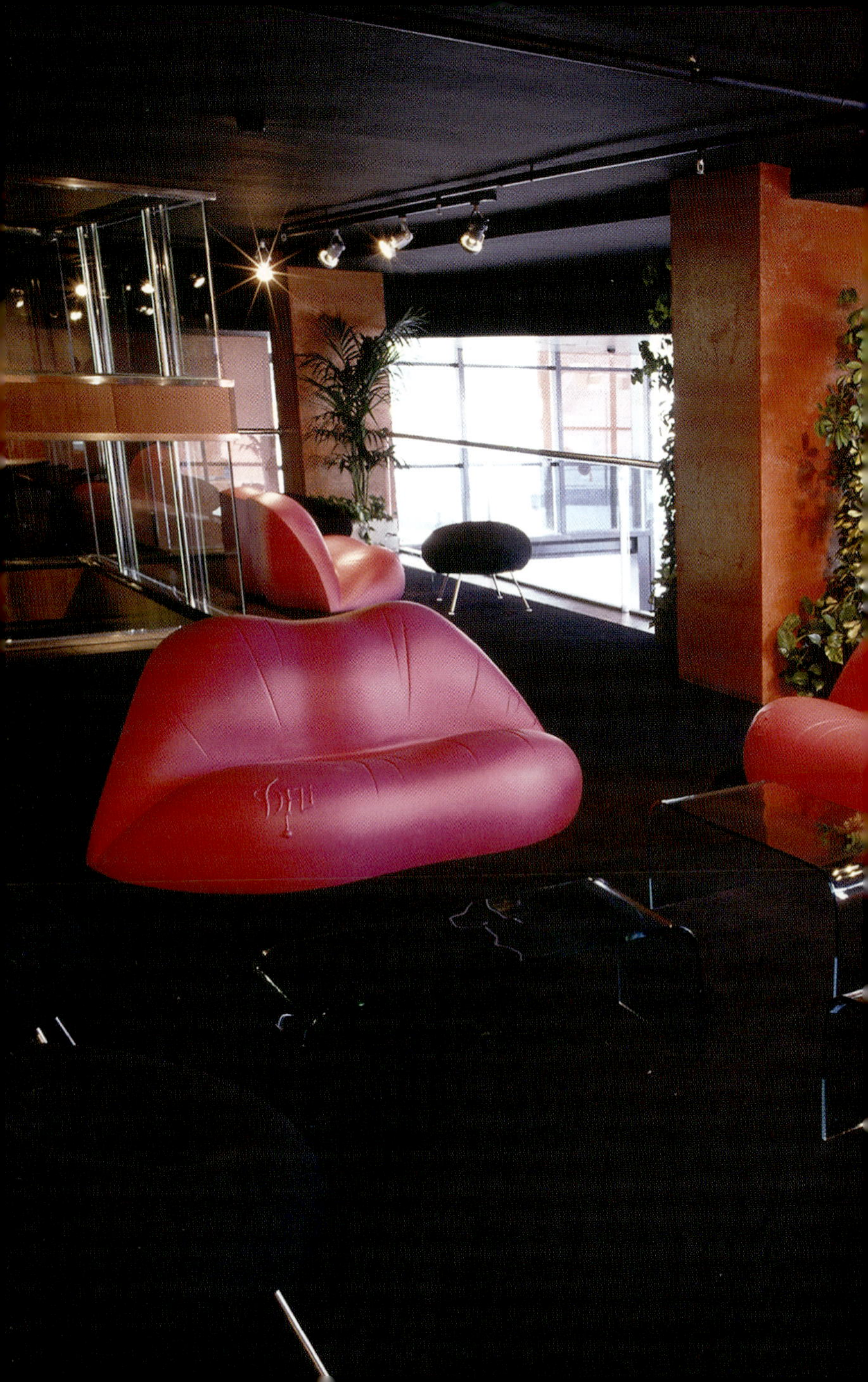

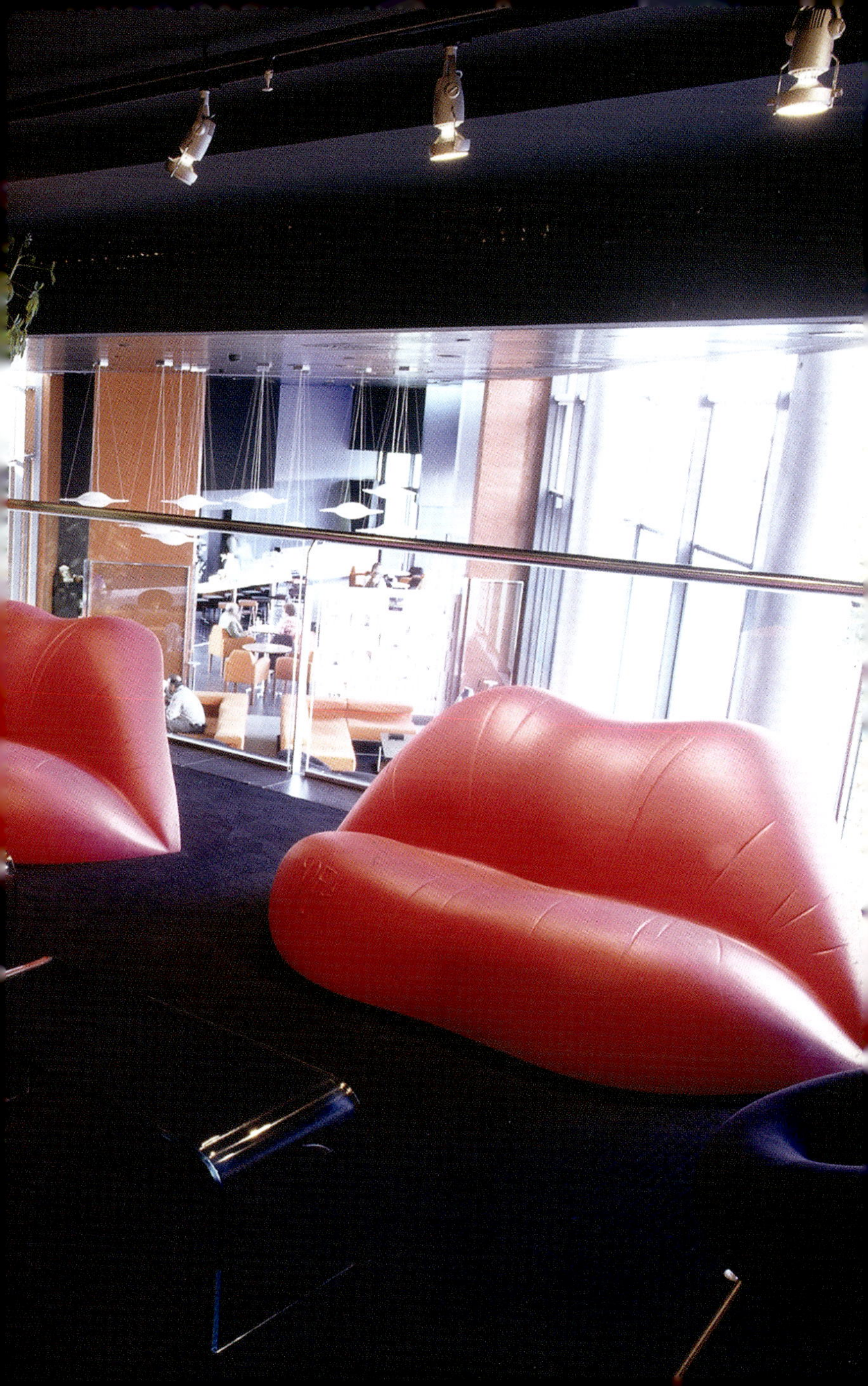

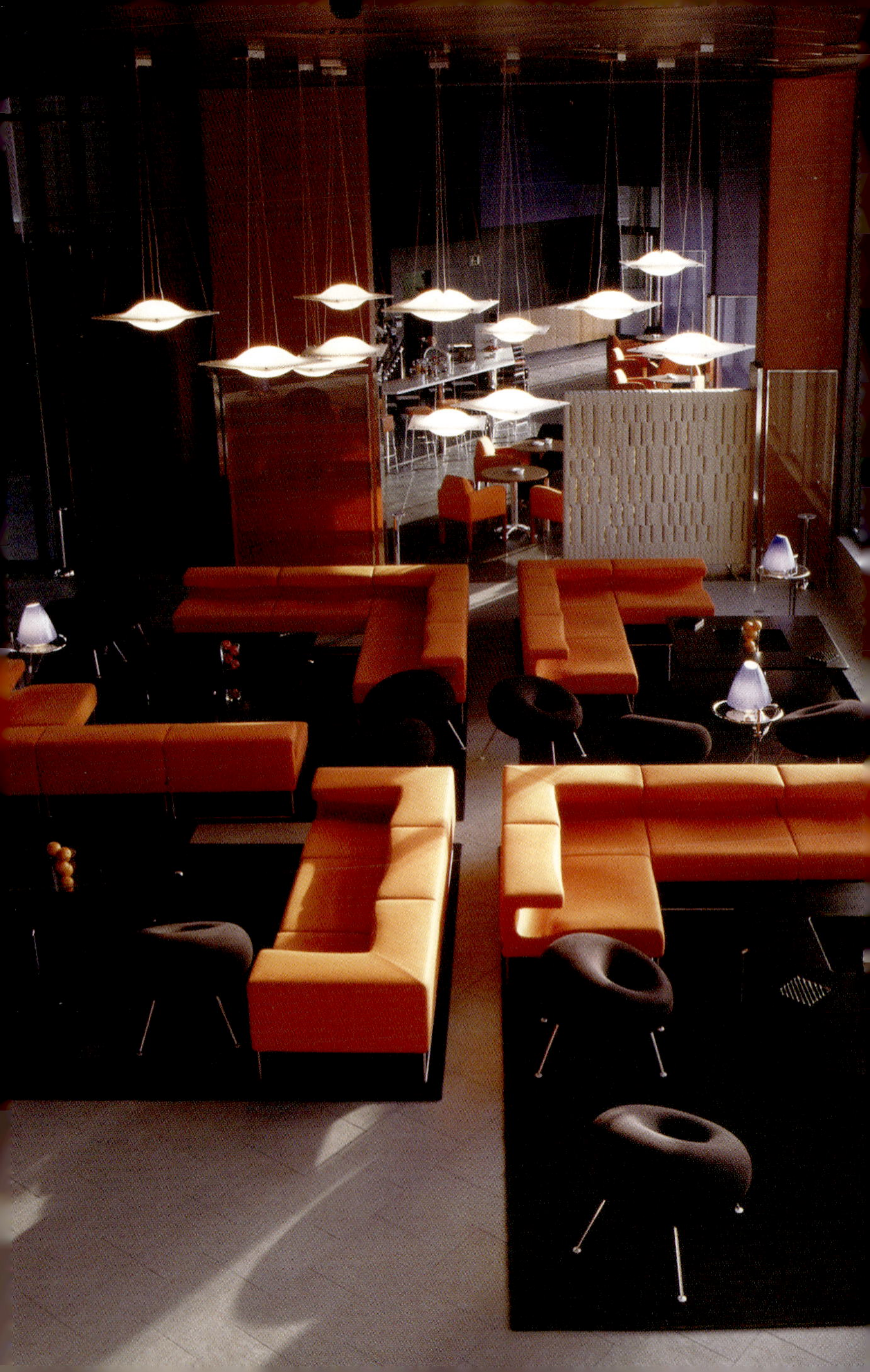

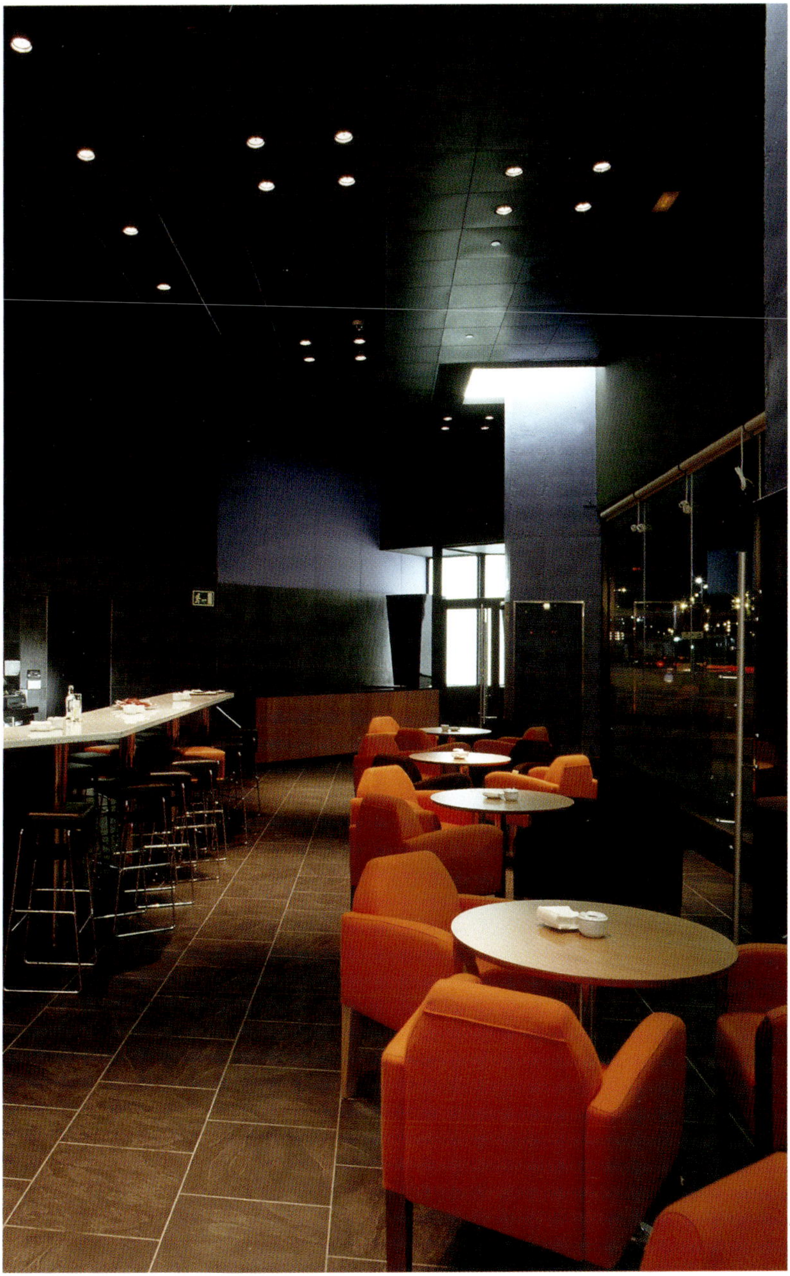

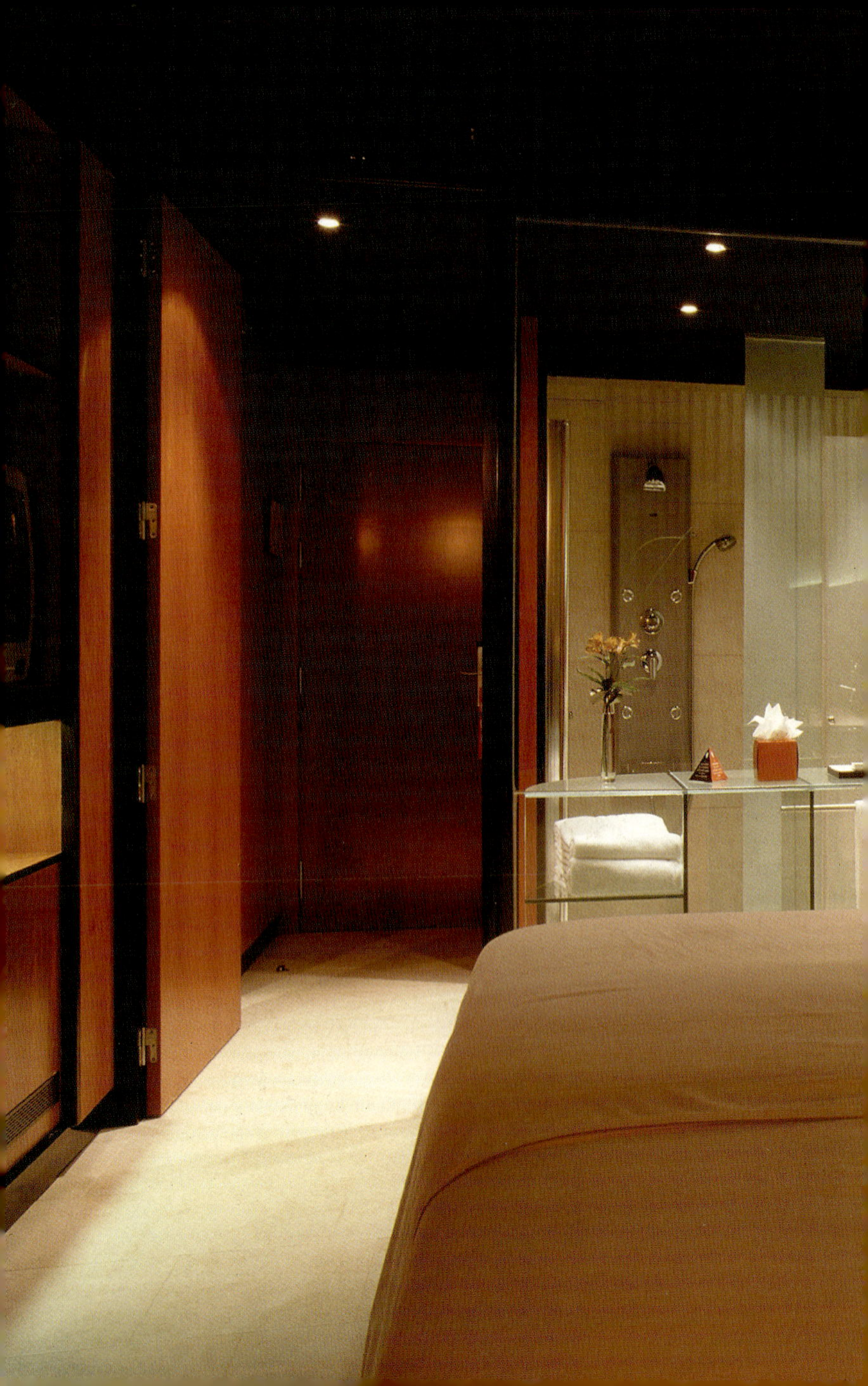

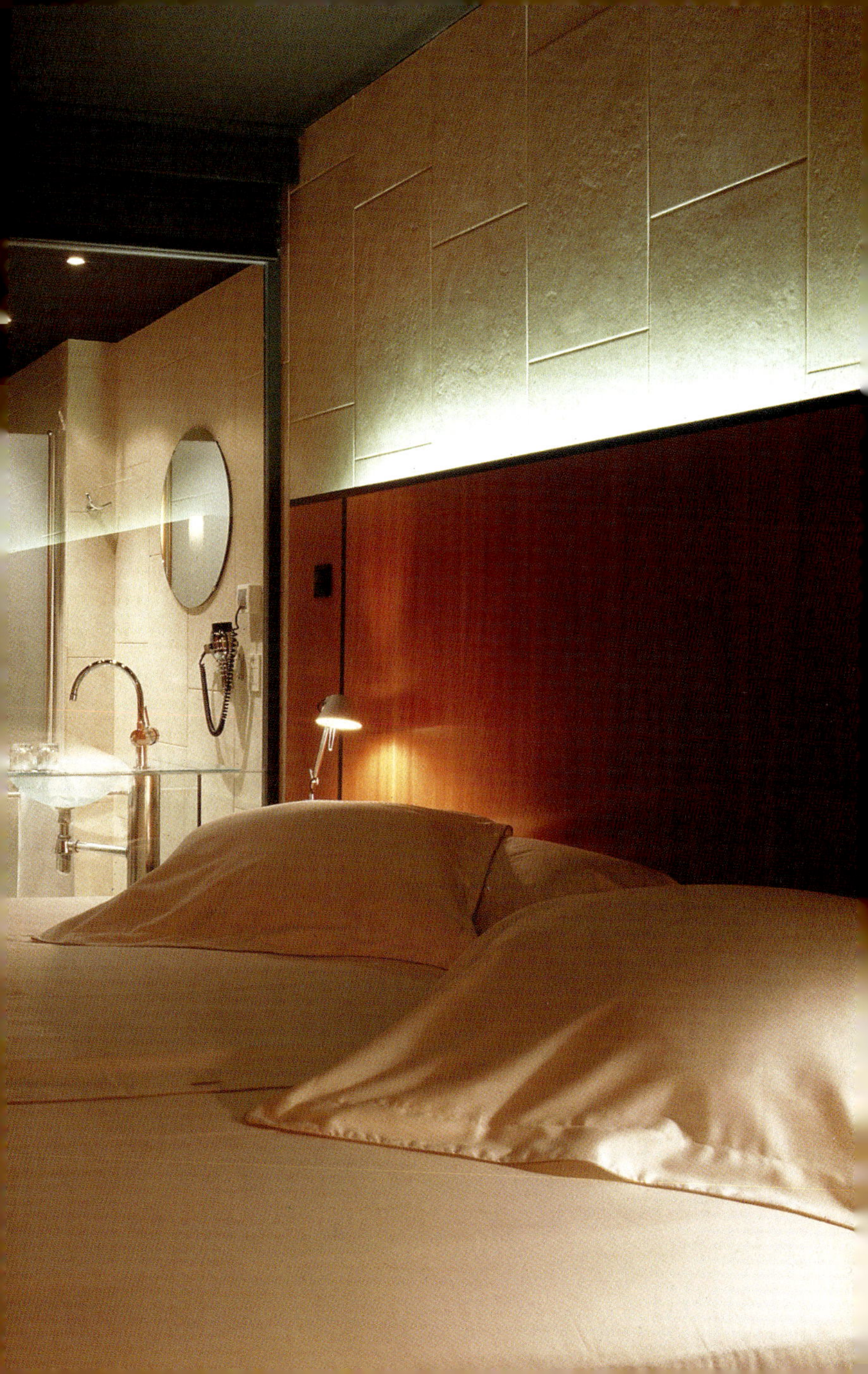

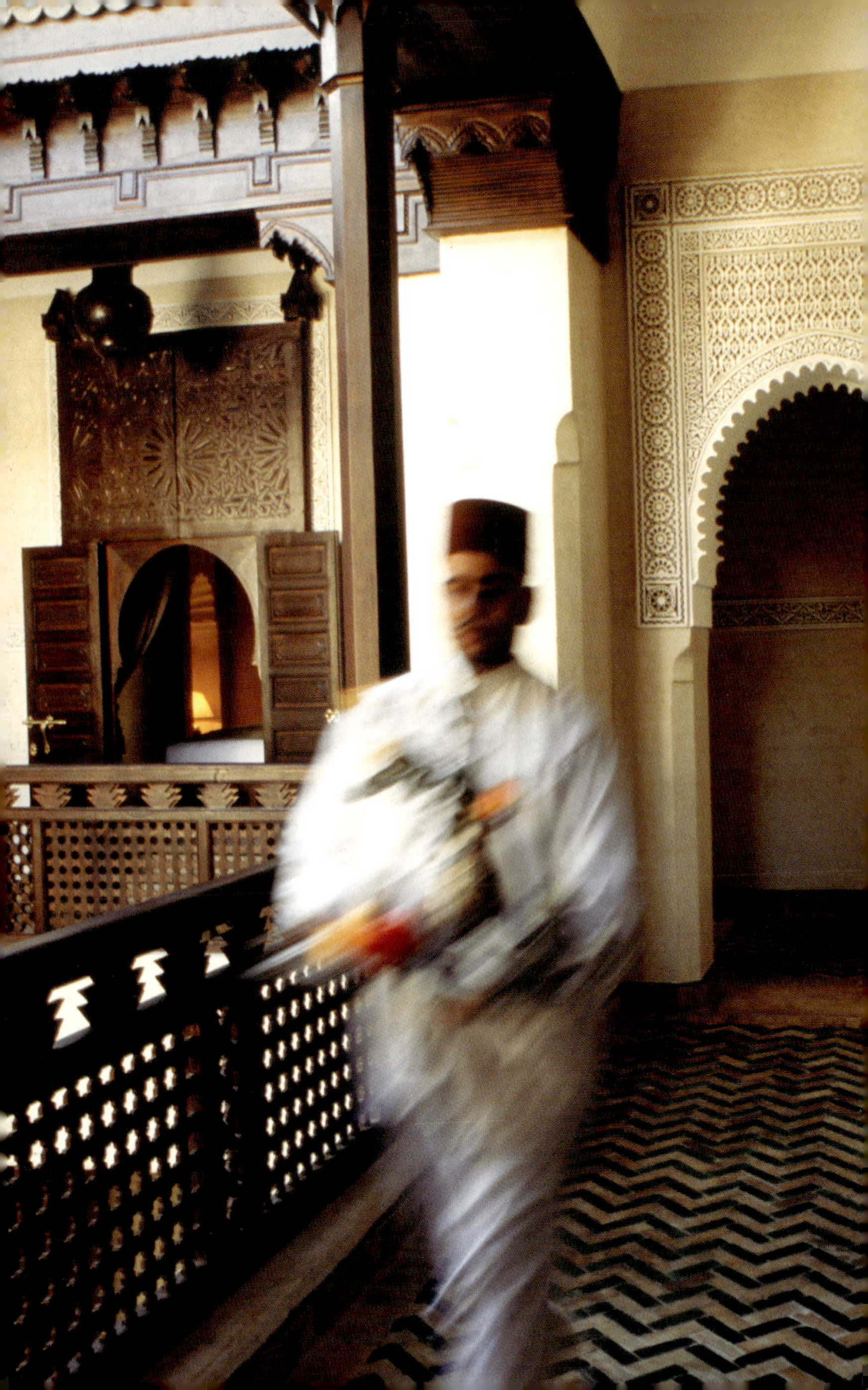

DAR LES CIGOGNES
A True Oasis of Calm in Marrakech

Architect: **Charles Boccara**

Date: 2004
Address: 108, Rue de Berima Medina, 40000 Marrakech, Morocco
Tel.: +212 24 38 27 40 Fax: +212 24 38 47 67
www.lescigognes.com
Photos: © Dar Les Cigognes

Location: Urban
Style: Moroccan luxury
Rooms: 11
Special features: 17th century structure, in-room fireplaces, central courtyards

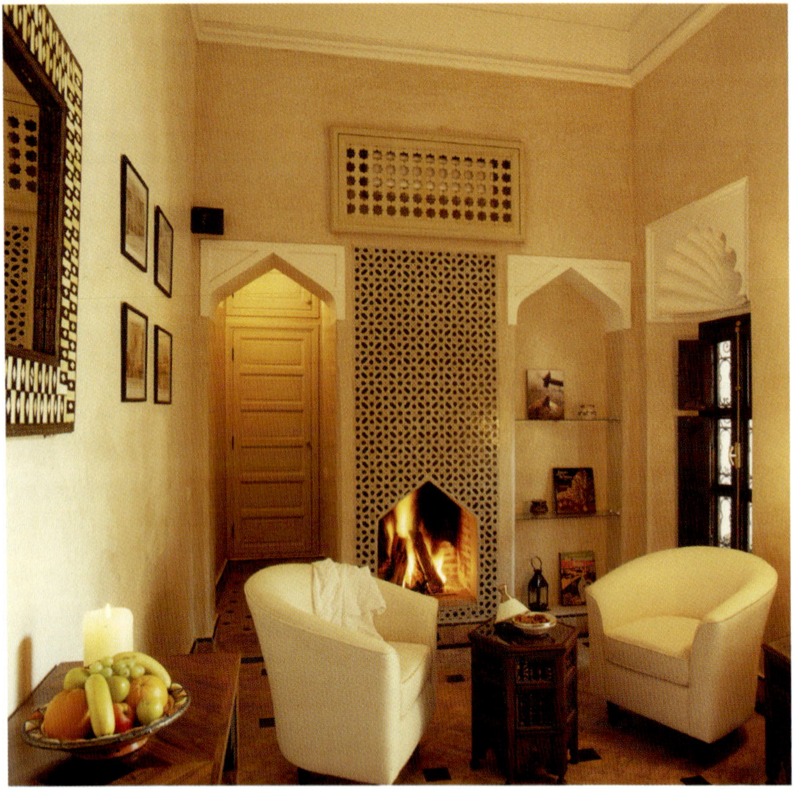

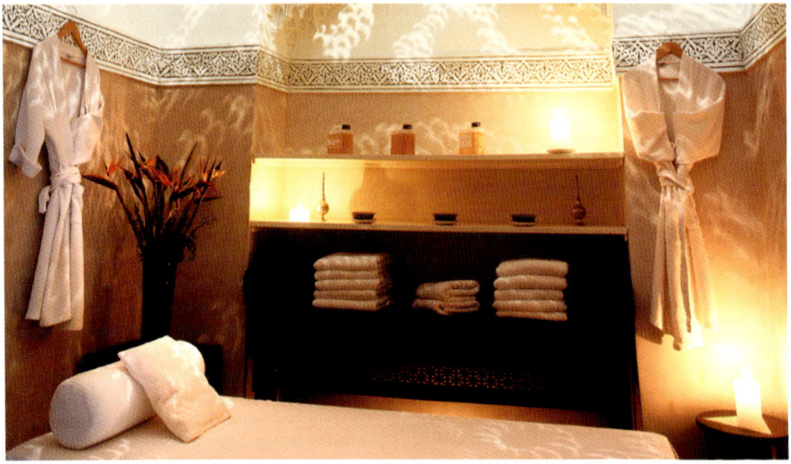

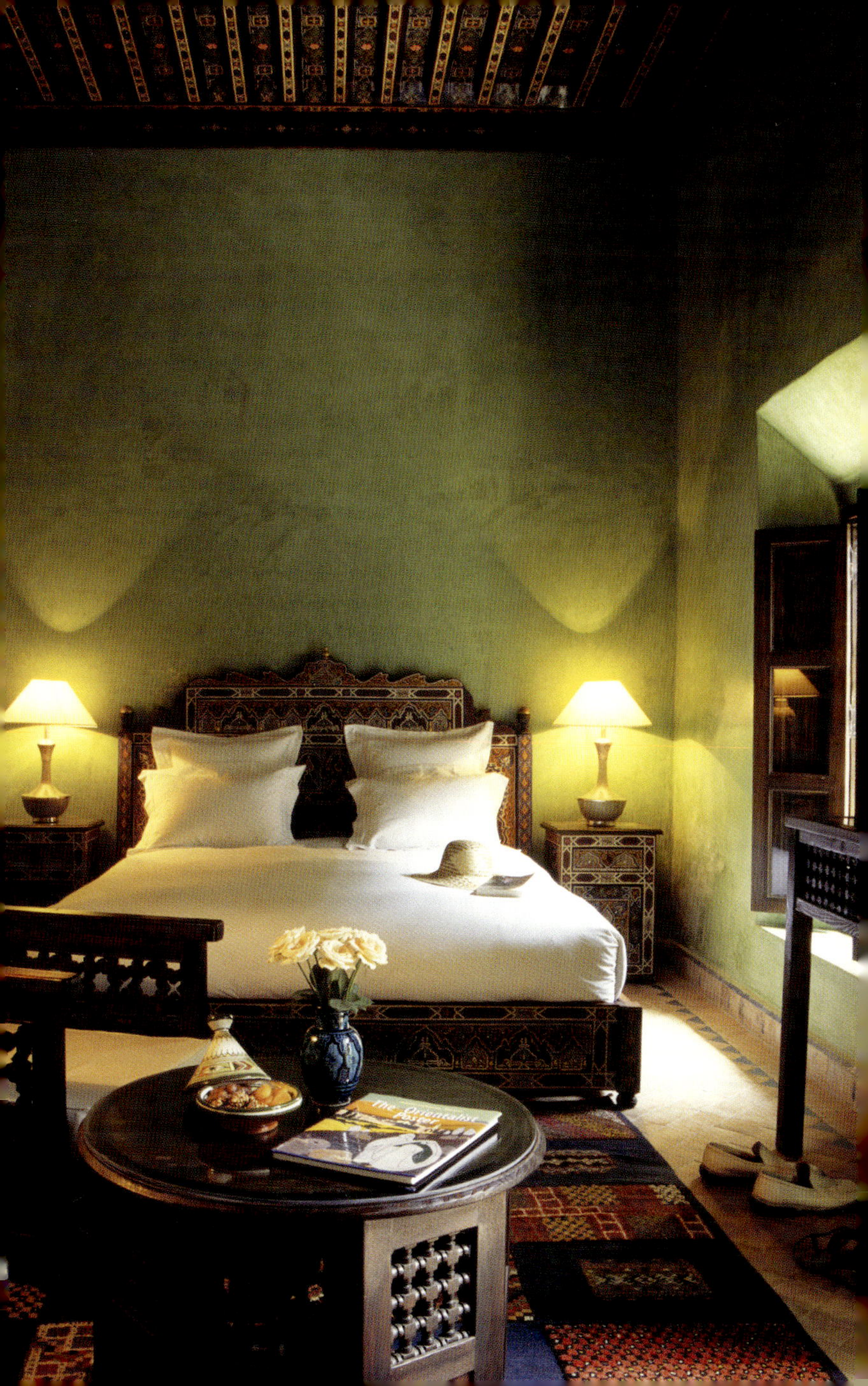
The Orientalist Poster

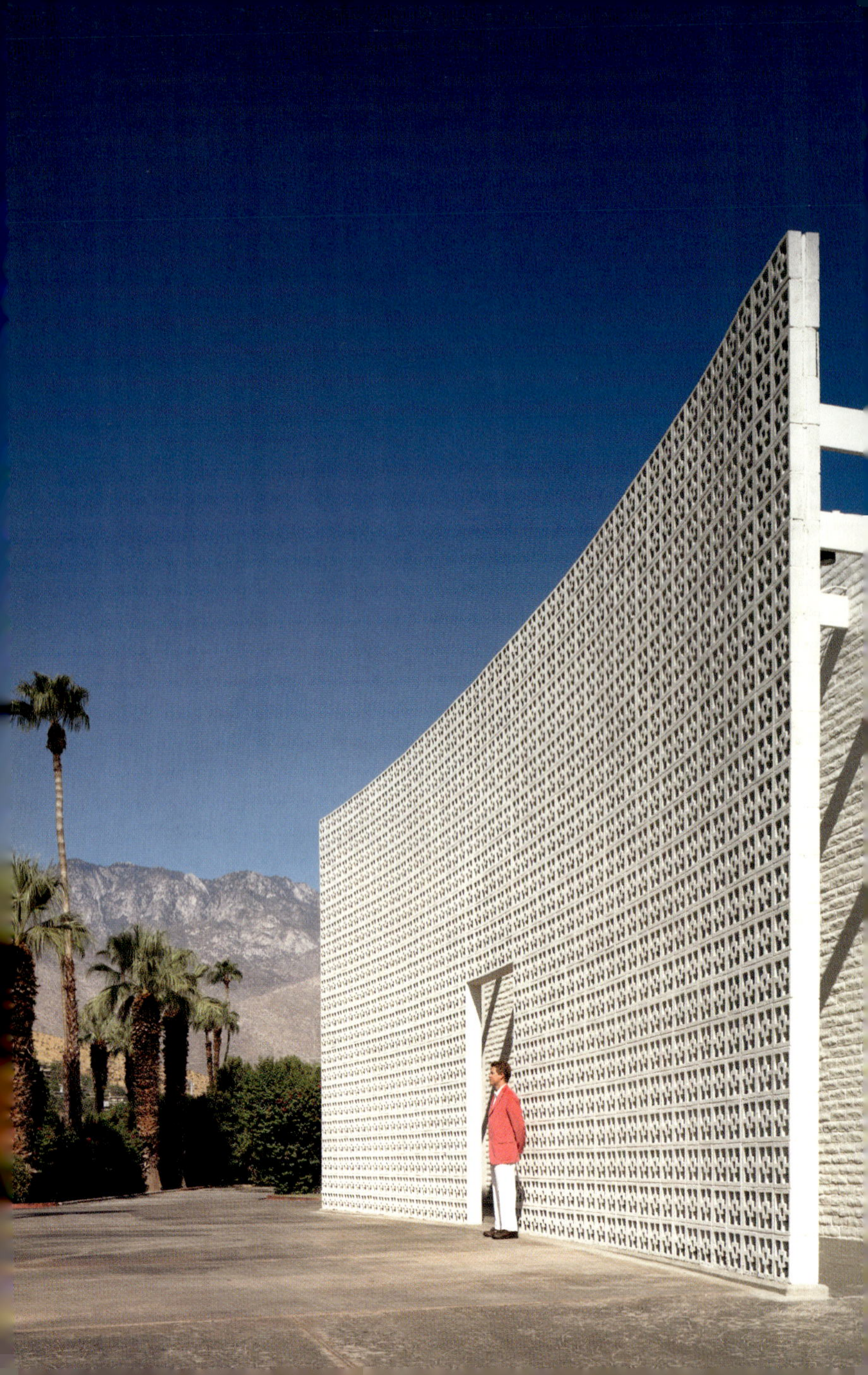

THE PARKER PALM SPRINGS
California's Desert Oasis

Architect: **Jonathan Adler**

Date: 2004
Address: 4200 East Palm Canyon Drive, Palm Springs, CA 92264, United States
Tel.: +1 760 770 5000 Fax: +1 760 324 2188
www.theparkerpalmsprings.com
Photos: © Nikolas Koenig

Location: Desert
Style: Bohemian retro chic
Rooms: 144, 1 two-bedroom house, and 12 villas
Special features: Yacht club spa, 930 m² banquet facility

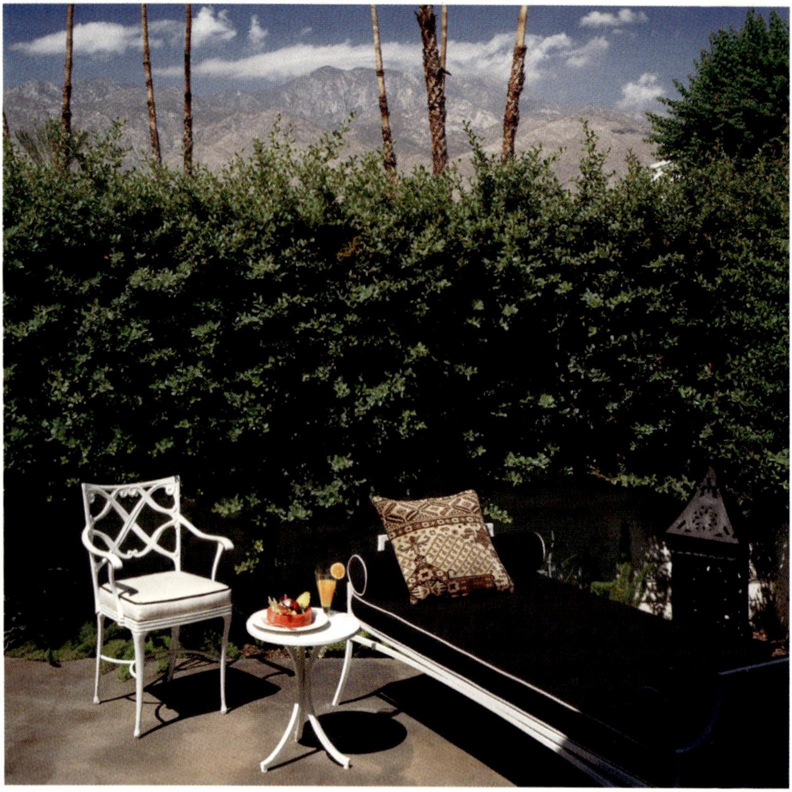

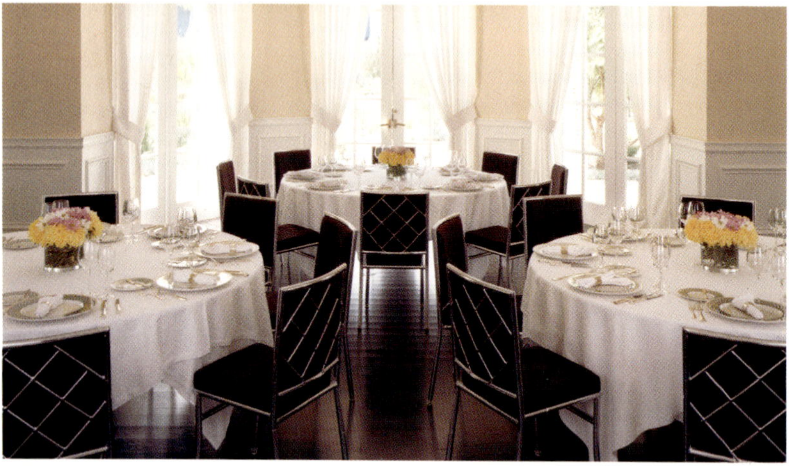

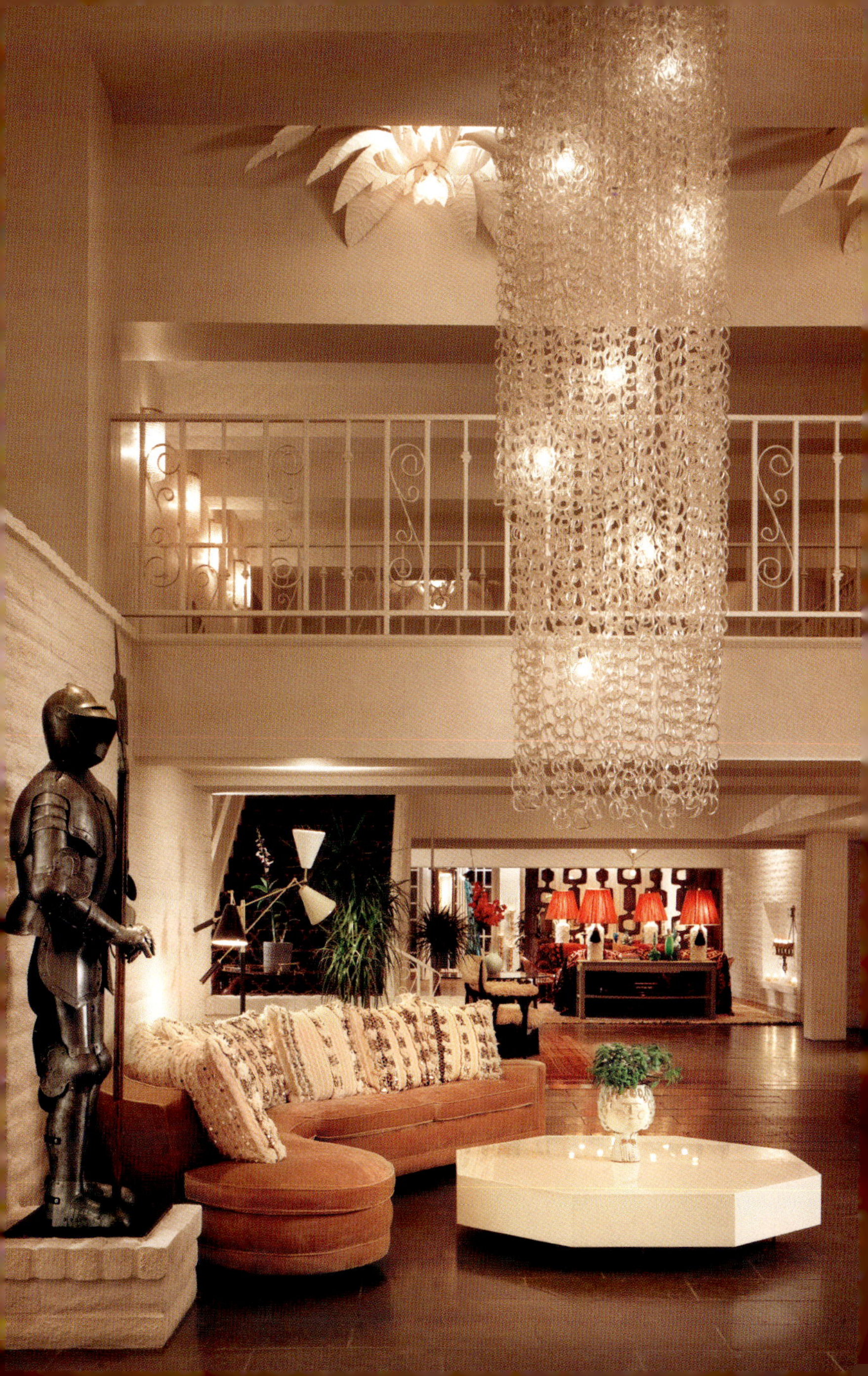

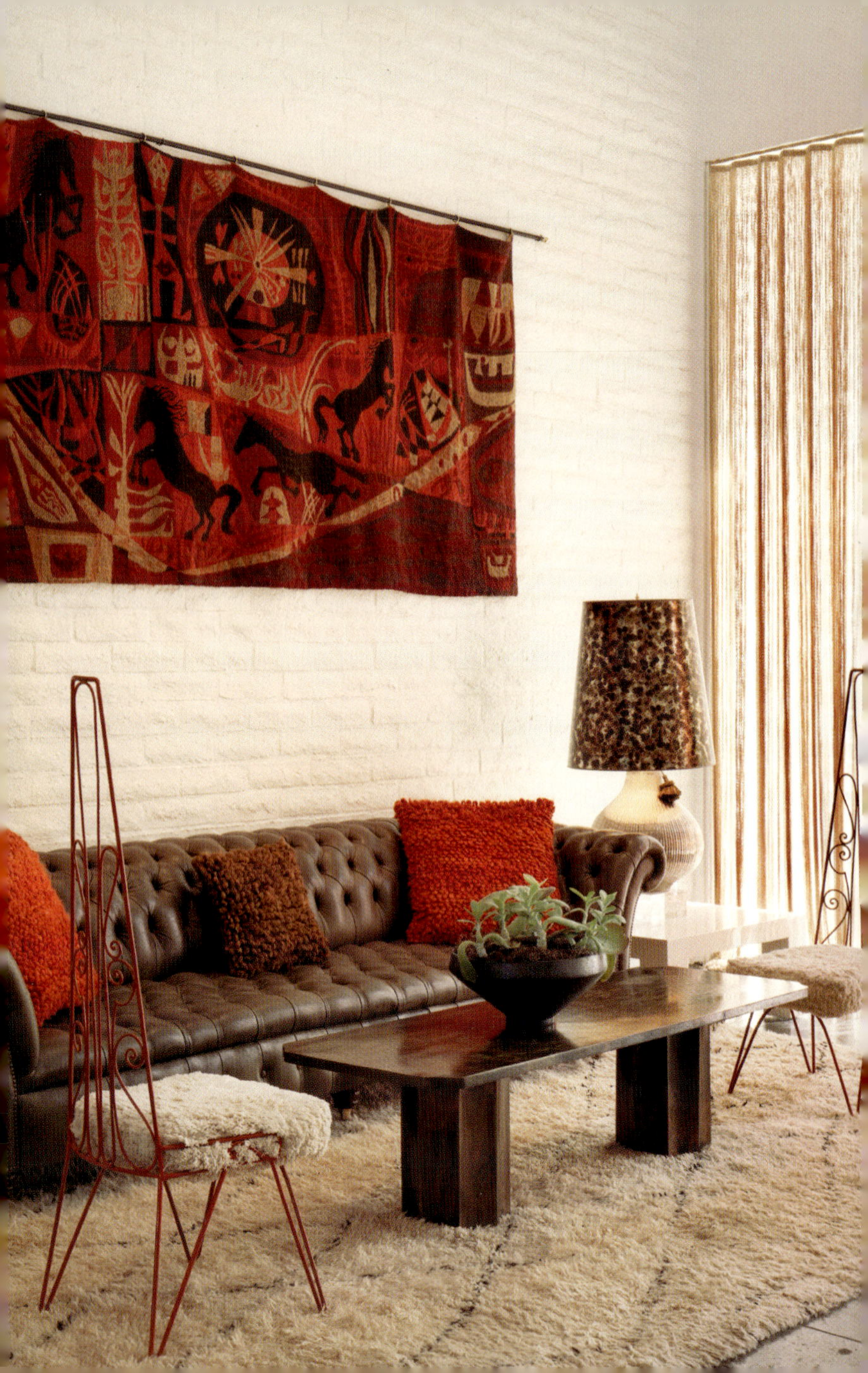

219

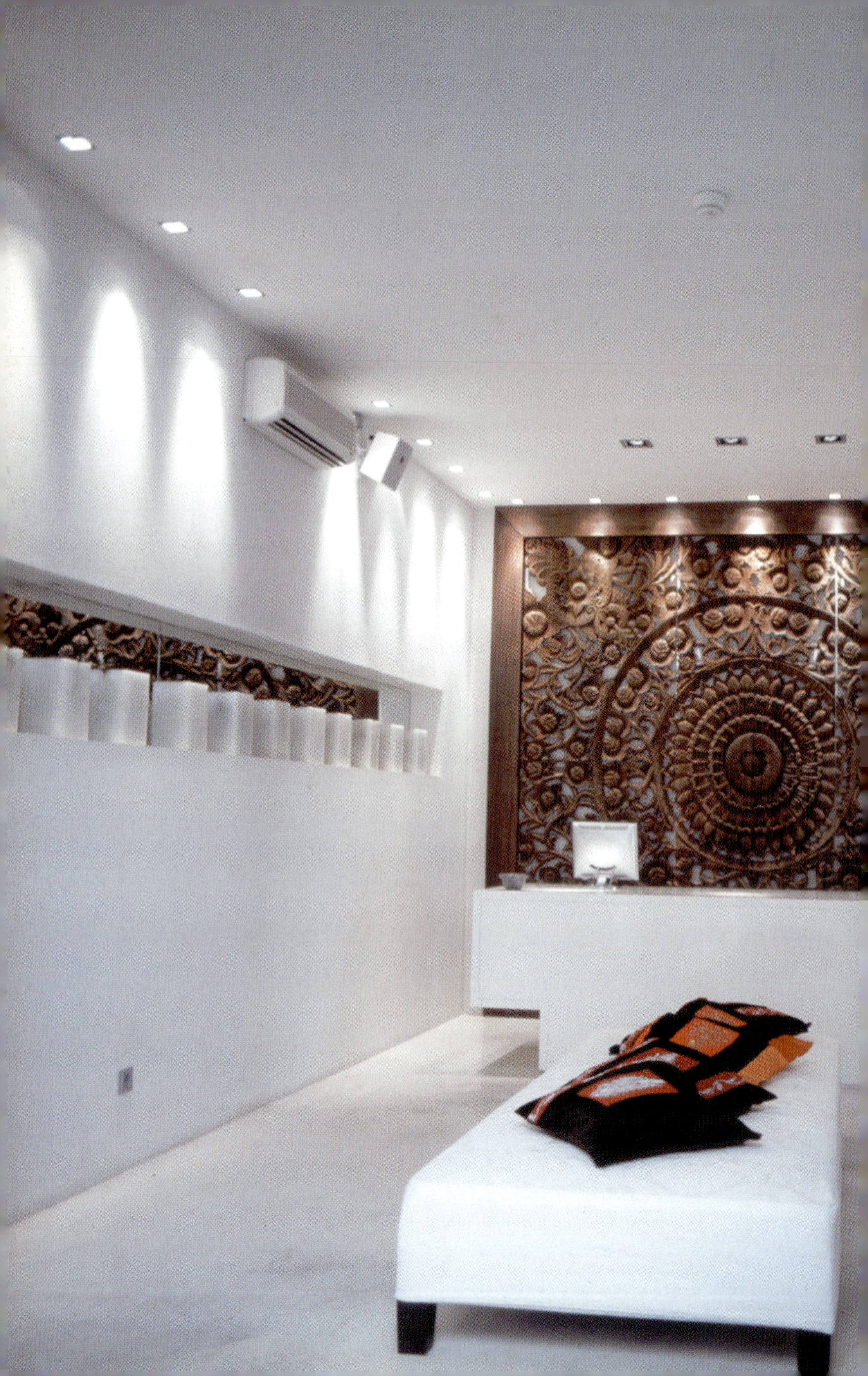

PURO
Urban Oasis

Architect: **Álvaro Planchuelo**

Date: 2004
Address: Monte Negro 12, 07012 Palma de Mallorca, Spain
Tel.: +34 971 425 450 Fax: +34 971 425 451
www.purohotel.com
Photos: © Puro

Location: Urban
Style: Exotic contemporary
Rooms: 26
Special features: Spa, two swimming pools, poolside cabanas, tennis courts

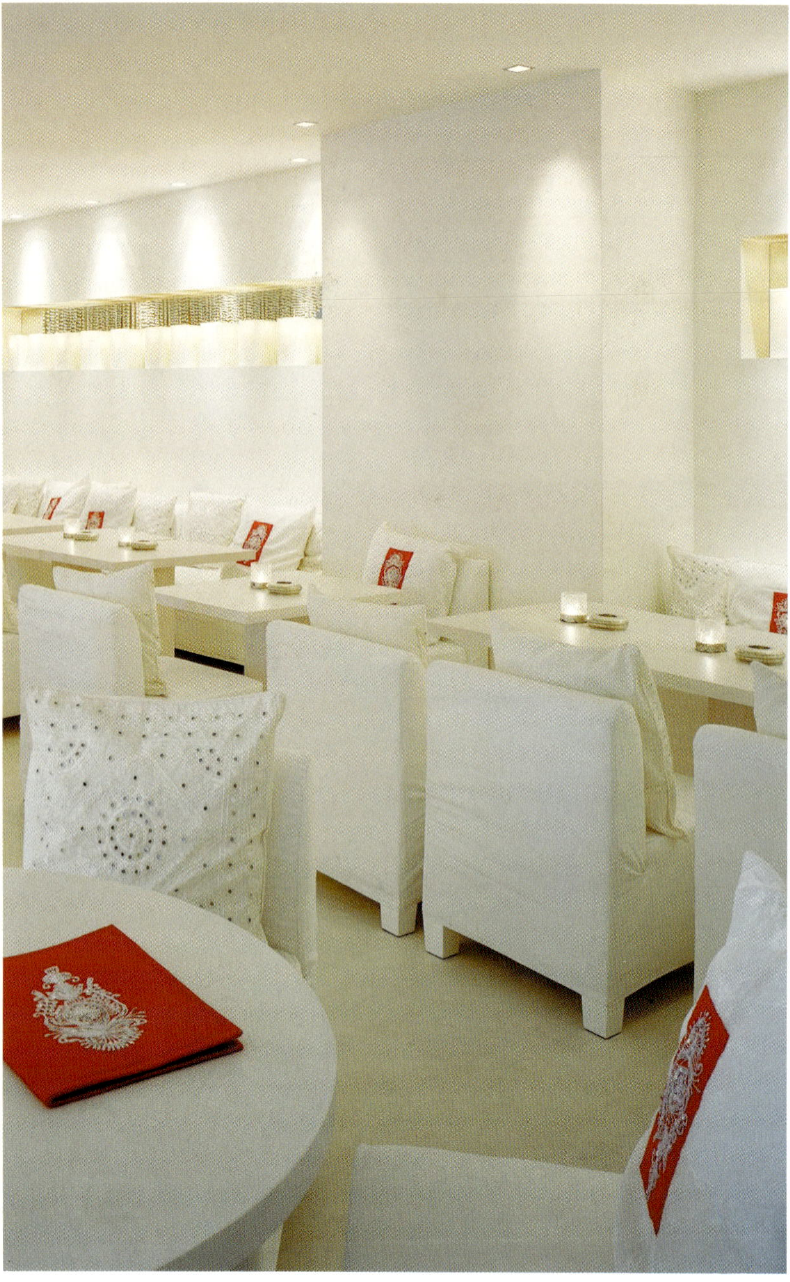

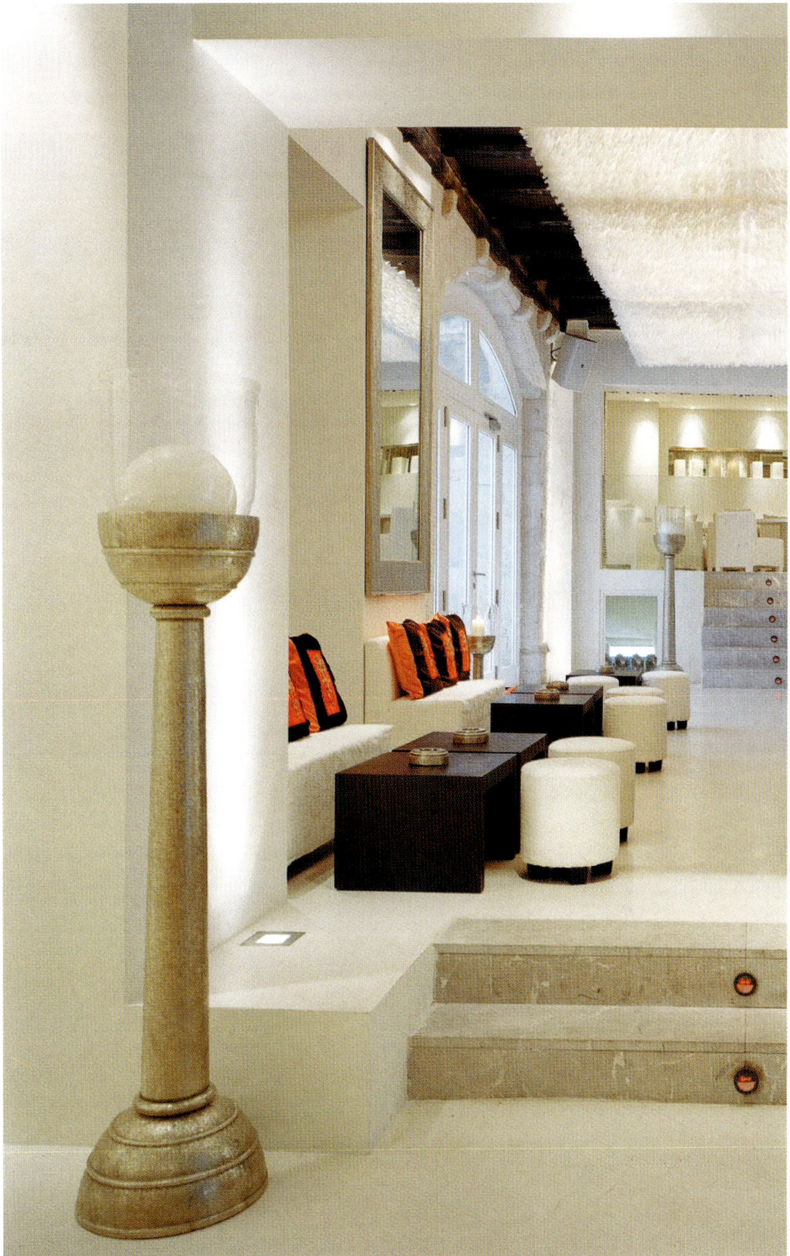

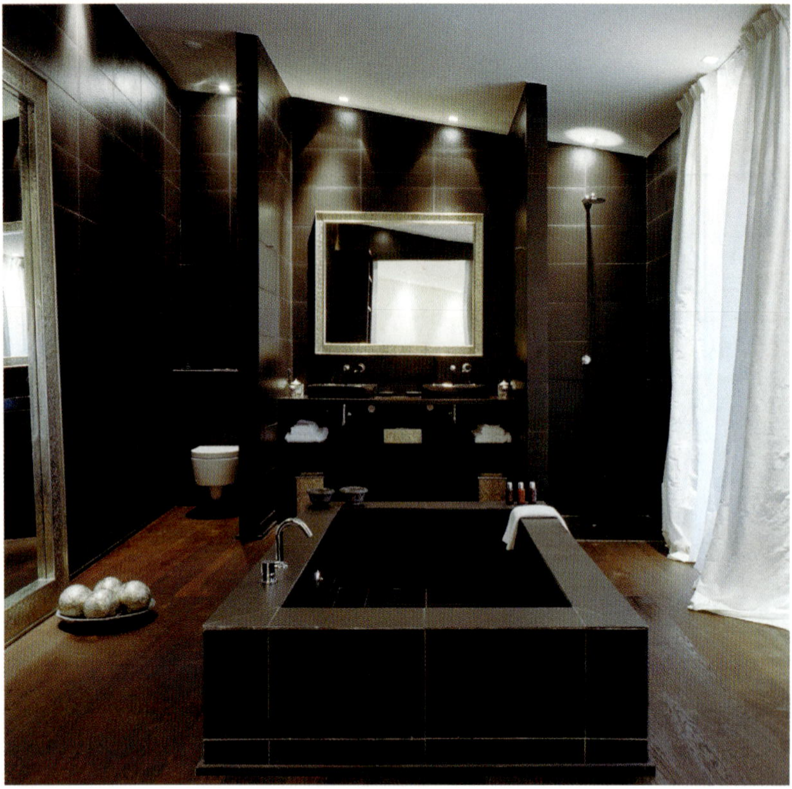

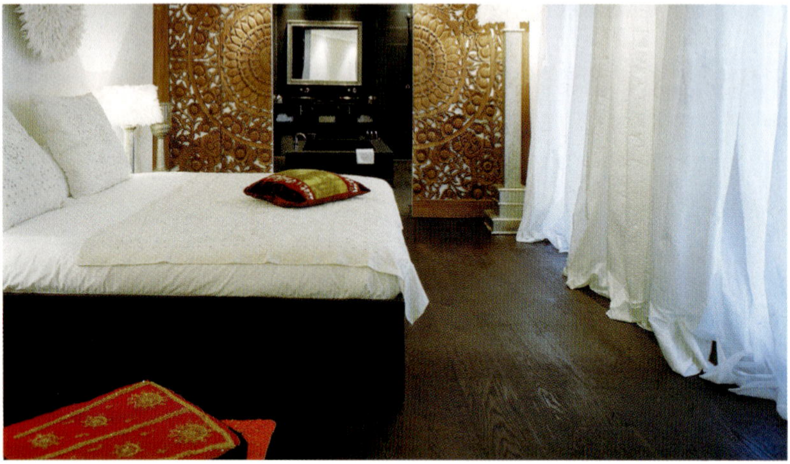

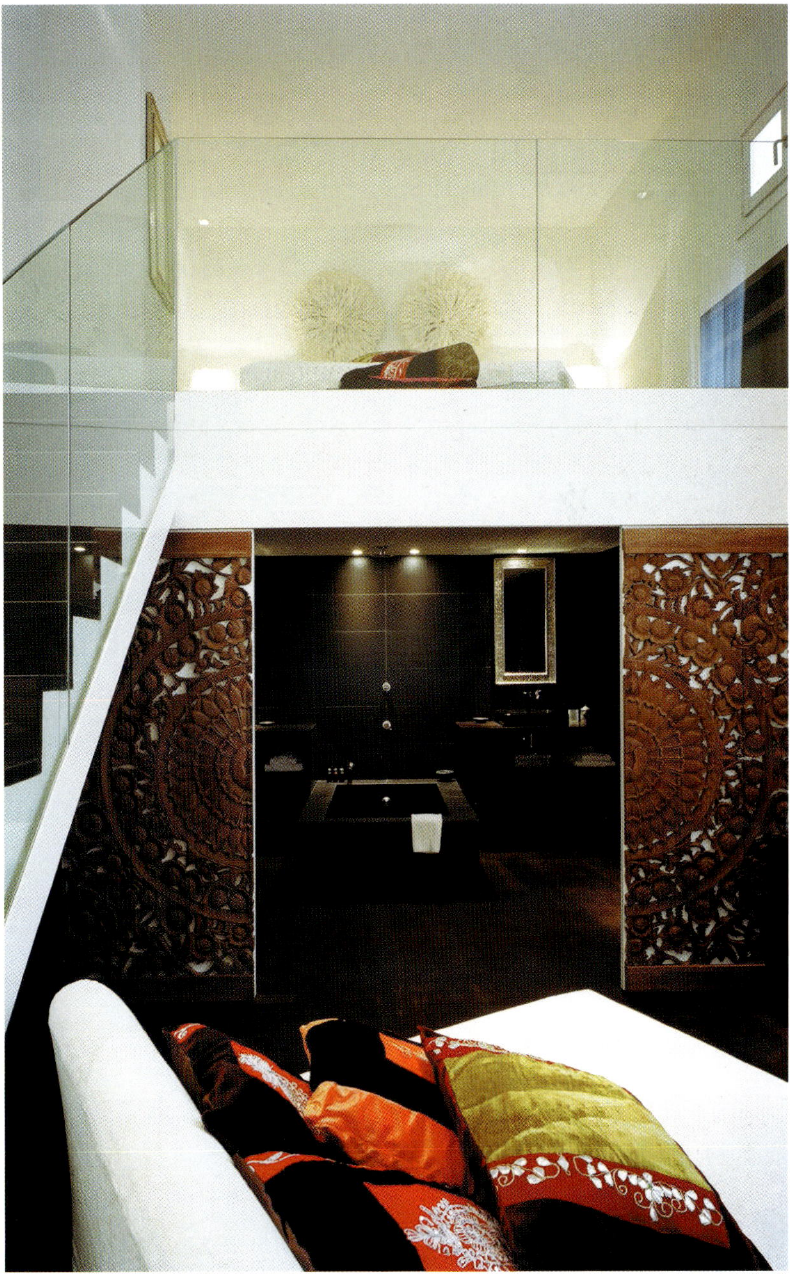

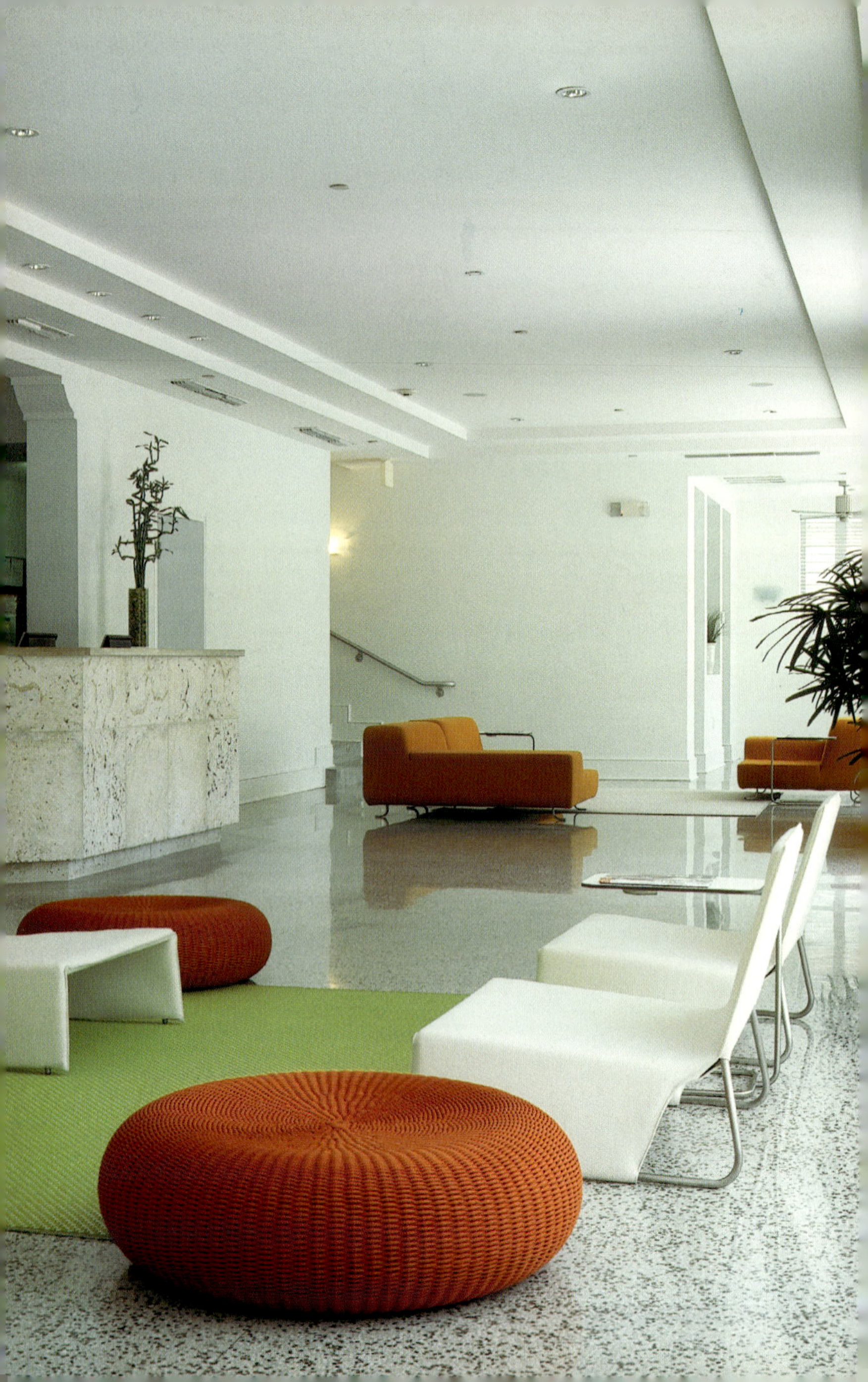

THE DORSET HOTEL
The Finest Boutique Hotel in the Heart of the Art Deco District

Architect: **Günther Domenig**

Date: 2004
Address: 1720 Collins Avenue, Miami Beach, FL 33139, United States
Tel.: +1 305 938 6000 Fax: +1 305 938 6001
www.dorsethotelmiamibeach.com
Photos: © Pep Escoda

Location: Beach
Style: Contemporary Art Deco
Rooms: 52
Special features: H_2O bath products, rooftop pool, solarium

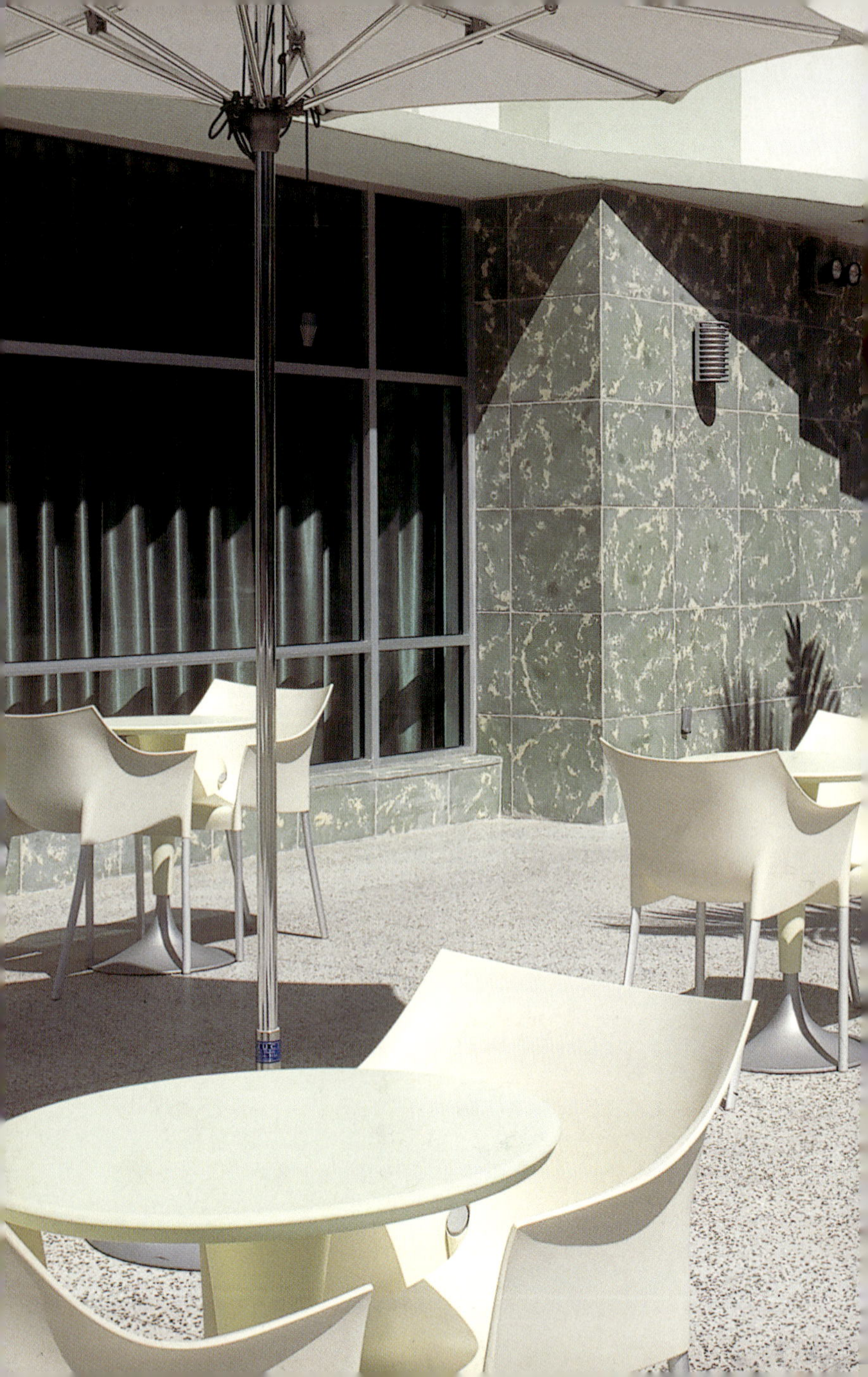

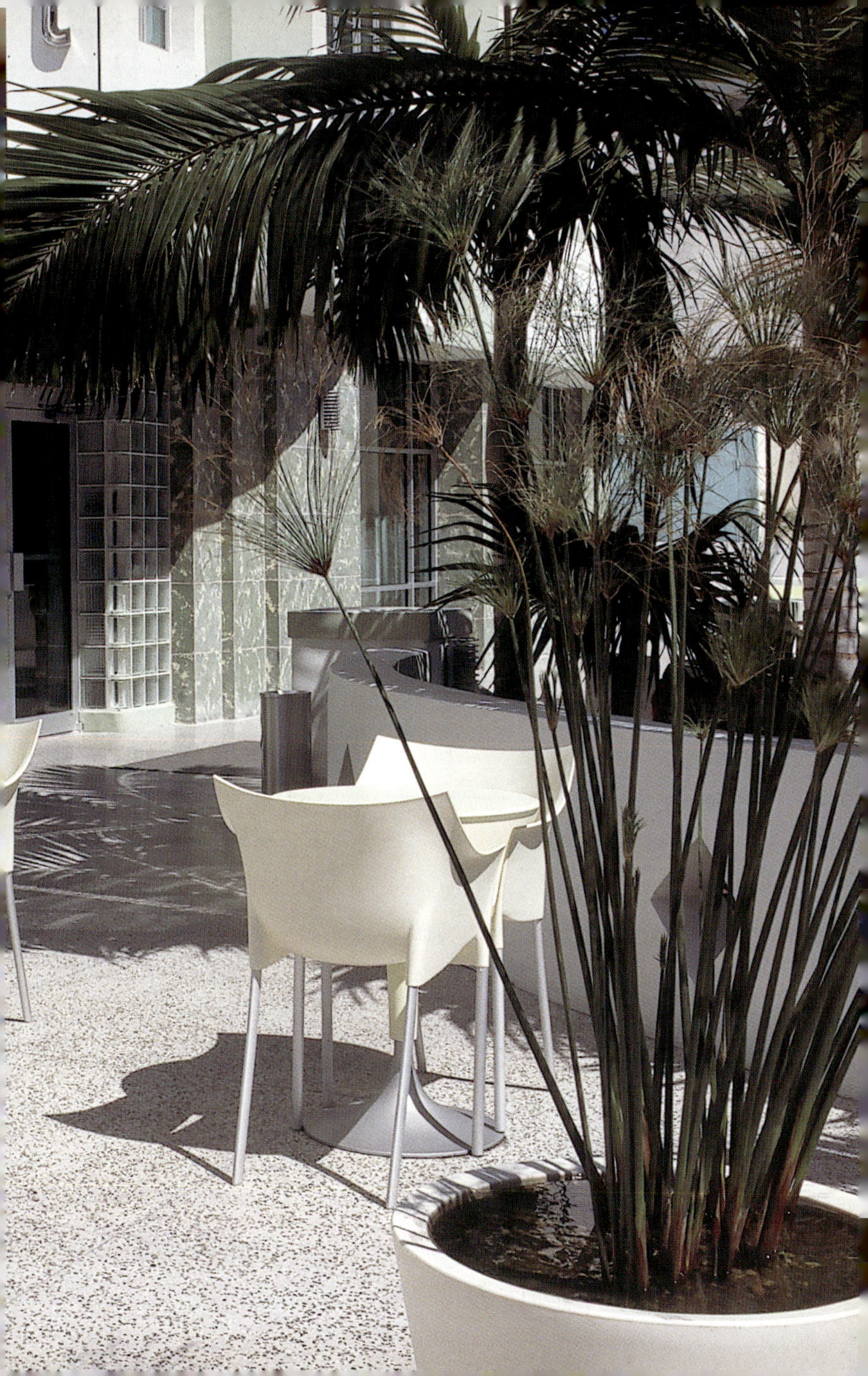

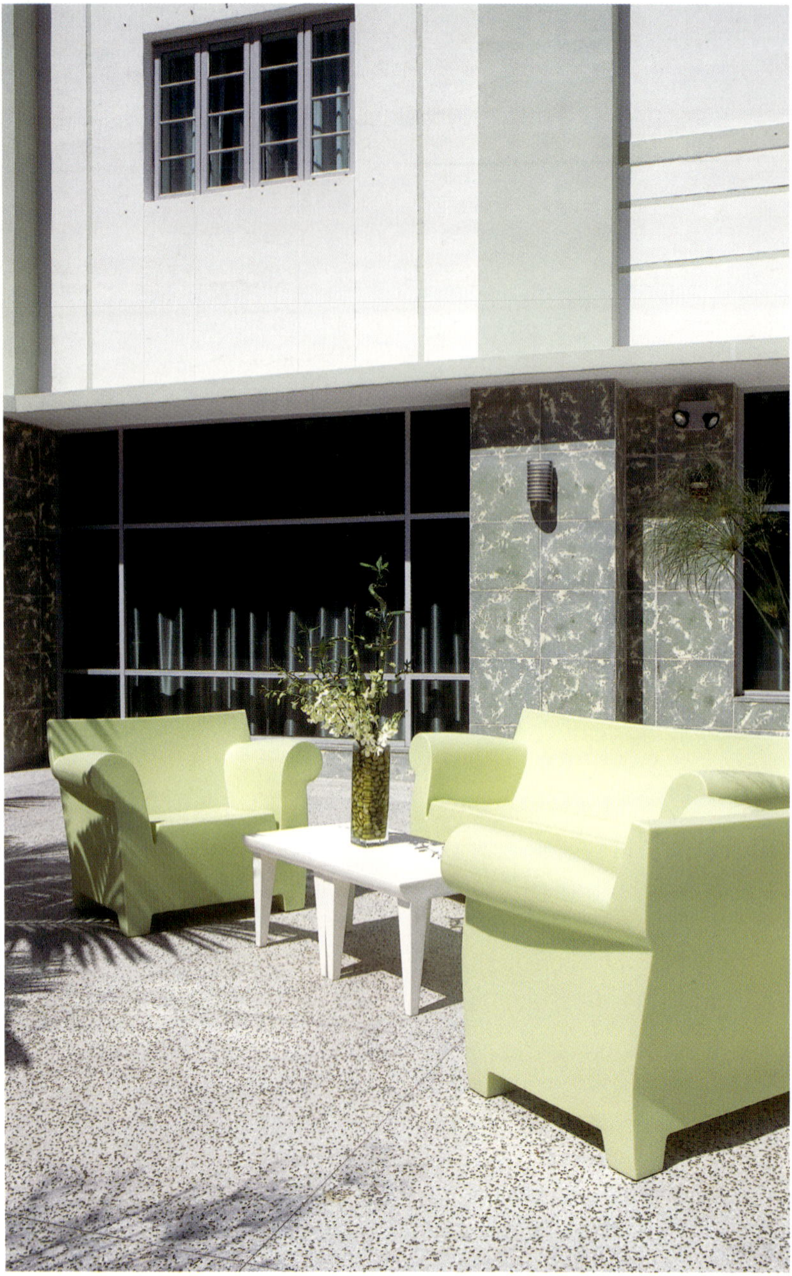

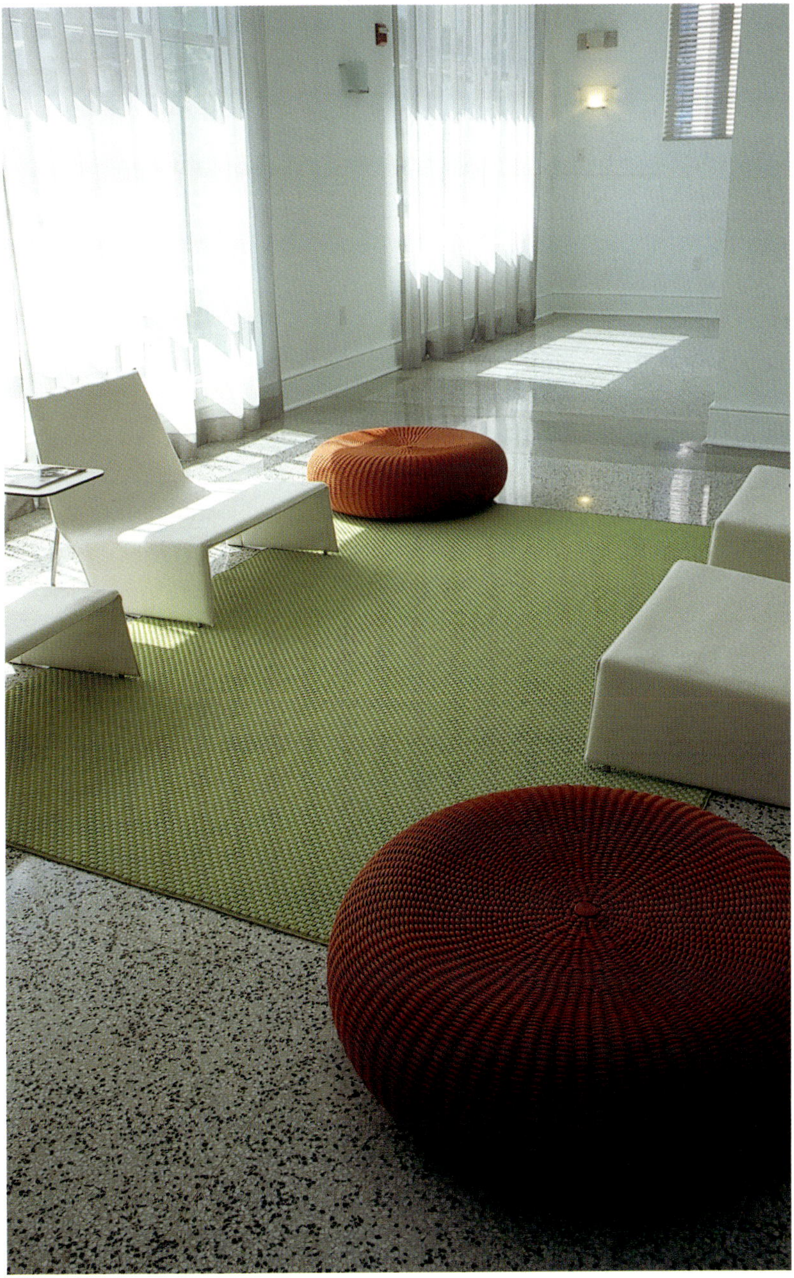

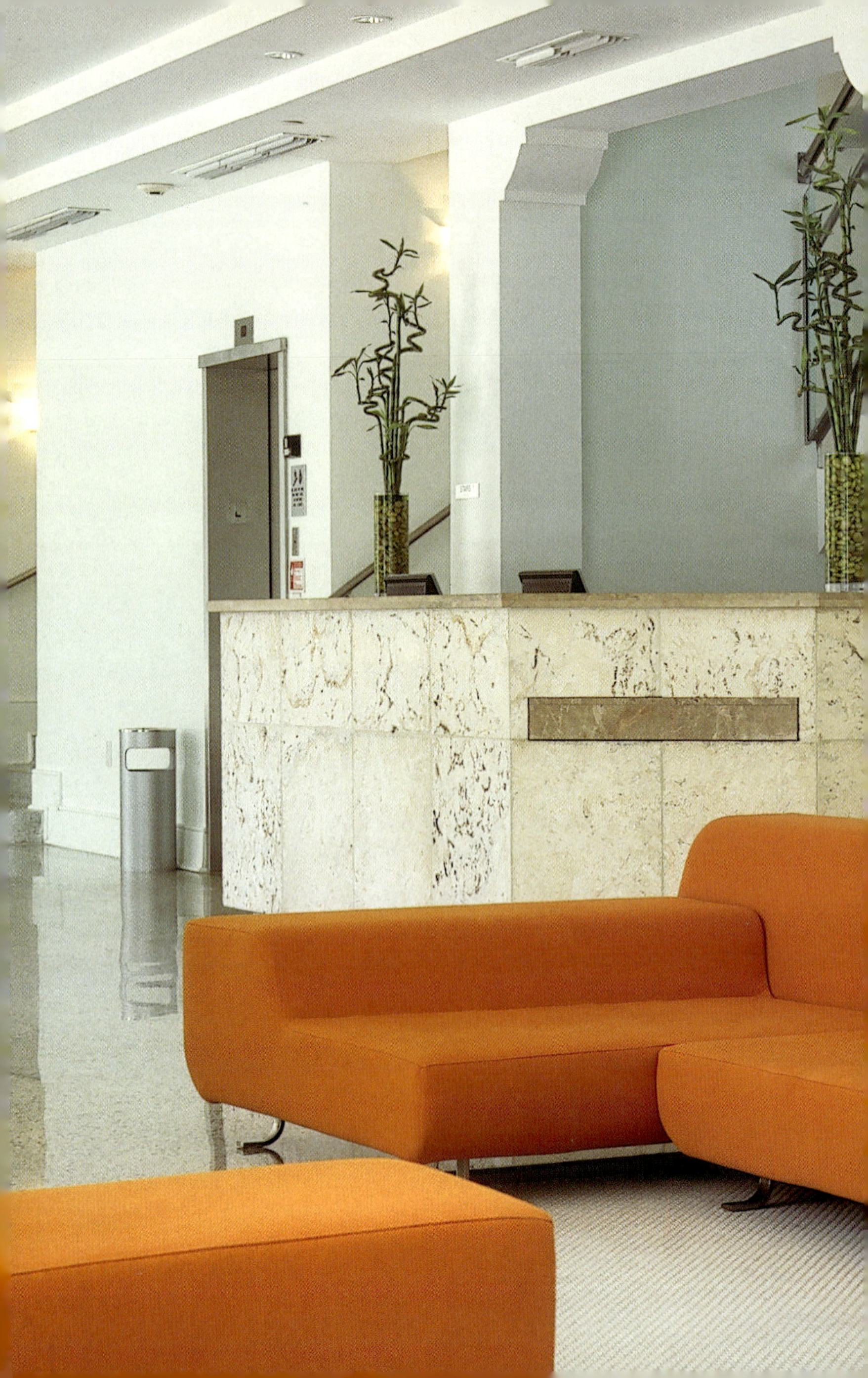

OFFICE

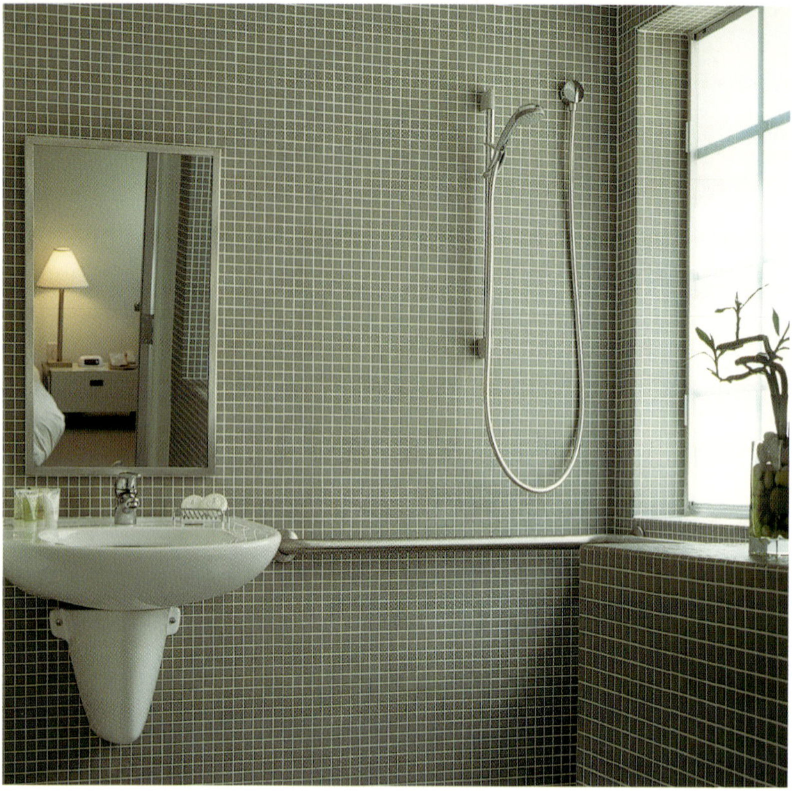

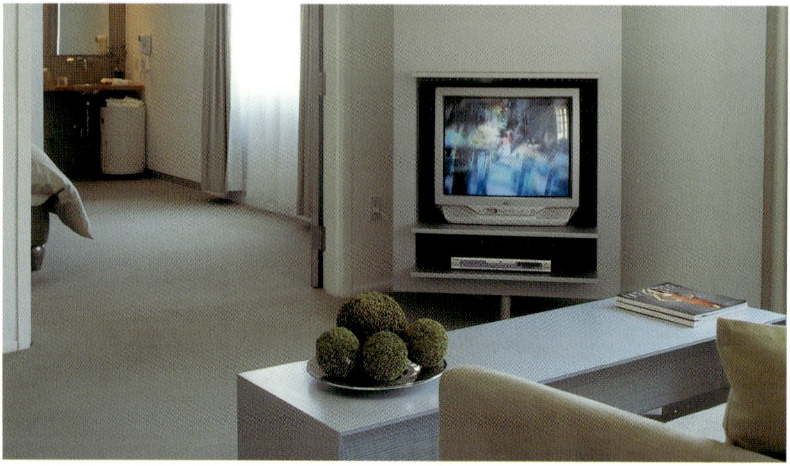

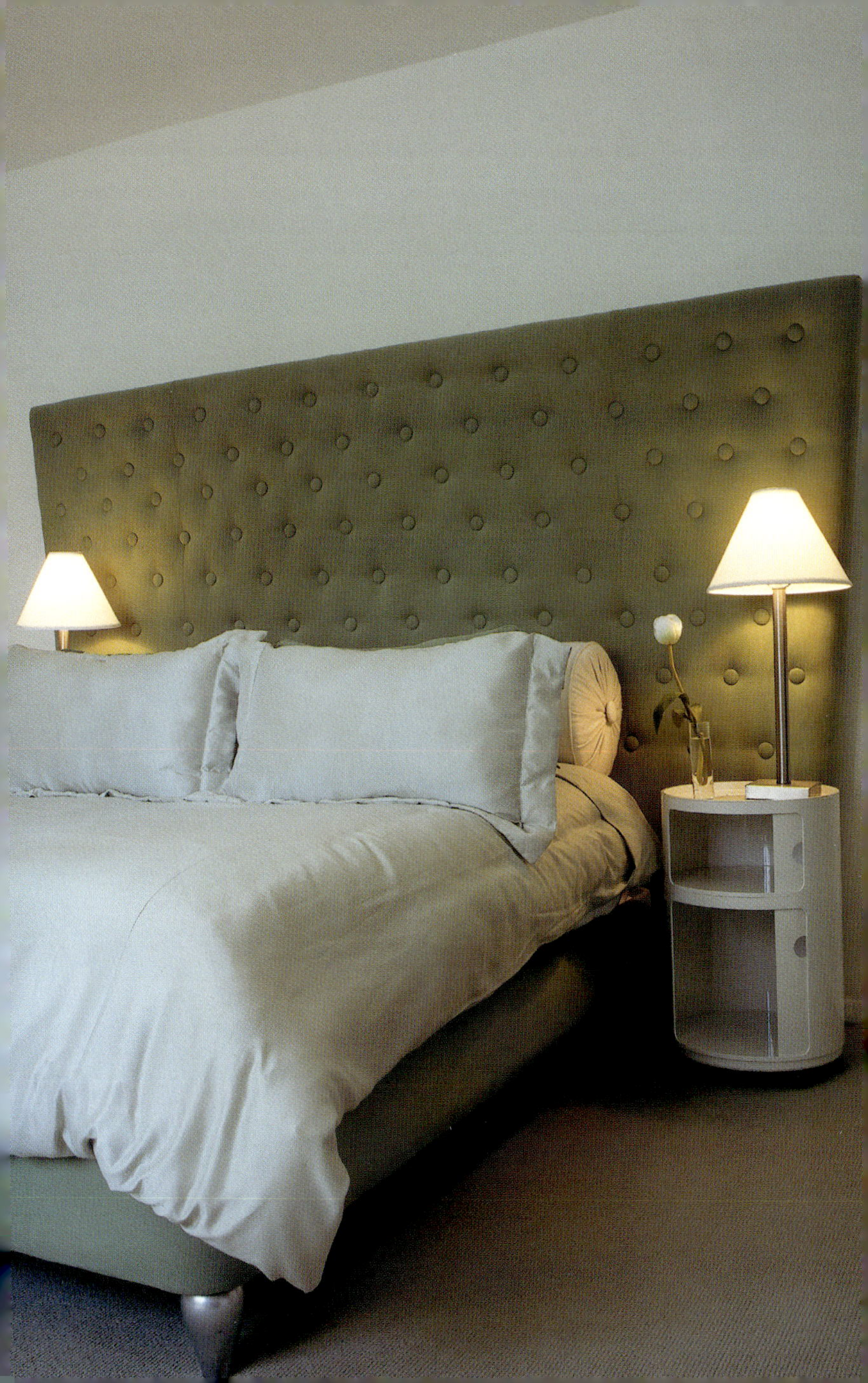

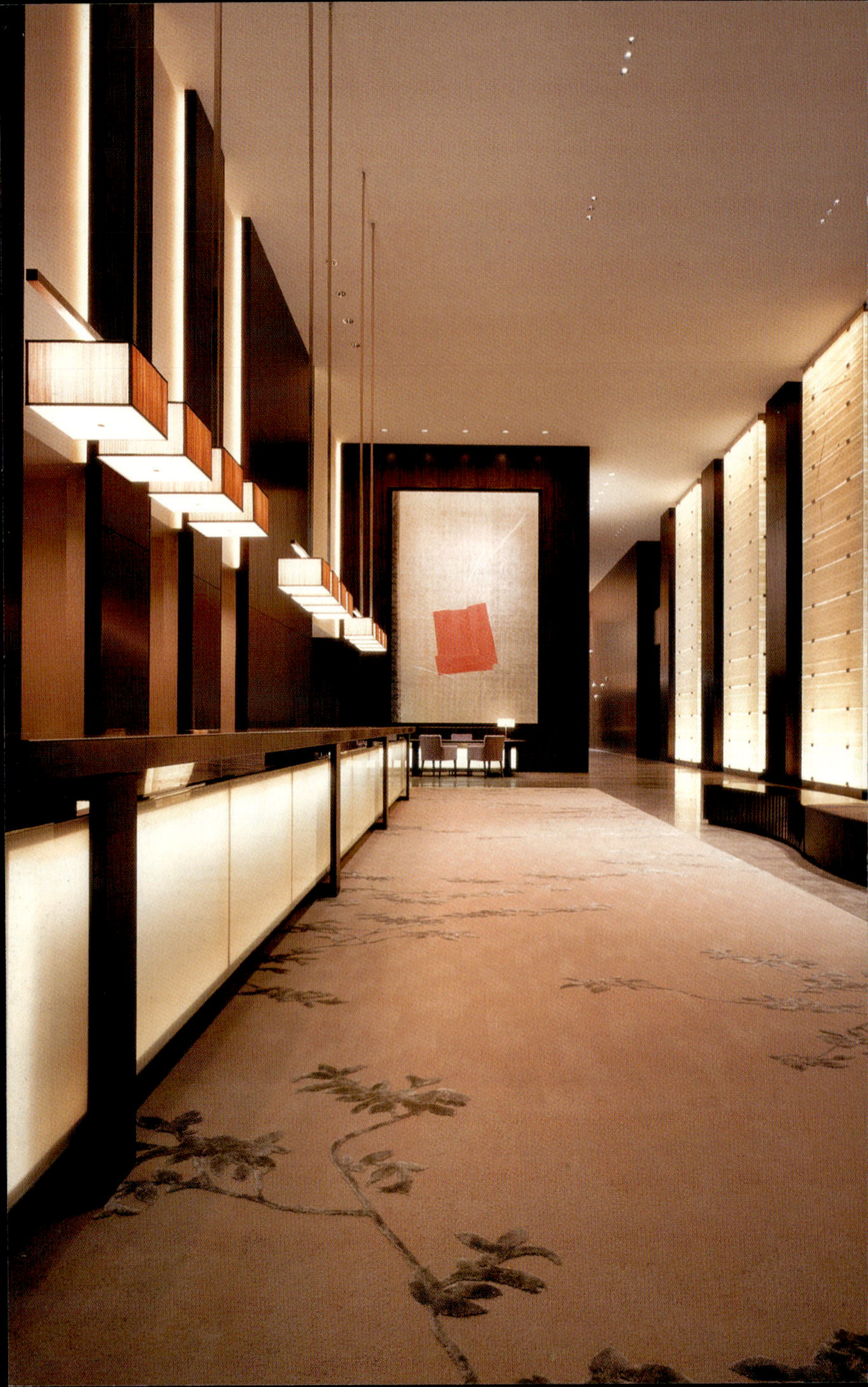

CONRAD TOKYO
Experience the Luxury

Architects: **Takenaka Corporation**
Interior designers: **GA Design International**

Date: 2005
Address: 1-9-1 Higashi-Shinbashi, Minato-ku, Tokyo 105 7337, Japan
Tel.: +81 3 6388 8000 Fax: +81 3 6388 8001
www.conradtokyo.co.jp
Photos: © Conrad Tokyo

Location: Urban
Style: Japanese modern luxury
Rooms: 290
Special features: Minimum 48 m² rooms with 37-inch plasma TV, satellite channels and wireless phone

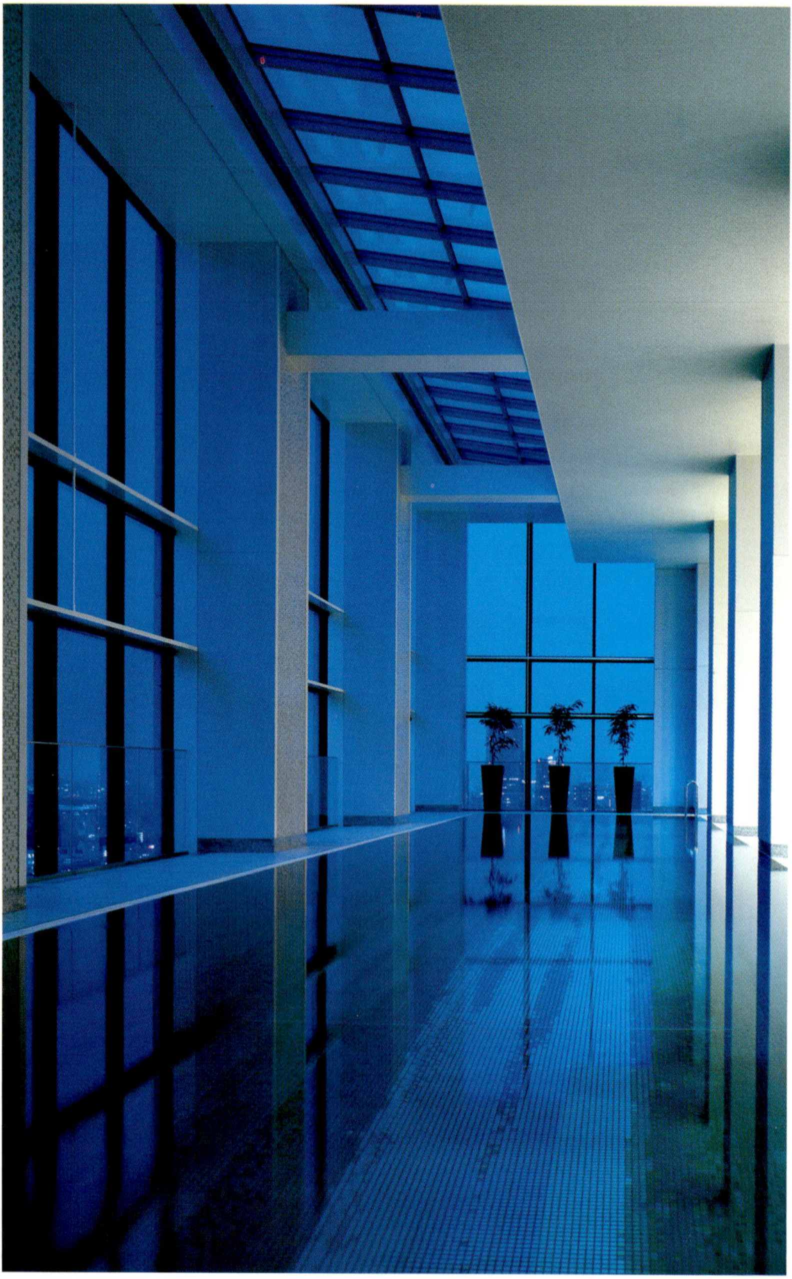

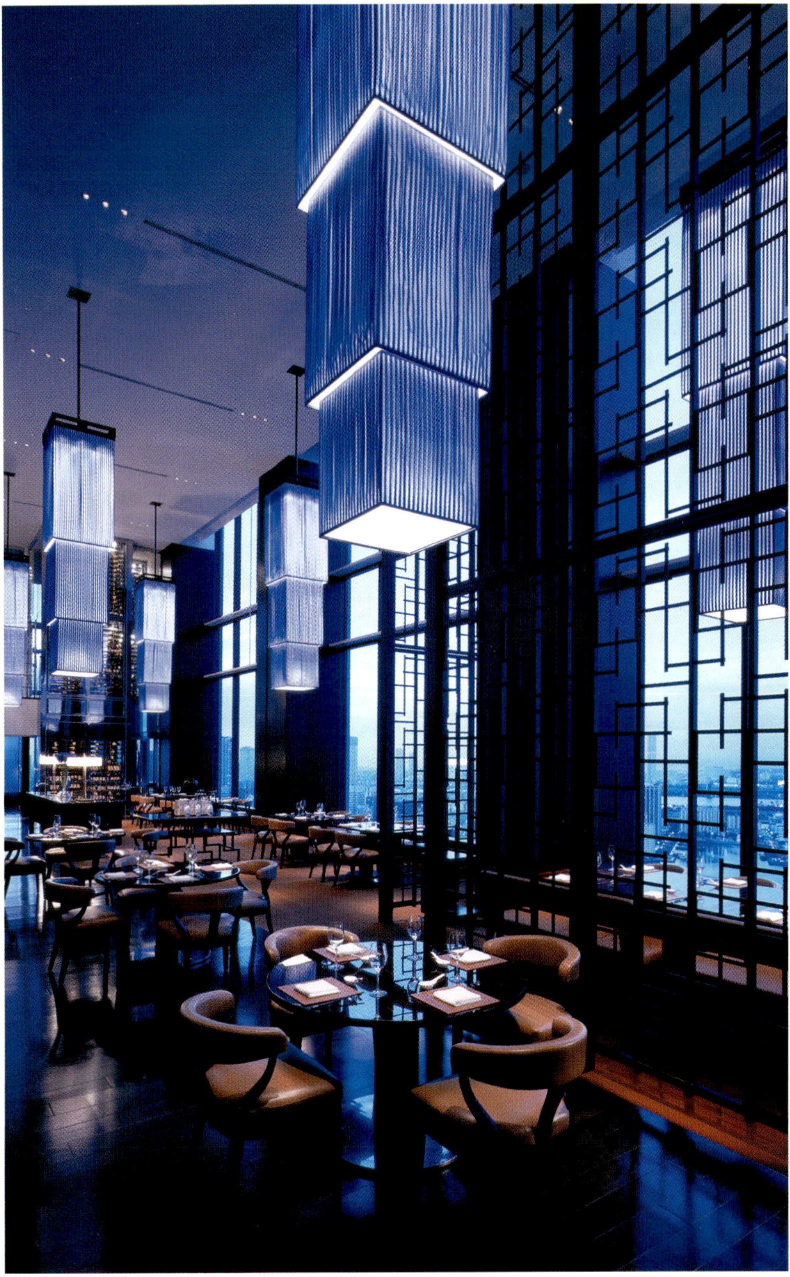

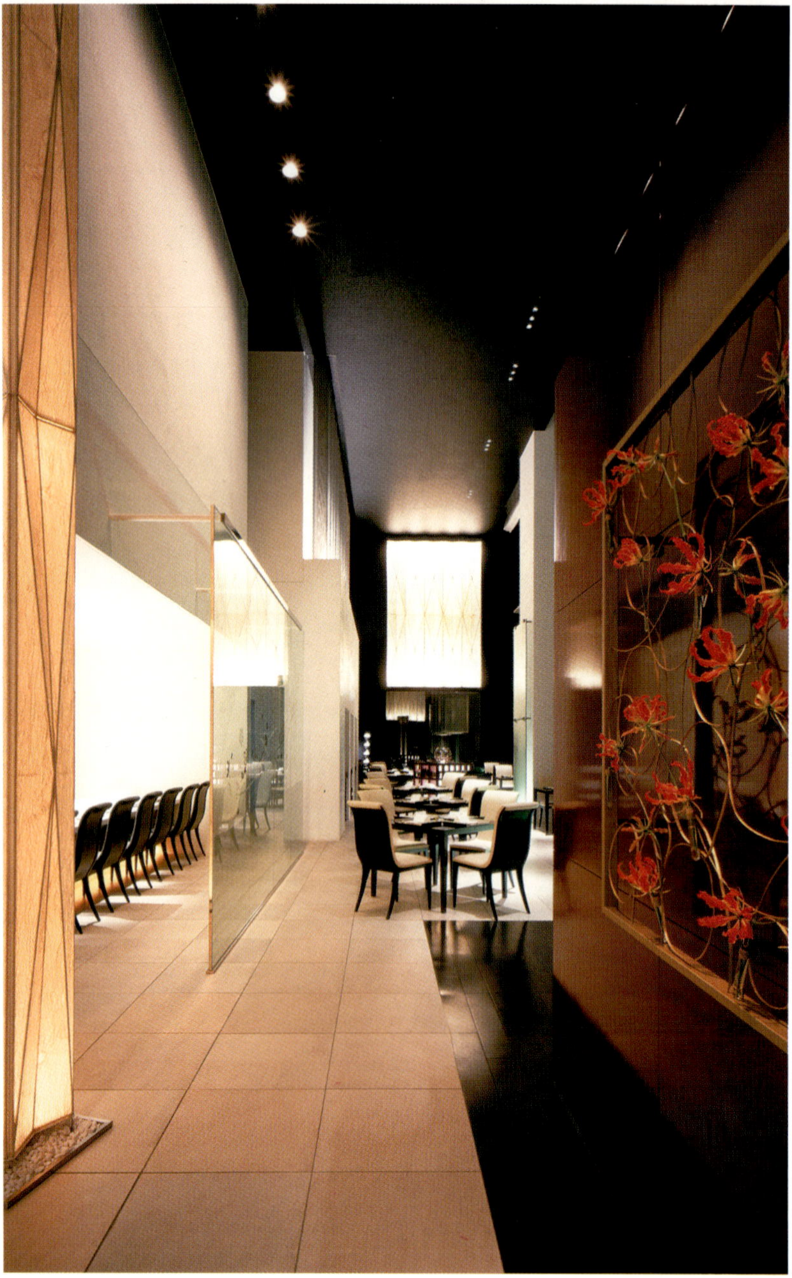

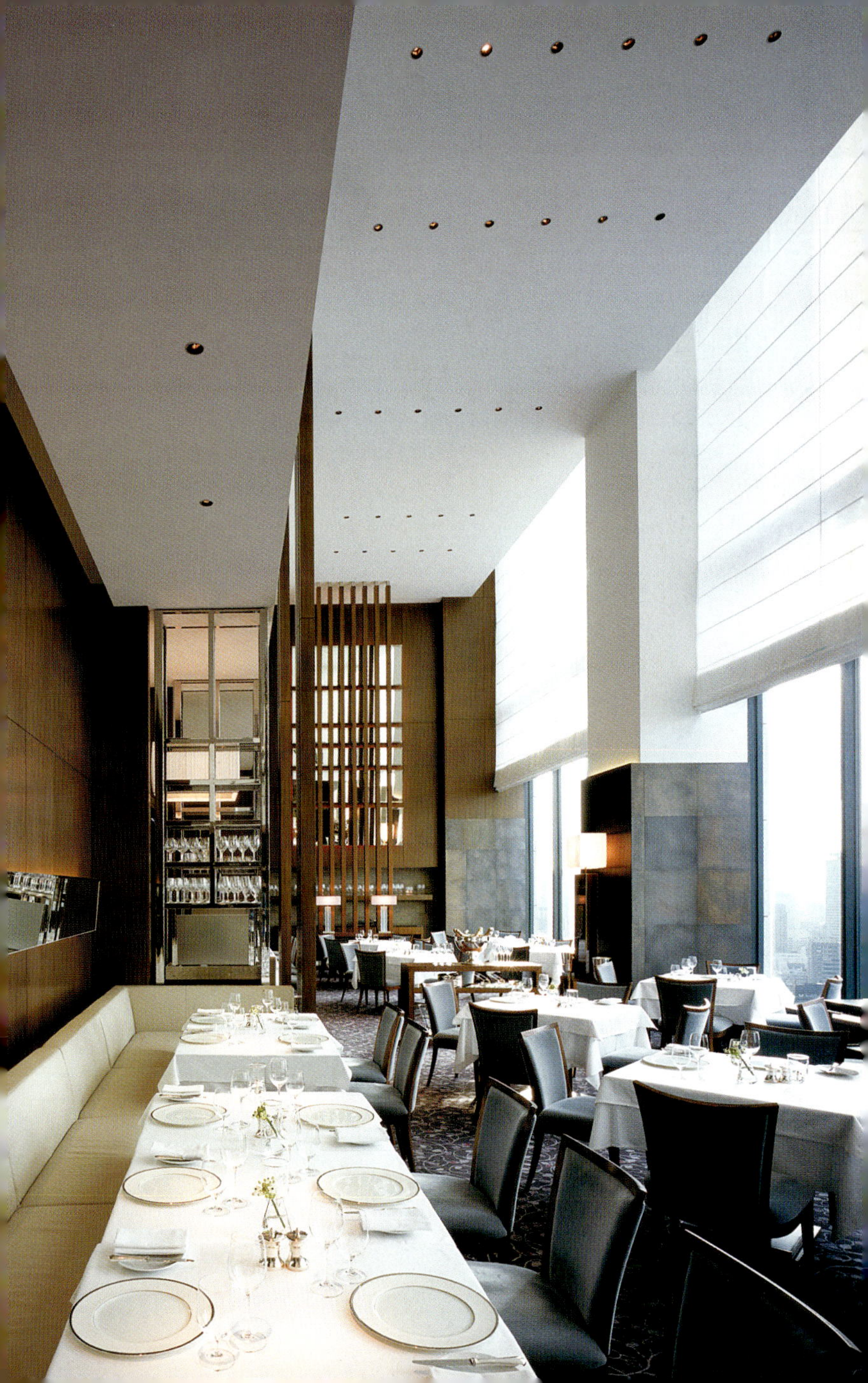

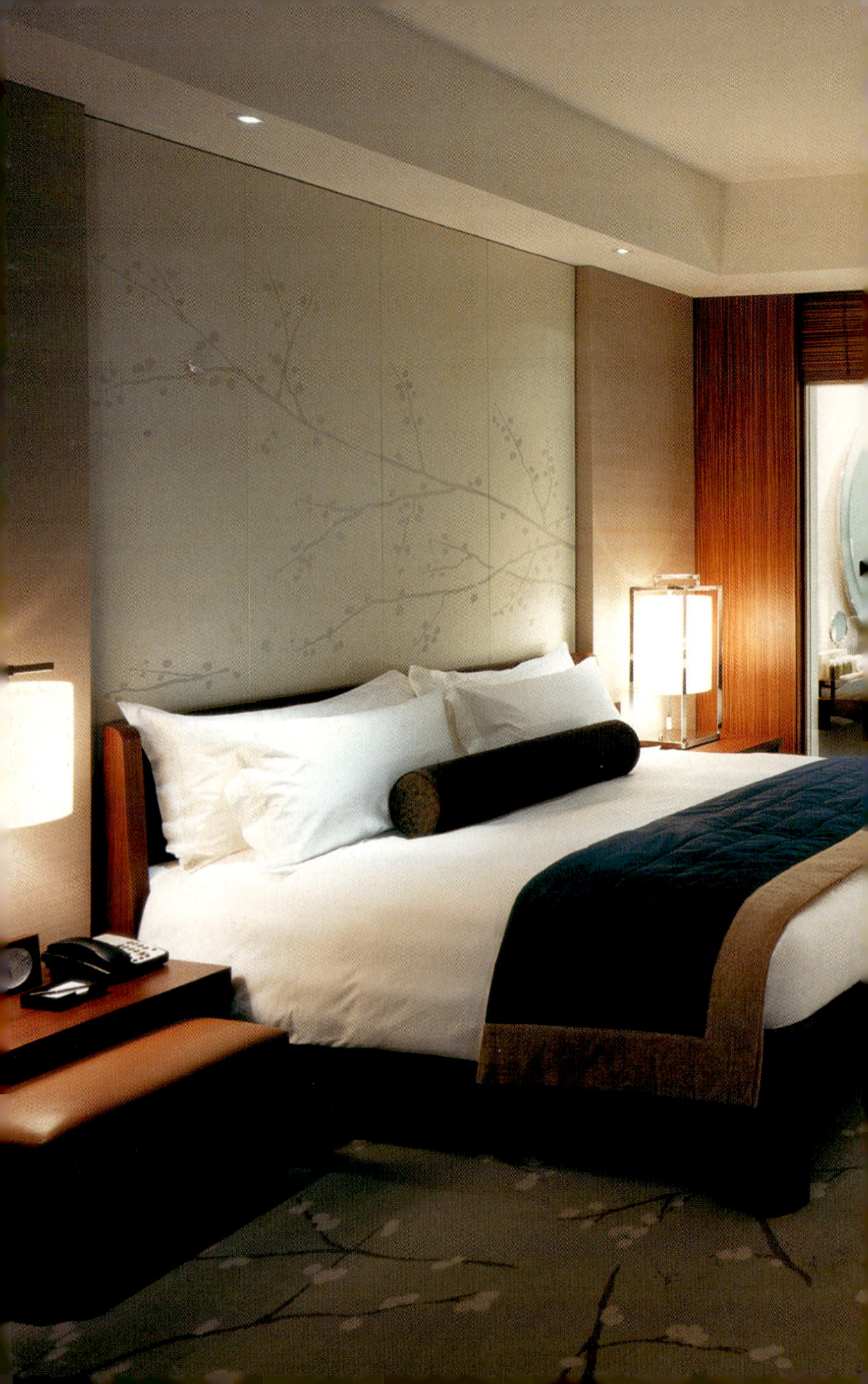

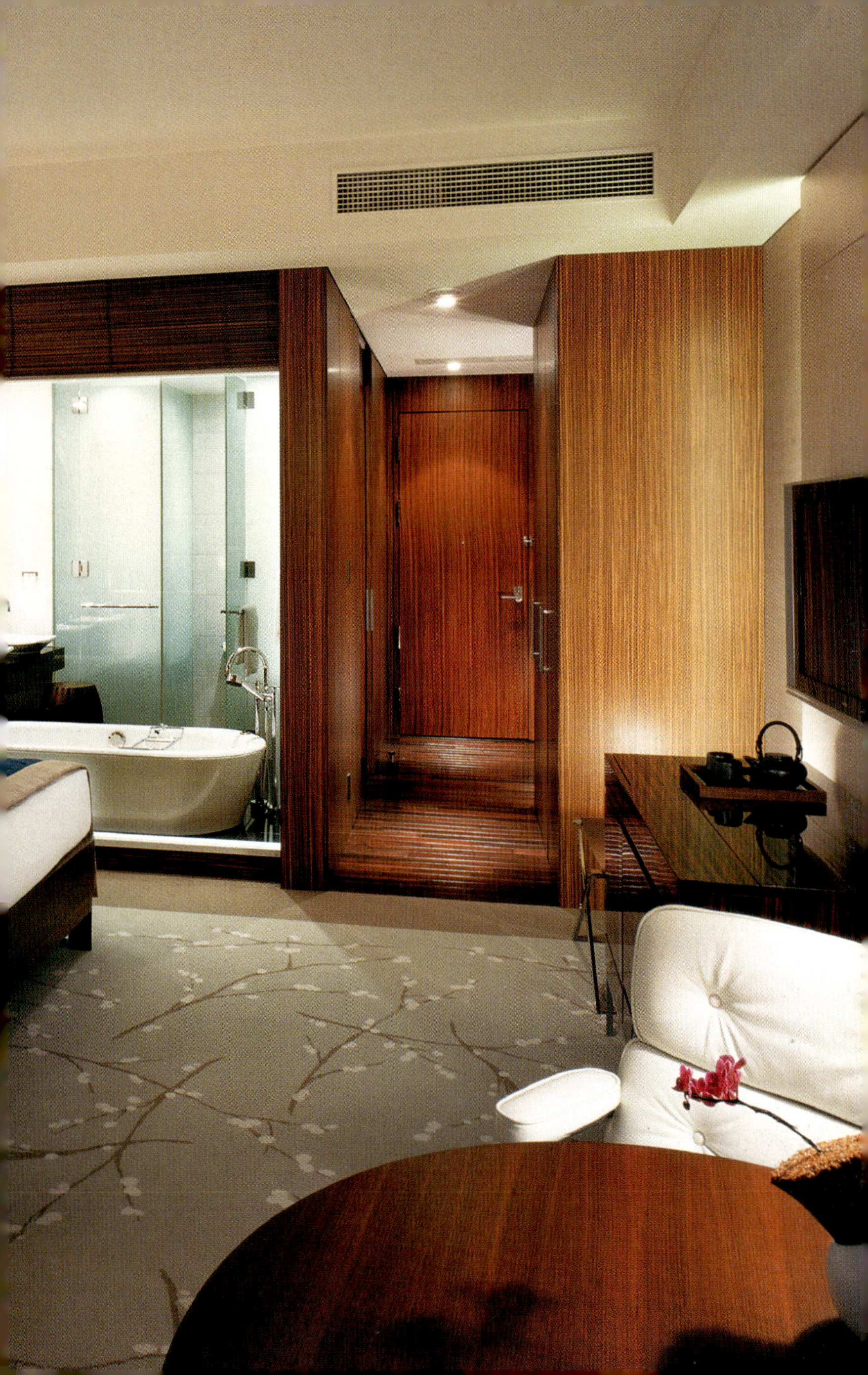

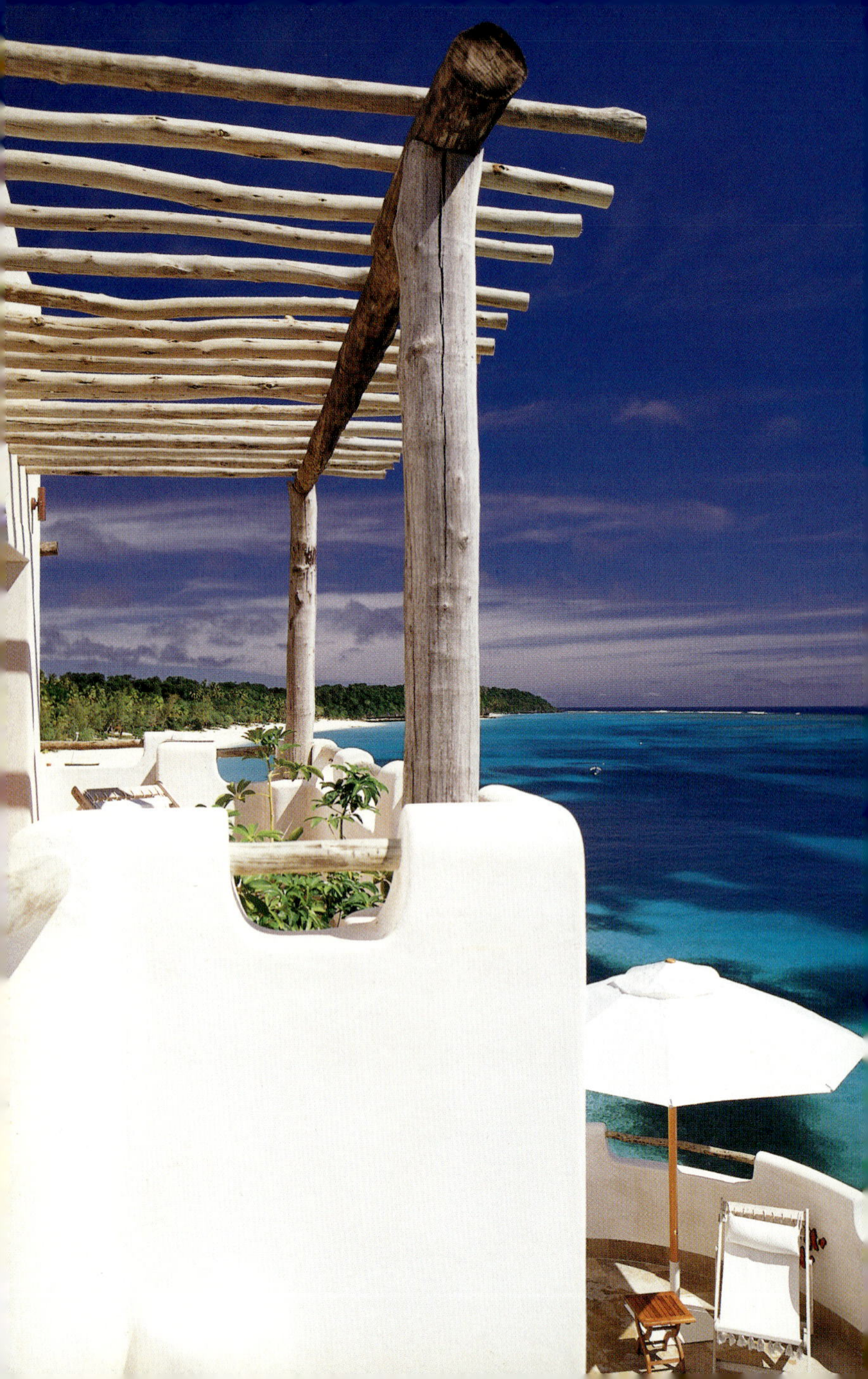

VATULELE RESORT
Fiji's Leading Resort

Architects: **Doug Nelson & Martin Livingston**
Creator: **Henry Crawford**

Date: 1990
Address: Vatulele Resort, Vatulele Island, Fiji Islands
Tel.: +44 13 7246 9818 Fax: +44 13 7247 0057
www.vatulele.com
Photos: © Earl Carter & Peter Carrette/Vatulele Resort

Location: Beach
Style: Cool casual Pacific
Rooms: 19 "bures" or villas, 1 Grand Honeymoon Bure and The Point Villa
Special features: All inclusive resort, scuba diving, wedding celebrations, no TV's, newspapers, telephones, money transactions or shoes

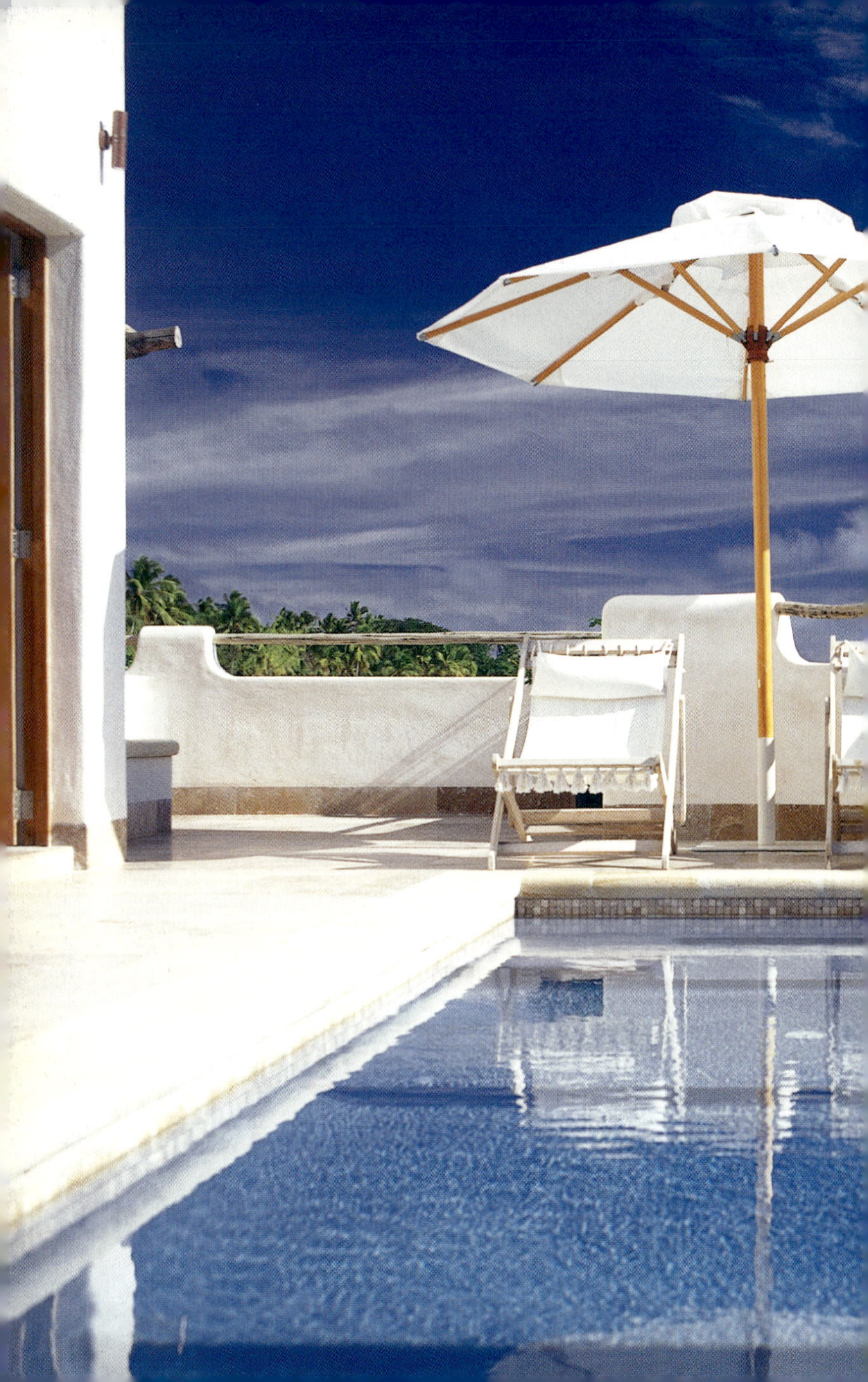

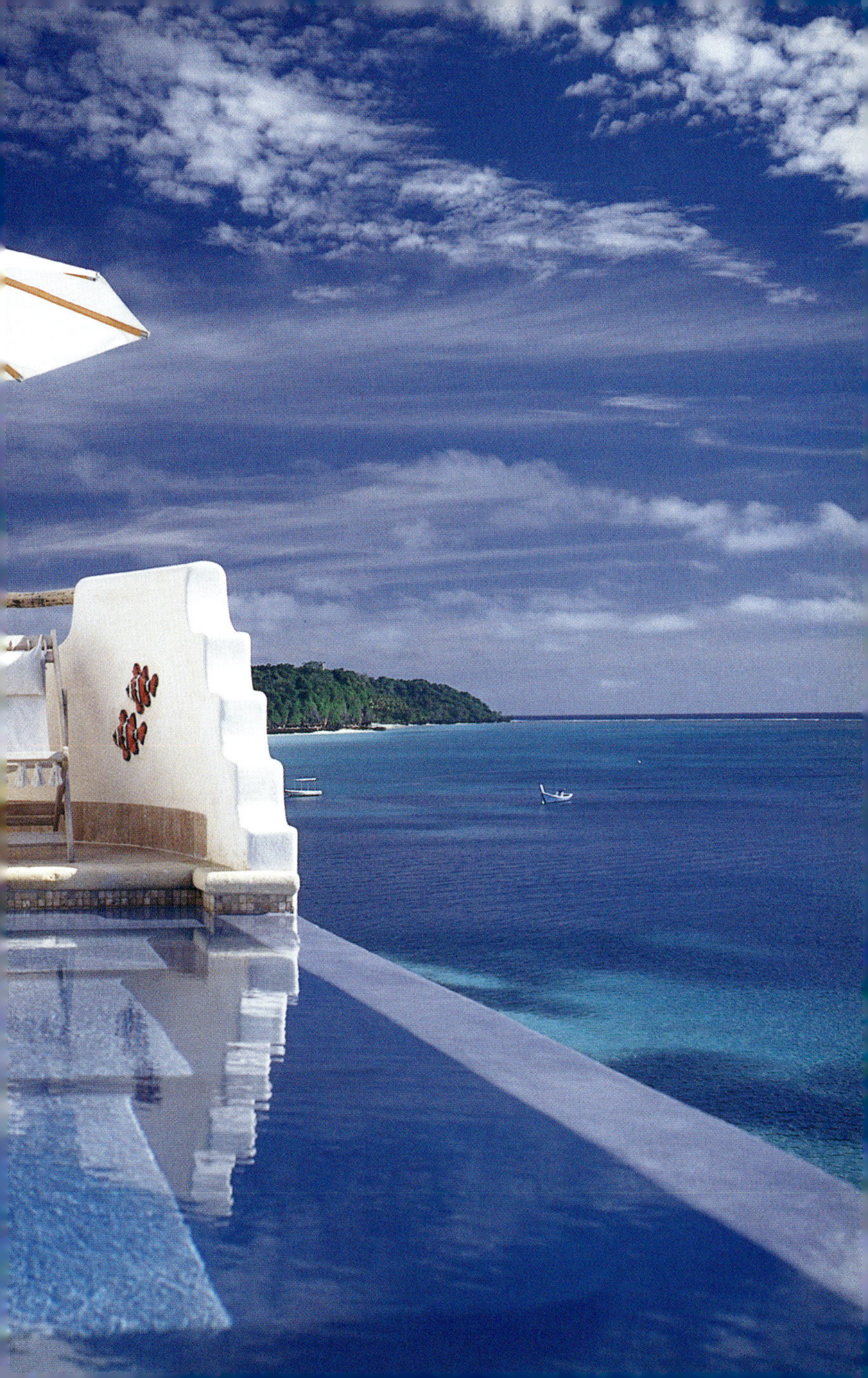

To private pool and sundeck

Entrance Path

Desk
Bar Area
Lounge
Lobby
Pool
Terrace

Upper Level

Bedroom
Ensuite

Lower Level

View to Beach

Resort's plan

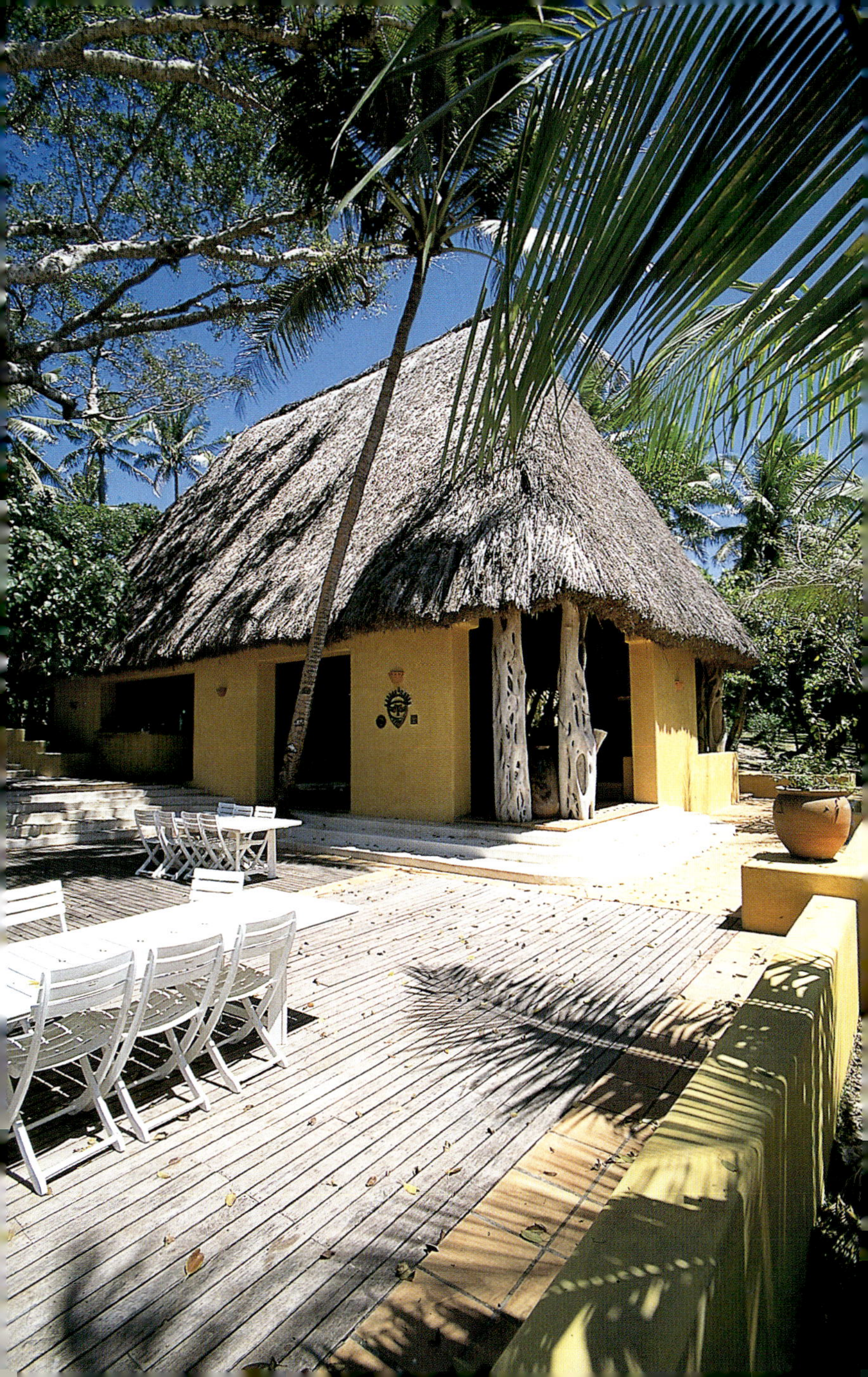

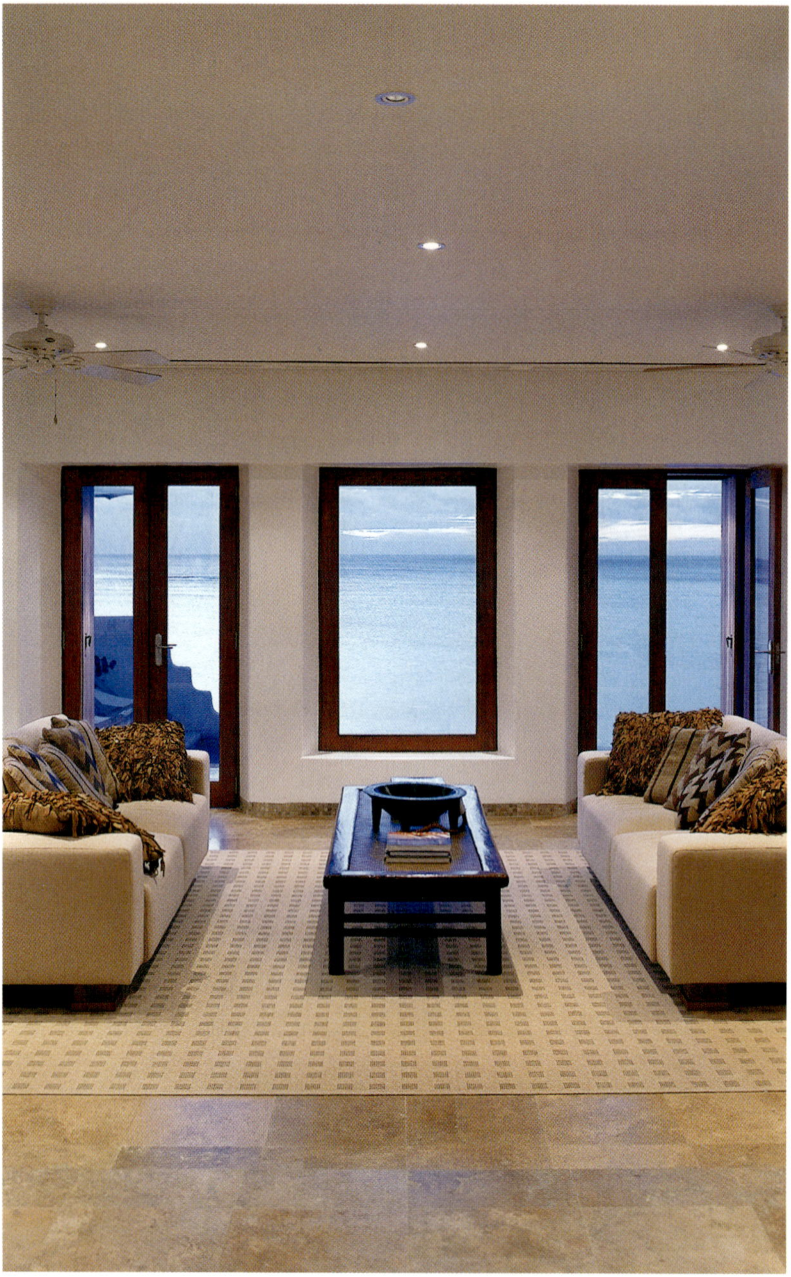

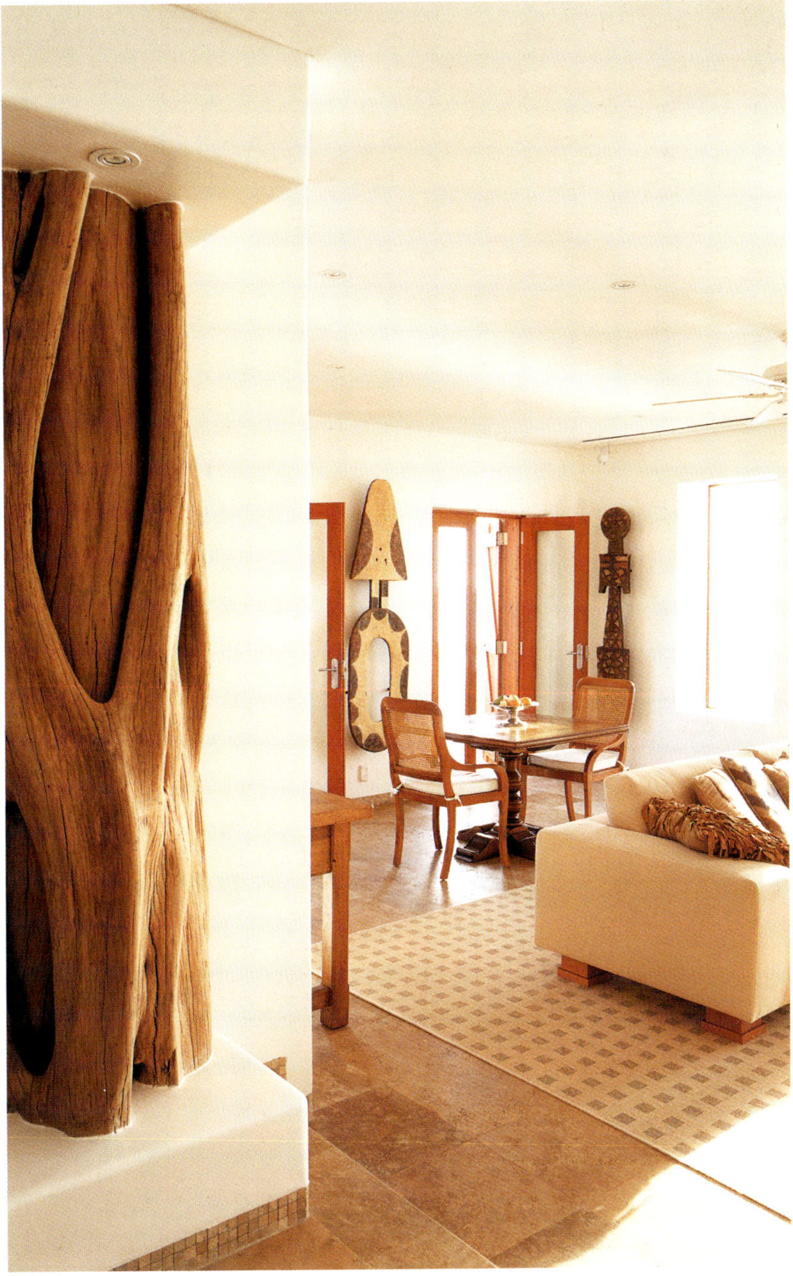

Children of the Sun
Fiji's Natural Heritage
Pacific Tapa
Bali Modern
Pacific Island Style

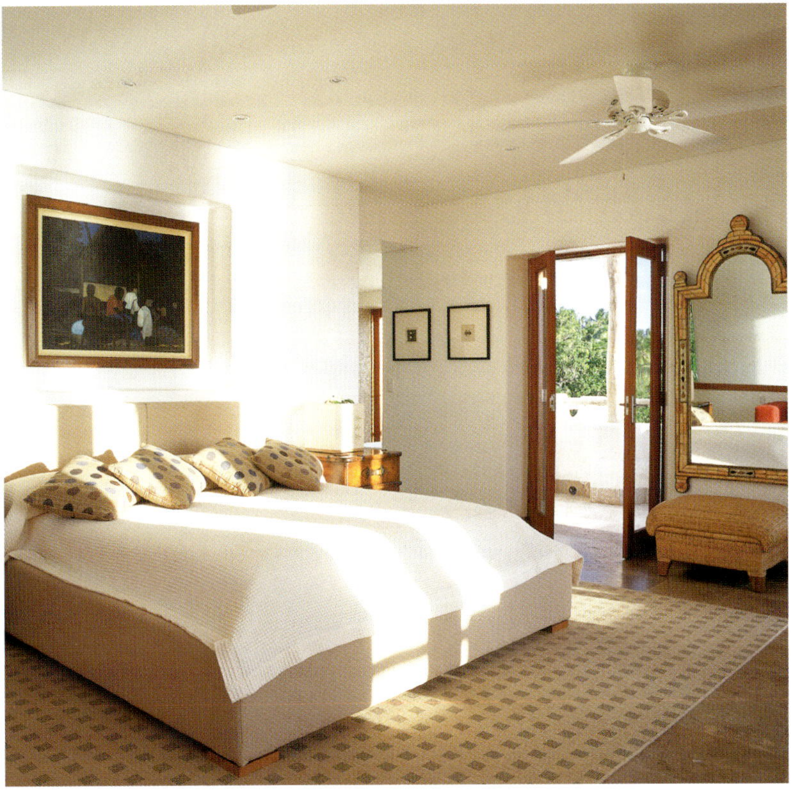

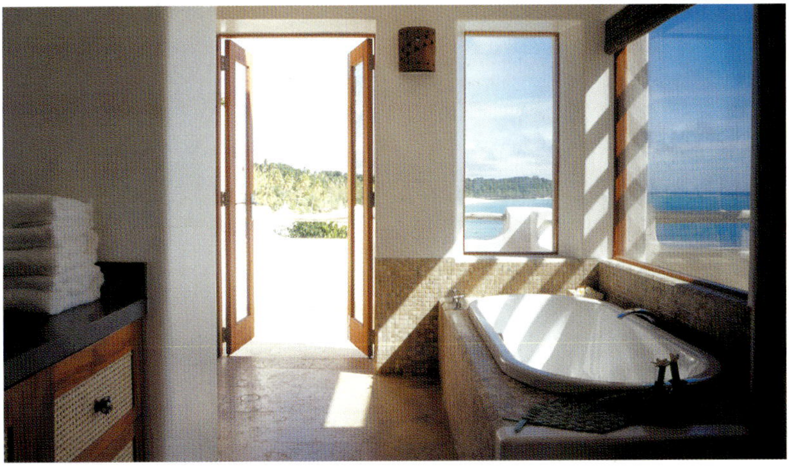

ARCHITECTS DIRECTORY

p. 12 **Jordan Mozer & Associates**
Address: 320 West Ohio, 7th Floor
Chicago, IL 60610, United States
Tel.: +1 312 397 1133
Fax: +1 312 397 1233
www.mozer.com

p. 22 **Angelos Angelopoulos**
www.angelosangelopoulos.com

p. 30 **Günther Domenig**
Address: Jahngasse 9/I
A-8010 Graz, Austria
Tel.: +43 316 827 753
Fax: +43 316 827 753-9
www.domenig.at

p. 36 **REAL Engineering d.o.o.**
Address: Šmartinska 152, Hala 6/II
1000 Ljubljana, Slovenia
Tel.: +386 1 585 2672

p. 42 **HPP – Hentrich-Petschnigg & Partner**
Address: Kaistrasse 5
40221 Düsseldorf, Germany
Tel.: +49 211 8384 0
Fax: +49 211 8384 185
www.hpp.com

p. 48 **Stephen Ryan**
Address: 7 Clarendon Cross, Holland Park
W11 4AP London, United Kingdom
Tel.: +44 20 7243 0864
Fax: +44 20 7243 3151
www.stephenryandesign.com

p. 58 **Kerry Hill Architects**
Address: 29 Cantonment Road
Singapore 089746, Singapore
Tel.: +65 6323 5400
Fax: +65 6323 5411
www.kerryhillarchitects.com

p. 68 **TMA Arquitectura**
Address: Avenida Diagonal 453, 3° 2°
08036 Barcelona, Spain
Tel.: +34 932 096 101
Fax: +34 934 145 236
www.tmaarquitectura.net

p. 74 **The Stephen B Jacobs Group, PC**
Address: 677 Fifth Avenue
New York, NY 10022, United States
Tel.: +1 212 421 3712
Fax: +1 212 752 4819
www.sbjgroup.com

p. 92 **Gail Behr**
Address: PO Box 1005
Plettenberg Bay, 6600 Cape Town, South Africa
Tel.: +27 44 533 0068
www.homework.co.za

p. 98 **Jean-Michel Gathy/Denniston
International Architects & Planners Ltd.**
Address: UBN Tower, 26th Floor, 10 Jalan P. Ramlee
50250 Kuala Lumpur, Malaysia
Tel.: +60 3 2031 3418
Fax: +60 3 2031 3422
www.denniston.com.my

p. 106 **Tadao Ando**
Address: 5-23 Toyosaki 2-Chome, Kita-ku
Osaka 531 0072, Japan
Tel.: +81 6 6375 1148
Fax: +81 6 6374 6240

p. 112 **Bruce Henderson Architects**
Address: 162 Toorak Road
South Yarra, Victoria 3141, Melbourne, Australia
Tel.: +61 3 9860 4000
Fax: +61 3 9866 4321
www.bh-architects.com

p. 118 **Paul Merrick Architects**
Address: 18 Bastion Square
British Columbia V8W 1H9, Victoria, Canada
Tel.: +1 250 480 7811
Fax: +1 250 480 5215
www.merrickarch.com

p. 124 **GCA Arquitectes Associats**
Address: Valencia 289
08009 Barcelona, Spain
Tel.: +34 934 761 800
Fax: +34 934 761 806
www.gcaarq.com

p. 134 **Philippe Starck**
Address: 8/20, Rue du Faubourg du Temple
75011 Paris, France
Tel.: +33 1 4807 5454
Fax: +33 1 4807 5464
www.philippe-starck.com

p. 142 **Zeppos-Georgiadi+Associates**
Address: 06 Likiou Street
10674 Athens, Greece
Tel.: +30 210 721 4706
Fax: +30 219 724 4407
www.zegegr.com

p. 148 **Gary Chang/Edge Design Institute Ltd.**
www.edge.hk.com
Shigeru Ban
www.shigerubanarchitects.com
Cui Kai/China Architecture & Design Research Group
www.cadreg.com.cn
Rocco Yim
www.roccodesign.com.hk
Antonio Ochoa-Piccardo/Soho China Ltd.
www.sohochina.com
Kengo Kuma
www.kkaa.co.jp
Kay Ngee Tan
www.kayngeetanarchitects.com
Nobuaki Furuya/Studio Nasca
www.studio-nasca.com
Seung H-Sang/Iroje Architects & Planners
http://iroje.com
Yung Ho Chang/Atelier Feichang Jianzhu
www.fcjz.com

p. 156 **Allan Powell Architects**
Address: 19 Victoria Street
St. Kilda, Victoria 3182, Melbourne, Australia
Tel.: +61 3 9534 8367
Fax: +61 3 9525 3615
www.allanpowell.com.au

p. 162 **Martin Hughes Architecture Interiors**
Address: 1:7 Axis Building
91 Lower Street Georges Bay Road, Parnell
PO Box 9608
Newmarket, Auckland 1149, New Zealand
Tel.: +64 9 379 4448
Fax: +64 9 303 3230
www.martinhughesdesign.com

p. 166 **Jean-Michel Gathy/Denniston International Architects & Planners Ltd.**
Address: UBN Tower, 26th Floor, 10 Jalan P. Ramlee
50250 Kuala Lumpur, Malaysia
Tel.: +60 3 2031 3418
Fax: +60 3 2031 3422
www.denniston.com.my

p. 172 **Aldo Rossi**
Address: Via Santa Maria alla Porta 9
20123 Milan, Italy
Tel.: +39 02 7201 0046
Fax: +39 02 8901 0633

p. 188 **MoHen Design International**
Address: 18, Alley 396, Wulumuqi South Road
Shanghai 200031, China
Tel.: +86 21 6437 0910
Fax: +86 21 6431 7125
www.mohen-design.com

p. 192 **Studio Gaia**
Address: 601 West 26th Street, Suite 415
New York, NY 10001, United States
Tel.: +1 212 680 3500
Fax: +1 212 680 3535
www.studiogaia.com

p. 200 **Oscar Tusquets Blanca**
Address: Cavallers 50
08034 Barcelona, Spain
Tel.: +34 932 065 580
Fax: +34 932 804 071
www.tusquets.com

p. 214 **Jonathan Adler**
Address: 7 Greene Street
New York, NY 10013, United States
Tel.: +1 212 942 8950
www.jonathanadler.com

p. 220 **Álvaro Planchuelo**
Address: Santa Engracia 30 6B
28010 Madrid, Spain
Tel.: +34 914 474 932
Fax: +34 914 480 457
www.alvaroplanchuelo.com

p. 226 **Günther Domenig**
Address: Jahngasse 9/I,
A-8010 Graz, Austria
Tel.: +43 316 827 753
Fax: +43 316 827 753-9
www.domenig.at

p. 236 **Takenaka Corporation**
Address: 1-13, 4-Chome, Hommachi, Chuo-ku
Osaka 541 0053, Japan
Tel.: +81 6 6252 1201
Fax: +81 6 6271 0398
www.takenaka.co.jp